1 PETER

In this commentary, Ruth Anne Reese offers a multidisciplinary study of 1 Peter that builds on contemporary scholarship and research methods. She explores the relationship of the letter to the Old Testament, as reflected in the themes of exodus, exile, suffering, and glory. Integrating sociological analysis, she offers insights into the social situation of the letter's audience that have grown out of postcolonial and empire criticism. Reese also explores the themes of majority–minority relationships, nonretaliation, and ethical living. Her study reveals a more subversive character to 1 Peter than is often posited.

Written in an accessible style, Reese's commentary provides overviews of important scholarly questions and points readers to a range of potential answers. It also features a "Closer Look" section on a significant topic in each passage, as well as "Bridging the Horizons" sections that connect the ancient context of 1 Peter with the contemporary world.

Ruth Anne Reese is Beeson Chair of Biblical Studies and Professor of New Testament at Asbury Theological Seminary. She is the author of *Writing Jude: The Reader, the Text, and the Author in Constructs of Power and Desire* and *2 Peter and Jude*.

NEW CAMBRIDGE BIBLE COMMENTARY

The New Cambridge Bible Commentary (NCBC) aims to elucidate the Hebrew and Christian Scriptures for a wide range of intellectually curious individuals. While building on the work and reputation of the Cambridge Bible Commentary popular in the 1960s and 1970s, the NCBC takes advantage of many of the rewards provided by scholarly research over the last four decades. Volumes utilize recent gains in rhetorical criticism, social scientific study of the Scriptures, narrative criticism, and other developing disciplines to explore the growing advances in biblical studies. Accessible jargon-free commentary, an annotated "Suggested Readings" list, and the entire *New Revised Standard Version* (NRSV) text under discussion are the hallmarks of all volumes in the series.

1 Peter

Ruth Anne Reese
Asbury Theological Seminary

CAMBRIDGE
UNIVERSITY PRESS

CAMBRIDGE
UNIVERSITY PRESS

University Printing House, Cambridge CB2 8BS, United Kingdom

One Liberty Plaza, 20th Floor, New York, NY 10006, USA

477 Williamstown Road, Port Melbourne, VIC 3207, Australia

314–321, 3rd Floor, Plot 3, Splendor Forum, Jasola District Centre, New Delhi – 110025, India

103 Penang Road, #05–06/07, Visioncrest Commercial, Singapore 238467

Cambridge University Press is part of the University of Cambridge.

It furthers the University's mission by disseminating knowledge in the pursuit of education, learning, and research at the highest international levels of excellence.

www.cambridge.org
Information on this title: www.cambridge.org/9781107137080
DOI: 10.1017/9781316480281

© Cambridge University Press 2022

First published 2022

A catalogue record for this publication is available from the British Library.

Library of Congress Cataloging-in-Publication Data
NAMES: Reese, Ruth Anne, author.
TITLE: 1 Peter / Ruth Anne Reese, Asbury Theological Seminary.
OTHER TITLES: First Peter
DESCRIPTION: Cambridge, United Kingdom ; New York, NY, USA : Cambridge University Press, 2022. | SERIES: New Cambridge Bible commentary | Includes bibliographical references and index.
IDENTIFIERS: LCCN 2021052532 (print) | LCCN 2021052533 (ebook) | ISBN 9781107137080 (hardback) | ISBN 9781316502068 (paperback) | ISBN 9781316480281 (epub)
SUBJECTS: LCSH: Bible. Peter, 1st–Commentaries. | BISAC: RELIGION / Biblical Studies / New Testament / General
CLASSIFICATION: LCC BS2795.53 .R44 2022 (print) | LCC BS2795.53 (ebook) | DDC 227/ .9207–dc23/eng/20211228
LC record available at https://lccn.loc.gov/2021052532
LC ebook record available at https://lccn.loc.gov/2021052533

ISBN 978-1-107-13708-0 Hardback
ISBN 978-1-316-50206-8 Paperback

Contents

Acknowledgments

I am grateful to Ben Witherington III for the opportunity to write on 1 Peter. Although I have been teaching this book for over 20 years, writing this commentary gave me the occasion to deepen my research on and understanding of the epistle. It has been a gift to explore it with students at a wide variety of levels as I have prepared this commentary. A special word of thanks goes to my research assistants: Kevin Southerland and Matthew K. Robinson.

Abbreviations

BAGD   Bauer, Walter, William F. Arndt, F. Wilbur Gingrich, and
Frederick W. Danker, *A Greek–English Lexicon of the New
Testament and Other Early Christian Literature*, second ed.
(Chicago: University of Chicago Press, 1979).

BBR   *Bulletin for Biblical Research*

BSac   *Bibliotheca Sacra*

BTB   *Biblical Theology Bulletin*

CBQ   *Catholic Biblical Quarterly*

CEB   Common English Bible

ESV   English Standard Version

HTR   *Harvard Theological Review*

IDB   George A. Buttrick, ed., *The Interpreter's Dictionary of
the Bible: An Illustrated Encyclopedia*, four vols.
(New York: Abingdon, 1962).

JBL   *Journal of Biblical Literature*

JECS   *Journal of Early Christian Studies*

JETS   *Journal of the Evangelical Theological Society*

JSNT   *Journal for the Study of the New Testament*

LCL   Loeb Classical Library

LSJ   Liddell, Henry George, Robert Scott, Henry Stuart Jones,
A Greek-English Lexicon. 9th ed. with revised supplement
(Oxford: Clarendon, 1996).

LXX   Septuagint

NA28   Nestle-Aland *Novum Testamentum Graece*, twenty-eighth edition

NASB   New American Standard Bible

NETS   New English Translation of the Septuagint

NIV   New International Version

NJB   New Jerusalem Bible

NLT   New Living Translation
NRSV   *New Revised Standard Version*
NTS   *New Testament Studies*
RB   *Revue Biblique*
RSV   Revised Standard Version
SJT   *Scottish Journal of Theology*
UBS5   *United Bible Studies, The Greek New Testament*, fifth edition
WTJ   *Westminster Theological Journal*
WW   *Word and World*

Ancient Sources

Aristotle

Eth. eud.   *Ethica eudemia*   *Eudemian Ethics*
Nic. Eth.   *Ethica Nichomachea*   *Nichomachean Ethics*
Pol.   *Politica*   *Politics*
Oec.   *Oeconomica*   *Economics*

Augustine

Ep. Eud.   *Epistolia Euodius*   *Epistle to Euodius*

Cicero

Pis.   *In Pisonem*   *Against Piso*

Dionysius of Halicarnassus

Ant. Rom.   *Antiquitates romanae*   *Roman Antiquities*

Philo

Leg. 1,2,3   *Legum allegoriae I, II, III*   *Allegorical Interpretation 1, 2, 3*
Cher.   *De cherubim*   *On the Cherubim*
Prob.   *Quod omnis probus liber sit*   *That Every Good Person Is Free*

Xenophon

Oec.   *Oeconomicus*   *Economics*

Map of Asia Minor

THRACE
Byzantium
Heraclea Pontica
Nicomedia
BITHYNIA
Nicaea
Cyzicus
Apamea Myrlea
Gordiucome-Juliopolis
MYSIA
Sangarius
PHRYGIA EPICTETUS
TOLISTOBOGII
Ilium
TROAS
Assos
GALA
Germe
Pessinus
Lesbos
Mytilene
Pergamum
AEOLIS
ABBAEITAE
Tiberiopolis
Aezani
Ancyra Phrygiae
Synaus
Thyatira
PROVINCIA
ASIA
PHRYGIA
Hierocaesarea
LYDIA
Sardes
Smyrna
Sebaste
Pisidian Antioch
Caesarea Trocetta
CILBIANI
Nicaea
Apamea Cibotus
Pappa Tiberiopolis
Chios
Magnesia by Sipylus
Nysa
Hierapolis
PISIDIA
Samos
Ephesus
Tralles
Laodicea
HOMANADENSES
Miletus
Priene
Aphrodisias
CARIA
Diocaesarea
Mylasa
Cibyra
Perge PAMPHYLIA
Attalia
Aspendus
Cos
Cnidus
LYCIA
Xanthus
Rhodes
Myra
Land over 1,000 metres
SCALE
0   50   100   150   200   250 km
0   50   100   150 miles
42°N
40°N
38°N
36°N
26°E   28°E   30°E   32°E

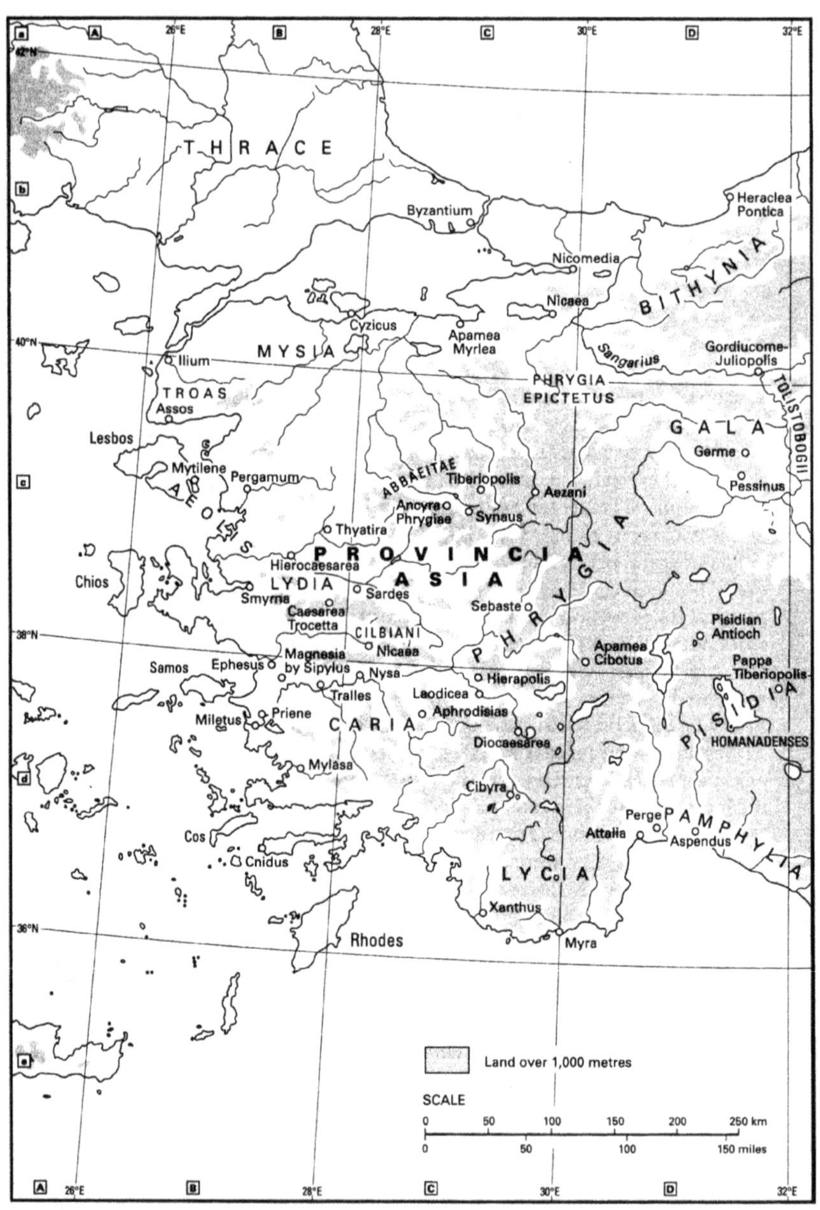

Asia Minor.

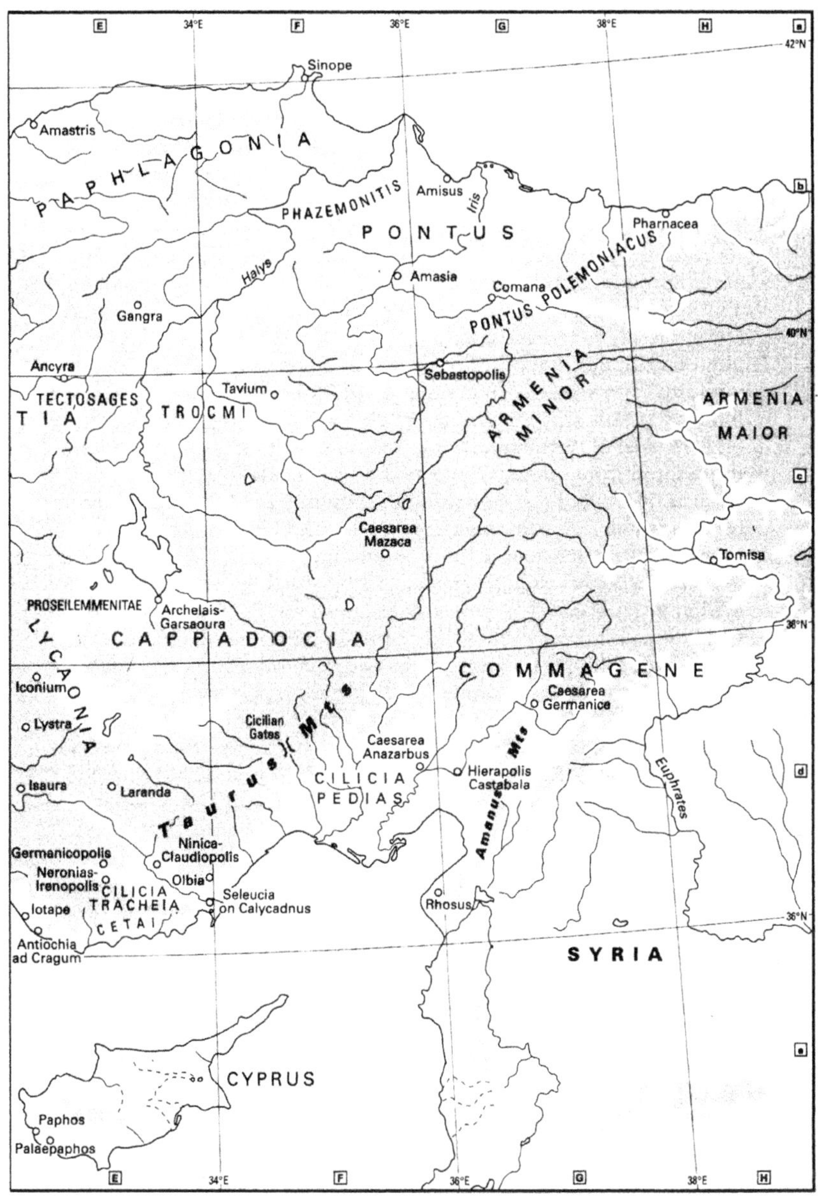
Sinope
Amastris
PAPHLAGONIA
PHAZEMONITIS
Amisus
Iris
PONTUS
Pharnacea
Halys
Amasia
Comana
PONTUS POLEMONIACUS
Gangra
ARMENIA MINOR
ARMENIA MAIOR
Ancyra
Sebastopolis
Tavium
TECTOSAGES
TROCMI
TIA
Caesarea Mazaca
Tomisa
PROSEILEMMENITAE
Archelais-Garsaoura
LYCA
CAPPADOCIA
COMMAGENE
Iconium
Caesarea Germanice
Lystra
ONIA
Cicilian Gates
Caesarea Anazarbus
Taurus Mts
CILICIA PEDIAS
Hierapolis Castabala
Amanus Mts
Euphrates
Isaura
Laranda
Germanicopolis
Ninica-Claudiopolis
Neronias-Irenopolis
Olbia
CILICIA TRACHEIA
Iotape
Seleucia on Calycadnus
Rhosus
CETAI
Antiochia ad Cragum
SYRIA
CYPRUS
Paphos
Palaepaphos
34°E
36°E
38°E
42°N
40°N
38°N
36°N

Introduction

What inspires people to read a text written two thousand years ago? For some readers, the biblical text carries a religious or spiritual message that they want to explore. Other readers may be drawn by curiosity about a text that was written long ago and which continues to influence the current political and cultural decisions of some members of the larger cultural milieu of the twenty-first century. Others may approach the text as an artifact of the ancient past with little connection to our current time. The reasons for reading the biblical text in general and 1 Peter in particular are various. The goal of this commentary is to introduce readers to the text of 1 Peter so that they can gain a deeper understanding of the message of the letter and become familiar with some of the most recent scholarship on it.

Reading an ancient text well involves making use of a variety of skills. It will help the reader if he or she is familiar with the history that shapes the first-century Greco-Roman world, the cultural values and ways of thinking that were important to the people of that time, and the literary artifacts of that society, including the Old Testament and other types of literature common at that time. These other types of literature include: apocalyptic literature which communicates a vision of the end times often mediated by an angelic messenger (e.g., Revelation and 1 Enoch); public and private letters written for a variety of audiences; and other types of works common at the time such as written speeches, novels, plays, histories, and geographies. All of these types of literature help us to understand the culture in which 1 Peter was written. In addition, the reader will be aided by being aware of the ways that humans make and communicate meaning, and will be careful to attend to the types of words that are used and the way they are used. Attention is given to quotations and metaphors, to allusions and analogies, and to the rhetoric and logic of the text.

Readers may understand that our ways of making meaning are embodied and experienced rather than disembodied and abstract. Our Western tradition has often disconnected reason and logic from the body and has identified metaphor, image, and the poetic as emotional and irrational. Yet, recent advances in our understanding of cognition have shown that metaphor derived from experience forms the central core of our ability to think.[1] Many of these metaphors are so deeply embedded in our thinking that we use them unconsciously as part of our everyday language. For example, we think of the person as a container – as having a space that can be filled with such things as knowledge, love, anger, or passion. And, continuing the metaphor, if a person is a container, then the space the person inhabits has an inside and an outside even as a container does.[2] These stock metaphors reflect our experience as embodied selves and form the scaffolding of our everyday life together and our capacity to communicate with one another. One of the challenges for interpretation is to understand not only the surprising metaphors that sparkle from the pages of the text but also the ordinary metaphors that reveal the building blocks of meaning. On the one hand, many metaphors are shared across cultural boundaries because they are rooted in shared human experiences.[3] Thus, everyone by virtue of their birth has some connection to family. On the other hand, even shared metaphors are transformed by the lived experiences of different peoples and different times. For example, the experience of family (a prominent metaphor in 1 Peter) in the Western world of the twenty-first century has significant differences from the experience of family in the first century. One of the tasks of the interpreter is to highlight similarities and differences between twenty-first-century experiences of and appropriation of the world and first-century experiences and appropriations. Failure to highlight these similarities and differences can lead to interpretations based on faulty

---

[1]   Bonnie Howe, *Because You Bear This Name: Conceptual Metaphor and the Moral Meaning of 1 Peter* (Leiden: Brill, 2006), 60.
[2]   Howe, *Because You Bear This Name*, 296.
[3]   Howe, *Because You Bear This Name*, 188.

connections, especially ones derived from thinking that our own metaphorical structures (e.g., our contemporary understanding of "family") are the same as the metaphorical structures used by the author of a first-century text. Some of this work will be carried out in the "A Closer Look" sections that highlight aspects of the historical and cultural realities of the time period we are examining. In addition, the main part of the commentary will also attend closely to metaphor and to the ways in which these metaphors press the readers of 1 Peter towards particular knowledge, resulting in certain behaviors.

Readers may also recognize that 1 Peter was never a purely informational letter but was designed to encourage those who read it and to exhort them to a particular type of life described as standing fast in the grace of God (5:12). While this commentary uses historical and theological material to illuminate 1 Peter, it also seeks to encourage contemporary readers of 1 Peter to consider what this exhortation written in the first century might mean for twenty-first-century readers. Here, the challenge is to engage the imagination of twenty-first-century readers in such a way that they might not only read the text but allow the text to read them and challenge them in ways that draw out a response. One metaphor that is being effectively applied to the work of interpretation is the metaphor of performance. Our interpretation of a text is a performance of that text, much as musicians interpret Bach when performing a work by the composer.[4] This commentary not only offers its own performance of the text but encourages readers to perform the text as well – both in their growing understanding of 1 Peter and in their appropriation of its wisdom. Some of this work will be done in the sections labeled "Bridging the Horizons."

The opening pages of this Introduction begin by laying a framework for understanding 1 Peter. This framework addresses such issues as the author and audience of the letter, the location to which it was sent, and the genre of the writing. It will also begin to take up some of the material that relates to the cultural setting of the letter, its place in the canon, and its theological significance.

---

[4]   Stephen C. Barton, "New Testament interpretation as performance," *SJT* 52:2 (1999): 179–208.

NEW APPROACHES

For centuries biblical studies, including the writing of commentaries, has been dominated by historical criticism. Historical criticism focuses on the sources of the text and its historical setting in order to facilitate understanding of the original meaning of the text. Over the centuries, historical critics developed a number of methods – including source criticism, form criticism, and redaction criticism – to help uncover the world behind the text and the development of the text itself. During the last fifty years, a variety of new methods have made their way into biblical studies. Sociohistorical methods offer new insights into the historical world by attending to the work of sociologists and anthropologists. These studies contribute to our understanding of social values (such as honor and shame) that drove the cultures of the first century. And when read alongside the biblical text they help current readers to hear it with an awareness of its sense for the original audience. Additionally, newer methods attended to the text itself by focusing on metaphor, narrative, and the use of the Old Testament in the New Testament (intertextuality). While historical-critical commentaries also note these types of issues, new research related to metaphor and cognition, the narrated nature of human existence, and intertextual relationships has transformed our understanding in these areas. Furthermore, scholars remind us that the readers of the first century were more likely illiterate and thus "hearers" rather than readers. A focus on memory and orality draws from contemporary sociology as well as from ancient handbooks on rhetoric and speech. Perhaps one of the greatest challenges to the dominance of historical criticism has come about through attending to the location of the reader or interpreter of the biblical text. New contributions have been made through the use of feminist and postcolonial criticisms that attend to the ways in which biblical texts have been heard and received by women and minorities. These types of criticisms also remind us of the power of the Roman Empire and highlight it as a ubiquitous background for the study of any New Testament book. One of the purposes of this commentary is to provide updated interaction with recent scholarly developments in the study of 1 Peter. There are many resources available in the historical-critical mode (and indeed the work of historical criticism has not been exhausted), but this commentary will also highlight a variety of new approaches and insights that draw from some of the more recent methods and approaches to have gained ground both in biblical studies more generally and in the study of 1 Peter in particular.

SETTING, POWER, AND MAJORITY–MINORITY RELATIONSHIPS

The book of 1 Peter is a letter written to small groups of Christians scattered across Asia Minor, a geographical region consisting of several provinces in the Roman Empire. In the first century, Rome was the center of the world. There, Caesar Augustus and the emperors who followed ruled as the head of a vast and expanding empire, holding together a territory stretching through parts of what is today Europe, North Africa, Turkey, and the Middle East. From Rome, Caesar wielded power over the provinces and set about continual expansion of the empire through conquest, especially to the north and west. Living in the central city of Rome or wielding power as a subordinate of Caesar brought honor, status, and recognition. Meanwhile, the provinces and their peoples gained and lost status and reputation depending on their relationship with Rome and the ruler of the empire. Provinces and cities that provided material support and honor for the empire were rewarded with monuments and benefactions that affirmed their commitment to the governing power of Rome.

By the latter half of the first century Asia Minor already had a long history of interaction with Rome. Around 129 BCE Rome had established its first province – Asia, part of current-day Turkey (see map of Asia Minor) – in the region when the king died and left his land to the Romans. About 50 years later, the region of Bithynia was also bequeathed to Rome. And in 66 BCE the general Pompey won the region of Pontus and went on to create one province with the name Bithynia-Pontus. Galatia was added by Augustus to the growing Roman Empire in 25 BCE.[5] By the mid to late first century BCE both the North African provinces and the provinces of Asia Minor were important regions with longstanding relationships with Rome. Of course, as provinces, these regions were subject to an immense tax burden which drained resources away from the local region towards Rome. Meanwhile, Rome became the

---

[5]   Travis B. Williams, *Persecution in 1 Peter : Differentiating and Contextualizing Early Christian Suffering*, Supplements to Novum Testamentum: 145 (Leiden: Brill, 2012), 354.

administrator of justice and peace in the provinces, replacing the kings that had once ruled these regions.

Asia Minor both gave and received benefits from its relationship with Rome. When Augustus first began to consolidate power after the battle of Actium (31 BCE), the provinces of Asia Minor recognized his position with various tributes such as adopting the Roman calendar and naming months after Caesar, minting new coinage, and erecting statues. "In 29 BCE Octavian [Augustus] gave permission to establish a ... *sacred precinct* for the goddess Roma and the heroized Julius Caesar in Nikaia and in Ephesos [Ephesus], and he instructed the [people] resident there to take part in their veneration."[6] The cult of the emperor would grow across Asia Minor and multiple temples were built to venerate the emperor both in the lifetime of Augustus and in the decades that followed. These temples tapped into a "religious veneration of the ruler and benefactor [that] was, however, nothing new in Anatolia. Not only had shrines to the goddess Roma long existed in several places, but cults of living Romans were also practiced in earlier times."[7]

Generally, the western provinces of Asia Minor (Asia, Galatia, Bithynia-Pontus) were relatively peaceful during the first century CE. In addition, this area was fertile and prosperous. Over the course of the first century, the region increased in wealth and had a strongly diversified economy. Of course, poverty still existed, but there is much to suggest that the region was generally economically stable and produced viable livings for its inhabitants.[8] The region had a wide variety of industries that produced goods for export, including wine, wheat, olive oil, pickled fish, fish sauce, wood, wool and other textiles, and products from mining including silver and salt. The region was also developed through the investment that Rome made in roads, cities, and governance. The only remaining map[9] of the Roman road system shows a well-connected region allowing for the transport of goods and services, as well as the deployment of military power

---

[6]   Christian Marek, Peter Frei, and Steven Rendall, *In the Land of a Thousand Gods: A History of Asia Minor in the Ancient World* (Princeton: Princeton University Press, 2016), 314, italics original.

[7]   Marek, Frei, and Rendall, *In the Land of a Thousand Gods*, 313.

[8]   Marek, Frei, and Rendall, *In the Land of a Thousand Gods*, 312–13.

[9]   *Tabula Peutingeriana*, thirteenth-century manuscripts held in the Austrian National Library.

when needed. The eastern province of Cappadocia, like Galatia, was rural. Cappadocia also formed part of the outer border of the Roman Empire. Military installations and the building of roads to transport soldiers and goods helped to fortify the border against invasion. The letter of 1 Peter is not addressed to cities but rather to regions. While the province of Asia had a number of prominent cities, many of the other areas addressed were rural in nature and maintained local social and religious traditions long after accepting rule by the Roman Empire. Such practices were maintained alongside allegiance to Rome. The book of 1 Peter is identified as coming to small groups of believers spread across the region of Asia Minor from the elder, Peter, an apostle of Jesus located in Rome (identified cryptically in 5:13 as "Babylon").

Both the writer and the recipients of 1 Peter were embedded in a deep hierarchical understanding of reality.[10] For Jews and Christians, at the top of the hierarchy was God. Below God were angels and then humans, then animals, and then plants. Other hierarchies were contained in the categories below God. In the first century, the emperor stood at the apex of the human category and below him were the senate, equestrians, governors, and magistrates. Far below these were peasants and slaves. The hierarchy could shift (after all, slaves of Caesar's household held more status than some free people), but that there was a hierarchy of position, honor, and status was a given reality in the first century. Most of the people directly addressed in the letter – slaves and wives, particularly – were among the least powerful people in the Roman Empire. Those addressed were not the rulers of the day nor the people whispering in the ears of the rulers with the hope that the empire might turn in their direction; rather, they were the lowly of the provinces. And while the provinces in which they were living were prosperous and fertile, the likelihood is that the communities who received 1 Peter "consisted of a mixed socioeconomic background ... some – although probably a very small percentage – would have been able to accumulate a moderate or even a substantial surplus of funds. Nevertheless ... the large majority of the readers would have found themselves in an unstable and precarious financial situation."[11] And while the letter is written from Rome and comes from the foremost of Jesus'

---

[10]   Howe, *Because You Bear This Name*, 228.
[11]   Williams, *Persecution in 1 Peter*, 128.

disciples, Peter too is a minority (a Jew) living in the majority (Gentile) culture of his day. He is writing from Rome where he is living as a foreigner separated from his home in Judea. He writes to others who have also come to experience minority status by virtue of their entrance into new relationship with God and with each other through their relationship with Jesus Christ. Thus, even in the midst of a fair amount of prosperity and the blessings of benefaction on the part of Rome, 1 Peter is still insider literature "responding to the needs of a multicultural, scattered, and vulnerable population."[12]

And here what we have learned from majority–minority relations in the twenty-first century can help us understand 1 Peter more fully. One of the realities of minority cultures is that they must live in two worlds and understand two languages. Minorities live within the cultural context of their minority community – this may include different foods, a different mother tongue, and different cultural values. At the same time, in order to survive, they must live and function within the majority culture as well. This means that they must be familiar with the language and culture and customs of the majority that surround them. On the one hand, they must be able to function and even flourish within that cultural setting. This can involve reproducing, "sometimes verbatim, the propaganda of the socially and politically dominant . . . in order to bend it to their favor by appealing to those elements of it that support their interests."[13] Those who belong to a minority culture are intimately aware of the messages and practices of the dominant culture. On the other hand, in order to retain their cultural identity, they cannot fully assimilate to the culture around them. Shively Smith notes that "1 Peter prescribes, in paraenetic fashion, a double consciousness in which its addressees observe two distinct cultural systems and oscillate between two parallel realities – [in this case], living under human authority and living under God's sovereignty."[14] In contrast, those born into a majority culture do not have to learn another language or another set of customs and conventions in order to thrive. In reality,

---

[12]   Shively T. J. Smith, *Strangers to Family: diaspora and 1 Peter's Invention of God's Household* (Waco, TX: Baylor University Press, 2016), 3.

[13]   Paul A. Holloway, *Coping with Prejudice: 1 Peter in Social-Psychological Perspective,* Wissenschaftliche Untersuchungen Zum Neuen Testament: 244 (Tübingen: Mohr Siebeck, 2009), 180–81.

[14]   Smith, *Strangers to Family,* 46.

majority culture persons may be unaware that minority cultures exist, or they may actively seek to undermine and/or destroy minority cultures that are different from their own. There is some debate, which will be addressed in the commentary on 1 Peter 1:1–2, about how the people addressed in this letter came to be a minority culture. But there is no debate on the fact that the group addressed is indeed a minority culture – a group of people described as living away from home (exiles or resident aliens) and scattered (Dispersion) across the provinces. This minority is being asked to live out their identity as the people of God in the context of a majority culture that ridicules and torments them for their belief. Culturally, the vast resources of power lie in the hands of the majority culture and the political systems that they control. Those who belong to a minority culture know this and yet they are not powerless. Work in postcolonial studies reminds us that "the weak also exercise agency and power through the multifarious means by which they resist their domination, whether in hidden or overt ways, and whether through linguistic means . . . or by physical acts . . .".[15] Peter's letter is designed to speak to their status in ways that encourage and empower them to live fully in a culture that they know and understand but to which they can never fully belong while belonging to the household of God. For twenty-first-century readers born into a majority culture, one challenge will be to place themselves into the minds of those living as a minority within a majority culture that is embedded in the structures of imperial control. One way that those, like myself, who belong to a majority context can try to understand majority–minority realities and colonial realities is by attending to the writings and stories of minorities who speak from within their context. Similarly, attention to the experiences of persecution experienced by Christians living in diverse times and places can also help us attend to the lived experiences of the first recipients of 1 Peter. Both of these stances require taking up a posture of listening and learning from those who in many ways find themselves in the same hierarchical position as the slaves and wives who first heard 1 Peter. Such attention includes listening to Christians who live as minorities in their nations, listening to

---

[15]   David G. Horrell, "Between conformity and resistance: Beyond the Balch-Elliott debate towards a postcolonial reading of First Peter," in Robert L. Webb and Betsy Bauman-Martin (eds.), *Reading First Peter with New Eyes: Methodological Reassessments of the Letter of First Peter* (London: T&T Clark, 2007), 118–19.

those who experience a wide variety of persecutions for their faith in Jesus, and attending to the narratives of those who have experienced refugee and alien status, especially because of their faith.

SITUATION

The household of God faced persecution as part of its experience of life in Asia Minor. In light of this situation, Peter indicates (5:12) that he wrote his letter to encourage the family of God, which was spread throughout the provinces of Asia Minor.

Commentators agree that those addressed by the letter faced a variety of difficult circumstances due to their identity as part of the household of God. These experiences are described in the letter as causing grief and are identified as various trials the group faces (1:6). Over the course of the letter, the description of what its recipients faced becomes clearer. In 2:12 their "good works"[16] result in slander, insults, and verbal attacks on their character from those who are not part of the household of God. They may experience abuse (indeed, they may already have done so) (3:9), suffering (3:14), or mistreatment (3:16) for doing what is good and right in the sight of God and the household of faith. In 4:12 their situation is described as a fiery ordeal that involves suffering (4:13) and being "reviled for the name of Christ" (4:14). The experience of suffering because of faith in Jesus Christ was varied and not monolithic. It is clear that Peter understands that the trials faced by Christians are not unique to his readership as he reminds them that "your brothers and sisters in all the world are undergoing the same kinds of suffering" (5:9).

Scholars have debated the nature of the persecution faced by the Christians in Asia Minor. Until recently the consensus was that the persecution they experienced was not orchestrated by the Roman government but was rather local and sporadic and consisted most often of verbal abuse and attacks from the local population.[17] This consensus position was in

---

[16]   See "A Closer Look" in the commentary on 1 Peter 2:12.

[17]   Williams, *Persecution in 1 Peter*, 4; Holloway, *Coping with Prejudice*, 36 notes, however, that "scholars of early Christianity make a serious mistake when they focus on the 'local and sporadic' nature of early Christian persecution ... and ignore this much more fundamental and abiding problem" of prejudice that amounts to hatred and leads to a very high threat level.

contrast to some who argued that the persecution was actively instigated through Roman authorities and had the full backing of the government.[18] Recent scholarship on the persecution experienced by the Christians in Asia Minor has drawn a more nuanced picture of the situation. Instead of seeing a hard and fast line between official persecution that involved torture, death, and the government on one side and unofficial persecution that involved local people, verbal abuse, and ostracism on the other, the work done by Williams shows a spectrum of experiences that ranges from verbal abuse by the local populous to prosecution and punishment by the government for one's faith. He argues that "the detrimental downturn in the legal status of Christians took place during the time of Nero ... and that after this point, all Christians (from the first century CE until the third century CE) shared the same perilous legal status: the profession of Christianity came to be seen as effectively illegal in that it was treated as a punishable offense if one was so charged before the governor's tribunal."[19] Williams refers to the status of Christians as "effectively" illegal because there is no official edict against Christianity prior to the third century.[20] However, it is clear that "Christianity is consistently treated throughout our period and across a broad range of sources as an actionable offense. To be a Christian is to be a criminal, and to be accused of being a Christian is to be accused of being a criminal."[21]

While the Roman government was not actively seeking out every Christian in the empire, it is worth noting that the governor of a province had enormous power to make judicial decisions regarding the cases before him and was also legally able to hand down the death sentence in cases that he heard. In the court system of the first century, the governor heard cases brought by private citizens, and this would include accusations against Christians based on their identity as followers of Jesus.[22] When it became clear that being a Christian was a criminal offense that would receive consideration and action from the governor, popular prejudice at the

---

[18] Williams, *Persecution in 1 Peter*, 7.
[19] Williams, *Persecution in 1 Peter*, 179.
[20] Williams, *Persecution in 1 Peter*, 203.
[21] Holloway, *Coping with Prejudice*, 65.
[22] William L. Schutter, *Hermeneutic and Composition in I Peter*, Wissenschaftliche Untersuchungen Zum Neuen Testament: 30 (Tübingen: J. C. B. Mohr, 1989), 14.

societal level became "a *lethal* threat for early Christians."[23] Neighbors could drag Christians to court and those who refused to recant their Christian faith would be put to death. Thus, the types of persecution that Christians in Asia Minor faced could range from verbal abuse by local neighbors to formal accusation and prosecution in the courts of the provincial governor. Such prosecution could result in the martyrdom of anyone who confessed their Christian status before the tribunal. At the same time, Williams reminds us that not all the recipients of 1 Peter "were equally prone to and necessarily expectant of Christian martyrdom."[24] While some might face that ultimate price for their belief, many others would live with lesser, though still real and painful, consequences for their life of faith. In light of these circumstances, 1 Peter is written as a word of encouragement to communities facing a variety of trials because of their faith.

This word of encouragement and consolation allows them to continue their "diaspora journey."[25] Martin sees their situation as a "scattered" people as the controlling metaphor for the epistle. They are a people who have been called and redeemed and reborn. They are heading towards the glory of God where they will obtain inheritance and salvation. "In between their beginning and destination is the time of their sojourn (1.17; 2.11; 4.2; 5.10) when they need to continue their journey."[26] In this context of suffering and persecution, Holloway argues that Peter's word of consolation is meant to help the audience cope with the prejudice they face. He presents three main ways in which they cope. The first, and most significant, is "disidentification" in which the group rejects a problematic identity and replaces it with a desired one; reminding oneself of this new identity is part of coping with prejudice. In this case, the group has rejected a previous way of life as morally inferior and futile and replaced it with the new identity of the holy family of God.[27] Second, the audience is encouraged to adopt behaviors that disprove negative stereotypes. So, Christians are

---

[23]   Holloway, *Coping with Prejudice*, 65, italics original.
[24]   Williams, *Persecution in 1 Peter*, 235.
[25]   Troy W. Martin, "The rehabilitation of a rhetorical step-child: First Peter and classical rhetorical criticism," in Webb and Bauman-Martin (eds.), *Reading First Peter with New Eyes*, 57.
[26]   Martin, "Rhetorical step-child," 57.
[27]   Holloway, *Coping with Prejudice*, 156–72.

encouraged to submit to those above them (rulers, masters, husbands) as a way of showing that the stereotypes that they reject order are untrue.[28] Finally, in 1 Peter negative outcomes such as the experience of grief or suffering are attributed to those outside the group or to the will of God. In this way, it is clear that those experiencing suffering bear neither blame nor shame for their situation.[29] This letter of consolation reminds the recipients that they are God's children, that they can practice good behavior, and that whatever suffering they may experience on this journey is short in light of the revelation of Jesus Christ yet to come. This is how the scattered Christian community participates in an eschatological journey towards full and final salvation.

AUTHORSHIP AND DATE

Peter in the New Testament

The letter begins with a standard epistolary opening that identifies the author of the letter as "Peter," a name that refers to the most prominent of Jesus' disciples, a fisherman from the shores of the Sea of Galilee. Peter was known by a number of names including Simon and Cephas, as well as the nickname "Peter," meaning "rock." In the synoptic gospels, the lists of the twelve apostles always begin with his name (Matt. 10:2; Mark 3:16; Luke 6:14). Only a few biographical details of Peter are offered in 1 Peter. He is identified as an apostle of Jesus Christ (1:1) and as a fellow elder and witness of Christ's sufferings (5:1). But the New Testament and extrabiblical materials from the first and second centuries help fill out the picture. Peter was a fisherman from Bethsaida, a town on the Sea of Galilee, where Greek would have been the main language and where there was only a small Jewish population (John 1:44). Prior to meeting Jesus, he had moved to Capernaum and was married (Luke 4:31–32). All of the Gospels recount Jesus' calling of Peter to follow him, although the details vary from one account to another (Matt 4:18–19; Mark 1:16–17; Luke 5:1–11; John 1:42). Throughout the gospel accounts, we find a man who raises questions,

---

[28]　Holloway, *Coping with Prejudice*, 174–91.
[29]　Holloway, *Coping with Prejudice*, 192–213.

speaks on behalf of the disciples, brashly asserts his capacity to follow Jesus even if that means death, and famously denies Jesus. And, especially in John's gospel, we see Jesus reaching out to restore Peter and commissioning him with "tending the flock" (John 21:15–19). This shepherding metaphor is also found in 1 Peter 5:2.

In Acts, Peter takes the lead as the followers of the risen Jesus wait for the Holy Spirit (1:15), and he boldly proclaims the message about Jesus as Messiah and Lord when the disciples have been filled with the Spirit (Acts 2). We see Peter as one of the leaders of the Jerusalem church, gifted as an evangelist and preacher of the good news. His ministry is connected with miraculous healings (Acts 3:6) and with bold testimony before the Jewish authorities (Acts 4:8–13; 5:29). It expanded beyond Jerusalem, and he was sent to Samaria to encourage the church there (Acts 8:14). The first conversion of a Gentile household took place through the work of the Holy Spirit and the obedient ministry of Peter (Acts 10) and found acceptance in Jerusalem because of Peter's testimony on behalf of the Gentiles of God's miraculous intervention (Acts 11:18). In Acts 12, we see that Peter is miraculously freed from prison and departs from Jerusalem. After that we encounter Peter one more time, at the Jerusalem Council (Acts 15), before he disappears from the narrative of Acts. There, he reminds the church of the way God used him to bring the message about Jesus to the Gentiles and argues that circumcision should not be required of Gentiles, a position that puts him closer to Paul's understanding than to the understanding of some others in the early church who thought that Gentiles who became followers of Jesus should take on the markers of Jewish identity.

Outside of 1 and 2 Peter, we encounter Peter in just two other New Testament books: 1 Corinthians and Galatians. In 1 Corinthians Paul identifies Cephas first among those who saw Jesus, thereby highlighting him and giving him a position of prominence (15:5). In addition, Paul indicates that there is a group of Christians in Corinth who identify with and follow the teachings of Cephas, the Aramaic surname of Simon Peter (1:12). When Paul discusses the way in which he has given up his rights in order to serve the Corinthians and fully proclaim the good news about Jesus, he identifies Peter as an example of one who exercises his right to receive financial support, allowing him to travel with his wife and engage in the ministry he has been given (1 Cor. 9:5–6). In 1 Corinthians, Paul portrays Peter as a leading apostle of the church whose influence is known and appreciated in the city of Corinth. In Galatians, Paul again identifies Peter as a leader, this time in the church in Jerusalem (1:18), and indicates that he met with him over the course of about two weeks. Moreover, Paul indicates that he and Peter agreed about the direction and purpose of their respective callings. Peter is identified as being sent to the circumcised and Paul as having a mission to the Gentiles (Gal. 2:7–10). Paul's identification of Peter as a leader in the early church does not mean that Peter was without faults. As was mentioned earlier, Peter was closer to Paul in his understanding of the practical implications of Christian faith, particularly as this related to requirements being placed on Gentiles such as keeping the Jewish food laws or being circumcised. But it is clear that not all the groups that formed in the early church were in complete agreement around these matters. Paul indicates that Peter, a Jew, was for a time eating with Gentiles, but stopped doing so when some Christians came from Antioch. They were associated with James, the brother of Jesus, and Peter was afraid of them as they supported a more traditional Jewish ethic related to circumcision (Gal. 2:11–14). Paul rebuked him for this failure to live consistently in relationship to the good news and the Gentiles. Paul saw Peter as a respected missionary and leader, but also as one who was not above reproach. It should be noted that while Paul identifies Peter as being sent to the Jews, it is clear that Peter is eating with and engaging with Gentiles. In other words, the identification of the missional focus of both of these apostles is not exclusive. Paul, we know, proclaimed the good news in synagogues and won followers from among the Jews while also turning his attention to Gentiles and God-fearers. Similarly, while Peter may have focused on a Jewish mission, Acts and Galatians both show an apostle who also ministered among the Gentiles.

Peter Outside the New Testament

In the book of Acts, we last see Peter at the council in Jerusalem. The books of Galatians and 1 Corinthians indicate that Peter was present in Syrian Antioch (Gal. 2:11) and in Corinth as well. But according to tradition, Peter eventually made his way to Rome, the powerful central city of the Empire. Today some scholars dispute this tradition, claiming that Peter was never in Rome.[30] However, the tradition of Peter's presence and martyrdom there is attested to early by *1 Clement* and other church fathers and is affirmed by a wide range of contemporary scholars, even if there is some dissent.[31]

In addition, a variety of written traditions related to Peter sprung up from the second century onwards. While these have been deemed apocryphal by the church, it is possible that some of the material contained in books such as the *Gospel of Peter*, the *Acts of Peter*, and the *Acts of Peter and the Twelve Apostles* date back to the early days of the church. However, determining the date of such materials, especially based on a limited number of manuscripts, is quite challenging. However, the proliferation of material around the person of Peter shows his prominence in the early church.[32]

Peter as the Author of 1 Peter

The early church uniformly affirmed that 1 Peter was written by the apostle Peter. However, over the last few centuries, this authorship has been called into question and many have now accepted that it was written by someone else after 70 CE. The question of the authorship of 1 Peter is directly tied to a long list of issues including, as Elliott notes, "genre, destination, historical and social situation, place and date of composition, the traditions it incorporates, its literary style, its proximity to other New Testament writings (especially of Paul and the Pauline circle) ... the position of the Roman Empire toward Christianity at the time of its composition, the function of pseudonymity within the early Christian literature, and of course its theological message."[33] This has made for a complex discussion of the authorship of 1 Peter in the contemporary period.

As many have recognized, the date and authorship of 1 Peter are intertwined. Tradition indicates that Peter was martyred in Rome during

---

[30]   Holloway, *Coping with Prejudice*, 156–72.

[31]   Oscar Cullmann and Helen K. Bond, *Peter: Disciple, Apostle, Martyr* (Waco, TX: Baylor University Press, 2011), 78.

[32]   F. Lapham, *Peter: The Myth, the Man and the Writings: A Study of Early Petrine Text and Tradition*, Journal for the Study of the New Testament: 239 (London; New York: Sheffield Academic Press, 2003).

[33]   John Hall Elliott, *A Home for the Homeless: A Social-Scientific Criticism of 1 Peter, Its Situation and Strategy: With a New Introduction* (Minneapolis: Fortress Press, 1990), 270–71.

the reign of Nero, which ended in June of 68 CE. This sets the boundary for the latest possible date of the letter if it is authored by Peter himself. The persecution of Christians by Nero began in 65 CE when Nero blamed Christians for the great fire that burned an enormous portion of Rome in the summer of 64 CE. If the fire was the beginning of the persecution experienced by Christians in Asia Minor, and if Peter is accepted as the genuine author of the epistle, then 1 Peter is most likely to have been written between 65 CE and 68 CE.

Early church attestation uniformly affirms Peter as the author of 1 Peter. Beginning with Origen, an early church father and scholar who wrote extensively on the New Testament and other subjects, the early church raised questions about the authorship of 2 Peter, but these questions never extended to the authorship of 1 Peter. External evidence from the earliest times attributes 1 Peter to Peter, the apostle of Jesus. First Peter is recognized as early as *1 Clement*, which is usually dated in the early 90s CE, although some have argued for a date for *1 Clement* as early as the 70s CE, which if accepted would provide very early attestation that Peter is indeed the author. First Peter is universally attributed to Peter by other early authors such as Polycarp and Irenaeus. In addition, the early church rejected other works attributed to Peter that were clearly pseudonymous, including the *Gospel of Peter* and *The Acts of Peter*. After careful examination of the evidence, Gene L. Green writes, "Taken all together, the early evidence for the authenticity of the letter is strong. Everything is as we would expect it to be, with the direct and indirect testimonies aligned and consistent. ... The testimonies regarding the authenticity of the letter harmonize completely and are corroborated by the ancient and universal voice of the early church."[34]

More recently, assessment of internal evidence has led many scholars to propose pseudonymous authorship for 1 Peter. These arguments are based on a number of concerns. First, the Greek of 1 Peter is polished and well written, and it has been argued that this does not reflect Peter's background as a fisherman from Galilee. However, it was common practice for authors to make use of scribes who had a great deal of flexibility in shaping the final written product. Second, many commentators understand 1 Peter as

---

[34] Gene L. Green, *Vox Petri: A Theology of Peter* (Eugene, OR: Cascade Books, 2019), 76–77.

addressing a situation of intense persecution that arises in a period later than the time of Nero, who died in 68 CE. Peter's martyrdom no later than 68 CE (and probably earlier) would thus eliminate him as the author. But the recent work by Williams shows that persecution began under Nero and continued in periodic and sporadic ways before being formalized in the third century. The intensity of the persecution varied by locale and could range from mostly verbal assault and intimidation through false accusations, imprisonment, and death. Third, some have objected to Petrine authorship based on internal considerations such as a lack of eyewitness accounting of the life and words of Christ, the use of the word "Babylon" to refer to Rome (a practice only found in other texts that can be dated after 70 CE and thus after the death of Peter), and questions about whether Christianity could have truly spread into the regions of Asia Minor by 68 CE. However, the purpose of the letter is not to recount the life of Christ but rather to offer encouragement to groups of Christians who are experiencing trials because of their faith. The words of Christ are not absent from the letter (e.g., 1 Pet. 3:14), but they bring a different focus and content to it. It is possible that Peter may have used the cipher "Babylon" to refer to Rome prior to 70 CE because of the precarious situation in which he found himself. And, it seems that Christianity spread far and wide soon after the experience of Pentecost. It was carried by Jewish visitors to Jerusalem and then enhanced by the scattering of Christians that took place in the years that followed. Our lack of knowledge of the early communities in Asia Minor should not lead us to assume that Christianity had not spread to these Roman provinces. Finally, those who support pseudonymous authorship often argue for a tradition of pseudonymity that was understood and accepted by the recipients and would not be seen as deceptive. However, those who make such arguments have not produced examples of personal letters that were read and received in this manner. Instead, most pseudepigraphical documents belong to other genres such as apocalypse, testament, and gospel.

Some who support pseudepigraphical authorship for 1 Peter sometimes suggest that 1 Peter was written and sent in Peter's name from the Petrine community gathered in Rome. John Elliott writes, "1 Peter originated from a *Petrine group* in Rome which included persons named Silvanus and Mark and an unnamed Christian 'sister' (5:12–13) and was sent in the name of the martyred apostle Peter, with whom this group had been most intimately associated, to the suffering Christian household communities in Asia Minor."[35] While a number of commentators have supported Elliott's view, David Horrell argues that 1 Peter is not distinctive enough to argue for authorship by a Petrine circle or for a distinctively Jewish-Christian perspective. Instead, he proposes a synthesis between Jewish-Christian (Jerusalem) and Pauline ideas reflected in the weaving together of diverse strands of the Christian tradition.[36] Nothing in the text of 1 Peter necessitates a "Petrine circle" for its production nor does the presence of multiple threads of the Christian tradition eliminate the possibility of Peter as the author.

Thus, while a number of objections to authorship by Peter have been raised over the last few centuries, it is best to understand 1 Peter as a word of encouragement written by the apostle Peter to scattered groups of Christians in Asia Minor who were experiencing various trials because of their faith. It is likely that the book was written after the time when Nero began to persecute Christians (65 CE) and before his death in 68 CE. However, even if one does accept pseudonymous authorship, arguing either for a date in the early 70s shortly after Peter's death or for a date, perhaps in the 90s, when more intense persecution was faced by the Christian community, it would still be clear that the pseudonymous author wished to appeal to the life and theology of Peter. The content of 1 Peter is fully in line with the theology and preaching of Peter presented in Acts and other parts of the New Testament.

In a discussion of the rhetoric of 1 Peter, Troy Martin focuses on the ethos of "each and every quality of the speaker that wins the sympathy of the audience."[37] In order for the audience to hear and respond well to the letter, they must develop rapport and trust in the author. Martin names a variety of ways in which 1 Peter develops Peter's ethos. His ethos is one of goodwill towards his audience (he wishes them grace and peace and refers to them as "beloved"), and of good sense, reflected in the wisdom that he shares. Also, he is a prominent apostle who has been called by God to shepherd the flock (1 Pet. 1:1; 5:1), and he is one who shares in the ethos of Christ as one who has

---

[35] Elliott, *A Home for the Homeless*, 272.
[36] David G. Horrell, *Becoming Christian: Essays on 1 Peter and the Making of Christian Identity*, Early Christianity in Context (London; New York: Bloomsbury, 2013), 42.
[37] Martin, "Rhetorical step-child," 62.

also experienced suffering on account of his commitment to God through Christ.[38] "The argument from *ethos* through the letter establishes the trustworthiness of the apostle Peter ... Petrine authorship, even if pseudonymous is essential to the argument of the letter."[39]

While the status and ministry of Peter are well established in the New Testament and in extrabiblical literature, there is no explicit record of Peter traveling to or ministering in Asia Minor. Nor does the author of 1 or 2 Peter claim to be the founder of the churches addressed in Asia Minor. We know that Paul visited the provinces of Cappadocia, Galatia, and Asia and established churches there, but we do not have evidence for a Pauline mission further north into Bithynia and Pontus. It is possible that 1 Peter is addressed to churches that were begun by Paul and whose mission then extended into regions that Paul had not visited. It is also possible that the churches that Peter wrote to were indigenous churches founded by people who were present in Jerusalem at Pentecost. Cappadocia, Pontus, and Asia are all listed as regions that heard the good news on the day the Holy Spirit empowered Peter's preaching in Jerusalem (Acts 2:9).

One of the most important observations that can be made about the audience of 1 Peter is that they are addressed as a group. Plural verb forms and plural pronouns are used throughout the letter. This is a challenge for twenty-first-century Western readers steeped in individual responsibility and in the identity of the self as distinct from the group. In 1 Peter the instructions that form a significant part of the book's teaching are directed to the group so that such things as holiness and good behavior are not the sole purview of the individual but are undertaken within the collective body of the church. While Western culture has long championed the position of the individual in distinction from the group, recent Western research has highlighted interdependency as a key feature that enhances the function of groups and teams.[40] Such research reminds us that individuals function

---

[38]   Martin, "Rhetorical step-child," 62–63.
[39]   Martin, "Rhetorical step-child," 63.
[40]   For one example, the idea of transactive memory in psychology suggests that couples who know each other well share memory tasks and in this way extend the individual capacity for memory through their partnership.

within social and relational structures and that even our memories and knowledge operate in cooperative ways. Our study of 1 Peter allows us to engage with a culture where group identity holds sway over the individual and where behavior is understood as pertaining to the group.

The letter of 1 Peter is addressed to a group identified as chosen exiles and people of the Dispersion located in the regions of Asia Minor, consisting of the provinces of Asia, Bithynia, Pontus, Galatia, and Cappadocia. Early commentators understood the recipients of the letter to be Jews who had joined the early Christian movement.[41] This opinion was based first on the view that Peter was the apostle to the Jews and Paul the apostle to the Gentiles (cf. Gal. 2:7). Second, the extensive use of the Old Testament pointed towards Jewish readers who valued and understood the Scriptures. Third, the earliest followers of Jesus were Jews and the Jews who were present in Jerusalem at the time of Pentecost were among those who carried the message of Jesus outward to the greater Roman Empire. The message about Jesus first spread through the Jewish synagogues before quickly extending out to God-fearers (Gentiles who were interested in the God of Israel but who had not converted to Judaism) and then beyond to Gentiles. If the letter was written in the mid to late 60s CE, then it is possible that Christianity may still largely be a Jewish affair. Fourth, the letter itself refers to those who are part of the "diaspora." This word was used to refer to Jews who were first scattered through exile in Babylon and who remained in Babylon after some had returned to Palestine. By the first century, the "diaspora" referred to the many Jews who were living scattered around the Mediterranean from Egypt to Asia to Rome. For these reasons, the early church fathers identified the audience of 1 Peter as Jewish Christians living in the communities of Asia Minor. For example, Eusebius of Caesarea writes, "Peter seems to have preached in Pontus, Galatia, Bithynia, Cappadocia and Asia to the Jews of the dispersion, and afterwards, having come to Rome, he was crucified head downwards, for he himself had asked to suffer so."[42] However, there is no indication within

---

41 Eusebius, Origen, Didymus, and other early Christian writers held this view. John Hall Elliott, *1 Peter: A New Translation with Introduction and Commentary*, The Anchor Bible: 37B (New York: Doubleday, 2000), 96.

42 Quoted in Gerald Lewis Bray and Thomas C. Oden (eds.), *James, 1–2 Peter, 1–3 John, Jude*, Ancient Christian Commentary on Scripture, New Testament (Downers Grove, IL: IVP Academic, 2000), 65.

the epistle itself that Peter visited the churches in Asia Minor or was their founder.

More recently, many scholars have argued that the audience is either mixed (composed of both Jews and Gentiles) or composed mainly of Gentiles. These views arose based on evidence in the epistle. First, there has been some question about whether the various practices that describe the recipients prior to their conversion could apply to Jews. These practices include such things as licentiousness, carousing, and idolatry (4:3). It is argued that these practices more appropriately refer to Gentiles. Second, there is a reference to "former ignorance" (1:14) that is hard to apply to Jews who might be in rebellion against the covenant but who were not ignorant of the covenant relationship God established with Israel. These references led some Western fathers to suggest that the audience was comprised of Gentiles.[43] Third, this view also fits well with the mainly Gentile population of the area. It is clear that Jews were present throughout Asia Minor and that some had prominent positions in society along with a level of wealth that allowed them to engage with the civic system. Yet, Jews remained a minority population and were often despised and denigrated because of their exclusiveness. They were known for keeping the Sabbath, refusing to worship in the local temples, and failing to participate in the civic duties of "serving" the city through contributions to building programs and campaigns.[44] If these were the characteristics by which Gentiles identified Jews, it seems hard to argue that the audience addressed in 1 Peter, an audience scattered throughout Asia Minor and not simply present in one location, has taken up the practices of Gentiles to such an extent that they have become just like those among whom they live.

However, Jobes rightly notes that none of these objections to a Jewish audience is insurmountable. The ignorance Peter describes is in the context of redemption (1:19) and while God's revelation did come through the Jewish people, they still lived apart from the redemption of God through Jesus Christ. There was also a long history of assimilation among some Jews that includes evidence of offering sacrifices to other gods.[45] Finally, throughout

---

43 Augustine and Jerome hold this view. Karen H. Jobes, *1 Peter*, Baker Exegetical Commentary on the New Testament (Grand Rapids, MI: Baker Academic, 2005) 23.

44 John M. G. Barclay, *Jews in the Mediterranean diaspora: From Alexander to Trajan (323 BCE–117 CE)* (Edinburgh: T&T Clark, 1996), 268–73.

45 Barclay, *Jews in the Mediterranean diaspora*, 321–26.

the Old Testament, the Jews are reprimanded for their quick abandonment of God in favor of idol worship. This begins first with the incident of the golden calf in Exodus 32 but is found throughout the history of Israel in such books as Judges and 1–2 Kings. It is quite possible for Jews to be idolaters and to participate in pagan practices in the places where they live.

There is no clear-cut argument that the audience must be either solely Jewish or Gentile. Instead, it is more likely that, as with most other New Testament churches, these churches consist of a mix of Jews, God-fearers, and Gentiles who have all chosen to follow God through faith in Jesus Christ. The letter itself does not explicitly address the ethnicity of the audience. There is no discussion such as we see in Romans 9–11 of tensions between Jews and Gentiles, nor are issues such as circumcision or eating meat sacrificed to idols addressed (e.g., Galatians, Acts 15). Instead, the audience is gathered together under one frame – chosen, and is instructed mostly in their relationships with one another as family and their relationships with those external to and hostile towards the church.

Questions about the audience of 1 Peter also extend to the situation of the audience. Peter identifies his audience as "exiles." We must ask whether they are literal or metaphorical exiles. The answers to these questions are significant because they impact (or should) the reader's understanding of the situation experienced by the letter recipients and the understanding of eschatology explored in the text. In order to answer the question of the audience's residential status (alien, exile, citizen?), we must explore the evidence supplied by the text and external evidence provided by knowing the context of Asia Minor.

John Elliott's groundbreaking work on the social condition and identity of the audience argued that the recipients of 1 Peter were literally resident aliens in Asia Minor. As people without the status of citizenship they would have faced barriers that impacted almost every facet of their lives. "Legally their status within the empire, according to both local and Roman law, involved restrictions concerning intermarriage and commerce ..., succession of property and land tenure, participation in public assembly and voting, taxes and tribute, the founding of associations ..., and susceptibility to severer forms of civil and criminal punishment."[46] This focus on

---

[46] Elliott, *A Home for the Homeless*, 37.

the social situation of the recipients of 1 Peter is a helpful corrective to previous commentators who often understood the recipients as being in exile from the world and therefore having a heavenly home towards which they were journeying. This can lead to interpretations of 1 Peter that sound more like the old gospel chorus "This World is Not My Home," which continues, "I'm just a passing through," than like a forthright acknowledgment of the reality of persecution given the church's new identity as God's chosen family.

The attention to the real social consequences of life as a resident alien in first-century Asia Minor is an important contribution to the study of 1 Peter. However, while the realities of exile were well known in Asia Minor, exile is also a defining Old Testament event in which the elite of Jerusalem and Israel were carted off by the empires of their day, though the poorest were left behind on the land. Despite the fact that not every Israelite experienced exile as a personal deportation, the reality of exile became a defining idea for Israel.[47] Embedded in the idea of exile are the important themes of judgment and hope (the promise of return), themes which are also prominent in 1 Peter but redefined in light of Christ. Familiarity with the reality of exile in the first century does not eliminate the potential that the designation "resident aliens" (NRSV: "exiles") is metaphorical. Rather, attention to the reality of exile in the first century along with attention to the event and idea of exile in the Old Testament provide the type of background needed in order to understand the social situation of the audience, whether they are literal or metaphorical resident aliens.

The question of the status of the audience concerns identity and how they obtained their status as resident aliens. If the audience is mainly Gentile or mixed, then it seems plausible to understand that they were living in Asia Minor prior to a decision to join the household of God; through their participation in the faith of the Christian community they have become like resident aliens to their own communities. In this case, they have not become resident aliens in a literal sense, but metaphorically they can be spoken of as having become aliens because they no longer participate in the customs of the dominant culture. Since the audience comes from a mix of cultures spread over a wide region, it is possible that

---

[47]   Andrew Mũtũa Mbuvi, *Temple, Exile, and Identity in 1 Peter*, T&T Clark Library of
       Biblical Studies (London: T&T Clark International, 2007), 22.

there were a variety of experiences among and within the various churches that were addressed. While it is possible that some of those to whom this letter was addressed were literally resident aliens who had fled from challenging situations, it is also possible that many of those addressed as resident aliens became such through their choice to become part of the family of God through faith in Jesus Christ. This metaphorical reading is also a reminder to contemporary readers of 1 Peter who belong to the majority or dominant culture of their region. Becoming part of the household of God has the very real potential to alienate Christians from the culture to which they formerly belonged. As Christians find themselves embedded in new social and theological norms, their old behavior and associations may become problematic and challenging. The letter of 1 Peter itself warns that believers should not be surprised when this comes to pass (4:12). Contemporary readers of 1 Peter who face persecution in a variety of forms on account of their faith may find encouragement and advice in this brief letter.

GENRE AND FORM

The epistle of 1 Peter follows standard Greco-Roman letter conventions. It begins with the identification of the author, the audience, a greeting and blessing, and ends with a short letter closing. The letter is, like many other New Testament letters, more literary than personal and designed to be read aloud within the context of a gathering of God's household. Some scholars have argued that the epistolary elements of the text have been added on to a document that served a different purpose. Two major suggestions have been put forward. First, some have suggested that the document is intended for new initiates to the Christian faith and should be seen as a baptismal sermon or liturgy.[48] However, proponents of this view have not been able to demonstrate what constitutes an early baptismal sermon or liturgy or that 1 Peter has these features. Others have argued that 1 Peter is composed of two or more letters (for instance, the first letter would be

---

[48]   Troy W. Martin shows that Bo Reicke, Oscar Brooks, and Ralph Martin hold some version of this view. Troy W. Martin, *Metaphor and Composition in 1 Peter*, Dissertation Series / Society of Biblical Literature: 131 (Atlanta: Scholars Press, 1992), 34–38.

1:13–4:11 and the second 4:12–5:11) written at the same time but meant for different churches. This suggestion addressed two issues. First, there are two doxologies (4:11; 5:11) and either one of them would provide a suitable ending to a letter. Understanding 1 Peter as a compilation would explain the inclusion of two doxologies. Second, there is a seeming intensification of the persecution addressed in the latter half of 1 Peter 4 where persecution is described as a "fiery ordeal."[49] But Peter has already indicated that the experiences of the communities he is addressing are varied (1:6). And, there is little to suggest that some parts of 1 Peter were meant for one church while other parts of the letter were meant for others. There is now a scholarly consensus that 1 Peter is a unified letter and should be studied as such.[50]

Some of the driving factors behind the different theories of composition had to do with the difficulty of identifying a major theme or purpose for the writing of 1 Peter. It has long been recognized that 1:3–12 forms an introductory setting for the letter that focuses on the blessings received from God and that 1:13–5:10 are a lived response to 1:3–12, but it has been much harder to narrow down the structure and themes of 1:13–5:10. Troy Martin has collected work that shows that 1 Peter focuses on instruction (what the Greeks called *paraenesis*), which is characterized by the use of the imperative, the presentation of moral examples, and an appeal to a certain way of life.[51] According to J. de Waal Dryden, "parenesis works in three primary modes: by providing moral advice, contextualizing moral instruction within worldview constructs, and reorienting affective commitments."[52] The letter Peter sends is designed to instruct the whole church in their life together as they contend with struggles and difficulties brought about by their adherence to faith in Jesus Christ. But it is not enough to inform or instruct, it is also necessary to direct the emotional (affective) response of the audience, and so we see that 1 Peter speaks often of love,

---

[49]   Proponents of this view include Hart, Wand, and Moule. Martin, *Metaphor and Composition in 1 Peter*, 32.

[50]   Williams, *Persecution in 1 Peter*, 349.

[51]   Martin, *Metaphor and Composition in 1 Peter*, 92–102.

[52]   J. de Waal Dryden, *Theology and Ethics in 1 Peter: Paraenetic Strategies for Christian Character Formation*, Wissenschaftliche Untersuchungen Zum Neuen Testament: 209 (Tübingen: Mohr Siebeck, 2006), 35.

fear, joy, and other emotions as Peter seeks to encourage a particular way of life in the midst of suffering.

The letter of 1 Peter was written to churches throughout the region of Asia Minor. It was intended to encourage and form communities of believers, as is evidenced by the address to groups scattered throughout the region to which it was addressed and the use of the plural form of "you" and plural verbs throughout. While all communities are made up of individuals, the focus of the letter is upon the life of the community as a whole. The letter was meant to be read publicly, and it is likely that Silvanus would have carried the letter from community to community and then read and interpreted the letter for those who gathered to hear it. Thus, the letter is a public document meant to be read and interpreted within the larger community rather than a private or personal communication between one individual and another. Both Greeks and Romans put a high value on the ability to speak well and persuade others. These skills were both taught in schools and were imbibed by listeners. A contemporary comparison might be the way in which contemporary culture places a high value on narrative and teaches filmmakers and others who produce cultural products the art of storytelling. At the same time, it is not necessary to study narrative theory in order to enjoy, critique, and engage in the ubiquitous narratives that make up our contemporary culture, whether these are found in movies, television, print, or other forms. Similarly, the art of rhetoric in all of its complexity was both taught and imbibed in first-century culture. Even authors who were not formally trained in rhetoric may make use of rhetorical structures that were common at the time. The letter, 1 Peter, clearly makes use of rhetorical strategies to persuade the audience to which it is addressed.

Three types of rhetoric were common in the Greco-Roman world: judicial, deliberative, and epideictic. Judicial rhetoric is the language of the law courts and deals in accusation and defense related to what has happened in the past. Deliberative rhetoric seeks to persuade or deter the audience from a course of action and is concerned with how that advice will play out in the future. Finally, epideictic rhetoric is the language of praise and blame and is oriented towards the present while also taking into account both the past and the future. Barth L. Campbell argues that 1 Peter is deliberative rhetoric aimed at persuading the audience to a future course of action, and he presents a clear progression of the argument from one part of 1 Peter to the next.[53] Lauri Thurén is more concerned with the underlying motivation that allows 1 Peter to be persuasive to its audience. He argues that there are both positive and negative motivations put in place by the author. As just one example, the audience is currently experiencing salvation (a positive experience that leads to praise and joy), and salvation will be fully revealed at the revelation of Jesus Christ (a potential negative as the audience may fear losing their salvation).[54] The negative and positive motivations are intertwined in such a way that they cannot and should not be understood separately. Attention to the various motivating factors behind the rhetorical structure in 1 Peter helps us hold together seemingly disjunctive aspects of the text. In addition, attending to the role of rhetoric in the text also allows us to notice such Asiatic features as long sentences, colorful expressions, aural repetition, and appeal to the emotions.[55] The study of the rhetoric used in 1 Peter has opened up our understanding of the motivations behind the text, the nature of using honor and dishonor to persuade the people of God to pursue good works in the face of suffering, and the sound of a letter that would have been read aloud in the gathered assemblies scattered across Asia Minor.

The letter also appropriates and weaves together a number of forms including a household code that extends from 2:11–3:12. Epistles employing multiple forms were known in the Greco-Roman world and appear elsewhere in the New Testament (e.g., Eph. 5:21–6:9; Col. 3:18–4:1), but the form is modified in 1 Peter. Instead of being addressed either solely to men like the Greco-Roman codes or to all members of the household in pairs (e.g., husbands and wives; masters and slaves) as in other New Testament letters, the household code of 1 Peter is first addressed to the whole household, then slaves, then wives, then (very briefly) husbands, and finally, the whole household once again. Such modifications of form to fit the message and situation of 1 Peter happen in the use of other forms as well. For example, in 1 Peter 2:4–8 the text presents a pesher-like

---

[53] Barth L. Campbell, *Honor, Shame, and the Rhetoric of 1 Peter*, Dissertation Series: Society of Biblical Literature: 160 (Atlanta: Scholars Press, 1998).

[54] Lauri Thurén, *Argument and Theology in 1 Peter: The Origins of Christian Paraenesis*, Journal for the Study of the New Testament: 114 (Sheffield: Sheffield Academic Press, 1995), 224.

[55] Ben Witherington, *New Testament Rhetoric: An Introductory Guide to the Art of Persuasion in and of the New Testament* (Eugene, OR: Cascade Books, 2009), 179.

interpretation of the "stone" passages in Isaiah and Psalms. Whether or not these verses were first put together for 1 Peter or came from another source, the letter offers an interpretation of the pesher so that the audience clearly understands that the word "stone" refers to Jesus. Some scholars have also suggested that 1 Peter makes use of hymnic material drawn either from the Scriptures (e.g., 1 Pet. 2:22–25, which draws on Isaiah 53 but arranges it to reflect Jesus' passion) or early Christian tradition (e.g., parts of 1 Peter 3:18–22). The epistle also contains beatitudes (3:14; 4:14), vice lists (2:1; 4:3), and moral instruction.

The epistle of 1 Peter clearly bears all the markers of an ancient letter that uses rhetorical strategies to communicate and contains a variety of recognized literary forms within it. Recent scholarship has also pointed out that the letter is embedded in a narrative worldview and that letters project a "narrative world."[56] Humans tell and refer to narratives in order to make sense of their world, and these narratives become guiding structures (e.g., "worldviews") for life and meaning. In a letter, such as 1 Peter, where the author and the audience share the same narrative worldview, the narrative does not need to be laid out explicitly but is rather implicit in the material of the letter. Conversion experiences, like those of 1 Peter's audience who have come to love and trust Jesus even though they have not seen him (1:8), alter previously held narrative worldviews, and an instructive epistle reinforces the new narrative worldview held in common by the author and audience. The author never lays out the "story" that he draws from; rather, it is assumed and drawn from throughout the letter. Dryden notes that "1 Peter utilizes an *implied* narrative that unifies all the 'salvation-historical' events it references. It describes a world that is governed by a story – the story of God's salvation."[57] Boring divides this narrative up into two parts: then and now. The past begins with God's foreknowledge of Christ before the creation of the world (1:20) and moves on to the salvation studied and looked for by the prophets (1:10). The definitive events of the narrative take place in the "now" when Jesus Christ is revealed. Here, the emphasis is upon Jesus' death and exaltation *and* upon the new life of the letter's recipients. Finally, the letter also emphasizes the goal of the

---

[56] M. Eugene Boring, "Narrative dynamics in First Peter: The function of narrative world," in Webb and Bauman-Martin (eds.), *Reading First Peter with New Eyes*, 15.

[57] Dryden, *Theology and Ethics in 1 Peter*, 66.

readers' faith as they move towards the end of history.[58] Ultimately, this implied narrative is shaped by Peter's theology, which is rooted in God's saving purposes.

Throughout 1 Peter the Scriptures of the early church, the books we now refer to as the Old Testament or Hebrew Bible, play a prominent role in the letter's theology and instruction. The Christology and ecclesiology of 1 Peter are both heavily shaped by being embedded in the Christology and ecclesiology of the Old Testament. The deep use of the Old Testament in 1 Peter is evidenced by the use of many direct quotations and allusions to Scripture throughout. Direct quotations are drawn from Leviticus, Psalms, Proverbs, Isaiah, Hosea, and Malachi. More broadly, the book alludes to Genesis, Exodus, Leviticus, Job, Psalms, Proverbs, Isaiah, Jeremiah, Ezekiel, and Daniel. In addition, there are allusions to Septuagint materials such as Sirach, Tobit, Maccabees, Wisdom of Solomon, and 1 Enoch, all of which demonstrates familiarity with a range of literature from the Second Temple period. While 1 Peter draws from a variety of books, there is a heavy concentration on the Psalms and Isaiah, and almost all of the direct quotations are drawn from these two books. Egan posits that this concentration is reflective of the popularity and availability of particular scriptural scrolls to the early Christian community and suggests that 1 Peter draws on the parts of the Old Testament that the first people to hear the letter would have been most familiar with.[59]

Those to whom Peter wrote were Greek speakers and Peter cited and referred to the Greek translation of the Scriptures, which we now refer to as the Septuagint or LXX.[60] There has been a significant expansion of interest

---

[58]   Boring, "Narrative dynamics in First Peter," 26–32.

[59]   Egan draws on the work of Detlef Fraenkel in *Verzeichnis der griechischen Handschriften des Alten Testaments*, Der Uberlieferung bis zum VIII. Jahrhundert, vol. 1, Gottingen: Vandenhoeck and Ruprecht, 2004; Patrick T. Egan, *Ecclesiology and the Scriptural Narrative of 1 Peter* (Eugene, OR: Pickwick Publications, 2016), 31.

[60]   Recent attention to Septuagint studies has reminded New Testament scholars of two significant facts. First, there were a variety of Greek translations of the Hebrew text, so it is anachronistic to refer to the LXX as if there were only one Greek translation. Second, just like the New Testament, the Septuagint is composed of varied manuscripts that have undergone their own process of transmission and correction. While we are not able to trace Peter's use of the Greek Scriptures back to a particular manuscript tradition, we should be wary of too easily attributing changes in Peter's citation of Scripture to the Hebrew text when these may be accounted for by variations in the translation, transmission, and correction of the Septuagint itself. Those interested in exploring the

in the use of the Old Testament in the New Testament, both in biblical studies in general and in the study of 1 Peter specifically. Older commentaries tended to reflect on the source from which Old Testament quotations were drawn and the Christological application of those quotations. But more recent attention to the use of the Old Testament in 1 Peter has focused on several new strands of inquiry. One area of study involves careful focus on the intertextual dimensions of interpretation. This work tends to focus on the use of quotations and allusions from the Old Testament, giving attention to the original passage from which a reference is drawn and the meaning of that passage in its original context. Then, the use of the passage in 1 Peter is explored and conclusions are drawn about its place in the argument, theology, and/or ethics of the book.[61] Another area of study involves exploring the way in which the Old Testament helps provide a narrative structure for 1 Peter, especially seen through a lens of continuity between Israel in the Old Testament and the people/household of God in 1 Peter. When interpreters understand a whole book or a large narrative as structuring the use of the Old Testament in 1 Peter, they generally use methods drawn from narrative studies.[62] Here recent work has focused on the story of redemption either associated with the larger narrative of God's redemption of Israel[63] or associated with the story of Israel as it is recounted in a particular text, such as Isaiah.[64] This recent work has deepened our understanding of the message that Peter communicates to the early Christian community – a message of salvation already embedded in Scripture, particularly the Psalms and Isaiah. Finally, in the most recent work on this subject, Benjamin Sargent argues that 1 Peter 1:10–12 lays out the interpretive lens that the author of 1 Peter used when interpreting Scripture for the community in Asia Minor. This hermeneutic has a dual-pronged approach that involves both Christology and the community. The prophets in 1:10–12 are those who sought to understand

---

Septuagint tradition more fully may consult Karen H. Jobes and Moisés Silva, *Invitation to the Septuagint*, 2nd ed. (Grand Rapids, MI: Baker Academic, 2015).

[61] G. K. Beale and D. A. Carson, *Commentary on the New Testament Use of the Old Testament* (Grand Rapids, MI; Nottingham, England: Baker Academic; Apollos, 2007), 1015–46.

[62] Abson Prédestin Joseph, *A Narratological Reading of 1 Peter* (London: Bloomsbury T&T Clark, 2013).

[63] Joseph, *A Narratological Reading of 1 Peter*.

[64] Egan, *Ecclesiology*.

Christ's sufferings and subsequent glories. This clearly points to the Christological lens through which the author of 1 Peter understood the Old Testament. At the same time, the prophets are described as serving not themselves but "you," the audience of 1 Peter. Sargent shows that the Old Testament is used in 1 Peter for the purpose of communal instruction. Indeed, according to Sargent, "the kerygmatic function of Scripture [the Old Testament] is subordinated to its paraenetic function. Scripture proclaims Christ and his sufferings so that the communities might be encouraged to live good lives."[65] The Old Testament is both a source of proclamation about Christ and of encouragement and instruction for the Christian community.

PURPOSE

Why did Peter write this letter to communities of Christians around Asia Minor? The letter serves several purposes: (1) encouragement and exhortation to remain faithful in the face of suffering caused by their new life of faith in Jesus Christ; (2) practical instruction in faithful living when faced with difficult and challenging circumstances brought on by persecution; and (3) reiteration of theological truths in order to support their life as a minority group among hostile outsiders.

In 1 Peter 5:12, it is explicitly stated that the purpose of the book is to offer encouragement (implying there is some discouragement on the part of the recipients, a reference to the conflict they were experiencing). The communities are instructed to stand fast in their faith when the temptation would be to waver. Part of standing fast is being prepared when suffering arises.

Throughout the letter, Peter recognizes the types of suffering that the churches may encounter (e.g., various trials [1:6]; being maligned as evil doers [2:12]; and fiery ordeals [4:12]). In these circumstances practical instructions for life as a resident alien in Asia Minor are offered. These instructions tend to be general rather than specific and describe advice and virtues that are widely applicable to churches scattered across a vast region. Instead of spelling out commands in detail, 1 Peter allows churches to work

---

[65] Benjamin Sargent, *Written to Serve: The Use of Scripture in 1 Peter*, Library of New Testament Studies: 547 (London: Bloomsbury T&T Clark, 2015), 48.

out the application of commands such as being holy, conducting one's self with reverence, and loving one another. At the same time, it is possible that the specific instructions given to slaves and to wives married to unbelievers may serve as examples for other members of the community who also experience suffering.

Finally, these instructions are deeply rooted in the narrative of Christ's suffering, death, resurrection, and ascension and serve to solidify the identity of the community as the household of God. For example, the instruction for the church to conduct itself in reverent fear (1:17) is followed by the reminder that Christians were redeemed with the precious blood of Jesus Christ. The ability of members of the church to live lives of holiness and good conduct is rooted in the reality that the church now belongs to the Lord who purchased them with his blood. Throughout the book, the theological and the practical are intertwined.

1 PETER IN THE CANON

First Peter is the second of seven letters known as the catholic (or general) epistles. When we look at ancient manuscripts that include the whole of the New Testament, we find these seven letters located either immediately following the book of Acts or, as in English Bibles today, following the Pauline epistles and the book of Romans. Recent scholars have argued that the seven catholic epistles should be understood as an intentional collection gathered together to represent the Pillars of the Jerusalem church (the family of Jesus: James and Jude; the prominent apostles: Peter and John) and to form a counterbalance to the collection of the Pauline epistles.[66] These seven epistles share a distinctive set of theological emphases that include human suffering as a test of the church's relationship to God, God's response to suffering is a word of truth that leads to salvation, the expectation that God's people will behave in a holy manner, and the right response to God in the face of suffering is embodied in loving works.[67] The letters of the catholic epistles collection, including 1 Peter, serve a

---

[66]   David R. Nienhuis and Robert W. Wall, *Reading the Epistles of James, Peter, John, and Jude as Scripture: The Shaping and Shape of a Canonical Collection* (Grand Rapids, MI: Eerdmans, 2013), 24, 35.

[67]   Drawn with modifications from Nienhuis and Wall, *Reading the Epistles of James, Peter, John, and Jude as Scripture*, 71.

distinctive purpose and carry a particular message within the canon along-side the Gospels, Acts, the Pauline letters and Hebrews, and the Apocalypse of John.

   Older scholarship posited various levels of dependence between 1 Peter and other books in the New Testament. Some argued that the author of 1 Peter knew and depended on the whole of the New Testament.[68] These arguments were based on linguistic parallels between 1 Peter and particular New Testament books.[69] Charles Bigg listed various parallels, but often rejected these parallels as too general to support the argument of dependence and argued against the reliance of Peter on Romans, Galatians, Ephesians, or 1 Timothy. At the same time, he thought there might be a shared relationship between 1 Peter and Titus, as both show concern for the position of elders and the behavior of various members of the Christian household.[70] Bigg posits more of a connection between James and 1 Peter but even here more recent scholarship has argued that "while James and 1 Peter are both addressed to communities in the diaspora, are both hortatory in tone with common appeal to Wisdom tradition, and are both intent on reinforcing the distinctions of insiders and outsiders, they also differ significantly in their general perspectives."[71] Overall, with the notable exception of Beare,[72] recent scholarship has rejected the dependence of 1 Peter on other New Testament books and instead argues that any affinities 1 Peter shares with other New Testament books come about due to the "use of a wide stream of Christian oral tradition."[73] Within this stream of oral tradition might be found hymns, creeds, various sayings attributed to Jesus, and some of the general teachings of the early church. There is no agreement among scholars about whether some materials in 1 Peter should be understood as examples of these particular forms or whether these materials reflect independent proclamation about Christ

---

[68] H. J. Holtzmann, *Lehrbuch der historisch-kritischen Einleitung in das Neue Testament* (Freiburg: J. C. B. Mohr, 1885) is cited as an example in Elliott, *1 Peter*, 20.

[69] Charles Bigg, *A Critical and Exegetical Commentary on the Epistles of St. Peter and St. Jude* (New York: C. Scribner's Sons, 1901), 20–22.

[70] Bigg, *A Critical and Exegetical Commentary on the Epistles of St. Peter and St. Jude*, 21.

[71] Elliott, *1 Peter*, 23.

[72] Francis Wright Beare, *The First Epistle of Peter: The Greek Text with Introduction and Notes*, 2nd ed. (Oxford: Basil Blackwell, 1958), 195.

[73] Elliott, *1 Peter*, 21.

that had not yet been formulated into formal hymns or creeds.[74] In 1 Peter 1:20, we see one example of such a short declaratory statement: "He was destined before the foundation of the world." Longer examples that may be hymnic or creedal in nature may be found at 2:6–8; 2:22–25; and 3:18–22. These longer statements sometimes display the use of parallelism or rhythmic cadence, but there is not sufficient correspondence with known hymns to argue with certainty that these are hymnic or creedal fragments.[75] These longer statements do show a use of Scripture, particularly from Isaiah and the Psalms, a use of the suffering servant motif from Isaiah 53, and a development of statements about the death, resurrection, and ascension of Jesus Christ, which the early church would have known and recognized. These same topics are touched on by the apostle Peter in the book of Acts (e.g., Acts 4:11; 3:13, 26; 2:29–33) showing a congruence between Peter's message and theology as it is portrayed in Acts and the teaching of 1 Peter.

While there continues to be debate about potential sources that 1 Peter may have made use of and about the relationship between 1 Peter and other parts of the New Testament, it is clear that the early church knew 1 Peter from early on and recognized it as apostolic. The letter of 1 Peter was included in the canon because it not only spoke to its original audience but because it was known and used in the earliest churches and continued to speak to the church across the first Christian centuries.

THE THEOLOGY OF 1 PETER

For some time, commentaries have focused on mainly historical-critical issues; however, more recently commentaries have been written that are informed by a variety of concerns such as sociology or anthropology, readerly locations, or even application.[76] One particular area of exploration over the last twenty-five years has been the recovery of an emphasis on the

---

[74] Elliott, *1 Peter*, 30.

[75] Elliott, *1 Peter*, 32.

[76] Ben Witherington, *Letters and Homilies for Hellenized Christians: A Socio-Rhetorical Commentary on 1–2 Peter*, Letters and Homilies (Downers Grove, IL: IVP Academic, 2007); Tokunboh Adeyemo (ed.), *Africa Bible Commentary* (Grand Rapids, MI: Zondervan, 2010); Scot McKnight, *1 Peter: The NIV Application Commentary from Biblical Text to Contemporary Life*, The NIV Application Commentary (Grand Rapids, MI: Zondervan, 1996).

theology of 1 Peter.[77] Before we turn to a brief consideration of the main theological foci of 1 Peter (God, Christ, church, salvation, and suffering), we must pause for a moment to address the question of what is meant by theology. Elsewhere I have defined theology as "our understanding of who God is, who humans are, what the cosmos is, and what the relationship(s) between these three are and can be."[78] In this approach, it is important to recognize both the contexts and knowledge that forms theological thinking (both that of 1 Peter and our own) since these impact the shape of the theology that emerges. The theology of 1 Peter must be considered within the contexts of suffering on account of faith, minority/majority relationships, the unfolding narrative of God's work in the world, and other considerations.

Some have questioned whether 1 Peter has a distinctive theology, arguing that it reiterates or synthesizes Pauline or early Christian theology without making a distinctive contribution. Others, like Joel B. Green, have argued that 1 Peter presents us not simply with a theology but with an example of what it looks like to live and think theologically in a particular context, the context of faith in the crucible of suffering. What is clear is that 1 Peter's theology focuses on God.[79] It begins with God's righteous activity of choosing those described as scattered exiles (1:1–2). They have been born again through the action of God made possible through the resurrection of Jesus Christ. God is the father who imparts a new identity to this group of exiles, shaping them into God's people. The people of God, God's household, come to resemble the Holy One (1:15) and to act in ways that reflect their relationship with God, made possible through Jesus Christ. God is repeatedly portrayed as one with authority: Father (1:3, 17, 23), Holy One (1:15), Judge (1:17), Ruler (3:22), and Creator (4:19) and thus as one to whom glory should be given, whether by those who malign believers (2:12) or by believers themselves (4:11). It is God who knows the work of the Messiah before the creation of the world and who raises the Messiah from the dead

---

[77]   Two notable examples of commentaries in this mode are Joel B. Green, *1 Peter*, The Two Horizons New Testament Commentary (Grand Rapids, MI: Eerdmans, 2007); Douglas Harink, *1 & 2 Peter*, Brazos Theological Commentary on the Bible (Grand Rapids, MI: Brazos, 2009).

[78]   Ruth Anne Reese, *2 Peter and Jude*, The Two Horizons New Testament Commentary (Grand Rapids, MI: Eerdmans, 2007), 3.

[79]   Elliott, *1 Peter*, 109–10.

(1:20). Jesus Christ will be the mediator and means of faith but it is God to whom faith is directed (1:21). In an epistle that focuses on the suffering experienced by those who have chosen trust in Christ, God's cornerstone (2:6), over rejection of the Messiah (2:8), Peter highlights God's righteousness and holiness and the call to become like God in behavior that imitates both the Holy One and Jesus Christ, the suffering servant (1:15–16; 2:21–25). It is the will of God that this imitation of both God and Christ results in the silencing of ignorant fools (2:15). Yet, if suffering continues, as God may will (4:19), it is clear that the inheritance God has stored up for God's household is securely kept, awaiting the day of judgment and the final salvation of those who believe (2:12; 4:5–6). Like other apocalyptic literature, 1 Peter clearly portrays God as the one who sets in motion the work of redemption, remains in control of that salvific activity, and brings it to conclusion on the day of judgment. Ultimately, though the church is suffering on account of faith, God remains in control. While 1 Peter clearly highlights God's authority, it also shows God's favor towards the church. It is God who brings about new birth for believers(1:3) and then protects them with God's power (1:5) so that they may finally receive the outcome of their faith – salvation (1:5, 9). It is God who gives grace to those who suffer (2:20) and it is God who supplies the gifts that are used by the church in service to one another (4:10–11). And, it is God who favors the righteous and the humble over the wicked and the proud (3:12; 5:5–6). In the end, the church places their faith and hope in God (1:21) and looks to the God who strengthens, restores, supports, and establishes them even if they do experience suffering on account of their faith (5:11).[80]

1 Peter's Christology with Special Focus on 1:19–21; 2:22–25; 3:18–22

Peter's Christology is complex. Throughout the epistle, theology and praxis are intertwined. At various points, Peter's Christology draws on the suffering, death, resurrection, ascension, and return of Jesus Christ. The Christology of 1 Peter forms the foundation for the life of the household of God as it experiences suffering. The first portion of 1 Peter 1:1–12 begins

---

[80] Peter H. Davids, *A Theology of James, Peter, and Jude*, Biblical Theology of the New Testament (Grand Rapids, MI: Zondervan, 2014); Green, *Vox Petri*; Green, *1 Peter*; Nienhuis and Wall, *Reading the Epistles of James, Peter, John, and Jude as Scripture*.

and ends with Christ. Peter has been sent by Jesus Christ. The personal name "Jesus" is never found alone in 1 Peter but is always accompanied by the Davidic title, Christ – the anointed king. However, the word "Christ" (Messiah, meaning "king") is found alone twelve times. The Davidic title, Christ, is used over twenty times in 1 Peter either on its own or in combination with the personal name "Jesus." Thus Peter emphasizes Jesus as the true king amid the churches' suffering caused by outsiders who see the good works done in service to that king as worthy of mockery and abuse. Jesus, the risen Messiah, both demonstrates a holy response to suffering and provides the means for the church to endure suffering with hope.[81]

1 Peter 1:1–12 sketches the Christological narrative which will unfold in the main body of the epistle. Jesus' suffering is first hinted at in 1:2 with the phrase "sprinkling of his blood." The Christians can only be sprinkled with blood because a sacrifice has happened on their behalf; such a sacrifice necessarily involves the death of that which is sacrificed. This is followed almost immediately with a comment on the "resurrection of Jesus Christ from the dead" (1:3). The resurrection of the true king is the source of life, hope, and salvation for the new household of God. But the author also realizes that the current experience of the household is one of grief and trials (1:6), yet this is not the end of the narrative. The household of God is awaiting the return of Jesus, the true king (1:7). At the very end of this opening section, Peter points to the prophets who searched for the time and place when the sufferings and glories of the Christ would take place. Through this comment Peter indicates that the narrative of Christ's suffering, resurrection, and return is not a surprise but is rather embedded in the prophetic promises of the Old Testament. And indeed, the things that the prophets saw were meant to serve the church, to help them understand the grace and salvation made available to them through the Messiah.

1 Peter 1:1–12 hints at the fuller narrative of Peter's Christology which will be explored and expanded in the chapters that come. When the major

---

[81]   Note that while the word "Christ" is sometimes used almost as a last name, it retains its titular sense, especially in contexts related to the suffering, death, resurrection, and return of Christ. Ben Witherington, "Christ," in Ralph P. Martin and Peter H. Davids (eds.), *Dictionary of the Later New Testament and Its Developments* (Downers Grove, IL: IVP, 1997) 152–60.

Christological passages are explored more fully, a narrative unfolds that becomes foundational for the suffering community. This narrative begins "before the foundation of the world" (1:20) and ends with the appearance of the chief shepherd (5:4). The appearance of Jesus Christ or God is spoken of throughout the book (1:7; 2:12; 4:13) and alludes to the day of judgment when good works and evil deeds will be fully revealed and honor and glory will be ascribed to those to whom they rightly belong. Between this beginning and end, Peter develops his Christology, beginning with sacrifice and suffering and moving towards ascension and triumph. He begins with the perfect sacrifice of Christ the unblemished lamb, which provides the ransom payment with which the children of God are purchased (1:18–19). Their identity is secured through the death of God's Son and their future is secured through the power of God that raises Christ from death. The proper response to such a sacrificial purchase and to the miraculous power of God is obedience (listening carefully and following what God has spoken), enabling one to live rightly in relationship to God and others.

But the reality is that even though this group of believers has a new identity as the children and household of God, they are facing suffering because of their faith in Christ. This letter is addressed to a community that suffers. As the book unfolds and Peter continues addressing the situation of the audience, he draws next on the example of Christ in the midst of suffering (2:21–25). First, the Messiah's response to suffering did not involve sin. In particular, he did not commit sins of speech. He did not lie, abuse, or threaten others. Instead, Christ entrusted himself to God, the just judge. In this way he carried sin on the cross, so that believers might experience freedom from sin and healing through his wound. Christ's sinlessness in the face of suffering sets an example for all those who suffer because of their faithfulness to God. At the same time, Christ's suffering brings about benefits for all those who follow him in their experience of suffering. It is important to point out that there are two different aspects of Christ's suffering: first, that which can be imitated and, second, that which is unique to Christ. The readers of 1 Peter are invited to imitate Christ's sinless response to suffering – not returning abuse for abuse or practicing deceitful speech. This is one means of living out the holiness to which they were called in 1:15–16. At the same time, there are aspects of Christ's suffering and death that are unique to Christ, including the bearing of our sins and the healing that Christ makes available through his suffering. But Christ's suffering is not the last word.

The suffering and death of Jesus Christ is followed by his resurrection from the dead (1:3; 3:21). This resurrection is the foundation of the living hope that the audience of 1 Peter inherits through their new birth (1:3). In 1 Peter, as elsewhere in the New Testament, the resurrection is attributed to God (1:21). Following the resurrection, Christ ascends in his resurrection body to heaven where he is at the right hand of God (3:22). There, angels, authorities, and powers are subject to him. Here, the focus is on the triumph of Christ over all that might oppose him. In a letter that returns again and again to the subject of suffering on account of faith in God, Peter places the triumphant ascension of Jesus Christ near the center of the book. Indeed, the most intense passages about suffering come in 1 Peter 4 shortly after the description of the ascension. Ultimately, the whole letter with its focus on suffering must be read in light of Christ's ultimate triumph over his enemies. Even if the followers of Christ may suffer now, that cannot be the end of the narrative, since Christ has triumphed over death and rules over his enemies. Yet ... believers still await the full unveiling of the glory of Christ the chosen, anointed king. For now, believers bear with suffering, so that at the moment of return they may shout with joy. Peter's narrative begins with the sacrifice of Christ, moves on to Christ's suffering and death, but then comes to the triumph of resurrection and ascension. Yet, the community of God's people also awaits the return of Christ. This is referred to in 1 Peter as the revelation of Jesus Christ (1:7) and comes to its culmination with the appearance of the chief shepherd (5:4) who sees and appreciates his flock, honoring them with recognition and the giving of a glorious crown to those who live faithfully in this life. This narrative of the suffering, death, resurrection, ascension, and return of Jesus the Davidic king provides the foundational message that the suffering community needs in order to live faithfully in this life with their hope set on God.

The Trinity in 1 Peter

The Trinitarian theology of the church only fully develops in the centuries following the New Testament writings. And yet, this letter opens with a proto-Trinitarian identification of the three with different functions: God the Father foreknows, the Spirit sanctifies, and the sacrificial blood of Jesus

Christ is sprinkled. The opening section of the book portrays three different activities, each one connected to a different person. And, as we explored above, both the identity of God and of Jesus Christ are more fully drawn out in the remainder of the letter. However, many commentators have said little about the Holy Spirit in 1 Peter because the Spirit is only mentioned a few times. And, some uses of the word Spirit are not always clear. In 1 Peter, we find both "the Spirit of Christ" (1:11) and the "Spirit of God" (4:14), along with the Spirit (1:2) and the Holy Spirit (1:12). *Pneumati* or "spirit" is also used in 3:18 and 4:6 and the commentary explores the meaning of its use there. But it is clear that there are two distinctive functions of the Holy Spirit that are highlighted in 1 Peter. First, it is the Spirit who is intimately connected to the work of sanctification (1:2), enabling the believers to fulfill the instruction to be holy as God is holy (1:15–16). Second, it is the Spirit who enables the proclamation of the good news (1:12). The Spirit is sent from heaven, which has been previously described as the place where God keeps the inheritance prepared for his children. Thus, it is God who sends the one who enables the proclamation of the message from God about the Son, Jesus Christ through whom they receive salvation. It is this word by which they receive new birth (1:25). In recent work, Lai has argued that the Spirit who sanctifies in 1:2 lies behind the concern the rest of the letter shows with holiness and good behavior.[82] The link between the holiness of God and sanctification by the Spirit reveals the intimate connection between God and the Spirit. Similarly, the link between the Spirit as the means of proclaiming the good news, the word of God as the seed of new birth, and the message about Christ, further highlights the participation of all three members of the Trinity in the salvation of the children of God.

Salvation

The epistle of 1 Peter begins by announcing the state in which the recipients of the letter live. They are God's chosen children who have been sprinkled with the blood of Jesus and sanctified by the Spirit. These children are living in exile and are thus not at home. Indeed, they are experiencing trials and persecution on account of their faith in Jesus Christ. While they are already

---

[82] Kenny Ke-Chung Lai, "The Holy Spirit in 1 Peter: A study of Petrine pneumatology in light of the Isaianic new exodus" (PhD dissertation, Dallas Theological Seminary, 2009).

born again as God's children (1:3, 23), they are also still growing into salvation (2:2). This growth is intimately connected with putting aside evil (2:1) and longing for that which nurtures growth (2:2). In this current life they face a battle against forces that seek to destroy them (2:11; 5:8). But they should not forget that they are God's people, called out of darkness and formed into God's royal and priestly household (2:9–10). They are already experiencing the salvation of God, which is transforming their lives (1:9, 15; 4:2–4). At the same time, 1 Peter has an eschatological horizon. There will be a day when Jesus Christ is fully revealed (1:7) and when God will judge humanity (4:5–6). Those who trust in God anticipate the fullness of salvation that will come at that last day (1:5). In this epistle, there is always more to salvation. It is not simply the experience of becoming children of God but is also the reality of continuing to grow in good conduct, faithfulness, and service. And, the fullness of salvation comes on the last day when the inheritance guarded by God will be shared with God's children (1:4). Then, they will no longer live in exile but will instead be at home in the full presence of God. The Old Testament imagery of the exodus (drawn from the book of Exodus) and the new exodus (drawn from the book of Isaiah) lie behind the story of salvation laid out in 1 Peter. The God who delivered the descendants of Abraham from Egypt formed them into the people of God at Sinai where they became a "priestly kingdom and a holy nation" (Exod. 19:6; Isa. 61:6). Centuries later, this same God would deliver Israel from Babylon, leading the Israelites once again through the wilderness and reminding them that they are God's chosen people (Deut. 10:15; Isa. 43:20). So too, the people who trust in God participate in the new exodus made available through the suffering of God's Son Jesus Christ. While they may find themselves in a time of exile, they know themselves to be God's people and anticipate the fullness of deliverance when they will no longer be in Babylon but will rather dwell with God.

Ethics in 1 Peter

The theology of 1 Peter provides the basis or motivation for the ethics of the book.[83] These motivations can be implicit. For example, the theological

---

[83] Fika Van Rensburg, "No retaliation! An ethical analysis of the exhortation in 1 Peter 3:9 not to repay evil with evil," in John T. Fitzgerald, Fika J. van Rensburg,

assertion that they are God's children becomes the basis for believing that their inheritance cannot be stolen from them and such belief gives the audience freedom to live out their beliefs while dwelling in a hostile culture.[84] Both implied and explicit ethical instruction occurs throughout the book. The explicit instructions that are given are general and addressed to a wide group scattered over a large geographical area rather than being confined to a specific church in one particular locale. This can be seen in the types of broad instructions that are given in the book such as "set your hope" (1:13), "be holy," (1:16), "have good conduct" (1:17), "love one another" (1:22), and "long for" spiritual sustenance (2:3). The weaving together of theology and ethics produces an ethos, a way of living together as a community, that is suitable for the church living in the midst of suffering.[85] When Peter instructs specific groups of people within the churches such instruction is given to large groups (to slaves and to wives of unbelievers) rather than specific individuals, and it is often given to serve as an example for the whole church of right patterns of living in the midst of suffering.

One of the questions that is necessarily raised by Peter's broad instructions derives from ways 1 Peter has been misread or used to hide or even excuse abusive behavior. This is particularly true in relationship to the instructions in 3:1–2 and 4:8. The former verses, 3:1–2, have been read to suggest that women should remain in abusive relationships with their husbands because that is the act of submission that the text requires of them.[86] Similarly, sometimes the suggestion that "love covers a multitude of sins" might be seen as an excuse to "sweep sin under the rug." Again, such hiding of sin can lead to the revictimization of those who speak up about abusive relationships or may suggest to victims of abuse that there is no point in coming forward because that is not "the loving thing to do." However, reading the text in this way ignores both the larger instructions of the book and the genre of the book itself. Peter is not directly discussing

---

and Herrie F. van Rooy (eds.), *Animosity, the Bible, and Us: Some European, North American, and South African Perspectives*, (Atlanta: Society of Biblical Literature, 2009), 222–24.

[84] Van Rensburg, "No retaliation!," 222.

[85] Van Rensburg, "No retaliation!," 229.

[86] Catherine Clark Kroeger and Nancy Nason-Clark, *No Place for Abuse: Biblical & Practical Resources to Counteract Domestic Violence*, 2nd ed. (Downers Grove, IL: IVP Books, 2010), 125–26.

how to deal with abusive actions or patterns that might take place in a church but is instead offering a word of encouragement and general instructions to a broad audience. At the same time, those very instructions (especially the instruction to be holy as God as holy (1:16) and the instruction to love one another earnestly (1:22)) indicate that abusive relationships are intolerable as they are neither holy nor loving. Finally, the other major focus of Peter's ethical instruction is on the performance of good works, which are understood as virtuous actions that reflect the identity of the audience as God's holy household and that have the potential to make God known to those outside the community.

SPECIAL SECTIONS

Each book in this commentary series, the New Cambridge Bible Commentary, contains special recurring sections labeled "A Closer Look" and "Bridging the Gap." The "Closer Look" sections are designed to highlight particular historical or cultural issues at greater length. These often provide exploration of structures, values, or ideas that were prominent in the ancient world. "Bridging the Gap" focuses on how we read and think about 1 Peter in the twenty-first century. This is especially important since issues related to empire, slavery, and women are still entrenched in our social discourse. However, our circumstances, our ways of thinking, and our understanding of political power in both the world and the church have changed over the centuries. Here, we attend to the shifting realities of our world, the changes in power, and the challenges of reading the biblical text in our world today.

Suggested Readings

This list of suggested reading focuses on recent works of scholarship in English as well as some commentaries.

PETER, THE APOSTLE

Bockmuehl, Markus N. A., *Simon Peter in Scripture and Memory: The New Testament Apostle in the Early Church* (Grand Rapids, MI: Baker Academic, 2012).

Cullmann, Oscar, and Helen K. Bond, *Peter: Disciple, Apostle, Martyr* (Waco, TX: Baylor University Press, 2011).

Helyer, Larry R., *The Life and Witness of Peter* (Downers Grove, IL: IVP Academic, 2012).

Lapham, F., *Peter: The Myth, the Man and the Writings: A Study of Early Petrine Text and Tradition*, JSNT 239 (London; New York: Sheffield Academic Press, 2003).

BACKGROUND AND HISTORICAL CONTEXT

Barclay, John M. G., *Jews in the Mediterranean Diaspora: From Alexander to Trajan (323 BCE–117 CE)* (Edinburgh: T&T Clark, 1996).

Barclay, John M. G., *Paul and the Gift* (Grand Rapids, MI: Eerdmans Publishing Company, 2015).

Brown, Jeannine K., "Just a busybody?: A look at the Greco-Roman topos of meddling for defining Ἀλλοτριεπίσκοπος in 1 Peter 4:15," *JBL* 125 (2006): 549–68.

Elliott, John Hall, "Elders as leaders in 1 Peter and the early church," *HvTSt* 64:2 (2008): 681–95.

Head, Peter M., "Letter carriers in the ancient Jewish epistolary material," in Craig A. Evans and H. Daniel Zacharias (eds.), *Jewish and Christian Scripture as Artifact and Canon*, Studies in Scripture in Early Judaism and Christianity: 13 (London: T&T Clark, 2009).

Hengel, Martin, *Crucifixion in the Ancient World and the Folly of the Message of the Cross* (Philadelphia: Fortress Press, 1977).

Holloway, Paul A., "Nihil Inopinati Accidisse – 'Nothing unexpected has happened': A Cyrenaic consolatory topos in 1 Pet 4.12ff," *NTS* 48 (2002): 433–48.

López, René, "Vice lists in non-Pauline sources," *BSac* 168 (2011): 178–95.

Marek, Christian, Peter Frei, and Steven Rendall, *In the Land of a Thousand Gods: A History of Asia Minor in the Ancient World* (Princeton: Princeton University Press, 2016).

Paschke, Boris A., "The Roman ad bestias execution as a possible historical background for 1 Peter 5.8," *JSNT* 28 (2006): 489–500.

Richards, E. Randolph, "Silvanus was not Peter's secretary: Theological bias in interpreting Διὰ Σιλουαψου ... Εγραψα in 1 Peter 5:12," *JETS* 43 (2000): 417–32.

Sanders, E. P., *Judaism: Practice and Belief, 63 BCE–66 CE* (London: SCM Press, 1992).

Schutter, William L., *Hermeneutic and Composition in I Peter*, Wissenschaftliche Untersuchungen Zum Neuen Testament: 30 (Tübingen: J. C. B. Mohr, 1989).

Seland, Torrey, *Strangers in the Light: Philonic Perspectives on Christian Identity in 1 Peter*, Biblical Interpretation Series: 76 (Leiden; Boston: Brill, 2005).

Trebilco, Paul R., *Jewish Communities in Asia Minor* (Cambridge: Cambridge University Press, 2006).

Veyne, Paul, *The Roman Empire*, trans. Arthur Goldhammer (Cambridge, MA: Belknap Press of Harvard University Press, 1997).

Williams, Travis B., *Persecution in 1 Peter: Differentiating and Contextualizing Early Christian Suffering, Supplements to Novum Testamentum*: 145 (Leiden: Brill, 2012).

Winter, Bruce W., "The public honouring of Christian benefactors: Romans 13:3-4 and 1 Peter 2:14-15." *JSNT* 11:34 (1988): 87-103.

Winter, Bruce W., *Seek the Welfare of the City: Christians as Benefactors and Citizens* (Grand Rapids, MI; Carlisle, Cumbria: Eerdmans; Paternoster Press, 1994).

SUFFERING, PERSECUTION, AND RESPONSE

Asumang, Annang, "'Resist him' (1 Pet 5:9): Holiness and non-retaliatory responses to unjust suffering as 'holy war' in 1 Peter," *Conspectus* 11 (2011): 7-46.

Byrley, Christopher, "Persecution and the 'adversary' of 1 Peter 5:8," *The Southern Baptist Journal of Theology* 21:3 (2017): 77-98.

Charles, Dominique, "'Votre Adversaire Le Diable Rôde Comme Un Lion Rugissant' (1 P 5,8)," *RB* 120:3 (2013): 405-22.

Horrell, David G., Bradley Arnold, and Travis B. Williams, "Visuality, vivid description, and the message of 1 Peter: The significance of the roaring lion (1 Peter 5:8)," *JBL* 132 (2013): 697-716.

Rensburg, Fika van, "No retaliation! An ethical analysis of the exhortation in 1 Peter 3:9 not to repay evil with evil," in John T. Fitzgerald, Fika J. van Rensburg, and Herrie F. van Rooy (eds.), *Animosity, the Bible, and Us: Some European, North American, and South African Perspectives* (Atlanta: Society of Biblical Literature, 2009), 199-230.

Williams, Travis B., "The divinity and humanity of Caesar in 1Peter 2, 3: Early Christian resistance to the emperor and his cult," *Zeitschrift Für Die Neutestamentliche Wissenschaft Und Die Kunde Der Älteren Kirche* 105:1 (2014): 131-47.

Williams, Travis B., "Reciprocity and suffering in 1 Peter 2, 19-20: Reading Χάρις in its ancient social context," *Biblica* 97:3 (2016): 421-39.

IDENTITY AND EMOTION IN 1 PETER

Hockey, Katherine M., *The Role of Emotion in 1 Peter*, Society for New Testament Studies Monograph Series: 173 (New York: Cambridge University Press, 2019).

Horrell, David G., *Becoming Christian: Essays on 1 Peter and the Making of Christian Identity*, Early Christianity in Context (London; New York: Bloomsbury, 2013).

Horrell, David G., "Between conformity and resistance: Beyond the Balch–Elliott debate towards a postcolonial reading of First Peter," in Robert L. Webb and Betsy Bauman-Martin (eds.), *Reading First Peter with New Eyes: Methodological Reassessments of the Letter of First Peter* (London: T&T Clark, 2007), 111-43.

Horrell, David G., "The label Χριστιανός: 1 Peter 4:16 and the formation of Christian identity," in David G. Horrell, *Becoming Christian: Essays on 1 Peter and the Making of Christian Identity*, *Library of New Testament Studies*: 394 (London: Bloomsbury T&T Clark, 2013), 164-210.

Smith, Shively T. J., *Strangers to Family: Diaspora and 1 Peter's Invention of God's Household* (Waco, TX: Baylor University Press, 2016).

Williams, Travis B., "Delivering oracles from God: The nature of Christian communication in 1 Peter 4:11a," *HTR* 113:3 (2020): 334-53.

Williams, Travis B., *Good Works in 1 Peter : Negotiating Social Conflict and Christian Identity in the Greco-Roman World*, Wissenschaftliche Untersuchungen Zum Neuen Testament: 337 (Tübingen: Mohr Siebeck, 2014).

USE OF SCRIPTURE IN 1 PETER

Bauckham, Richard, "James, 1 and 2 Peter, Jude," in D. A. Carson and H. G. M. Williamson (eds.), *It Is Written: Scripture Citing Scripture* (Cambridge: Cambridge University Press, 1988).

Christensen, Sean M., "Solidarity in suffering and glory: The unifying role of Psalm 34 in 1 Peter 3:10–12," *JETS* 58 (2015): 335–52.

Elliott, John Hall, *The Elect and the Holy: An Exegetical Examination of I Peter 2:4–10 and the Phrase "Basileion Hierateuma"* (Eugene, OR: Wipf and Stock, 2005).

France, R. T., "First century Bible study: Old Testament motifs in 1 Peter 2:4–10," *Journal of the European Pentecostal Theological Association* 18 (1998): 26–48.

Horrell, David G., "Jesus remembered in 1 Peter? Early Jesus traditions, Isaiah 53, and 1 Peter 2.21–25," in Alicia J. Batten and John S. Kloppenborg (eds.) *James, 1 & 2 Peter, and Early Jesus Traditions* (New York: Bloomsbury, 2014), 123–50.

Jobes, Karen H., "Got milk?: Septuagint Psalm 33 and the interpretation of 1 Peter 2:1–3," *WTJ* 64 (2002): 1–14.

Jobes, Karen H., "'O taste and see': Septuagint Psalm 33 in 1 Peter," *Stone-Campbell Journal* 18 (2015): 241–51.

Johnson, Dennis E., "Fire in God's house: Imagery from Malachi 3 in Peter's theology of suffering (1 Pet 4:12–19)," *JETS* 29 (1986): 285–94.

Mbuvi, Andrew Mũtũa, *Temple, Exile, and Identity in 1 Peter*, T&T Clark Library of Biblical Studies (London: T&T Clark International, 2007).

Sargent, Benjamin, *Written to Serve: The Use of Scripture in 1 Peter*, Library of New Testament Studies: 547 (London: Bloomsbury T&T Clark, 2015).

Shaw, David M., "Called to bless: Considering an under-appreciated aspect of 'doing good' in 1 Peter 3:8 – 17," *BTB* 50:3 (2020): 161–73.

SLAVES, WIVES, AND HOUSEHOLD CODES

Bain, Katherine, *Women's Socioeconomic Status and Religious Leadership in Asia Minor: In the First Two Centuries C.E.*, Emerging Scholars (Minneapolis: Fortress Press, 2014).

Balch, David L., *Let Wives Be Submissive: The Domestic Code in 1 Peter*, Society of Biblical Literature Monograph Series: 26 (Chico, CA: Scholars Press, 1981).

Batten, Alicia J., "Neither gold nor braided hair (1 Timothy 2.9; 1 Peter 3.3): Adornment, gender and honour in antiquity," *NTS* 55 (2009): 484–501.

Bird, Jennifer G., *Abuse, Power and Fearful Obedience: Reconsidering 1 Peter's Commands to Wives*, Library of New Testament Studies: 442 (London; New York: T&T Clark International, 2011).

Carter, Warren, "Going all the way?: Honoring the emperor and sacrificing wives and slaves in 1 Peter 2.13–3.6," in Amy-Jill Levine and Maria Mayo Robbins (eds.), *Feminist Companion to the Catholic Epistles and Hebrews* (London: T&T Clark Intl, 2004), 14–33.

Davids, Peter H., "A silent witness in marriage: 1 Peter 3:1–7," in Ronald W. Pierce, Rebecca Merrill Groothuis, and Gordan D. Fee (eds.), *Discovering Biblical Equality: Complementarity without Hierarchy* (Leicester: IVP, 2004), 224–38.

Dinkler, Michal Beth, "Sarah's submission: Peter's analogy in 1 Peter 3:5–6," *Priscilla Papers* 21 (2007): 9–15.

Forbes, Greg W., "Children of Sarah: Interpreting 1 Peter 3:6b," *BBR* 15 (2005): 103–7.

Horrell, David G., "Fear, hope, and doing good: Wives as a paradigm of mission in 1 Peter," *Estudios Bíblicos* 73:3 (2015): 409–29.

MacDonald, Margaret Y., "Beyond identification of the topos of household management: Reading the household codes in light of recent methodologies and theoretical perspectives in the study of the New Testament," *NTS* 57 (2011): 65–90.

Martin, Troy W., "Dating First Peter to a hairdo (1 Pet 3:3)," *Early Christianity* 9:3 (2018): 298–318.

Moxnes, Halvor, "The beaten body of Christ: Reading and empowering slave bodies in 1 Peter," *R&T* 21 (2014): 125–41.

Nugent, John C., "The 'weaker sex' or A weak Translation?: Strengthening our interpretation of 1 Peter 3:7," *Priscilla Papers* 32:3 (2018): 8–11.

Patterson, Orlando, *Slavery and Social Death: A Comparative Study* (Cambridge: Harvard University Press, 1982).

Schroeder, Joy A., "John Chrysostom's critique of spousal violence: Full text finder results," *JECS* 12:4 (2004): 413–42.

Wallace-Hadrill, Andrew, "Domus and insulae in Rome: Families and housefuls," in David L. Balch and Carolyn Osiek (eds.), *Early Christian Families in Context: An Interdisciplinary Dialogue* (Grand Rapids, MI: Eerdmans, 2003), 3–18.

SOCIOLOGICAL AND RHETORICAL APPROACHES TO 1 PETER

Balch, David L., *Let Wives Be Submissive: The Domestic Code in 1 Peter*. Society of Biblical Literature Monograph Series: 26 (Chico, CA: Scholars Press, 1981).

Bechtler, Steven Richard, *Following in His Steps: Suffering, Community, and Christology in 1 Peter*, Society of Biblical Literature Dissertation Series: 162 (Atlanta: Scholars Press, 1998).

Campbell, Barth L., *Honor, Shame, and the Rhetoric of 1 Peter*, Society of Biblical Literature Dissertation Series: 160 (Atlanta: Scholars Press, 1998).

Elliott, John Hall, *A Home for the Homeless: A Social-Scientific Criticism of 1 Peter, Its Situation and Strategy: With a New Introduction* (Minneapolis: Fortress Press, 1990).

Hanson, Kenneth C., "How honorable! How shameful! A cultural analysis of Matthew's makarisms and reproaches," *Semeia* 68 (1994): 81–111.

Himes, Paul A., *Foreknowledge and Social Identity in 1 Peter* (Eugene, OR: Pickwick Publications, 2014).

Holloway, Paul A., *Coping with Prejudice : 1 Peter in Social-Psychological Perspective*, Wissenschaftliche Untersuchungen Zum Neuen Testament: 244 (Tübingen: Tübingen Mohr Siebeck, 2009).

Martin, Troy W., "The rehabilitation of a rhetorical step-child: First Peter and classical rhetorical criticism," in Robert L. Webb and Betsy Bauman-Martin (eds.), *Reading First Peter with New Eyes: Methodological Reassessments of the Letter of First Peter*, Library of New Testament Studies: 364 (London: T&T Clark, 2007), 41–71.

Pearson, Sharon Clark, *The Christological and Rhetorical Properties of 1 Peter*, Studies in Bible and Early Christianity: 45 (Lewiston, NY: E. Mellen Press, 2001).

Thurén, Lauri, *Argument and Theology in 1 Peter: The Origins of Christian Paraenesis*, Journal for the Study of the New Testament Supplement Series: 114 (Sheffield: Sheffield Academic Press, 1995).

Webb, Robert L., "Intertexture and rhetorical strategy in First Peter's apocalyptic discourse: A study in sociorhetorical interpretation," in Robert L. Webb and Betsy Bauman-Martin (eds.), *Reading First Peter with New Eyes: Methodological Reassessments of the Letter of First Peter* (London: T&T Clark, 2007), 72–110.

Winter, Bruce W., *New Testament Rhetoric: An Introductory Guide to the Art of Persuasion in and of the New Testament* (Eugene, OR: Cascade Books, 2009).

METAPHOR IN 1 PETER

Achtemeier, Paul J., "Newborn babes and living stones: Literal and figurative in 1 Peter," in Maurya P. Horgan and Paul J. Kobelski (eds.), *To Touch the Text: Biblical and Related Studies in Honor of Joseph A Fitzmyer, SJ.* (New York: Crossroad, 1989), 207–36.

Howe, Bonnie, *Because You Bear This Name: Conceptual Metaphor and the Moral Meaning of 1 Peter* (Leiden: Brill, 2006).
Martin, Troy W., "Christians as babies: Metaphorical reality in 1 Peter," in Eric F. Mason and Troy W. Martin (eds.), *Reading 1-2 Peter and Jude: A Resource for Students* (Atlanta: Society of Biblical Literature, 2014) 99–112.
Martin, Troy W., *Metaphor and Composition in 1 Peter*, Society of Biblical Literature Dissertation Series: 131 (Atlanta: Scholars Press, 1992).
Martin, Troy W., "Tasting the Eucharistic Lord as usable (1 Peter 2:3),"*Catholic Biblical Quarterly* 78:3 (2016): 515–25.
Tite, Philip L., "Nurslings, milk and moral development in the Greco-Roman context: A reappraisal of the paraenetic utilization of metaphor 1 Peter 2.1–3." *JSNT* 31 (2009): 371–400.

NARRATIVE APPROACHES TO 1 PETER

Boring, M. Eugene, "Narrative dynamics in First Peter: The function of narrative world" Robert L. Webb and Betsy Bauman-Martin (eds.), *Reading First Peter with New Eyes: Methodological Reassessments of the Letter of First Peter* (London: T&T Clark, 2007), 7–40.
Joseph, Abson Prédestin, *A Narratological Reading of 1 Peter* (London: Bloomsbury T&T Clark, 2013).

WORKS ON 1 PETER 3:18–4:6

Crawford, Matthew R., "'Confessing God from a good conscience': 1 Peter 3:21 and early Christian baptismal theology," *JTS* 67 (2016): 23–37.
Dalton, William Joseph, *Christ's Proclamation to the Spirits: A Study of 1 Peter 3:18-4:6*, Analecta Biblica (Rome, Italy: Pontifical Biblical Institute, 1989).
Geiger, Stephen, "A word about baptism: Ἐπερώτημα in 1 Peter 3:21," *Wisconsin Lutheran Quarterly* 113 (2016): 204–9.
Grudem, Wayne A., "He did not descend into hell: A plea for following Scripture instead of the Apostles' Creed," *JETS* 34:1 (1991): 103–13.
Horrell, David G., "Who are 'the dead' and when was the Gospel preached to them? The interpretation of 1 Pet 4.6," *NTS* 49 (2003): 70–89.
Marcar, Katie, "In the days of Noah: Urzeit/Endzeit correspondence and the flood tradition in 1 Peter 3–4," *NTS* 63:4 (2017): 550–66.
Reicke, Bo, *The Disobedient Spirits and Christian Baptism: A Study of I Peter III. 19 and Its Context* (Eugene, OR: Wipf & Stock, 2005).
Westfall, Cynthia Long, "The relationship between the Resurrection, the proclamation to the spirits in prison and baptismal regeneration: 1 Peter 3:19–22." in *Resurrection*, Journal for the Study of the New Testament Supplement Series: 186 (Sheffield: Sheffield Academic Press, 1999) 106–35.
Yates, Jonathan P., "Salvation through water?: 1 Peter 3:20–21 in the ancient Latin tradition," *Worship* 92 (2018): 492–510.

THEOLOGY AND ETHICS IN 1 PETER

Beetham, Christopher A., "The eschatology of 1 Peter: Considering the influence of Zechariah 9–14," *JETS* 58:1 (2015): 197–99.
Breed, Gert, "The diakonia of the elder according to 1 Peter," *In Die Skriflig* 50:3 (2016): 1–8.
Davids, Peter H., *A Theology of James, Peter, and Jude*, Biblical Theology of the New Testament (Grand Rapids, MI: Zondervan, 2014).

Downs, David J., "'Love covers a multitude of sins': Redemptive almsgiving in I Peter 4:8 and its early Christian reception," *JTS* 65 (2014): 489–514.

Dryden, J. de Waal, *Theology and Ethics in 1 Peter: Paraenetic Strategies for Christian Character Formation*, Wissenschaftliche Untersuchungen Zum Neuen Testament: 209 (Tübingen: Mohr Siebeck, 2006).

Dubis, Mark, *Messianic Woes in First Peter : Suffering and Eschatology in 1 Peter 4:12–19*, Studies in Biblical Literature: 33 (New York: P. Lang, 2001).

Elliott, John Hall, *Ecclesiology and the Scriptural Narrative of 1 Peter* (Eugene, OR: Pickwick Publications, 2016).

Green, Gene L., *Vox Petri: A Theology of Peter* (Eugene, OR: Cascade Books, 2019).

Green, Joel B., "Embodying the Gospel: Two exemplary practices." *Journal of Spiritual Formation & Soul Care* 7:1 (2014): 11–21.

Horrell, David G. and Wei-Hsien Wan, "Christology, eschatology and the politics of time in I Peter," *JSNT* 38 (2016): 263–76.

Liebengood, Kelly D., *The Eschatology of 1 Peter : Considering the Influence of Zechariah 9–14*, Society for New Testament Studies Monograph Series: 157 (New York : Cambridge University Press, 2014).

Martin, Troy W., "Emotional physiology and consolatory etiquette: Reading the present indicative with future reference in the eschatological statement in 1 Peter 1:6," *JBL* 135:3 (2016): 649–60.

Martin, Troy W., "The present indicative in the eschatological statements of 1 Peter 1:6, 8," *JBL* 111 (1992): 307–12.

Michaels, J. Ramsey, "St. Peter's passion: The passion narrative in 1 Peter," *WW* 24 (2004): 387–94.

Volf, Miroslav, "Soft difference: Theological reflections on the relation between church and culture in 1 Peter," *Ex Auditu* 10 (1994): 15–30.

RECENT MAJOR ACADEMIC COMMENTARIES

Achtemeier, Paul J., *1 Peter: A Commentary on First Peter. Hermeneia* (Minneapolis, MN: Fortress Press, 1996).

Elliott, John Hall, *1 Peter : A New Translation with Introduction and Commentary*, The Anchor Bible: 37B (New York: Doubleday, 2000).

Goppelt, Leonhard, *A Commentary on I Peter*, Ferdinand Hahn (ed.), trans. John E. Alsup (Grand Rapids, MI: Eerdmans, 1993).

Michaels, J. Ramsey, *1 Peter*, Word Biblical Commentary: 49, David Allan Hubbard and Glenn W Barker (eds.), (Waco, TX: Word Books, 1982).

OTHER SIGNIFICANT COMMENTARIES

Adeyemo, Tokunboh (ed.), *Africa Bible Commentary* (Grand Rapids, MI: Zondervan, 2010).

Beale, G. K. and D. A Carson, *Commentary on the New Testament Use of the Old Testament* (Grand Rapids, MI; Nottingham, England: Baker Academic; Apollos, 2007).

Beare, Francis Wright, *The First Epistle of Peter: The Greek Text with Introduction and Notes*, second ed. (Oxford: Basil Blackwell, 1958).

Best, Ernest, *1 Peter*, New Century Bible Commentary (Grand Rapids, MI: Eerdmans, 1982).

Bigg, Charles, *A Critical and Exegetical Commentary on the Epistles of St. Peter and St. Jude* (New York: C. Scribner's Sons, 1901).

Bray, Gerald Lewis and Thomas C. Oden, *James, 1–2 Peter, 1–3 John, Jude*, Ancient Christian Commentary on Scripture, New Testament (Downers Grove, IL: IVP Academic, 2000).

Davids, Peter H., *The First Epistle of Peter*, The New International Commentary on the New Testament (Grand Rapids, MI: Eerdmans, 1998).

Donelson, Lewis R., *I & II Peter and Jude: A Commentary*, first ed., The New Testament Library (Louisville: Westminster John Knox Press, 2010).

Dubis, Mark, *1 Peter: A Handbook on the Greek Text*, Baker Exegetical Commentary on the New Testament (Waco, TX: Baylor University Press, 2010).

Edwards, Dennis R., *1 Peter*, Tremper Longman and Scot McKnight (eds.), Story of God Bible Commentary, New Testament Series: 17 (Grand Rapids, MI: Zondervan, 2017).

Feldmeier, Reinhard, *The First Letter of Peter: A Commentary on the Greek Text* (Waco, TX: Baylor University Press, 2008).

Forbes, Greg W., *1 Peter*, Exegetical Guide to the Greek New Testament, Robert W. Yarbrough and Andreas J. Köstenberger (eds.) (Nashville, TN: B&H Academic, 2014).

Green, Joel B., *1 Peter*, The Two Horizons New Testament Commentary (Grand Rapids, MI: Eerdmans, 2007).

Grudem, Wayne A., *1 Peter*, Tyndale New Testament Commentaries (Nottingham, England: IVP Academic, 2009).

Harink, Douglas, *1 & 2 Peter*, Brazos Theological Commentary on the Bible (Grand Rapids, MI: Brazos, 2009).

Hort, F. J. A., *The First Epistle of St Peter I.I–II.17* (London: Macmillan, 1898).

Jobes, Karen H., *1 Peter*, Baker Exegetical Commentary on the New Testament (Grand Rapids, MI: Baker Academic, 2005).

Keener, Craig S., *1 Peter: A Commentary* (Grand Rapids: Baker, 2021).

McKnight, Scot, *1 Peter: The NIV Application Commentary from Biblical Text. . .to Contemporary Life*, The NIV Application Commentary (Grand Rapids, MI: Zondervan, 1996).

Nienhuis, David R., and Robert W. Wall, *Reading the Epistles of James, Peter, John, and Jude as Scripture: The Shaping and Shape of a Canonical Collection* (Grand Rapids, MI: Eerdmans, 2013).

Reicke, Bo, *The Epistles of James, Peter, and Jude*, Anchor Bible Commentary (Garden City, NY: Doubleday, 1964).

Schreiner, Thomas R., *1, 2 Peter, Jude*, The New American Commentary: 37 (Nashville, TN: Broadman & Holman, 2003).

Selwyn, Edward, *The First Epistle of St. Peter: The Greek Text with Introduction, Notes and Essays* (London: Macmillan, 1958).

Senior, Donald and Daniel J. Harrington, *1 Peter, Jude and 2 Peter*, Sacra Pagina Series (Collegeville, MN: Liturgical Press, 2008).

Watson, Duane Frederick and Terrance Callan, *First and Second Peter*, Paideia: Commentaries on the New Testament (Grand Rapids, MI: Baker, 2012).

Witherington, Ben, *Letters and Homilies for Hellenized Christians: A Socio-Rhetorical Commentary on 1–2 Peter*, Letters and Homilies for Hellenized Christians (Downers Grove, IL: IVP Academic, 2007).

Commentary

1 PETER 1:1–2: LETTER OPENING

[1] Peter, an apostle of Jesus Christ, To the exiles of the Dispersion in Pontus, Galatia, Cappadocia, Asia, and Bithynia,

[2] who have been chosen and destined by God the Father and sanctified by the Spirit to be obedient to Jesus Christ and to be sprinkled with his blood: May grace and peace be yours in abundance.

The opening of a letter serves to establish the relationship between the writer and the recipients and to introduce significant themes that will recur in the letter. Like typical Greco-Roman letters, 1 Peter begins with the name of the author and the people addressed followed by a greeting or blessing. Peter[1] identifies himself as the author and adds the description "apostle of Jesus Christ," meaning a person sent to do the work of establishing and instructing churches. Peter identifies the recipients broadly using three categories: "chosen," "exiles," and residents of the "dispersion." In Greek, the first word describing the audience is "chosen." It is only after they are recognized as chosen that they are identified by their experiences of exile and being scattered, dispersed. "Divine election is . . . an integral part of the author of 1 Peter's answer to the social ostracism and persecution of his readers."[2] It is their chosen status that highlights their unique identity, that gives them courage to resist assimilation, and that allows them to modify their behavior in accordance with the instruction of the one who has called them. In 1 Peter

---

[1]   See the Introduction under "Authorship and Date" for a more extensive discussion of the authorship of 1 Peter.

[2]   Paul A. Holloway, *Coping with Prejudice: 1 Peter in Social-Psychological Perspective*, Wissenschaftliche Untersuchungen zum Neuen Testament: 244 (Tübingen: Mohr Siebeck, 2009), 138.

1:3–2:10, a wide variety of images is used (e.g., new birth [1:3]; obedient children, [1:14]; and living stones [2:4]) to remind members of the church that they have been chosen by God. They are chosen according to the *prognōsis*, the foreknowledge, of God the Father. The experience of the audience is one of social displacement; they are experiencing alienation and scattering. In this context, God's foreknowledge is not predetermination but rather serves as "a word of comfort . . . and assures the audience of their place in the plan of God."[3]

From the very beginning of the letter, Peter encourages members of the church by assuring them of their status as people who have been selected by God. God's choice of a group of people echoes the Old Testament and God's choosing of the people of Israel (cf. Exod. 19; Isa. 43:20).[4] This calls to mind the great story of God's deliverance of the people of Israel from the hand of Pharaoh in Egypt.[5] After they received the gift of deliverance, they came to Mount Sinai and there enacted a covenant with the God who rescued them from bondage and oppression. God, out of his grace and mercy, chose this group of people to be his treasured possession (Exod. 19:2; Deut. 14:2). God's choosing of Israelites to be his people begins at Sinai but is reiterated throughout the history of Israel and especially by the prophet Isaiah (Isa. 43:20; 45:4; 65:9). Those whom God has chosen are his beloved children.[6] In 1 Peter 1:1–2, Peter tells his readers that they are chosen by God and identifies them in ways that echo the identity of Israel. From the very beginning of 1 Peter, the audience of the epistle is identified as a group of people chosen by God the Father. The election that Peter describes is the corporate election of God's people, the church.[7] Throughout 1 Peter 1:1–2:10, familial language, such as we see here with the reference to God as father, plays a prominent role in securing the identity of the audience.[8]

---

[3] Paul A. Himes, *Foreknowledge and Social Identity in 1 Peter* (Eugene, OR: Pickwick Publications, 2014), 182. After an exhaustive study of *prognōsis*, Himes argues that the word does not have the meaning "foreordain."

[4] For further comments on the use of the Old Testament in 1 Peter see the Introduction.

[5] F. A. Chamy, "Royal priesthood: The new exodus framework of 1 Peter 1:1–2:10" (MA thesis, Trinity International University, 2016), 24.

[6] Joel N. Lohr, *Chosen and Unchosen: Conceptions of Election in the Pentateuch and Jewish-Christian Interpretation*, Siphrut 2 (Winona Lake, IN: Eisenbrauns, 2009), 31.

[7] For more on corporate election see Matthew W. Bates, *Salvation by Allegiance Alone: Rethinking Faith, Works, and the Gospel of Jesus the King* (Grand Rapids, MI: Baker, 2017), 170–71.

[8] See commentary on 1 Peter 1:3 ff. for a fuller description of the family metaphor.

These chosen ones are also called *parepidēmois* (NRSV, "exiles"). This Greek word has a range of meanings – "sojourners," "resident aliens," "strangers," or "temporary residents"[9] – related to the idea of living in a strange place, thus, in the NRSV, "exiles." These chosen ones are not able to live in the comfortable manner associated with being at home in familiar cultural environments. They face all the dangers and uncertainty contained in that experience. Their location is further identified with the description that they are part of the dispersion and are scattered among the five provinces of Asia Minor. The dispersion or diaspora originally referred to those who remained behind after Jews were allowed to return to Israel. Many who were part of the dispersion settled into their new locations and lived there for generations. This was a different experience from that of exile. By the first century, there were Jews living all around the Mediterranean world. Those who lived outside of Israel were identified as part of the diaspora. Brueggemann distinguishes between exile and dispersion (diaspora) by indicating that "'exile' leads to an expectation of a return home to 'normalcy.' By contrast 'diaspora' is a practice of life and faith among those who are far from home … with no serious expectation of 'returning home' or returning to an old normalcy."[10] Still, those who were part of the dispersion were not fully at home in the places where they lived. They continued to see themselves as outsiders and to be regarded by others as outsiders. Both of the opening descriptions of the audience – exiles and dispersion – point to minority experiences of displacement and insecurity in an unfriendly and hostile world.

The letter is sent to five provinces in Asia Minor, what is current day Turkey.[11] It would have traveled from church to church as the carrier most likely walked along the Roman roads that cross the five provinces. Some have suggested that the order in which the provinces are listed relates to the order of delivery. In this view, the letter carrier most likely brought the letter from Rome to the eastern part of Pontus. After this the carrier would

---

[9]   BAGD; J. P. Louw and Eugene Albert Nida, *Greek-English Lexicon of the New Testament: Based on Semantic Domains* (New York: United Bible Societies, 1988), two vols.

[10] This is quoted from the foreword by Walter Brueggemann published in Lee Beach, *The Church in Exile: Living in Hope after Christendom* (Downers Grove, IL: IVP Academic, 2015), 12.

[11] Further information on the five provinces can be found in the Introduction under "Setting, Power, and Majority–Minority Relationships."

have turned south through the eastern portion of Galatia and on into Cappadocia before once again turning west and north to return to Bithynia, the western portion of the joint province of Bithynia–Pontus.[12] The carrier of the letter, most likely Silvanus (5:12), would have read the letter aloud to the churches and interpreted it. First Peter is called a "general" or "Catholic" epistle because it is addressed to a general audience of churches rather than to one specific church or person, and also because of the general nature of the instructions that are laid out for the churches. No particular churches, cities, or people are addressed in the letter.

A Closer Look: Aliens, Exiles, and Dispersion in the Empire

In 1 Peter, three interrelated descriptions of the audience are used. The words "exiles" and "diaspora" (or dispersion) are found in 1:1 while "aliens" is found in 1:17 and 2:12. These words describe particular realities in the first century. The words that are used for exiles (*parepidēmoi*) and aliens (*paroikoi*) both refer to strangers who reside in a place that is not their home. The first word, which NRSV translates as "exiles," is probably better understood with a translation that captures the transitory nature of the idea. Thus we might speak of "those temporarily residing abroad" (New English Translation) or "those who reside as aliens" (New American Standard Bible). Both of these capture the tenuous nature of the life of the sojourner.

The word *paroikoi* (NRSV, "aliens") also designates the resident alien, but in the social world of the first century that designation fitted within a social hierarchy and afforded a type of legal status. Those at the apex of the political system laid claim to the status of citizen. Below them were the resident aliens who were marked out as being foreign, strange, and outsiders. And below these were strangers, freedmen, and slaves.[13] Those known by the designation *paroikoi* were marked by experiences of "social separation, cultural alienation and a certain degree of personal deprivation."[14] This group of people had a legal, recognized standing in society that gave them greater status than those who were transient or enslaved, but the *paroikoi* experienced restrictions based on their status. They could not vote or participate in the political assemblies of citizens. Obtaining a legally recognized marriage was only possible with a special exemption as marriage was legally restricted to citizens. Similarly, the resident alien had to obtain special permission to engage in commerce, to purchase land, and to pass land on to heirs. A resident alien was neither able to inherit a legacy

---

[12]   John Hall Elliott, *1 Peter: A New Translation with Introduction and Commentary*, The Anchor Bible: 37B (New York: Doubleday, 2000), 84–93.

[13]   John Hall Elliott, *A Home for the Homeless: A Social-Scientific Criticism of 1 Peter, Its Situation and Strategy: With a New Introduction* (Minneapolis: Fortress Press, 1990), 25.

[14]   Elliott, *A Home for the Homeless*, 25.

nor to become the heir of a Roman citizen. In addition to all this, resident aliens were subject to harsher punishment in both civil and criminal judgments.[15]

Peter also refers to his audience as a group of people who are part of the diaspora (also referred to as the dispersion [NRSV], or scattering). The dispersion refers to the scattering of the Jews. After the Jewish experience of deportation (722 BCE for the northern kingdom and 586 BCE for the southern), Jews became scattered among many nations. Some of the very poorest remained in the land of Israel (2 Kings 25:12), many fled to Egypt (cf. 2 Kings 25:26 and Jer. 43:7), and others were taken to exile in Babylon. Jews living in the dispersion were expected to testify to the nations around them about the character of their God by maintaining a distinctive way of life to affirm their covenant relationship.

> Acknowledge him before the nations, O children of Israel;
>> for he has scattered you among them.
> **4** He has shown you his greatness even there.
> Exalt him in the presence of every living being,
>> because he is our Lord and he is our God;
>> he is our Father and he is God forever.
>
> (Tobit 13:3, 5–6, NRSV)

However, various levels of assimilation took place over the centuries that followed their deportation. Some became highly assimilated Greek speakers and were willing to participate in festivals and games even though these were dedicated to pagan gods.[16] At the other end of the spectrum were Jews who maintained fidelity to their God alone and who resisted cultural assimilation by refusing to participate in common social festivals and activities that were seen as opposing Jewish values.

After the exile, when Jews were allowed to return to Jerusalem, only some returned from Babylon. Over time, Jews scattered to many parts of the known world. In some locations such as Alexandrian Egypt there were high concentrations of diaspora Jews. We have significant knowledge of the lives and habits of diaspora Jews living in both the countryside and capital city of Egypt, but our knowledge about the lives of Jews in other parts of the Roman Empire is more limited.[17] The concentration of Jews living in Alexandria, the literary work of Jewish authors like Philo (an Alexandrian Jew), and the favorable conditions of the Egyptian climate and geology have allowed the recovery of much information about diaspora life in

---

[15]   Elliott, *A Home for the Homeless*, 25.

[16]   E. P. Sanders, *Judaism: Practice and Belief, 63 BCE–66 CE* (London: SCM Press, 1992), 216.

[17]   John M. G. Barclay, *Jews in the Mediterranean Diaspora: From Alexander to Trajan (323 BCE–117 CE)* (Edinburgh: T&T Clark, 1996), 13.

first-century Egypt. Less is known about the diaspora experience elsewhere in the Roman Empire. While we can, to some extent, extrapolate from the lives of Jews in one part of the empire to the lives of those living elsewhere, we must continue to be cautious and aware that local conditions varied from one province to another.

It is clear that diaspora Judaism existed in the provinces of Asia Minor. Significant populations of Jews were known in major cities such as Miletus, Sardis, and Ephesus. By Roman decree, Jews were allowed to pursue their worship in synagogues, to observe their religious calendar, and to keep the Sabbath.[18] The residents of Asia Minor often saw Jews as prosperous. Diaspora Jews in Asia Minor supported the temple in Jerusalem with regular contributions, and this could anger local residents who saw the dispersion of funds to a foreign God and temple as a betrayal of civic responsibilities in their own locale.[19] Barclay regards these Jewish "communities as significant entities, represented by influential individuals able to fight for redress . . . there is evidence for Jews both as Roman citizens and as citizens of their own cities, and in general one can only explain Gentile hostility on the grounds that the Jewish community was of influence and importance."[20]

The dispersion (exile and diaspora) was seen as a symbol of God's judgment upon his chosen people. However, over time, as Jews came to live throughout the Roman Empire, it came to be seen as a term that might refer more generally to the scattering of God's people and to the idea that God's people were meant to hold a position of honor among the nations. But, when Jerusalem was overthrown and destroyed in 70 CE, diaspora once again took on a meaning more closely related to the theme of scattering as a sign of God's judgment.[21] The use of the term "dispersion" in 1 Peter has led many commentators to argue for a largely Jewish audience for the letter, while others have understood all three of these terms as metaphorical descriptions of either a Gentile or ethnically mixed church.[22]

Together these three designations (exiles, aliens, and dispersion) for Peter's audience all point to a group of people whose experience is defined as being away from home – the place of security and familiarity. Theirs is the position of outsiders – tenuous and vulnerable, susceptible to mistreatment and oppression, and looked upon with scorn and mistrust by those with greater status and power.

---

[18] Barclay, *Jews in the Mediterranean Diaspora*, 270–71.

[19] Barclay, *Jews in the Mediterranean Diaspora*, 268.

[20] Barclay, *Jews in the Mediterranean Diaspora*, 276.

[21] David G. Horrell, "Between conformity and resistance: Beyond the Balch-Elliott Debate towards a postcolonial reading of First Peter," in Robert L. Webb and Betsy Bauman-Martin (eds.), *Reading First Peter with New Eyes: Methodological Reassessments of the Letter of First Peter* (London: T&T Clark, 2007), 125–6.

[22] See the section on "Audience" in the Introduction for further details.

After establishing the relationship between author and audience, Peter also describes the relationship of the audience with God the Father, the Spirit, and Jesus Christ. The expansion on the letter opening in **v. 2** is unusual as each member of the Trinity is explicitly noted in relationship to the identity of the recipients, even though the early church has not yet developed a full-orbed theology of the Trinity. The recipients have been identified at the beginning as chosen exiles living in the dispersion. Now it becomes clear that these very ones who are experiencing alienation are chosen and known by God the Father, participate in a state of holiness/ sanctification in which they are set apart for God's purposes through the work of the Spirit, and have a purpose that includes obedience since they have been sprinkled with the blood of Jesus Christ. Part of the good news that Peter declares to those who have been chosen is that they have entered into new life through their knowledge of God, the work of the Spirit, and the cleansing blood of Christ. The recipients are invited to respond to this good news with obedience. This introduction is the beginning of a pattern in 1 Peter where theological statements are intertwined with ethical instruction about the types of behavior expected of those who have received new life.

The phrase "to be sprinkled with his blood" has its roots in the cross *and* in the Old Testament. Throughout the New Testament, the blood of Christ refers to the sacrificial death of Jesus Christ on the cross (e.g., Heb. 10:19; 1 John 1:7). The blood of Christ is connected to the new covenant that Jesus Christ makes with those who follow him, those who become the community of his people, the church. In the Old Testament, God covenanted with the people of Israel after he rescued them from slavery in Egypt. In Exodus 24:2–8, Moses communicates the words of the Lord and the people respond with a promise of obedience (v. 3). Moses then ratifies the covenant between God and Israel by taking blood from the sacrifices offered and sprinkling it (*kataskedasen*[23]) over the people. Although the words for sprinkling in Exodus and 1 Peter are not the same, the combination of obedience and ratification with blood make the references in 1 Peter a likely

---

[23] The Greek word for "sprinkling" in 1 Peter (*rhantismos*) is uncommon, and appears only six times in the Bible: 1 Peter 1:2, Heb. 12:24, and four times in Numbers 19. In Numbers 19, the sprinkling is an act of purification after various events that result in uncleanness.

allusion to the account in Exodus. The association of Christ's sacrifice with the ratification of a new covenant strengthens the allusion. On the one hand, Moses brokered a covenant at Sinai, but now a far more perfect covenant is on offer in which the recipients have been chosen by their Father, made holy by the Spirit, and entered into covenant relationship through Jesus Christ. At one and the same time, Christ is the sacrifice offered on their behalf and his blood is the means by which the communities' covenantal bond with Jesus Christ is ratified. The recipients of this letter do not earn their way into relationship with Christ by their obedience. Rather, God chooses, the Spirit enables holiness, and Christ's sacrificial blood ratifies the covenant. And the chosen exiles – those experiencing distress because of their alienation from home – respond to the good news with obedience.

Many other New Testament letters begin with reference to God and Jesus, but Romans is the only other New Testament letter that introduces all three members of the Trinity in the opening sentence and specifies roles for different members of the Trinity. Although the doctrine of the Trinity will develop over the first few centuries of the early church, the opening of 1 Peter demonstrates the beginning of early Trinitarian theology. Father, Son, and Holy Spirit will continue to have distinct roles throughout the book, both in relationship to each other and to the Christians living in exile. In 1 Peter, God is repeatedly associated with authority (e.g., Father 1:2; Judge 1:17; Creator 4:19). Similarly, Jesus Christ is associated with the narrative of redemption (suffering, death, resurrection, ascension, and return). Here, the introduction of the Spirit as the one who sanctifies may serve as an indicator that the Spirit in concert with God and Jesus Christ stands behind the emphasis on holiness and purity in this epistle even if the Spirit is not mentioned as frequently.[24]

Finally, Peter blesses his readers by expressing the desire that grace and peace will be multiplied in the recipients' lives. This is a standard Christian greeting expressed in many New Testament letters that reflects Jewish understandings of God's favor and desire that God's people experience wholeness and tranquility. The description of these qualities as things to be

---

[24]   Kenny Ke-Chung Lai, "The Holy Spirit in 1 Peter: A study of Petrine pneumatology in light of the Isaianic new exodus" (PhD dissertation, Dallas Theological Seminary, 2009), 182–83.

multiplied in the lives of believers is unique to 1–2 Peter and Jude. While this is a standard Christian greeting, it also reflects the early understanding of life as a follower of Jesus. Those who are known by God, designated as holy, and provided with purpose through obedience and cleansing are given the gift of relationship with God. Grace is a gift from God, a set of benefits that they receive. In 1 Peter this will include new birth, all of its benefits, and finally salvation.[25] In addition, those who have experienced trouble gain peace through Christ in a world full of tumult. Peter will write about God's grace in every chapter (1:10, 13; 2:19–20; 3:7; 4:10; 5:5, 10, 12) and peace begins and ends the book (5:14). In a world that understands Caesar as the great benefactor who gives gifts and promulgates peace, Peter points his readers to a different source of favor and peace – God. Those people who feel displaced find themselves gifted with relationship and at peace in the presence of God.

The familiar markers (author, audience, and greeting) of a letter are in place. Several themes of the book including alienation, familial identity, and holiness have been introduced. The opening verses also tell us that this is not an ordinary letter about daily life or specific needs sent from one individual to another. Rather, the description of the recipients as those who are chosen by God, sanctified by the Holy Spirit, and sprinkled with the blood of Jesus indicates that the letter is a theological and literary document designed to encourage a group of people living in troubled circumstances and scattered over a wide area.

A Closer Look: Peter in the Tradition

Peter is the best known of Jesus' twelve disciples. Originally a fisherman (Mt. 4:18), Peter and his brother Andrew left their nets to follow Jesus. Throughout the Gospels, Peter speaks often. He famously identifies Jesus as the Christ, a title that refers to Jesus as God's chosen king, the anointed one or Messiah (Mark 8:29). He also boldly asks Jesus a variety of questions. It is Peter who asks how many times forgiveness must be offered to one who has wronged him (Matt. 18:21). And it is Peter who declares that the disciples have left everything and then asks what they will receive in return (Matt. 19:27). And then it is Peter who makes the audacious

---

[25]   Travis B. Williams, "Reciprocity and suffering in 1 Peter 2,19–20: Reading Χάρις in its ancient social context," *Biblica* 97:3 (2016) 429.

declarations that Jesus must never suffer and die (Matt. 16:22; Mark 8:32) and states that he would never leave or deny Jesus (Matt. 26:35; Mark 14:29; Luke 22:33). But Peter is also well known for warming himself over a fire in the courtyard of the high priest and then denying his relationship with Jesus (Mark 14:66–72) Finally, at the end of the Gospels, we see Peter running towards the tomb and stooping to look in (Luke 24:12; John 20:3–7). In the final chapter of the Gospel of John, Jesus encounters Peter at the Sea of Galilee where Peter has gone with his companions to fish. And just as, in Matthew's gospel, Jesus called to Peter, who was in a boat, so now at the end of John's Gospel, Peter once again sees Jesus from a boat, and when he recognizes that it is the Lord, he swims to the shore. There, Jesus has prepared a meal of fish for the disciples and Jesus once again calls Peter. This time the call is to "tend my flock." Such a call is a reference to caring for God's people, and the reference to a "flock" is a common metaphor for God's people, a reference that will be a prominent part of Peter's instructions to leaders in 1 Peter 5:1–4. After Jesus' ascension, Peter is gathered with others in the upper room and leads in the process of choosing a disciple to replace Judas (Acts 1:15–26). And then at Pentecost when the Holy Spirit descends upon the waiting group of Jesus' followers, Peter is empowered to proclaim the good news message of the death and resurrection of Jesus. Through the work of the Holy Spirit and the message that was proclaimed, the church is birthed in a first wave of conversion (Acts 2). In the next section of Acts, we see Peter as a disciple who brings healing (3:1–10) and continues proclaiming the good news (3:11–26) in ways that mirror the ministry of Jesus who also healed and proclaimed good news. Peter's continued preaching and church leadership result in multiple imprisonments (4:3; 5:18; 12:3). Peter is repeatedly presented as one of the most important leaders in the early church, and it was through him and his willingness to go to the house of a Roman centurion that the Lord first brought the message about Jesus Christ to the Gentiles (Acts 10–11). And when others might have required Jewish identity signs such as circumcision and food laws to be applied to Gentiles, Peter agreed with Paul that such things should not be required of the Gentiles (Acts 15). The book of 1 Peter does not focus on its author, but does contain references to the words of Jesus and to the eyewitness experiences of Peter. However, a letter that introduces its author as the apostle Peter draws on the knowledge of the early church about the experiences of Peter that are known and communicated in the Gospels and Acts. The letter presents Peter as an apostle, one who has been sent and commissioned by Jesus for the work of planting churches and making disciples. In 1 Peter 5:1, when Peter turns his attention to church governance, he identifies himself as a fellow elder and as one who witnessed the suffering of Christ. In the letter we encounter Peter, the mature apostle, instructing a flock that is not at home and reminding them of both their identity and their responsibilities.

Bridging the Horizons: For those readers who live in countries where the free practice of religion is upheld, it may be difficult to relate to the experience of exile, dispersion, and alienation experienced by the audience of 1 Peter. Yet, those who experience a new covenantal identity as God's chosen ones and receive the cleansing that is made available through the blood of Jesus and the work of the Holy Spirit face the same call to live a life of obedience to the one who has brought them into new relationship. It is the life of obedience to God that has the potential to lead to alienation from all that surrounds us that is not from God. When Christian practice closely mirrors the practice of the larger society of which it is a part, it is appropriate to ask whether the members of the church are fully living out the obedience to which they are called. Such obedience may be deeply costly as those among whom the church resides come to see Christians as strangers in their midst. In the event of any alienation, readers are invited to remember Peter's wish that God's favor will be multiplied many times over and that wholeness and tranquility will abound in their lives.

1 PETER 1:3–12: THE NEW BIRTH INTO SALVATION

[3] Blessed be the God and Father of our Lord Jesus Christ! By his great mercy he has given us a new birth into a living hope through the resurrection of Jesus Christ from the dead,

[4] and into an inheritance that is imperishable, undefiled, and unfading, kept in heaven for you,

[5] who are being protected by the power of God through faith for a salvation ready to be revealed in the last time.

[6] In this you rejoice, even if now for a little while you have had to suffer various trials,

[7] so that the genuineness of your faith—being more precious than gold that, though perishable, is tested by fire—may be found to result in praise and glory and honor when Jesus Christ is revealed.

[8] Although you have not seen him, you love him; and even though you do not see him now, you believe in him and rejoice with an indescribable and glorious joy,

[9] for you are receiving the outcome of your faith, the salvation of your souls.

[10] Concerning this salvation, the prophets who prophesied of the grace that was to be yours made careful search and inquiry,

[11] inquiring about the person or time that the Spirit of Christ within them indicated when it testified in advance to the sufferings destined for Christ and the subsequent glory.

[12] It was revealed to them that they were serving not themselves but you, in regard to the things that have now been announced to you through those who brought you good news by the Holy Spirit sent from heaven—things into which angels long to look!

After beginning with a standard letter opening that clearly identifies the sender, the recipients, and the work of God in their lives, Peter moves to another form, "blessing," which expresses praise for God. Peter's praise begins in v. 3 and develops over the course of one long Greek sentence that describes the work God does on behalf of the audience. By beginning the first main section with a focus on the praise of God and the benefits that believers receive through their relationship with God, Peter establishes goodwill with his audience while introducing important themes, such as salvation and suffering, which will continue in the rest of the book.[26] The sentence ends in v. 12 although most English translations break up the sentence into more manageable parts with the insertion of periods. The whole of what follows in vv. 3–12 is part of the praise and worship of God and celebrates the gracious gift of salvation first named in v. 3 and brought to its final summation in v. 12. We will examine the sentence in three sections: vv. 3–5 focus on God and the identity of those who have received new birth; vv. 6–9 focus on the experiences of the letter recipients; vv. 10–12 focus on salvation.

While Peter begins with praise directed towards God, his attention turns very quickly to Jesus Christ and will come to include the work of the Spirit as well (v. 12). Once again, we see early Trinitarian ideas at work in the opening segments of 1 Peter. As in v. 2, the persons of the godhead are not static and there is a generative and transformative relationship expressed that is directed outward towards the chosen exiles who are now further identified as family members of the Trinitarian God. God is not identified as a singularity or an autonomous, all-powerful being. Rather, God, who has already been identified as Father in v. 2, is now identified in v. 3 as the Father of our Lord Jesus Christ. Jesus Christ is also identified by his relationship to his followers. He is "our lord," the master, the one to whom they give obedience and through whom they receive initiation into the new

---

[26]   Barth L. Campbell, *Honor, Shame, and the Rhetoric of 1 Peter*, Dissertation Series: Society of Biblical Literature: 160 (Atlanta: Scholars Press, 1998), 57.

covenant (vv. 2–3). In 1 Peter the members of the Trinity are understood both in relationship to each other and to believers.

> ### A Closer Look: Fathers, Children, and Households in the Greco-Roman World
>
> Within the Roman Empire there were a variety of ethnic configurations of the family. In the Roman family, fathers held the most important role as the head of the household (*paterfamilias*) and exercised authority over all the other members of the household, including their adult sons. A household included a man and his wife, their children, and any slaves they might own. When Roman children grew up they often moved out of their father's house and established households of their own. However, they remained bound to their father by the flow of money made available to them by him. And control of family resources, including the inheritance, remained with the father until his death.[27] These families were typically small.[28] Both Greek and Jewish family structures were larger and more extended than the Roman family structure and often multiple generations lived together in one household. Greek and Jewish fathers also retained considerable power in their families, although to a lesser extent than Roman fathers.[29] Fathers tended to be disciplinarians who focused on helping children grow up to be good members of society. At the same time, they showed care and concern for their children.[30] A father provided his household with honor, which was one of the keys to status in the first century. Those with greater authority, stronger patronage networks, and high social positions accrued more honor, while lowly households accrued less honor. When Peter names God as the father of Jesus Christ and as one who has begotten children, God is associated with great honor and is identified as exercising authority over the household and its resources, including the inheritance.
>
> Children receive the gift of life from their parents. They therefore have legitimate obligations to show respect and obedience to their parents. Dionysius of Halicarnassus writes "that they [children] should honour and obey them in all things, both in their words and actions."[31] A child was expected to bear a resemblance to their father not only in looks but also in disposition and character.[32] Children were obligated to act in ways that brought honor rather than dishonor, shame, or disgrace to the family.

---

[27] Holloway, *Coping with Prejudice*, 163.

[28] Paul Veyne, *The Roman Empire*, trans. Arthur Goldhammer (Cambridge, MA.: Belknap Press of Harvard University Press, 1997), 71–72.

[29] James S. Jeffers, *The Greco-Roman World of the New Testament Era: Exploring the Background of Early Christianity* (Downers Grove, IL: IVP, 1999), 239–40.

[30] Jeffers, *The Greco-Roman World of the New Testament Era*, 247.

[31] *Ant. Rom.* 2.26 (LCL).

[32] David Arthur deSilva, *Honor, Patronage, Kinship & Purity: Unlocking New Testament Culture* (Downers Grove, IL: IVP, 2000), 187.

Mothers provided early sustenance and guidance for children. Then, around age six, the father began to oversee the education of the child within the home. The educational goal was to enable the child to function in the world and to move from external enforcement of values to the internalization of honorable and moral ways of living. When Peter refers to his audience as "obedient children" (1:14) and enjoins them to be holy as the one who called you is holy (1:15), he is drawing on a common first-century understanding of the family. Obedience was expected of children as was living a moral life that resembled the character and values of one's father.

Wives/mothers often managed the household, cared for babies and young children, and participated in the larger business of the family unit, such as farming, fishing, or pottery making. Managing the household included planning so that the food from one harvest would last until the next. Failure to plan well could lead to poor nutrition, hunger, or even starvation when food was not plentiful.[33] When Peter instructs his readers to long for "pure, spiritual milk" (2:2), he is drawing on a motherly image of good tasting, pure milk. All milk comes from mothers, and Peter will go on to remind them that they have tasted this milk and found it good (2:3).

This brief look at fathers, children, and mothers and the way these categories are applied to God and the audience of 1 Peter is a reminder of the predominance of the metaphor of home, household, and family throughout the epistle.[34]

The recipients of the letter are those who are *anagennēsas*, who "are begotten again or born again" (v. 3). The Greek word used for "begotten or born again" occurs only in 1 Peter (vv. 3, 23) and nowhere else in the New Testament or the Septuagint (LXX). It is a compound word derived from the suffix *ana* (with the general meaning of "up" and the more specific meaning here of "repetition" thus "again"), which is combined with *gennaō* (mostly referring to the male activity of begetting but also to the female activity of giving birth [BAGD]). The portion of 1 Peter that begins here and extends to 2:10 is focused on issues of identity. Peter seeks to shore up the identity of his beleaguered audience. He begins by identifying God as the father of Jesus and then by identifying his audience as those "begotten" by God. They share in the same familial relationship as that between God the Father and the Son, Jesus Christ. Peter specifies that the life the exiles

---

[33]　Andrew Wallace-Hadrill, "Domus and insulae in Rome: Families and housefuls," in David L. Balch and Carolyn Osiek (eds.), *Early Christian Families in Context: An Interdisciplinary Dialogue* (Grand Rapids, MI: Eerdmans, 2003), 190.

[34]　Elliott makes this case extensively in his work. Elliott, *A Home for the Homeless*.

now have is one that came into being on account of God's mercy. They do not deserve the new life they have received nor have they earned it; rather it is a gift, an act of God's kindness and compassion.

Like all newborns, the chosen exiles are born into a particular familial context. The audience have their origin as children of God because of God's mercy. A child does not conceive itself or plan its existence. Instead, the beginning of life and new birth is simply gift. These reborn children are welcomed into the family with three gifts. Each gift is a reality that is present now and will come to its fullness in the future. Peter denotes these grace-filled contexts with the same preposition (*eis*, meaning "into") repeated three times. They are born into a living hope, an inheritance, and a future salvation.

Hope is a necessary element for life in the present. Those without hope wither away in despair. At the same time, hope by its nature is unseen in the present (Rom. 8:24) and oriented towards the future. The hope that Peter's audience experiences is modified by the adjective "living," which contrasts with such ideas as "dead" or "false" hope. Their new birth into a state of living hope takes place through the resurrection of Jesus Christ from the dead. The connection between living hope and Jesus' resurrection cannot be overlooked. Jesus himself experienced persecution that led to his death on the cross. But God raised him from the dead, vindicating his life, his message, and his sacrifice and enabling now, in this world, new birth, life, and identity for all those who belong to Christ. Those who are hearing this letter face the challenges of persecution and life in a society that does not know or trust their message, but they are members of the same family and belong to the same father who raised Jesus from death. Their living hope as children of God is based on Jesus' resurrection. This is the source of their living hope as they cope with a hostile social setting.

As God's children, they have an inheritance. This too is a current reality. They know their Father has an inheritance to pass along. The inheritance is already secured, and this current knowledge about the future strengthens their faith. Their inheritance has three qualities. It is imperishable, undefiled, and unfading. Nothing can happen that will destroy this inheritance. It is guaranteed. It is not subject to the threats that destroy earthly inheritance but is safe and secure in the presence of God, in heaven.

God's promise that his children will receive an inheritance is familiar. In the Old Testament, God made a covenant with Abraham that he would have children who would inherit the land God promised. God grew and sustained that family and fulfilled his promise to them, and the language of inheritance became a regular way of identifying the land God gave them.[35] Now God's children are once again provided with an inheritance. This time it is an inheritance that cannot be destroyed or taken away. In Asia Minor true resident aliens had limited rights to legally pass on an inheritance of property (if they possessed it) or land tenure. Those addressed as resident aliens, whether having become so through political exile or through obedient faith, now find themselves the children of the greatest father and benefactor. Those whose faith brought them defamation and trouble find that in their identity as God's children they can be assured that God almighty is protecting their inheritance. Indeed, it is kept in heaven, the place where God dwells, for them. But not only is the inheritance protected, it also becomes clear that they themselves are too (the word for "guarded" is derived from the context of guarding cities and prisons) by the power of God through faith for salvation.

Before Peter introduces the third reality, "salvation," his long sentence takes a digression. After describing the inheritance, he has to mention where and how that inheritance is secured. And once he has filled out the nature of the inheritance, he also describes in further detail whom the inheritance is for. In the midst of this expansion on the inheritance we come across the little phrase "through faith." In the first five verses of the book, God does so much. He is the one who chooses, who begets, who keeps an inheritance and protects its recipients. But this little phrase reminds us of the part that is played by those who experience new birth. They trust. In so doing they show their loyalty to their father and patron and thus honor their father. "Firm trust in God becomes a source of stability for the believer, allowing him or her, in turn, to be a reliable client of God and friend of fellow believers (Col. 1:5)."[36]

And now we come to the third state into which believers enter through new birth: salvation.[37] It too is a reality that they experience now while still

---

35   See Exod. 13:32, Chamy, "Royal priesthood," 40.
36   deSilva, *Honor, Patronage, Kinship & Purity*, 145.
37   Like the other two, this one is also introduced with the preposition *eis*. However, there is debate over whether this third use of the preposition is truly parallel. Many scholars understand "into salvation" as a parallel with the living hope and the inheritance of vv. 3–4 and a further modification of the new birth. Paul J. Achtemeier, *1 Peter:*

awaiting its fullness. The salvation they anticipate is described as "ready to be revealed in the last time." Salvation is described using a word (*hetoimēn*) that is sometimes used in contexts where a group is called to a meal that is ready. Similarly, the way that salvation is described in 1 Peter has a quality that is both "now," it is ready, and a quality that is "not yet" but rather future, the revelation will occur in the last time. For the first time, the theme of the "last time," which is repeated in 1 Peter, is introduced. The early church understood the last time as the time in which they were currently living. In the life, death, resurrection, and ascension of Jesus, God inaugurated the last time. So, the author of Hebrews can write "in these last days" to refer to his own time (Heb. 1:2). At the same time, the early church anticipated a final triumphant return of Jesus Christ in which the whole world would see and acknowledge Jesus as the true ruler of the world (e.g., Phil. 2:9–11). The fullness of salvation will be realized for those who have experienced new birth when they are together in the presence of the one who has made the way for them, through his resurrection from the dead, into the full presence of God. In 1 Peter, salvation is presented as an event that is unfolding and that will be fully realized upon the return of Jesus Christ. This salvation has implications for the life that they live and it will be fully realized on this earth when Jesus Christ returns.[38] In other words, 1 Peter is not advocating an otherworldly life of faith in which one's soul flies away to heaven but is rather portraying "heaven" as the secure bank where the church's inheritance is held until that day when Jesus Christ returns and salvation is realized in all its fullness, when God and God's people dwell together. This salvation is not something they earn.

A Commentary on First Peter, Hermeneia (Minneapolis, MN: Fortress Press, 1996), 97; Greg W. Forbes, *1 Peter*, Exegetical Guide to the Greek New Testament, Robert W. Yarbrough and Andreas J. Köstenberger (eds.), (Nashville, TN: B&H Academic, 2014), 19. However, others have suggested that *eis* shows purpose and modifies "being protected" (*phrouroumenous*) – Mark Dubis, *1 Peter: A Handbook on the Greek Text*, Baker Exegetical Commentary on the New Testament (Waco, TX: Baylor University Press, 2010), 8 – so that those who received new birth are guarded with the purpose of receiving salvation. Jobes sees the *eis* as modifying "being protected," but identifies it as a temporal marker: Karen H. Jobes, *1 Peter*, Baker Exegetical Commentary on the New Testament (Grand Rapids, MI: Baker Academic, 2005) 89–90. However, since salvation in 1 Peter is not purely in the future, it is likely that "into salvation" describes a third aspect of the new birth.

38 N. T. Wright, *The Resurrection of the Son of God*, vol. 3 of Christian Origins and the Question of God (Minneapolis, MN: Fortress Press, 1996), 465–66.

Rather, it is what results from God's choosing and begetting of them. Their response is lived out in a life of faithful hope in the Father who has given them life, identity, hope, and inheritance.

Verses 6–9 focus on the present experience of the audience. The audience rejoices in God and in the gift of new birth, which is the subject of vv. 3–5. They rejoice in their status and identity as chosen children of the Father who have received a living hope through the resurrection and an imperishable inheritance guarded by God. They anticipate joyfully the salvation they will receive when Jesus is fully revealed. The emotion they experience is joy. But, at the very same time, they experience obstacles to their joy: suffering.[39]

A Closer Look: Emotions in the Greco-Roman World

First Peter, like other biblical books, incorporates emotions such as joy, distress, hope, and fear among others. Emotions are culturally conditioned responses and are not universally shared across every culture. Sometimes there is a tendency to associate emotions with the irrational or with chaotic behavior, but emotions do have their own logic and contain both cognitive and physiological components that are experienced as a whole process.[40] Both Greco-Roman and Jewish writers demonstrate careful attention to emotions in their writing. While we do not know the physiological experiences some underwent when they felt joy or distress, we can study the objects of emotions.

Emotions are an interpretive lens. The same experience can produce different emotional responses depending on the way in which that experience is interpreted. For example, one person may shake a fist at another person. Someone who perceives that action as a threat will feel fear, but someone who perceives that action as a provocation may experience anger. The emotional response becomes an interpretive lens. That interpretive lens forms a basis for action. People tend to move away from things that produce negative emotions and towards things that produce positive emotions.[41] The cultural groups to which an individual belongs provide an emotional map that enables individuals to respond in emotionally appropriate ways to people and events that occur in their contexts. In the first century there were several

---

[39]   Lauri Thurén, *Argument and Theology in 1 Peter: The Origins of Christian Paraenesis*, Journal for the Study of the New Testament: 114 (Sheffield: Sheffield Academic Press, 1995) 100.

[40]   Katherine M. Hockey, *The Role of Emotion in 1 Peter*, Society for New Testament Studies Monograph Series: 173 (New York: Cambridge University Press, 2019) 26.

[41]   Hockey, *The Role of Emotion in 1 Peter*, 31.

ways of understanding emotions. Three of the most significant ideas about emotions are found in the work of the Stoics, of Aristotle, and the Septuagint.

Stoicism was a philosophy that first began around 300 BCE in Athens and was influential into the third century CE. It was the leading philosophy among the Romans of the first century and was a highly integrated understanding of life. In English the word "stoic" has come to be applied to someone who does not show emotion; however, the Stoics wrote and thought extensively about both negative and positive emotions. Emotions were understood within the context of the mind and soul, which the Stoics understood as material substances to which emotions were subject. One of the keys to the Stoic way of life was regulating the passions (emotions) through mental assessment of those emotions. The four passions that Stoics discussed were fear, desire, grief, and mental pleasure.[42] Other emotions were understood as subcategories of these four passions. The first three of these are found in 1 Peter. The goal of Stoic philosophy was to achieve a way of life that was in accordance with the natural mental state and led to virtuous behavior. To achieve this goal required monitoring and assessing emotions to ensure they led to the proper end. Those which did not, such as fear and grief, should be excised or avoided. In 1 Peter, there is no suggestion that emotions should be avoided or that only some emotions are appropriate.

In contrast to the Stoics, others preferred a middle or moderate way. Aristotle thought that emotions were states that produced pleasure or pain (*Nic. Eth.* 1105b). Emotions were engaged well when the emotion that was experienced or expressed fit with the circumstance that produced it and was of the appropriate intensity. Aristotle gave the following example: "one can be frightened or bold, feel desire or anger or pity, and experience pleasure and pain in general, either too much or too little, and in both cases wrongly; whereas to feel these feelings at the right time, on the right occasion, towards the right people, for the right purpose and in the right manner, is to feel the best amount of them, which is the mean amount—and the best amount is of course the mark of virtue" (*Nic. Eth.* 1106b).[43] The right amount of emotion expressed in the right way and for the right reasons was a mark of virtue and thus of honor. The ancient art of rhetoric often appealed to emotions to help persuade listeners to take up the course of action that a speaker proposed.[44] Throughout 1 Peter, we see the author working to dispel the audience's emotions of shame and fear. While they might feel fear, that fear should drive them towards

---

[42] Hockey, *The Role of Emotion in 1 Peter*, 59.

[43] H. Rackham (ed.), "Aristotle, *Nichomachean Ethics*," Perseus Digital Library, Tufts University.   www.perseus.tufts.edu/hopper/text?doc=urn:cts:greekLit:tlg0086.tlg010 .perseus-eng1:1106b

[44] Troy W. Martin, "Rhetorical step-child," 67.

good behavior in relationship to God (cf. 1:17). At the same time, awareness of the benefits they have received from God also brings joy. Peter urges his audience to live with confident trust in God and to realize that they have honor and worth in the sight of God.

We also see emotions expressed in the Jewish literature of the Second Temple period, particularly in the Septuagint. This literature helps us to see another way of understanding emotions in the Greco-Roman time period. While Jewish literature written in or translated into Greek makes use of the same terms for emotions that are used in other Greek literature, they are used in different contexts. In addition, some words for emotions, such as the verb "rejoice," are used extensively in the LXX but are absent from other Greco-Roman literature. Because the LXX does not provide an extensive discussion on the nature of emotion, Hockey directs attention to the contexts in which emotions are used and the objects of the emotions. Again, going back to the observation about "rejoice," we can ask what the object of that rejoicing is. "In the LXX rejoicing was oriented towards God ... but was specifically occasioned by his just judgments, mercy, and salvation. We find two of these highlighted in 1.3–9: mercy and salvation."[45]

Hockey argues that in 1 Peter "through his use of emotions, the author is showing the audience how to perceive reality and therefore also how to position others and the self."[46] In other words, Peter is not merely recording the emotions of his audience but is advocating that his readers take a certain emotional stance towards the world that they inhabit. They are able to take this emotional stance for three reasons. First, the object of their emotion is God, and they can trust that the emotions they experience in relationship to that object will lead them towards the goal that they desire: new birth, mercy, and salvation. Second, as members of a new family, they are receiving instruction from their new community about the types of people and experiences in their reality that should bring about positive emotions (e.g., joy and hope) and what kinds of people and experiences should bring about negative emotions (e.g., sorrow or fear). As they grow in their new identity as the family of God, they will come to an ever deeper experience of the positive emotions associated with the object of their affection, Jesus Christ, and will endure grief or pain in order to reach the fullness of salvation for which they long. Third, they will encounter a variety of emotions including mercy, hope, fear, joy, grief, and brotherly affection. These should not be surprising in their context and are not to be avoided but rather used to further their faithful response to God's salvation.

---

[45]　Hockey, *The Role of Emotion in 1 Peter*, 117.
[46]　Hockey, *The Role of Emotion in 1 Peter*, 38.

There is some discussion about the object of the believers' joy in v. 6. Do they rejoice in the last time (end of v. 5) when they anticipate that Jesus will be revealed? Such a reading would require that the present tense verb "rejoice" be understood with a future sense. This is a possible understanding of the Greek tense that is supported by grammarians and reflected among the early church fathers, later Latin commentators, and early English translations.[47] Usually, this interpretation of the verb is correlated with their present experience of grief and with the idea that joy and grief are mutually exclusive, particularly in the ancient understanding of joy and grief as opposite emotions that cannot exist simultaneously. The second option argues that they rejoice in God and the benefits of the new birth described in vv. 3–5. This would allow the present tense "rejoice" to retain its present sense of current rejoicing.[48] This position also allows for the present tense of "rejoice" in both vv. 6 and 8 while accounting for the context of vv. 3–5. In 1 Peter 1:3, it is God's mercy that is the cause of God's action of new birth on behalf of the chosen exiles. And in 1:5 salvation is highlighted as an outcome of God's protection and the believers' faith. Mercy and salvation are gifts the believers receive from God. Hockey points out that, "The benefits the believers have received are not to be rejoiced in as isolated items in themselves; they are their possession only because of God's mercy towards them and through Christ. Thus, it is this relationship [with God] that is central to joy."[49] However, this position must still address the relationship between rejoicing and grieving or suffering. Hockey suggests a more expansive view of the present so that it refers to the "whole time-frame in which the believer currently sits—the current epoch before the eschaton" rather than to a particular moment in time.[50] Verbal aspect reminds us that the aorist tense, "although experiencing sadness" (*lupēthentas*), is the unmarked tense and that other tenses, such as the present, are more marked and thus have more emphasis. So, the emphasis falls on the state of rejoicing – a rejoicing that takes place

---

[47]   This reading is supported by Troy W, Martin, "The present indicative in the eschatological statements of 1 Peter 1:6, 8," *JBL* 111 (1992): 307–12; Troy W. Martin, "Emotional physiology and consolatory etiquette: Reading the present indicative with future reference in the eschatological statement in 1 Peter 1:6," *JBL* 135:3 (2016): 649–60.

[48]   For discussion see Achtemeier, *1 Peter*, 100.

[49]   Hockey, *The Role of Emotion in 1 Peter*, 125.

[50]   Hockey, *The Role of Emotion in 1 Peter*, 120.

now and, in light of the last time mentioned at the end of v. 5, continues into the future.

In **vv. 6–9**, more of the situation that the exiles face is revealed. What is interesting is that rather than being laid out with attention to the facts, their situation is laid out in emotional terms: rejoicing and grieving. The source of the believers' joy is both the person and gifts of God in vv. 3–5. God and the mercy that God displays are a source of joy as are the gifts of God, such as new birth, mercy, and salvation. In addition, v. 8 shows that the person of Jesus Christ, whom they love even though they have not seen (v. 8), is also connected to their experience of rejoicing. In between these two experiences of joy, Peter introduces the grief or pain (*lupēthentas*) they experience because of the various trials that they face. Their experience of suffering is surrounded by the emotion of joy.[51] These residents of the five provinces of Asia Minor are experiencing, or anticipate experiencing, sadness and emotional distress because of a variety of suffering and trials. As the book unfolds, it becomes more evident that these are trials of various types. Travis Williams suggests a spectrum of trials that may have confronted the Christian in Asia Minor. At one end of the spectrum was a mixture of social ostracism and verbal abuse that had the potential to flare up into violence, and on the other end were experiences such as being accused and tried as a Christian before the governor's tribunal. Such trials could be brought by local adversaries and would not be a systematic attempt by the Roman government to persecute all Christians, but would still present a real threat of lethal consequences for Christian identity.[52] These negative experiences cause emotional distress. Hockey understands the verb here as an emotional state of distress rather than as generalized suffering. Thus, the joy expressed in vv. 6 and 8 is in contrast to the distress experienced because of the various trials they face, and the joy they currently experience tempers the distress that lasts "for a little while."[53] Here it seems that 1 Peter anticipates both the conditional and the transitory nature of their suffering. The phrase "even if" points to the possibility of trials but not to their certainty. And the exiles may suffer "for a little

---

[51] Hockey, *The Role of Emotion in 1 Peter*, 128.

[52] Travis B. Williams, *Persecution in 1 Peter : Differentiating and Contextualizing Early Christian Suffering*, vol. 145 of *Supplements to Novum Testamentum* (Leiden: Brill, 2012), 300–16.

[53] Hockey, *The Role of Emotion in 1 Peter*, 129.

while," but their suffering will not last forever. Many seek to avoid grief and suffering, but Peter instructs the churches to rejoice in God and God's gifts in the midst of grief caused by a variety of trials. In this way, Peter introduces a key subject of the epistle: suffering on account of one's faith and the response to such suffering.

Tests or trials are referred to in 1 Peter 1:6–7. In v. 6 the grief that the Christians experience comes about because of trials (*peirasmoi*).[54] In **v. 7** the idea of testing is repeated using the verb "to test" (*dokimazō*) and a cognate noun. There are two ways to think about this type of test. First, it can be a test that determines whether something is genuine (NRSV). Second, it can be a test that determines the value of something (NASB). The English Standard Version (ESV) captures a bit of both senses with the translation "the tested genuineness of your faith." Verses 6–7 both point to the trials and testing that face those who stand firm in their faith in Jesus Christ. Faith that is tested by suffering is more precious than gold, which is described as perishable, even though its purity has been tested with fire. Faith endures while gold perishes. The picture that Peter appeals to is that of a refiner's fire. Metallurgy was well known in the ancient world and the image of the refiner's fire is known in Greco-Roman literature, the Old Testament, and Second Temple Jewish Literature. For example, in Jer. 6:27 God says to the prophet, "I have made you a tester and a refiner among my people so that you may know and test their ways" (*dokimazō* is used three times in this verse). This is followed by a description of the bellows and the fire, parts of the refining process (Jer. 6:29). But this is not the most likely source of the image in v. 7. The Old Testament passages alluding to refining are used in a context that indicates that God's people have gone astray and are in need of purification. In contrast, some of the quotations that come from other Jewish literature describe God's testing as an affirmation of the righteous. For example, Wisdom 3:1 begins by stating that the righteous are in the hands of God. Wisdom 3:2–5 show that those who observe the experience of the righteous might see them as simply dying or suffering, but in reality (vv. 5–6) they have been tested and approved by

---

[54] While this word sometimes refers to temptation, it is used repeatedly in a wide variety of secular Greek literature to refer to the testing of character and should be understood as trials or tests here. Craig A. Evans and Stanley E. Porter (eds.), *Dictionary of New Testament Background* (Downers Grove, IL: InterVarsity Press, 2000), 1207–11. Article I.

God. Wisdom 3:6 uses the same word (*dokimazō*) as 1 Peter 1:7 when it says, "as gold in the furnace, he tested them, and as a sacrificial whole burnt offering, he accepted them" (New English Translation of the Septuagint [NETS]). Wisdom 3:7–8 describes the righteous as ones who shine (v. 7) after the time of testing, and who will come to "judge the nations and rule over peoples." In other words, the time of successful testing is followed by being honored, a pattern that is similar to the pattern of testing followed by glory in 1 Peter 1:7. Similarly, in Sir. 2:1–6 there is a depiction of a close link between faith that has been tested and the testing of precious metals. Gold was a valuable metal in the first century, but in the eyes of God faith that has endured despite various trials is even more precious. The faith of the believers is tested by the trials that they endure, and the result of faithful endurance in the face of suffering is praise, glory, and honor directed towards Jesus Christ when he is fully revealed at the second coming.

Honor was a core value across both Jewish and Greco-Roman culture in the first century. One of the important ways that people obtained honor was by having others speak well of them or praise them for their deeds and their reputation as honorable people. Praise is the act of expressing approval for someone. The tested faith of those who have endured trial due to their commitment to Jesus results in their favorable recognition when Jesus is revealed. Hort indicates that while "praise" is often used of both humans and God, "glory" and "honor" more properly belong to the realm of the divine.[55] There is a gradation upward from praise to glory and honor. Similarly, glory is the enhancement of one's reputation, often for carrying out extraordinary deeds.[56] For those suffering because of their faith, the temptation to abandon faith in Christ and return to a former life would be strong, but Peter encourages them with the reminder that enduring testing brings glory and honor. These are the very virtues valued by the cultures of the first century. The followers of Jesus receive praise, glory, and honor when Jesus is revealed at the last day. The wording here in 1 Peter 1:7 with the preposition *en* (in) does not have to be exclusively

---

[55] F. J. A. Hort, *The First Epistle of St Peter I.I-II.17: The Greek Text with Introductory Lecture, Commentary, and Additional Notes* (London: Macmillan, 1898), 44.

[56] "[C]oncern for others leads to enhancement of one's δόξα [glory] or reputation" (BAGD).

temporal. It can also have an instrumental sense, so that the revealing of Jesus is also an unveiling of those who have trusted their Lord and thus are worthy of praise from the world around them.[57] In 1 Peter the testing of faith, fiery trials, and eschatology are all linked together. Testing and trials occur now, but at the final revelation of Christ suffering will cease and recognition of the praiseworthy nature of Christians will rise.

Verse 8 indicates that the recipients of the letter were not eyewitnesses to the life of Christ. They had not seen Jesus, but despite their lack of eyewitness experience in the past, they love Jesus Christ. Larry Hurtado, writing about Paul, makes an observation that can also be applied to 1 Peter. He observes that few discuss the "strong affective tone" of Paul's messianic Christology. Judaism emphasized God's love, but the *Messiah's* love, and affective love for Messiah, is "to my knowledge, without precedent or analogy in other forms of Second Temple Jewish messianic discourse. One factor helping to account for this might be that Paul's messianic figure is a real, known person of then-living memory, whereas most other types of ancient Jewish messianism projected some future, as yet unidentified figure."[58] Even though they have not and do not see Jesus Christ, they have come to love this person whom others had indeed seen in person. Their experience is an ongoing, active experience of love in the present.

In addition, they do not see Jesus now, but they believe (*pisteō*). Their belief is not an intellectual assent to the facts of Jesus' life, death, and resurrection; rather, their experience of Jesus is embedded in the emotional ties of deep relationship, the bonds of love, trust, and joy that draw people closer together. These bonds grow out of the sacrifice that Christ offers on their behalf (the sprinkled blood of the new covenant and the resurrection from the dead) that are foundational to their living hope. There is a deep emotional connection to the one whose revealing (v. 7) they anticipate. And their experience of new birth and cleansing solidify their trust in one whom they have not seen in the flesh.

Their joy is so deep that it is "indescribable" (v. 8), beyond words. And their joy is glorious. On the one hand, the "glory" of v. 7 is something they

---

[57]   Hort, *The First Epistle of St Peter I.I–II.17*, 44.
[58]   Larry W. Hurtado, "Paul's messianic Christology," in *Paul the Jew: Rereading the Apostle as a Figure of Second Temple Judaism* (Minneapolis, MN: Fortress, 2016), 115–16.

anticipate when Jesus is revealed. On the other hand, the joy that they experience now is already filled with glory and will continue to be filled with glory (*dedoxasmenē* is a perfect participle used as an adjective, which can indicate an action already completed but with continuing significance or relevance). The exalted nature of the joy that they experience contrasts deeply with the grief, trials, and testing of vv. 6b–7. In other words, the life of the believer is one in which they already experience "glory" in their current joy and anticipate sharing in the divine glory to come at the revelation of Jesus Christ. Glory is part of the Greco-Roman framework of honor and here the clients of Jesus participate in the greatness, honor, and fame of their patron Jesus Christ when he is revealed.

The outcome of their faith is that they are currently receiving (present participle) the salvation of their souls. The Greek word for soul (*psuchē*) refers to "human beings in their entirety as *living beings* animated by the breath of God (Gen. 2:7). [In other words,] ... personal selves as living beings and not their 'spiritual souls' alone, are the object of divine salvation."[59] The logical result of trust in the one who has given new birth is to receive what is anticipated – full salvation. In v. 5, salvation is anticipated as a future event that will be unveiled on the last day. In **v. 9**, salvation is an ongoing present experience. Peter's view of salvation is not static. He sees salvation as God's deliverance from sin and futility (1:18), as a present experience of new birth (1:3, 9), and as a future reality that will unfold out of the revelation and triumph of Jesus Christ (1:5; 3:21–22).

In **vv. 10–12**, the long sentence that began in v. 3 draws to a close with an emphasis on the salvation that Peter's readers are already experiencing and the completion of which they can anticipate. This salvation is further described as "the grace that was to be yours." While some have described the grace that is spoken of here as the inclusion of the Gentiles in God's plan of salvation,[60] it is probably better to understand it as another way of talking about the salvation that comes through the sufferings and subsequent glories of the Messiah.[61] Such grace demonstrates both God's favor towards the exiled audience of 1 Peter and the beneficial gift they have

---

[59]   Elliott, *1 Peter*, 344.
[60]   Edward Selwyn, *The First Epistle of St. Peter: The Greek Text with Introduction, Notes and Essays* (London: Macmillan, 1958), 252.
[61]   Leonhard Goppelt, *A Commentary on I Peter*, Ferdinand Hahn (ed.), trans. John E. Alsup (Grand Rapids, MI: Eerdmans, 1993), 96.

received in and through the Messiah. The prophets, most likely a reference to the Old Testament prophets, who prophesied about this grace, searched, and carefully inquired about the grace Peter's readers have received. The prophets had two questions to which they carefully attended. They wanted to know "who" and second "when."[62] It was the Spirit of Christ who made clear to the prophets beforehand the content of the good news that Peter's readers have now received. The phrase "the Spirit of Christ" only occurs here and in Rom. 8:9. Old Testament prophets clearly experienced prophecy through the Spirit (1 Sam 10:6; Hosea 9:7; Joel 2:28). In 1 Peter the prophetic Spirit is directly connected to Christ. Some have argued this refers to the preexistent Christ who is described as foreknown from the foundation of the world (1:20).[63] Others have argued that this is the Spirit that came upon Christ at his baptism.[64] Still others contend that the Spirit active in prophecy had already been experienced in prior times but is now understood fully from the perspective of God's work through his Son Jesus Christ.[65] Jobes indicates that the point here is that "the Spirit who was the agent of revelation to the prophets of old is the same Spirit of Christ known to the first-century church."[66] Verses 10–12 invite us to think about time – the time beforehand during which the prophets prophesied, the experience they had of the Spirit of Christ testifying to them before the events unfolded, the events themselves (the sufferings and glories of Christ), and the experiences of the readers who have received this good news through the ministry of the prophets and proclamation enabled by the Holy Spirit (v. 12). Across this great span of time, the Spirit of Christ and the Holy Spirit are working for the benefit of the readers, those in the early church.

The specific content that the Spirit of Christ related to the prophets concerned the sufferings and glories of the Christ: his passion and the resurrection and ascension to follow. In his life, ministry, and death Jesus experienced a variety of types of suffering. He knew the suffering of being

---

[62]   The word *tina* can be either an interrogative adjective modifying *kairon* with the meaning "which or what sort" of time, or it can be an interrogative pronoun (who or whom). This second meaning fits well with 1 Peter where *tis* is used as a pronoun elsewhere (e.g., 3:13).

[63]   Achtemeier, *1 Peter*, 111.

[64]   Beare, *The First Epistle of Peter: The Greek Text with Introduction and Notes*, 66.

[65]   Goppelt, *A Commentary on I Peter*, 99.

[66]   Jobes, *1 Peter*, 101.

despised by those in his hometown who did not understand his ministry (Luke 4:24–29), of being misunderstood by those who were close to him (Mark 8:31–33), of being betrayed (Luke 22:3–4) and denied (Mark 14:68–70) by his disciples, and of being crucified by those in power (Matt 27:26–44). Most likely, 1 Peter focuses on the suffering related to his passion as also seen in 2:22–23. But the prophets foresaw both suffering and glory. Glory is a state of splendor and greatness that is also connected to fame, honor, and renown. Throughout the Old Testament, glory is ascribed to God. And God's glory is particularly connected to God's presence with his people at Mount Sinai: there, the covenant that was enacted was characterized by glory (Exod. 24:16). For Jesus Christ, his glory comes about through the resurrection in which the new life that he receives from God vindicates his suffering and death and verifies the truth of his teaching and the efficacy of his sacrifice. Luke 24:26 shares this same unfolding of suffering and glory. The Messiah had to die, but after death comes the glory of the resurrection and new life (cf. Luke 24:46–47). Those to whom this particular letter was written are already experiencing suffering and trials (vv. 6–7) and anticipate receiving glory if they steadfastly endure suffering on account of their faith (v. 7). They can look to Jesus as their example of one who also suffered and then received glory, but Jesus is not simply the example. He is also the Messiah, the one chosen by God, to bring about full salvation at the completion of time.

In **v. 12** it becomes clear that the witness that the prophets received was not for their own benefit but for the benefit of Peter's readers. Indeed, the prophets are described as serving Peter's audience with their work of seeking out and inquiring about the time and person who would bring God's gift to the believers and the proclamation of Messiah's suffering and glory. Now, it is these truths that are proclaimed through those who brought the good news to them by means of the Holy Spirit who was sent from heaven. Almost as an aside, Peter adds, "things into which angels long to look." This brief statement reminds the audience of the favor they have experienced through hearing and responding to the good news. It also reminds them of their elevation above the angels, having been the recipients of the good news about Jesus. The status of the believers is elevated in these verses. Although they are experiencing suffering, they are served by the prophets of old and are enabled to look into and understand realities that angels wish they could explore.

Recent work on vv. 10–12 has focused on its role as an interpretive lens through which to understand the use of the Old Testament in 1 Peter. Two major suggestions have been put forward. First, Joel B. Green has argued that we can rightly see the Old Testament as Christian Scripture because it testifies to the one plan of God. This plan is made known through the Spirit of Christ and now comes to focus in Christ and is proclaimed and affirmed by the church through the Holy Spirit. The unity of Old and New Testament comes about because "Scripture's subject and focus is God, whose identity is found in three persons, Father, Christ, and Spirit."[67] God's redemptive plan is consistent between both testaments. Green following Peter argues that this is so because "the Christ in whom Christians place their trust and now worship is the same Christ who long ago revealed the ways of God in the Scriptures. Interpretively, then, Israel's Scriptures are not predictions that Christ would fulfill, but rather testify to the Christ . . . who first inspired them."[68] This becomes a model to help us understand the use of Scripture in 1 Peter. Green points to the use of the prophet Isaiah in 1 Peter 2:21–25 as an example of God's consistent purposes so that "the suffering of Christ and the suffering of Yahweh's righteous servant" both bring about salvation for sinful people.[69] In this way, 1 Peter 1:10–12 reveal a consistency between the Old and New Testament that is rooted in God and made available through Christ and the Spirit. In contrast, Benjamin Sargent has argued that we should see discontinuity rather than continuity between the Old Testament prophets and the use of Scripture in 1 Peter. He argues that vv. 10–12 indicate that the prophets were searching diligently regarding the person through which and time when the sufferings and subsequent glories of the Christ would be revealed. Verse 12 then follows with the statement that "It was revealed to them that they were serving not themselves but you." Sargent argues that "Because the Prophets 'served not themselves but us', Scripture is viewed by Peter as primarily describing things of importance to the early Church."[70] Thus, Peter can utilize Scripture as if it were written directly for the benefit of the church. This comes through in two main ways:

---

[67]   Joel B. Green, *1 Peter*, The Two Horizons New Testament Commentary (Grand Rapids, MI: Eerdmans, 2007), 254.

[68]   Green, *1 Peter*, 251.

[69]   Green, *1 Peter*, 252.

[70]   Benjamin Sargent, *Written to Serve: The Use of Scripture in 1 Peter*, Library of New Testament Studies: 547 (London: Bloomsbury T&T Clark, 2015), 31.

instruction and proclamation. The Scriptures are written both to teach the church significant truths about the Messiah and to proclaim the good news of salvation that has come about through Jesus Christ. Ultimately, according to Sargent, this teaching function of Scripture will be the means of shaping the identity of the church because "the Prophets spoke to serve the very communities to who Peter writes."[71]

A Closer Look: Suffering, Redemption and Status in the Ancient World

First Peter makes a significant contribution to the biblical theology of suffering. In the Old Testament there were prevailing ideas that those who suffered did so because they had sinned. This type of theology can be seen in the dialogue of Job's friends who urge him to repent so that he can return to God (e.g., Job 22:21–26). Meanwhile, Job argues that he has done nothing wrong and indeed wishes to present his case before God so that he can be vindicated (Job 5:8). God counters the argument of the friends that Job must have sinned; instead, the end of the book of Job recounts God's sovereign nature and refutes the mistake of the friends. A similar idea persists in the New Testament. In John 9:1–2, Jesus and his disciples encounter a man who is blind from birth. The disciples assume that the blind man's condition is the result of sin and ask whether it was the man himself or his parents who sinned. Jesus replies (9:3) that neither of them sinned but rather his blindness was for the purpose of revealing God's glory. Jesus refutes the idea that all suffering is the result of sin. Some suffering may indeed be the result of sin on the part of the person who is suffering, as even 1 Peter acknowledges, but both the Old and New Testament refute the idea that all suffering is a recompense for wrongdoing on the part of the one who suffers. The letter of 1 Peter is clear that believers may experience suffering. And Peter also distinguishes between suffering for wrongdoing (e.g., 2:20; 4:15) and suffering that is directly tied to the choice to follow Jesus Christ (1:6–7; 2:19; 4:16). Those who suffer because of faith are in a different situation than those who suffer because of sin or those who suffer because of general troubles in this world (e.g., sickness, loss, disaster). In the eyes of God the status of those who suffer for their faith is elevated and they are worthy of God's favor (e.g., 2:20).

Bridging the Horizons: In the major opening section of 1 Peter, the audience is reminded of their new identity as the children of God who belong to the family of

---

[71]   Sargent, *Written to Serve*, 49.

God. Their Father is utterly reliable and protective of them and of their inheritance. The emotional response to their new familial identity is one of joy even if they experience suffering for a time on account of this new identity. They can expect honor if they endure faithfully the suffering they experience on account of their faith and such endurance demonstrates the genuine nature of their faith. These familial ties also involve the emotional bonding of family members who rejoice in what God has done for them and who love and trust Jesus Christ, the one who has made this new life possible through his death and resurrection. They can be confident that the salvation they have received has both been anticipated from long ago and is also now specifically revealed for them. They have been recipients of the good news about Jesus Christ proclaimed through the power of the Holy Spirit. They are chosen and special in the eyes of God – indeed, perhaps they are even to be envied by the angels who long to look into these things – even if they are aliens in the eyes of the world around them.

1 PETER 1:13–2:10: LIVING IN RESPONSE TO NEW BIRTH

1 Peter 1:13–2:3: Growing in Holiness and Love as God's Children

[13] Therefore prepare your minds for action; discipline yourselves; set all your hope on the grace that Jesus Christ will bring you when he is revealed.

[14] Like obedient children, do not be conformed to the desires that you formerly had in ignorance.

[15] Instead, as he who called you is holy, be holy yourselves in all your conduct;

[16] for it is written, "You shall be holy, for I am holy."

[17] If you invoke as Father the one who judges all people impartially according to their deeds, live in reverent fear during the time of your exile.

[18] You know that you were ransomed from the futile ways inherited from your ancestors, not with perishable things like silver or gold,

[19] but with the precious blood of Christ, like that of a lamb without defect or blemish.

[20] He was destined before the foundation of the world, but was revealed at the end of the ages for your sake.

[21] Through him you have come to trust in God, who raised him from the dead and gave him glory, so that your faith and hope are set on God.

[22] Now that you have purified your souls by your obedience to the truth so that you have genuine mutual love, love one another deeply from the heart.

[23] You have been born anew, not of perishable but of imperishable seed, through the living and enduring word of God.

²⁴ For "All flesh is like grass and all its glory like the flower of grass. The grass withers, and the flower falls,

²⁵ but the word of the Lord endures forever." That word is the good news that was announced to you.

2:1 Rid yourselves, therefore, of all malice, and all guile, insincerity, envy, and all slander.

² Like newborn infants, long for the pure, spiritual milk, so that by it you may grow into salvation –

³ if indeed you have tasted that the Lord is good.

Those who are chosen by God, given new birth, and honored with the gift of salvation are instructed to live in particular ways. In the Greek text, there are five imperative verbs (hope [1:13], be holy [1:15], conduct yourselves [1:17], love one another [1:22], desire [2:2]) that structure this section that extends from 1:13 to 2:3. In many English translations, including the NRSV, there are a lot more than five imperative verbs. This reflects the choice of translators to understand the Greek participles in this section as having an imperatival force. Generally, the imperatival use of the participle in the New Testament is rare and if the participle can adequately be connected to the main verb it should be translated in a way that reflects that. However, there are clear examples of the imperatival participle in 1 Peter such as the participles at 2:18 and 3:1.⁷² Other scholars have thought that either Aramaic and/or Greek were both developing in a way that brought more use of the imperatival participle into the language and that this is reflected in 1 Peter.⁷³ Despite this argument, many contemporary scholars have seen the quantity of imperatival participles in 1 Peter as being limited to clear examples such as are seen in 2:18; 3:1; 3:8–9, and 4:7–10. However, a participle that is in close relationship to an imperatival verb can derive imperatival force from the relationship with the main verb while still being a participle. Thus Forbes indicates that participles can have a double duty in which they function with imperatival sense *while also* carrying adverbial sense.⁷⁴ In 1 Peter 1:13–2:3, the use of five imperatival Greek verbs alongside many participles shows that the author of 1 Peter was able to distinguish between the participle and the imperative. This commentary will discuss the

---

⁷² Daniel B Wallace, *Greek Grammar beyond the Basics: An Exegetical Syntax of the New Testament* (Grand Rapids, MI: Zondervan, 2008), 650–52.

⁷³ Forbes, 1 Peter, 6.

⁷⁴ Forbes, *1 Peter*, 7.

participles in relationship to the main verb that they accompany rather than treating them as imperatives. This normal adverbial function of the participle is often an important means of giving further nuance to the instruction of the main imperative. These participles may carry imperatival meaning but that meaning is subordinate to the main imperatival verb. In instances later in the book where the imperatival participle is clearly used, this will be discussed more fully (see 2:18 and 3:1 in particular). Finally, as with each section of 1 Peter, this section of the text is embedded in the Scriptures of the early church and contains a variety of quotations and allusions to the Old Testament, which will be explored in greater depth.

Verse 13 begins with "therefore," which acts as a hinge between 1:3–12 and what follows. In vv. 3–12 Peter has turned the hearers' attention to the praise of God and the identity that they derive from their new birth into the family of God. In the cultures of the first century, those who have been born into a particular family are expected to live in ways that bring honor to the family.

Their identity is one that is being tested but in which they are persevering through the gracious gift of salvation that they received. In this passage, Peter will lay out a response to that gift. The first of five imperatives is found in v. 13. Each imperative verb is plural and should be read as something like "all of you" are to take up this action. The whole community of believers is to live together as the family of God that has experienced the gift of salvation. These instructions are a means to living that life together. Peter's first instruction to his readers is that they are to "set their hope." This instruction is preceded by two participles describing behavior that accompanies it. The opening phrase is translated by the NRSV as "prepare your minds for action," but a more literal rendering of the phrase (found in the marginal note of the NRSV) is "gird up the loins of your mind." The Greek phrase *anazōsamenoi tas osphuas* meaning "girding up the loins" literally refers to the action undertaken by anyone wishing to work, run quickly, or fight in a battle who must first gather up the folds of the long garment worn by most first-century males and tie it about the waist so that it does not get in the way. The whole phrase "girding up the loins of your mind" is a metaphor that NRSV rightly, if less colorfully, translates as being prepared. Before a reader can set their hope, they need to take action to prepare their mind. The action described is in the aorist tense, which indicates that preparation happens before a person sets their hope, just as people gird up their garments prior to the activity they are to undertake. At the same time, a person must also be completely sober (*nēphontes*). Again, the participle is used metaphorically, this time to refer to being self-controlled, but it is in the present tense indicating an ongoing need to be restrained, levelheaded, and disciplined. These two metaphors together present a picture of a person who is prepared for action as needed while being calm, attentive, and restrained. These are the circumstances[75] under which Peter instructs his readers to "set their hope." The imperative is, as Michaels notes, "the first of many aorist imperatives in 1 Peter ... These aorists can be called 'programmatic'; they have the force of directives, setting a course for the churches to follow in the days ahead."[76] Hope is a future-oriented emotion in which a person anticipates receiving a future benefit.[77] In the Old Testament, the object of hope is frequently the Lord.[78] And hope in the Old Testament is also directed towards attributes of God, such as mercy,[79] and actions of God, such as speech and decisions.[80] In these cases, it is clear that those who hope are not simply hoping in the attributes of God but are hoping in God and God's capacities. In 1 Peter, the object of hope is most directly "grace," which refers to the gift of salvation made available to God's children and that demonstrates favor towards them.[81] Grace is being brought (passive participle) to them when Jesus Christ is revealed. The subject of "being brought" is left unstated, though the NRSV has made the subject explicit with the translation "that Jesus Christ will bring you when he is revealed." However, since in Greek Christ is the object of the revelation, it is probably better to understand God as the one who brings grace and also, by implication, reveals Jesus Christ. An expanded translation would read "hope on the grace being brought by God when Jesus Christ is revealed." The hope of the recipients is the same type of hope that is found repeatedly

---

[75]   The participles are most likely adverbial descriptions of attendant circumstances. See Achtemeier, *1 Peter*, 118.

[76]   J. Ramsey Michaels, *1 Peter*, Word Biblical Commentary: 49, David Allan Hubbard and Glenn W Barker (eds.) (Waco, TX: Word Books, 1982), 55.

[77]   Hockey, *The Role of Emotion in 1 Peter*, 208.

[78]   For example, LXX: Ps. 13:6; 15:1; 17:3, 30; 20:8; 21:3–11 (where hope in both its noun and verbal forms is used) 30:2; 117:9.

[79]   For example, LXX: Ps. 32:18; 51:10; 146:11.

[80]   For example, LXX: Ps. 118:42–43, 74, 114.

[81]   Cf. commentary on 1 Peter 1:10.

in the Old Testament – hope in God and in the grace that God offers. But now that grace is understood as favor that is received through the person of Jesus Christ and is brought to its fullness on the day when Jesus returns. The revelation of Jesus Christ has already been mentioned in v. 7 where the same phrase occurs. There it refers to the day when Christ will return, and it should be understood with that meaning here as well. It is possible that "when he is revealed" also refers to the revelation that has already taken place in the good news of Jesus' life, death, and resurrection. While both meanings are possible, the focus on hope, a future-oriented emotion rooted in trust, and the earlier eschatological orientation of v. 7 point towards the future revealing of Jesus in the last day. The recipients of the letter are to be prepared for action and to have a disposition of self-control as they orient themselves towards hope because of the grace that they are already receiving and will continue to receive until the day God fully reveals Jesus Christ and the salvation promised in 1:9 is finalized.

Elliott suggests that the instruction to hope is part of a small inclusio:

A Hope (v. 13)
  B Holiness (vv. 14–16)
  B¹ Holiness (vv. 17–21b)
A¹ Hope (v. 21c)[82]

Hope in God and knowledge of the grace that has been received surrounds the teaching on holiness and serves as a further reminder that a life of holiness comes about in the context of hope.

In **vv. 14–16** Peter once again emphasizes familial language while now drawing out the instruction to be holy. **Verse 14** begins with the description "like obedient children," which recalls to the hearer's mind their identity as a child begotten by God the Father and given living hope, an inheritance, and salvation (vv. 3–5). Now, the hearer is reminded that someone born into the household of God is instructed to be an obedient child. In both Jewish and Greco-Roman culture, obedience as a character trait was expected of children. This expectation extended into adulthood as an adult son remained subject to his father.[83] Peter's readers would not have found

---

[82] Elliott, *1 Peter*, 355.

[83] "But the lawgiver of the Romans gave virtually full power to the father over his son, even during his whole life, whether he thought proper to imprison him, to scourge him, to

it odd to understand themselves as children, whether grown or not, who had a responsibility of obedience to their Father, but they also knew that the Father to whom they belonged extends mercy, grace, and salvation to them, qualities that would not necessarily have been expected from earthly fathers.

A life as an obedient child who has entered into a new family is to be different from the former life. Peter lays out a contrast (*alla*, but) between "not being conformed to former desires in your ignorance" (v. 14) and living in conformity to "the Holy One who called you" (v. 15). The choice that is presented is between continuing to be molded by the patterns that come from one's former ignorant desires or allowing oneself to be molded by the Holy One, a reference to God, drawing on the Old Testament (e.g., 2 Kings 19:22; Job 6:10; Ps. 71:22). In this context, the phrase "former desires" points towards unholy cravings, passions, and lusts which controlled a person's life before their entry into a new family through new birth. The audience is described as being ignorant. As those who have come to be born again by God through Jesus, this ignorance extends to all those who do not know the ways of God and the salvation made possible through Jesus Christ. In contrast to the old life, the new life is to be lived in conformity with the Holy God. To be holy is to be set apart. When the word "holy" is used to describe God it refers to God's unique nature as one who is completely pure, uncontaminated, and distinct from all that is evil or unholy. While God is set apart by God's very nature, God has sought to be present with humanity from the beginning of creation, first in the Garden of Eden and then through special covenantal relationship with Abraham and Israel. In

put him in chains and keep him at work in the fields, or to put him to death, and this even though the son were already engaged in public affairs, though he were numbered among the highest magistrates, and though he were celebrated for his zeal for the commonwealth. Indeed, in virtue of this law men of distinction, while delivering speeches from the rostra hostile to the senate and pleasing to the people, and enjoying great popularity on that account, have been dragged down from thence and carried away by their fathers to undergo such punishment as these thought fit; and while they were being led away through the Forum, none present, neither consul, tribune, nor the very populace, which was flattered by them and thought all power inferior to its own, could rescue them. I forbear to mention how many brave men, urged by their valour and zeal to perform some noble deed that their fathers had not ordered, have been put to death by those very fathers, as is related of Manlius Torquatus and many others. But concerning them I shall speak in the proper place." (Dionysius of Halicarnassus, *Ant. Rom.* 2.26, LCL, 319, (Cambridge, MA: Harvard University Press, 1937).

order that God could dwell with human beings who were sinful and ritually unclean, God instructed Moses to build a tabernacle, a dwelling place for God in the Israelite camp where God could be present in holiness and where God's people could approach him through covenant membership and the sacrificial system. In 1 Peter, God's temple is now made up of the living stones of God's church (1 Peter 2:4–5, 9) and allusions to this new temple and the holy people who constitute it happen throughout 1 Peter.[84] This Holy God is one who calls. Calling is reminiscent of the Father who calls the names of his children, and here that calling extends an invitation and summons to a new life. Peter now introduces the second imperative of 1:13–2:3: be holy in all your behavior. This instruction is followed immediately in v. 16 with a reason drawn from Scripture, "*for* it is written, 'You shall be holy, for I am holy.'" The phrase that is quoted here is a formula drawn from Leviticus where it occurs prominently in chapters 11, 19, and 20.[85] The book of Leviticus is itself located in a narrative that extends from Exodus 19 through Numbers 10.[86] This is the narrative of God's formation of the people of Israel at Sinai through the enacting of the covenant. Within the context of a narrative that focuses on God's gracious deliverance of Israel, God's holy character, and the means (covenant and sacrifice) of entering into relationship with God, chapters 11, 19, and 20 of Leviticus describe practices that set apart the people of God from those around them. Leviticus 11 sets out the restricted dietary practices of God's people. Leviticus 19 is the beginning of what has been labeled the holiness code – a portion of Leviticus describing the behaviors of God's holy people. Leviticus 19 in particular deals with a wide variety of behavior, from honoring one's parents at the beginning of the chapter (v. 3) to having just weights and balances (v. 36) at the end. To be holy is to be set apart and invited to participate in the very nature of God. Just as God dwelt in holiness among his people, so too God calls his people to holiness both

---

[84] Andrew Mūtūa Mbuvi, *Temple, Exile, and Identity in 1 Peter*, T&T Clark Library of Biblical Studies (London: T&T Clark International, 2007), 70–128.

[85] The phrase is found with minor variations at Leviticus 11:44, 45; 19:2; 20:7, 26. Patrick T Egan, *Ecclesiology and the Scriptural Narrative of 1 Peter,* (Eugene, OR: Pickwick Publications, 2016), 78.

[86] John Oswalt, *Called to Be Holy: A Biblical Perspective* (Nappanee, IN: Evangel Publishing House, 1999), 28. Oswalt notes that this can be broken up into five parts roughly labeled Covenant (Exod. 19–24]; Tabernacle (Exod. 25–40); Worship (Lev. 1–17]; Holiness code (Lev. 18–27); and Preparation to depart Sinai (Num. 1–10:11).

in relationship to God and in relationship to others. In 1 Peter this holiness is clearly contrasted with a former way of living. It is clear that holiness is not simply the offering of sacrifices or entry into relationship with God but that rather holiness is to govern all of life in its particularities, details, and material realities. However, the holiness code is not simply a list of rules and regulations but is part of God's loving instruction (*torah*) that sets the parameters of life in relationship with God. Such holy behavior is an imitation of the holy nature of God and a gift to one's neighbors since holy living is good for the community. The people are to be like the one to whom they belong and since that one is holy, they too are to live holy lives. Peter draws on this quotation in v. 16 to substantiate the turn from an old life controlled by evil desires to a new life in which obedient children come to resemble the one who fathered them.

The familial language of this section continues in **v. 17**. The opening "if" of v. 17 should be understood as introducing a stated reality[87] and could be translated as "*since* you invoke as Father the one who judges all people impartially according to their deeds." Two images are brought together in this phrase. The already familiar image of father (vv. 2, 3) is now joined with the image of the impartial judge. There is some tension between these two images. On the one hand, children anticipate that a good father will show partiality to his children, choosing them over others. The biblical tradition speaks frequently of God as father. In Deuteronomy 32:6 the Lord is described as the father who created "you," which is reminiscent of God's fatherly activity in 1 Peter 1:3. The Psalmist identifies God as the father of the fatherless (68:5) and the Psalmist cries out to God as his father (89:26). The prophet Isaiah speaks of God as the Father who redeems (63:16) and who shapes his children like a potter (64:8). Alongside these references that speak to the compassion and generative activity of God are many references to the faithful relationship of God to the ancestors of Israel. In other words, God's identity as Father is not an image of an authoritarian ruler but of the compassionate head of a household who desires the best for his children even when that best requires discipline. This image of the Father is recognizable even in the Greco-Roman culture that saw fathers as the ultimate household authority. Ideally such authority was not wielded for

---

[87] Elliott, *1 Peter*, 364.

the sake of slavish obedience but for the betterment of the family. In contrast to the father who is partial to his children, the ideal judge was expected to be impartial. Both the Old Testament (Deut. 16:19) and Greco-Roman custom speak to the cultural expectation of the impartiality of judges.[88] Just as God is identified as Father throughout the Old Testament so too God is identified as judge. 1 Samuel 2:10 speaks of the Lord who "will judge the ends of the earth." And Psalms 96:10 states that God "will judge the peoples with equity." God's judgment is based on the works, meaning the deeds and behavior, of each individual. God the Father is also God the impartial judge of all humanity, and God does not show favoritism and does not excuse the misbehavior of anyone, God's children or otherwise. The children may invoke (*epikaleisthe* can mean "appeal" in legal contexts[89]) God as their father but must not forget God's role as judge.

The third imperative, "live in reverent fear," appears in the context of life before the one who is both Father and judge. The NRSV captures the sense of *phobos* well. When fear is directed towards God it often means "reverence" or "respect" and is associated with a sense of awe. But a translation that only focuses on reverence or respect can gloss over the root sense of "fear" that *phobos* often carries, and the judge's courtroom is a place of fearful trembling and not simply awe. Thus, the translation "reverent fear" captures well the attitude the believers are to have. God is the compassionate Father, but this should not be taken lightly or flippantly. The new life that a believer lives should be conducted with reverence and awareness of the power that brought them forth. Verses 15 and 17 share a cognate word (*anastrophē*) that denotes conducting oneself according to certain principles that are good and upright. This word is used repeatedly in the next couple of chapters as Peter focuses intently on the behavior of the believers who live in exile.[90] As members of God's household, they are to conduct themselves in ways that are good and reflect the family to which they belong. The judge of what constitutes right behavior is not the culture or context in which they live but God. In a culture that values honor and assigns honor based on proper behavior in the eyes of the culture, Peter

---

[88] Luke Ming-Mou Tsai, "Brothers in dispute: A socio-economic and legal analysis of the litigants in the church of Corinth" (PhD, Dallas Theological Seminary, 2016), 164.

[89] Campbell, *Honor, Shame, and the Rhetoric of 1 Peter*, 67.

[90] Expanded comments on exile can be found in the commentary on 1 Peter 1:2.

sets up God as the judge in the court of reputation and gives a command that urges the whole community to strive towards a way of life different from that of their neighbors.[91]

Verses 18–21 provide support for the preceding instruction to "live in reverent fear" (v. 17). Peter answers the question, "why should we live in this manner?," by indicating that their living in reverent fear is tied to what they know about how they were ransomed. Verses 18–21 form another long sentence with one main verb in the Greek text: "you were ransomed." Verse 18 spells out the negative side of the equation indicating what was insufficient for their ransom and what they needed to be ransomed from. Verse 19 describes the price that was actually paid. The emphasis on the negative is temporary and serves to heighten the reception of the positive assertion that follows.[92] Verses 20–21 further describe the Messiah and those who believe.

Peter's audience know that they were not ransomed with perishable things like silver and gold (vs. 18). This statement points to an allusion to Isaiah 52:3 which speaks of the Lord redeeming Israel without silver. In 1 Peter the emphasis is that the price paid for them was *not* an earthly amount of silver and gold, which is subject to the decay and destruction of this world. Even these precious metals (especially gold) that are not known for their decay are not comparable to the price that was actually paid in order to redeem or ransom them. There are two backgrounds for the word *lutroō*, which appears in v. 18. First, it was a term used to describe money paid to buy the freedom of a slave or prisoner of war. The slave then either belongs to a new master or may be set free. Thus, Peter portrays the audience of the letter as having a former way of life that is a life of captivity and bondage; they have now been bought out of that way of life and belong to God. Second, "ransom" is rooted in the Old Testament where God is described as redeeming Israel. The verb is first found in Exodus 6:6 where God gives Moses the following message for Israel: "I am the LORD, and I will free you from the burdens of the Egyptians and deliver you from slavery to them. I will *redeem* you with an outstretched arm and with mighty acts of judgment." God is repeatedly identified as the one who ransoms Israel (Exod. 15:13; Deut. 7:8; 9:26; 13:6; 15:15; 24:18; 1 Chron. 17:21;

---

[91] deSilva, *Honor, Patronage, Kinship & Purity*, 58.
[92] Dubis, *1 Peter*, 21.

Ps. 77:15; Micah 6:4). In Isaiah's prophetic proclamation to Zion he says, "You were sold for nothing, and you shall be redeemed without money" (Isa. 52:3). While Isaiah depicts a redemption without money echoing Isaiah 45:13 and the declaration that Israel will be released by Cyrus without payment, in 1 Peter the focus is on a price *beyond* any monetary price. Peter understands the redemption made available in Christ through the lens of God's deliverance of Israel from bondage in Egypt *and* through the lens of the new exodus, the return from exile, in the prophet Isaiah. But this redemption in 1 Peter is far greater than liberation from a national oppressive regime and is instead redemption from futility.

Peter begins with the hopeful reminder of their ransom before turning to *what* they are ransomed from – the futile ways of their ancestors. Neither their ransom, nor what they inherited from their family circumstances, nor the price that was needed to redeem them are new to this audience. The apostle is reminding them of something they already know, a fundamental teaching of the apostles about God's redemptive work (e.g., Titus 2:14). Those who have become part of the family of God know that their participation in this new life was costly as it meant leaving behind their ancestors' valued ways, which are now described as futile. Elliott shows that Greco-Roman literature evaluated "things handed down from the ancestors" positively and gave honor to wisdom drawn from antiquity.[93] But Peter identifies these ways of living as fruitless or empty in their outcomes. In discussions about the audience of 1 Peter, this verse has been used to argue that the majority of the readers may have been Gentiles because Peter would not describe God's covenant people, the Jews, as having ancestors whose way of life was futile.[94] However, the contrast here is not between Jews and Gentiles but between those who have experienced new birth and belong to the family that God is now forming, and those who have not yet come into relationship with God through the blood of Jesus Christ. God is making a new covenant in Christ and is inviting the whole world, Jews and Gentiles, into new relationship through the person of Jesus Christ. In other New Testament books we find futility associated with the worship of false gods (Acts 14:11–15), with dissension and quarreling among Christians (Titus 3:9), and with thinking that one's way of life is

---

[93]   Elliott, *1 Peter*, 370.
[94]   Elliott, *1 Peter*, 96.

religious though it contains little self-control or true religious action such as helping those in need (James 1:26–27). Futility can be found in both the worship of other gods and in the failure to live into God's covenant. While the futility of previous ways of life may be different for Jews and Gentiles, the need for new birth (v. 3), salvation (v. 5), and the grace of God (v. 10) are universal. And, Peter reminds his audience that the salvation and wisdom that he shares with them come from "before the foundation of the world" and thus are even more ancient than the salvation and wisdom they received from their fathers.[95]

Verse 19 begins with a contrast (*alla*, but) between the price that was not paid, gold and silver, and the price that *was* paid for the redemption of believers. They were bought with the precious blood of Christ. The blood of Christ is described with the adjective *timios*, which is related to the noun "honor," and is used here to describe Jesus' blood as being precious and having exceptional value, a value far greater than gold or silver.[96] Campbell notes that Christ's "shed blood is precious because it is shed according to God's plan (cf. v. 20) and thus honorably. If the suffering of Jesus is honorable, so is that of those it ransoms."[97] This precious blood is compared to a lamb without defect or blemish. This alludes to the sacrificial lambs of the Old Testament, and the Passover lamb itself, where the offerings were required to be animals that were perfect in every way.[98] While the Old Testament offerings are not described using exactly these words, it is clear that a perfect animal was to be brought for sacrifice (e.g., Lev. 1:3; 3:1; 4:23, 28; 5:15). Having just alluded to Isaiah 52 in 1 Peter 1:18, it is possible that v. 19 refers to the passage in Isaiah 53 in which the servant is described as a lamb (Isa. 53:7).[99] Jesus is referred to as a lamb in John's Gospel (John 1:29, 36) and Acts 8:32 also points us to a Christological understanding of Isaiah 53. Revelation, using a different word, *arnion*, refers to Jesus repeatedly as "lamb" (e.g., Rev. 5:6; 6:1; 7:9; 12:11). Egan argues that, in combination with the quotation on holiness from Leviticus, "Peter reads Isaiah and Leviticus together, with the suffering servant

---

[95] Elliott, *1 Peter*, 371.
[96] BAGD
[97] Campbell, *Honor, Shame, and the Rhetoric of 1 Peter*, 74.
[98] For examples see Exodus 12:5 and Numbers 6:14.
[99] It is clear from 1 Peter 2:21–25 that Peter was intimately familiar with Isaiah 53, so such a brief reference is quite possible.

representing a unique 'lamb' for the offering. Peter connects the sin offering of Leviticus to Christ by means of the suffering servant of Isaiah 53."[100] The covenantal context of Leviticus is joined to the prophetic word of Isaiah to show the fulfillment of God's covenant promises in Jesus Christ. When Peter reminds readers of the perfect sacrifice offered on their behalf, he once again alludes tangentially to the cultic context of the temple in which such sacrifices take place. The reference to the precious blood of Christ evokes the cross already alluded to in 1 Peter 1:2 ("sprinkled with his blood") and is perhaps reminiscent of the covenant symbolized by Jesus' blood at the Last Supper (Matt 26:28; Mark 14:24; Luke 22:20). John's Gospel also portrays Jesus as the sacrificial lamb offered for the forgiveness of sins (John 1:29) and the blood of Jesus as the source of life for those who believe (John 6:53–56). The blood of Christ was the price paid for the ransom of those in bondage to their former way of life (cf. Acts 20:28).

In **v. 20** Peter further describes Christ as being known by God (NRSV "destined") before the foundation of the world and being made known in these last times. These two references to time bracket the daily reality in which the chosen exiles live. In the narrative backstory that lies behind 1 Peter, the story begins before creation, "the foundation of the world," and ends with the final salvation that will be revealed when Christ returns. The epistle of 1 Peter hints at other points along the timeline of God's story: God's rescue of the Israelites from Egypt and the covenant made with them at Sinai; the search by the prophets to understand the grace and salvation of God (1:10–12); the experience of exile that colored Israel's understanding of history (1:2); the sacrifice of Jesus Christ as the lamb of God (1:19); the resurrection that brought hope (1:3); and the anticipated return in the last time (1:5). While Peter does not put these references into chronological order, these hints in the first chapter point to the way in which the early church understood time and the narrative structure that lay behind the letter to the chosen exiles. At a more sweeping level, Joel B. Green lays out the following timeline for the narrative: Primordial time → Time of ignorance → Revelation of Jesus at the end of the ages → Liberation → Time of alien life → Revelation of Jesus Christ.[101] In this narration of time,

---

[100]   Egan, *Ecclesiology*, 58.
[101]   Green, *1 Peter*, 36.

Green accounts for the preexistence of Christ before the creation of the world and for the ignorance of those who did not see and acknowledge the Creator (Wis. 13:1). From the perspective of the audience, their own ignorance (v. 18) was followed by their experience of the revelation of Jesus Christ even though this happened at the cross and through resurrection in a time that either coincides with or is prior to their experience of the revelation. Having experienced new birth (1:3), they still live as aliens and exiles (1:1, 17; 2:11) awaiting the final revelation of Jesus Christ.[102] Christ was known (the implied meaning is that Christ was known by God) long before the believers' experience of exile and estrangement. And, now, Christ is revealed in the last days. These last days begin with the incarnation of Christ and extend into the age when Christ's reign will be complete. Thus the author of Hebrews can write "in these last days" when referring to the present circumstance (Heb. 1:2). The emphasis in v. 20 falls on the last few words "for your sake." All of this – God's choosing of Jesus Christ before the world was made and the life, death, and resurrection of Jesus Christ – happened for the benefit of the church.

The church are those who through Jesus Christ believe in God (**v. 21**), who raised Jesus from death and gave glory to him. Notice that believers trust is oriented towards God and made possible through Jesus Christ. God is further described as the one who raised Christ from death. God is the author of salvation and Christ is the agent and means of that salvation. In the opening chapter of 1 Peter, hope is repeatedly connected to the resurrection, which is a distinctive activity of God. Jesus is never described as raising himself but always as being raised by God. Jesus' life is deeply connected to the life and power of God. Similarly, in 1 Peter, believers are born into a living hope that they received through the resurrection of Jesus (1:3). Believers also do not give life to themselves but rather receive it from outside themselves as a gift from God. In 1:13 the hope of believers is focused on the grace being brought to them when Jesus is revealed. Now, their hope is once again oriented towards God because they have seen God at work raising Jesus Christ from death. Without the resurrection, there could be no revelation of Christ as the living one who has conquered death and offers salvation to those whose life is defined by exile.

---

[102] Green, *1 Peter*, 37.

Not only does God raise Jesus Christ from death, but he also gives him "glory." Glory is used repeatedly in the Old Testament to describe the presence of God dwelling with his people, whether on the mountain or in the tabernacle or temple (e.g., Exod. 24:16; 40:34; 1 Kings 8:11). God's glory is often associated with splendor and light, but can also be terrible and consuming (e.g., Lev. 9:23; Deut. 5:24–27), and God does not share his glory with idols or with others but retains it for himself (Isa. 42:8). In 1 Peter, God gives glory to Jesus, elevating his status and showing his relationship to the Father. Vs. 11 already identifies the "sufferings of Christ and the subsequent glories" (the cross, the resurrection, and the enthronement of Christ). Once again, in a set of verses (vv. 18–21) that focus on the theology of Christ's atonement, the movement is from the blood (death) of Jesus to his resurrection and glorification. These theological truths are put together not to write a treatise on proper theology but rather so that the faith and hope of believers are "set on God." As believers recognize the sacrifice of Jesus Christ and the work of God in the resurrection, they find that their hope and faith are more securely located in God himself.

The fourth instruction, "love one another deeply from the heart," is the main verb (in the imperative) governing **vv. 22–23**. Prior to the command, which is at the end of v. 22, Peter lays out the conditions that make the command possible: "Now that you have purified your souls by your obedience to the truth so that you have genuine mutual love . . .". Peter indicates that this purification is something that has already happened and is something in which the audience participates. The verb "purify" (*hagnizō*) is used in both the LXX and the New Testament to refer to ritual purification that enables those who have performed the proper cleansing to participate in the sacrifices and feasts related to worship (e.g., Exod. 19:10; John 11:55), but in 1 Peter purification is tied to obedience to the truth. Both purity and obedience resonate with much of the material that Peter has already laid out in 1:1–21. The audience have already experienced purification (1:2) and have already been called to holy ways of being and living that reflect the character of God (1:15–16). The perfect active sense of the verb signifies that purification has begun, and it continues. The "souls" that are purified refers to the whole person, each a member of God's chosen community, and does not simply refer to an internalized experience. The phrase can be translated as "have purified yourselves" (see, New International Version [NIV], New Jerusalem Bible [NJB], Common English Bible [CEB]). All the members of the church have been cleansed at the time of conversion through the Holy Spirit and have entered into new covenant relationship with God through sprinkling with the blood of Jesus (1:2). Now this purification continues by means of "obedience to the truth." The truth is the message of the good news that Peter has just summed up as their redemption from futility by means of the precious blood of Jesus Christ (1:18–19). Obedience is a thread that traces its way through the first chapter. First, the cleansing of readers is for the purpose (*eis*) of obedience (1:2), then they are described as obedient children who belong to a particular family (1:14), and now their conversion is characterized as related to obedience to the truth. Obedience begins as a willingness to receive the good news message about purification and continues as behavior that glorifies the Lord who has purchased believers with his blood. Through obedience God's children honor their benefactor and the gift they received. The purification of the believer is both derived from their conversion, *and* it is an active work in which they participate by obeying the one who has redeemed them (1:18). The temptation is to see purification as only God's work, but purification is also the work of God's children and is accomplished by responding with obedience to the good news. Such obedience moves a believer towards genuine brotherly love; the purification of the members of the community benefits the community. Commentators note that throughout 1 Peter theological assertions (like the reference to holiness) are interwoven in complex ways with imperative instructions (like the command to love one another) showing one way in which Peter holds together his understanding of God and the practical implications that result.[103] As 1 Peter progresses, this trait of obedience among believers will contrast with the disobedience of others (1 Pet. 2:8; 3:1; 4:17) who reject the good news of Christ's redemptive work.

The familial language of this section continues with the purpose statement "so that you have genuine mutual love." In Greek *philadelphia* refers to "brotherly" or "familial" love that is now directed towards one's fellow Christians, those who are part of the new family of God. This family love is to be genuine, without pretense, and is produced from a clean heart.[104]

---

[103] For example, Lewis R. Donelson, *I & II Peter and Jude: A Commentary*, first ed., The New Testament Library (Louisville, KY: Westminster John Knox Press, 2010), 51.

[104] This verse contains a number of challenging textual variants and translational issues that the NRSV notes in the margins of the translation. These include the question of

Entrance into God's family through the sanctifying work of the Holy Spirit and the blood of Jesus Christ results in a new kind of genuine family love for people with whom one shares no biological kinship. This is now summed up in the command to "love one another deeply from the heart." Elliott notes that "'Love' . . . entailed both an inward feeling of attachment expressed in an outward manifestation of loyalty to God, Jesus, and fellow group members and an unrelenting commitment to this group's values and beliefs." Already, 1 Peter 1:8 notes the love that the church has for Christ, which manifests in faith and joy. Now, their love that began with Jesus Christ is oriented towards their new kinship group. The person who has been cleansed by the blood of Christ is capable of love for the community that is constant and pure because (**v. 23**) they have experienced new birth.

Both 1 Peter 1:23 and 1:3 use the same word (*anagennaō*) for "born anew" to identify the new life and familial relationship of the audience. (See the comments at 1:3 for a fuller discussion of *anagennaō*.) This new birth takes place through the "imperishable seed." "Seed" here may be a double entendre. Fathers bring about new life through their seed, and "seed" can also refer to the seed of a plant. This potential double meaning relates back to the familial metaphor of new birth in v. 23 and forward to the plant metaphor of v. 24. Once again Peter distinguishes between the perishable and the imperishable. In vv. 18–19 perishable gold and silver was contrasted with the precious blood of Christ. In v. 23 perishable seed (whether referring to seeds that are planted in the ground or to sperm) is contrasted with the imperishable seed of God's word. Unlike the transitory seed that can decay or be destroyed, God's word is "living and enduring." The imperishable nature of God's word derives from the nature of the living God. From the beginning of the biblical narrative, God is associated with

whether the word *ektenōs* should be translated as "deeply" or "constantly." Many commentators lean towards "constantly" because this fits well with the context that follows where God's word is understood as imperishable and thus enduring over time (Dubis, *1 Peter*, 37; Elliott, *1 Peter*, 387). One textual variant concerns whether the brotherly love flows from "the heart" or from "a pure heart." In some early manuscripts the word *katharas* is missing; however, other early manuscripts do include the word. Because the words for pure and heart are very similar (*katharas* and *kardia*), scribes may have omitted the first word while copying because they thought they had already written it (Elliott, *1 Peter*, 387). Even if the word "clean" is not included, the verse begins with the language of purification, and it can be understood that the brotherly love envisioned by Peter is pure in its nature.

God's word which calls the world into being (Gen. 1) and through which God speaks. Moses, Aaron, and the prophets all heard the word of God or the word of the Lord (v. 25). And Christ himself came to be known as the Word through which God was made known in the world (John 1:1–18). God and God's speech are intimately intertwined.

Verses 24–25 provide support from Scripture for the imperishability of God's living and abiding word. Once again there is a contrast between the perishable (grass and wildflowers) and the imperishable (the word of the Lord). The support relies on a quotation made up of lines from Isaiah 40:6–8[105] where "all flesh," referring to humanity, is compared to grass that dries up and flowers that fall off thus portraying human existence as fragile and perishable.[106] The fragility of humanity's condition has already been noted with reference to "futile ways inherited from your ancestors" (v. 18). Now this frailty is extended to all of humanity. Humanity does have some glory (even as do the grass and the flowers). Jesus' saying is one example of the glory of the flowers of the field: "Consider the lilies of the field, how they grow; they neither toil nor spin, yet I tell you, even Solomon in all his glory was not clothed like one of these" (Matt. 6:28–29). But for all their beauty, the grass and flowers last only a day before being burned up (Matt. 6:30) and indeed Solomon is no longer with us and his kingdom was splintered upon his death. The glory of humanity, however powerful it might be at one particular moment, is as transitory as grass and wildflowers. It is nothing compared to the enduring nature of the word of the Lord. In contrast, the word of the Lord remains forever.

When New Testament authors cite the Old Testament, the quotation that they cite often carries with it a reference both to the particular lines of the Old Testament passage and a reference to the larger context in which that passage is found. Isaiah 40 is a hinge point in the greater book of Isaiah. Isaiah 1–39 has a stronger focus on the sin of Israel and the judgment the people experience as a consequence of that sin. But Isaiah 40 begins with words of comfort and introduces the remainder of the book

---

[105] There are some differences between the quotation of Isaiah 40:6–8 in 1 Peter and the text of the LXX, but these do not make a significant difference to the interpretation. The LXX text differs from the Hebrew in that Isaiah 40:7 ("The grass withers, the flower fades, when the breath of the LORD blows upon it; surely the people are grass.") is left out of the LXX translation of the text.

[106] Dubis, *1 Peter*, 39.

of Isaiah with its focus on God's redemption of the people out of exile and the way that God provides so that the people can return home. This theme is often referred to as "the new exodus," and elements of it are evident in 1 Peter. These include the deliverance from the "futile ways inherited from your ancestors," which resonates with the deliverance of Israel from Egypt and Babylon. God brought the Israelites out of Egypt, through the desert, and into the promised land. Isaiah retells this story, and applies it to the new situation. Now, the Israelites are brought out of Babylon where they have been in exile and God prepares a way of return for them to Jerusalem. Similarly, Christians who are currently living in exile have already been delivered from futility and anticipate the final fulfillment of their journey in their experience of salvation at the revelation of Jesus Christ.[107] This larger context of deliverance from exile forms the backdrop of the quotation from Isaiah 40. In the context of Isaiah 40, Israel is assured that the promise of God, the promise of comfort, peace, forgiveness, and a way home are secure because the word of God lasts forever. Peter uses both the words of Isaiah 40:6–8 and the larger context of Isaiah 40 and following to assure his readers that their new birth through the imperishable word of God is also secure. Their identity as members of God's family is secure in contrast to their status as aliens and exiles. This new birth secures for them new familial identity with all of its accompanying honor, hope, salvation, and other benefits. These remain secure because unlike the flowers in the field, God's word does not perish or fade.

At the end of v. 25 it becomes clear that the "word of the Lord" refers to the good news message that was proclaimed to the followers of Jesus.[108] "[W]hen 1 Peter speaks of the *rhema*, "word" that was preached to them in the gospel, Peter has in mind the *specific rhema* of Isaiah 40, namely the promise of restoration from exile. Thus, 1 Peter equates the good news of what has happened in Christ with Isaiah 40's glorious hope of Israel's restoration."[109] The love that Christians have for one another

---

[107] Mbuvi, *Temple, Exile, and Identity in 1 Peter*, 32.

[108] Although v. 23 describes the living word (*logos*) of God and vv. 24–25 speak of the word (*rhema*) of the Lord, these two Greek words can be used interchangeably and the use of *rhema*, "word" in v. 25 should be understood as deriving from its use in the Isaiah quotation.

[109] Mark Dubis, *Messianic Woes in First Peter: Suffering and Eschatology in 1 Peter 4:12–19*, Studies in Biblical Literature: 33 (New York: P. Lang, 2001), 53.

flows out of the purifying impact of the gospel and their obedient response to the good news. Love is made possible because of their new birth. And the new birth is secured by the eternal word of God made available to them through the proclamation of the good news (v. 25), a proclamation enabled by the Holy Spirit (1:12).[110]

We come to **2:1**, which connects to what came before with a "therefore" (*oun*) and introduces a further development in the familial metaphor. Current research on metaphors shows that they are drawn from one domain and applied to another.[111] First Peter 2:1–3 is part of an extended metaphor related to babies, hunger, milk, and tasting. Together, these parts of the extended metaphor are applied to the Christian's growth in salvation (2:2). When studying metaphors it is important to identify the source domain(s) the metaphor is drawn from in order to help readers understand the way the metaphor is being used in the new setting. Karen Jobes' work shows that Psalm 33 LXX (English Psalm 34) is a significant background source for our understanding of the metaphor "craving pure spiritual milk."[112] Following her, other scholars have proposed additional attention to another potential source domain: the Greco-Roman background of milk, nursing, and wet nurses.[113] Together, these scholars have pressed into the near consensus that "craving pure spiritual milk" should be understood as "craving Scripture or the word of God."[114] In order to understand the new direction they propose, we will need to unpack 1 Peter 2:1–3.

The response in **2:1** to the instruction to love completely is to lay aside the activities and attitudes that destroy the loving, familial community. The Greek word for "lay aside," *apotithēmi*, can be used literally of taking off clothes, but is used here metaphorically to describe laying aside things that are of no value in the church's communal life together. Taking off the

---

[110] James D. G. Dunn, *Baptism in the Holy Spirit: A Re-examination of the New Testament Teaching on the Gift of the Spirit in Relation to Pentecostalism Today* (Philadelphia: Westminster Press, 1970), 220–21.

[111] Troy W. Martin, "Christians as babies: Metaphorical reality in 1 Peter," in Eric F. Mason and Troy W. Martin (eds.), *Reading 1–2 Peter and Jude: A Resource for Students* (Atlanta: SBL, 2014).

[112] Jobes, *1 Peter*, 137–41.

[113] Troy W. Martin, "Tasting the Eucharistic Lord as usable (1 Peter 2:3)," *Catholic Biblical Quarterly* 78:3 (2016): 515–25; Philip L. Tite, "Nurslings, milk and moral development in the Greco-Roman context: A reappraisal of the paraenetic utilization of metaphor 1 Peter 2.1–3," *JSNT* 31 (2009): 371–400.

[114] Jobes, *1 Peter*, 132.

behaviors that are listed is both loving towards the other members of the community *and* a demonstration of the holiness that God's children should practice (1:14–16). There are a number of vice lists in the New Testament (e.g., Col. 3:5–8; Rom. 1:29–30; 1 Cor. 5:10–11) and the idea that the new life in Christ involves the removal of sin and a turn to a new way of living is consistent in Scripture. The vice list in 1 Peter begins with the broadest term "evil" or "malice" (*kakia*) which can refer generally to wickedness or vice but in the context of the list signifies "a mean-spirited or vicious attitude or disposition."[115] It is the opposite of "virtue" (*aretē*) and such an attitude has no social worth or value in the Christian community. "Guile" is the second item Christians are to lay aside. There is no room in the Christian community for any deceit, cunning, or treachery or for the crafty underhanded thinking and methods that inform such behavior. The third item is "insincerity" (*hupokrisis*) from which we get our word "hypocrisy." This is the exact opposite of the "sincere (*anhupokritos*) brotherly love" envisioned in 1:22. Hypocrisy is the act of creating "a public impression that is at odds with one's real purposes or motivations."[116] Often, such hypocrisy can be used to mislead and manipulate others. The fourth item to be put aside is "envy," the desire to have assets, advantages, and possessions that belong to another. Envy of others within the community would undermine the ability to practice genuine love for others. Finally, the last item on Peter's list is "slander," that is evil speech or defamation directed at another. Three times in the list, Peter repeats the word "all," so that it is clear that the recipients should lay aside *all* things related to malice, guile, and slander.

A Closer Look: Vice Lists

Vice lists were well known in both Jewish and Greco-Roman literature from the time of the first century. Although the Old Testament has only a few examples of possible vice lists (Jer. 7:9; Hosea 4:2), it certainly identified numerous sins to be avoided so that God's people could maintain their holiness (e.g., Lev. 17–18). In contrast, the Hellenistic world, beginning with Aristotle, developed long lists of virtues and vices. These were often contrasted with each other and put forward as a

---

[115]　BAGD
[116]　BAGD

way of encouraging the audience to virtuous behavior.[117] For example, Aristotle compares vices, virtues, and the mean between them. Just a few examples from his long list show how virtue and vice are viewed in relationship to one another:

Boastfulness	Self-deprecation	Sincerity
Flattery	Surliness	Friendliness
Subservience	Stubbornness	Dignity
Luxuriousness	Endurance	Hardiness[118]

Aristotle describes envy (the fourth vice in 1 Peter's list): "Envy consists in being annoyed at prosperity more often than one ought to be, for the envious are annoyed by the prosperity even of those who deserve to prosper."[119] He then goes on to draw out the opposite of "envy," as failure to be annoyed at those who prosper undeservingly. In other words, the virtues and vices are understood in relationship to each other and to their opposites.

Closer to the first century, vice lists appear in the writings of a number of Greco-Roman authors. Cicero in a venomous speech against Piso accuses him of a long list of vices saying, "You may in the past have thought [Lucius Piso] merely dishonest, cruel, light-fingered; you may more recently have found him greedy, groveling, headstrong, arrogant, deceitful, perfidious, shameless, impudent; but you may take it from me that he is the last word in voluptuousness, in licentiousness, in baseness, in villainy."[120] Accusing the former consul of Rome of these vices was a way to undermine his character and draw attention to his treatment of others. During the first century Dio Chrysostom, who lived in the province of Bithynia (cf. 1 Pet. 1:1) in Asia Minor addressed the city of Tarsus. In his address he reminds the audience that the elimination of vices allows for the promotion of unity. The vices that he identifies are "envy, greed, contentiousness, the striving in each case to promote one's own welfare at the expense of both one's native land and the common weal."[121] While not all lists were the same, and some were much more extensive than others, they all show a common interest in identifying vices that should be avoided and that when indulged reveal the true character of the person. Communities that wanted to live together in harmony were communities that valued virtues over vices.

---

[117]   René López, "Vice lists in non-Pauline sources," *BSac* 168 (2011): 181.

[118]   Aristotle, *Eth. Eud.* 2.3.4–5 (LCL 285: 250–51).

[119]   Aristotle, *Eth. Eud.* 2.3.4–5 (LCL 285: 252–53).

[120]   Cicero *Pis.* 27.66 (LCL 252:218–219).

[121]   Dio Chrysostom. *Discourses 31–36.* Translated by J. W. Cohoon, H. Lamar Crosby. LCL 358. Cambridge, MA: Harvard University Press, 1940, 355.

Vice lists were also found in Jewish literature during the intertestamental time period. This literature often coupled lists of vices with the language of sin. For example, 1 Enoch 91:7 reads, "When sin, oppression, blasphemy, and injustice increase, crime, iniquity, and uncleanliness shall be committed and increase (likewise)." Similarly, in Jewish literature, vices are sometimes associated with spirits who lead people into error as in the *Testament of Reuben*:

First, the spirit of promiscuity resides in the nature and the senses. ⁴ A second spirit of insatiability, in the stomach; a third spirit of strife, in the liver and the gall; a fourth spirit of flattery and trickery, in order that through excessive effort one might appear to be at the height of his powers; ⁵ a fifth spirit of arrogance, that one might be boastful and haughty; a sixth spirit of lying, which through destructiveness and rivalry, handles his affairs smoothly and secretively even with his relatives and his household. ⁶ A seventh spirit of injustice, with which are thefts and crooked dealings, in order that one might gain his heart's desire. (3:2–6)[122]

Both Jewish and Greco-Roman culture knew and used lists of vices. These could be used as guidance to encourage proper behavior, as a means of denouncing ones enemies, or as a means of encouraging communal unity. Most Greco-Roman authors thought that people had the capacity to choose virtuous behavior over vices. But some Jewish authors associate the vices with spiritual forces. "Within the NT, virtue-and-vice lists are adapted to the needs of the rhetorical situations addressed (e.g., Gal. 5:19–23; 2 Pet. 1:5–7)."[123] In 1 Peter, Christians receive new birth as a gift from God with the expectation that the new life they receive is one that embodies holiness and shuns vices.

In **2:2** the familial metaphor continues. His readers are described metaphorically as newborn babes and as such they are given the final imperative command of this section: "long for," "desire," or "crave" (*epipothēsate*). The word for longing is used in the Old and the New Testament to describe a deep longing, often for good things such as desiring God (Ps. 42:1), the place where God dwells (Ps. 84:2), God's commandments (Ps. 119:131), and God's salvation (Ps. 119:174). In the New Testament this longing is

---

[122] "Testaments of the twelve patriarchs, the sons of Jacob the patriarch: Testament of Reuben, the firstborn son of Jacob and Leah," in James H. Charlesworth (ed.), *The Old Testament Pseudepigrapha: Apocalyptic Literature & Testaments*, vol. 1 (New York: Doubleday, 1984).

[123] Duane Frederick Watson and Terrance Callan, *First and Second Peter*, Paideia: Commentaries on the New Testament (Grand Rapids, MI: Baker, 2012), 43.

sometimes attached to the desire to see people (Rom. 1:11; Phil. 1:8; 2:26) as well as longing for heaven (2 Cor. 5:2). In 1 Peter, Christians are to have a strong desire for milk just as a hungry newborn baby wants only one thing – milk. In this verse, three pieces of the familial metaphor come together. The Father has begotten children (1:3, 23) causing them to come into existence; the children are the newborn babies (2:2); and the longing they have is for milk (2:2), the sustenance produced only by mothers. While the text explicitly identifies God as Father (1:3), the identification of God as mother is only implicit through the mention of milk.

The milk they are to long for is described with the adjectives "pure" (*adolos*) and "spiritual" (*logikos*). The first adjective refers to something that is unadulterated, that has not been watered down. In the market place, unscrupulous venders sometimes diluted milk that was for sale, but this milk is the real, genuine nourishment that Christians need. It is the best quality milk available, a concern shared by ancient writers who wrote about nursing, milk, wet nurses, and mothers.[124] Galen notes that the highest quality milk is the milk that is fit for its purpose or use.[125] In 1 Peter, this is the milk appropriate to growth in salvation. The adjective "spiritual" (*logikos*) is more challenging to translate. Various English translations give it the meaning "spiritual" (NRSV, NIV, New Living Translation [NLT], ESV) even though it is not the word for spiritual (*pneumatikos*, which occurs in 2:5), while others translate it as "milk of the word" (NASB, CEB) even though it does not take that form in Greek (*tou logou*). The word is used only here and in Rom. 12:1 ("your spiritual/ reasonable worship/service;" *tēn logikēn latreian*), which means that there is little usage to compare it to in the New Testament. It is related to the noun *logos*, "word, reason." By virtue of an association between *logos* and *logikon* many interpreters have come to the conclusion that the milk that Christians are to crave is "the word of God."[126] However, 1 Peter does not choose the common word *logos* to describe the milk but the uncommon adjective *logikon*. Recent work has shown that *logikon* can have the meaning "true to its real nature."[127] In the context of 1 Peter, Jobes argues that

---

[124] Tite, "Nurslings," 387.
[125] Tite, "Nurslings," 393.
[126] Jobes, *1 Peter*, 132 shows this is the consensus among major commentators. Calvin and Michaels are exceptions.
[127] Jobes, *1 Peter*, 136 following Louw and Nida.

this means something along the lines of "milk that is true to the nature of the new eschatological reality established by the resurrection of Jesus Christ and into which Peter's readers have been reborn (1:3)."[128] In other words, that which Christians are to crave is broader than only craving Scripture ("the word") and is instead about craving the truest, highest quality experience of salvation made possible through Jesus Christ.

Their longing for milk is to result in "craving the moral transformation necessary to sustain life in Christ."[129] The best possible outcome for a baby who eagerly drinks a mother's milk is growth. A baby who does not drink will fail to thrive or may even die. Christians who drink eagerly from the unadulterated gift of new life as milk will experience the appropriate result – growth into salvation. The readers already know that their Father is protecting them so that through trust in God they can experience the full and final revelation of salvation in the last time (1:5), and they know that the result of loving and trusting Jesus Christ is receiving the outcome of their faith – an ongoing life of salvation (1:9). This is the same salvation that the prophets (1:10) searched for and spoke of and which came through the precious blood of Jesus Christ (1:11, 19–20).

Peter ends his exhortation to long for divine milk with a brief allusion from Psalm 34:8: "O taste and see that the Lord is good." In the Psalm, the verb is an imperative, but in 1 Peter it has changed to an indicative that is part of a conditional clause with the meaning "since you have tasted." Peter does not need to instruct them to taste but rather assumes that they have already done so. In addition, Peter leaves out the words from the Psalm "and see" so that the quotation now focuses on tasting, a reference that furthers the metaphor of milk in the previous verse. Both Martin and Tite point to the ancient understanding of infant nutrition to develop their understanding of the metaphor of "tasting" in relationship to milk. In the first century doctors thought that the infant was nourished by blood in the womb and that when the baby was born that blood was redirected to the breasts where it then provided nourishment as milk.[130] Both scholars also agree that in the ancient world nutrition was based on the principle

---

[128] Jobes, *1 Peter*, 140.

[129] Karen H. Jobes, "'O taste and see': Septuagint psalm 33 in 1 Peter," *Stone-Campbell Journal* 18 (2015): 241.

[130] Martin, "Tasting the Eucharistic Lord as usable (1 Peter 2:3)," 521; Tite, "Nurslings," 384.

that "like nourished like." Tite will use this idea to suggest that, unlike Jobes who rejects a connection to the word, the Logos, "[t]he 'like-to-like' motif draws the reader of 2.1–3 back to the source of the new birth in 1.23, inclusive of the 'precious blood of Christ' at 1:19" and asserts that the metaphor refers to "the high quality word-like milk."[131] More recently, Martin, using the same principle and noting that Psalm 34 was used in the eucharistic liturgies of the early church, argues that when Christians are reminded that they have tasted the "goodness" (also translated as "usable" or "wholesome" food) of the Lord, they are being reminded of the eucharistic body and blood of the Lord.[132] The whole experience of salvation made available through Jesus Christ, the Scripture as the word of God, and the celebration of Christ's supper are all means of growth in salvation. What they taste is "the goodness or kindness of the Lord." In some manuscripts the word for goodness (*chrēstos*) has been changed to Christ (*christos*). The two words only differ by one letter and it is possible that the ancient pronunciation was identical or extremely close.[133] The word for goodness may have been deliberately chosen as a play on the word Christ. The word "Lord" (*kurios*) refers to Jesus whom Peter describes as "our Lord Jesus Christ" (1:3). *Kurios* is one of the usual titles given to Jesus by the early church, and it can certainly have this meaning here. While it is possible to argue that "Lord" refers to God in 2:3, it quickly becomes clear that 2:4 refers to Jesus as a living stone chosen and precious before God and 2:4 hangs on the end of 2:3 as a relative pronoun (e.g., literally, "to whom by coming …"). So, in 1 Peter 2:3, it is best to understand "Lord" as referring to Jesus Christ.

Bridging the Horizons: In most of Western culture today there is a laissez-faire attitude towards behavior and even character. We often hear messages that communicate that one should do whatever makes one happy or brings one pleasure. Self-control and restraint are laughed at or seen as a waste of time. Indeed, one of the highest values of Western culture is individualism with its focus on individual rights and on the differentiation of the self (both within and from the family). This

---

[131] Tite, "Nurslings," 393.
[132] Martin, "Tasting the Eucharistic Lord as usable (1 Peter 2:3)," 524–25.
[133] Achtemeier, *1 Peter*, 148.

often manifests in weaker commitments to groups, especially when individuals sense that the group no longer serves their individual goals or needs. In the midst of this context, Christians are challenged to take up the imperatives in this section of 1 Peter. These imperatives are given in a context that is deeply aware that neither this day nor this life are the end of reality. Rather, Christians look towards the day when Jesus Christ will be fully revealed. The church's experience of rebirth and of God's grace in the present allow hope for the day when God will fully reveal the savior, Jesus Christ. Christians are to be prepared and calm as they set their hope on the fullness of that revelation.

Hope is something that our culture can appreciate. During the coronavirus pandemic of 2020 and 2021 many experienced hopelessness because of the overwhelming losses they faced, including death, disease, loss of work, and loss of community. Depression, anxiety, and despair increased. Some then described receiving vaccination as an experience that brought them hope that was connected to the promise of a return to "normal life" and the hope that there would be less death, disease, and despair. This is one demonstration of the connection that hope has to life, living, and the future. The object of hope in 1 Peter is the completion of the salvation they have begun to experience through the resurrection of Jesus Christ from the dead.

Both the object of hope and the response to the salvation that God offers are distinctively Christian. Those who have been born into a new family are instructed to look like their Father, to be molded into the very depths of God's character, the holiness that makes God so wholly other and fearsome, for God is what we are not but what we are becoming. As Oswalt puts it, God "is calling them [God's people] to share his unique character, one that will alter how they approach every aspect of their lives."[134] Even though almost every church speaks of the doctrine of holiness, there is a range of teachings about holiness in the wider church. Some have taught that we are not able to become righteous but rather are only able to receive the imputed righteousness of Christ. Others have asserted that Christians are able to keep God's command to be holy through the infilling and power of the Holy Spirit. Between these two positions is a range of others.[135] To be holy does not mean to be "perfect" in the English sense of the word but rather to be completely yielded to the will of God, to be the obedient children of God. As obedient children, Christians do not resist the voice and direction of God and instead seek eagerly to do that which the Father asks of them. There is no intentional or deliberate sin in the life of such a

---

[134] Oswalt, *Called to Be Holy*, 33.
[135] Keith W. Drury, *Holiness for Ordinary People*, twenty-fifth anniversary ed. (Indianapolis, IN: Wesleyan Publishing House, 2009), 42–50.

believer. However, the believer is not static as if having arrived at a destination. Instead, he or she continues to grow in relationship with Christ and experience deeper love of God and greater love and service towards those around them.

Peter begins his letter by reminding his recipients of the new birth, new life, and salvation that they have received through the gracious gift of Jesus Christ. This gift of new life from God the Father through Jesus Christ is available today to those who believe. This new life is a distinctive life in which the character of God's holy love infused into the life of the believer overcomes sin and empowers the believer for service. Sometimes Christians have thought of "holiness" as a list of rules – things that either should or should not be done and have come to associate "holiness" with what is really legalism. But Peter's calling to holy behavior is a calling to be like the Father and to bear the Father's character. It is made possible by the new birth that Christians have received and is set in the context of faithful hope in the ultimate redeemer. In that context, it is both possible and necessary that God's people be set apart as distinctively different in a broken world.

Conduct yourselves with reverent fear. Western culture today is full of irreverence, a lack of respect for others and for God. And while there may be threats that strike real fear into various communities, fear of God is generally a thing of the past. Some have argued that irreverence taps into the deep pain of our culture, and that Christians in Western culture need to attend to the pain and suffering that is expressed through various forms of irreverence.[136] At the same time, the Christian community must ask itself what it means to conduct itself in reverent fear while living openly, honestly, and vulnerably within the larger culture. The Christian church must embrace its identity as children of God and recognize that doing so entails living in accord with God's character. Any status and standing that the Christian community has must be had first before the eyes of God. The culture around the church may or may not see the behavior of God's people as precious or honorable, but those who belong to the family of God must look to God, rather than culture, as their judge. Such godly conduct must give up the futile ways inherited from ancestors; this often means giving up what feels right or natural for ways of living that are distinct from the culture. Currently, this means refusing to worship at the altar of materialism and consumerism (whether the consumption of goods or experiences); putting aside violence and revenge; neither upholding nationalism nor seeing patriotic loyalty as a defining characteristic of being Christian. Positively, this means being continual seekers for truth, honesty, and integrity; upholding a culture

---

[136] Cindy Brandt, "Irreverence is the new reverent," *Huffington Post*, 22 July 2014, www.huffingtonpost.com/cindy-brandt/irreverence-is-the-new-reverent_b_5608381.html accessed September 21, 2017.

that celebrates life as a gift from the Creator; and recognizing the need for living in ways that generate peace and flourishing for neighborhoods, cities, and ultimately, the world. The capacity to live in such a way has been bought for followers of Christ with the blood shed on the cross for their redemption from all sin, bondage, and oppression.

Love one another completely. Christians prepare themselves to love by purifying their hearts with obedience to the truth. There is an interesting mix of effort and humility in this stance. On the one hand, Christians have received the gift of Jesus' sacrifice that redeems them from futile ways of living (1:18–19), and they recognize that the Holy Spirit does the work of making us holy (1:2). On the other hand, Christians employ the gift that they receive so that the purity of their lives grows as they obey the one they love (1:8, 22). For Peter, what does it mean to have a pure life? Purity happens within the context of the Christian community (spoken of metaphorically as family). The Father brings new children into being and blesses them with hope and an inheritance; the children respond with obedience that seeks to imitate the one who gave them life (1:14–16). For Westerners the word "truth" in the phrase "obedience to the truth" can be a pitfall. Some may still wish to attach truth to the Enlightenment project that sought one universal truth to govern all things; others have consigned truth to the relative and perspectival. But when Peter calls his audience to purify themselves through obedience to the truth, he is asking them to obey that which has already been laid out for them as truth – their relationship with the Father who has chosen them, the Spirit who has made them holy, and the Son who has sacrificed his blood on their behalf. Obedience to the truth is more than intellectual assent to reasonable assertions about theological dogma; it is behavior ordered in relationship to God and God's truth about Jesus Christ, his suffering, death, resurrection, ascension, and enthronement. As the children of God, Christians are enabled by God to have clean hearts that imitate God and to take up and live out the same loving, just, and merciful actions that God has demonstrated towards them. And just as God's action is other-centered – God does not give himself life but rather gives life to his children – so too the pure lives of God's children are also other-focused. The purity that is found within the familial relationship with God is extended to familial relationships with other children of God, the brothers and sisters formed through shared participation in the new birth given by God. Fellow members of the Christian community are to be loved with genuine familial affection. Indeed, the instruction is to love one another completely. Such love that is reflective of the Father and family to which they belong resembles the sacrificial love that Jesus demonstrated when he gave his life on behalf of the whole world. If we want to know if we have loved well, we might ask ourselves whether our love has been other-oriented and whether those around us have experienced our love as oriented in such a way. In other words, it is not enough to think that one has loved in an other-oriented way; the other should be able to affirm that they have been the recipients of love.

The final instruction in this major section is for Christians to desire the unadulterated true milk that causes them to grow in their salvation. They are to put off those things that do not nurture their growth in Christ's salvation. In a culture that is full of "spin" and where phrases like "alternative facts" and "fake news" have become common, Peter identifies malice, deceit, insincerity, and duplicity as undermining the character and practice of Christian community. When even Christians come to value winning at all costs or obtaining power in any way feasible, they are no longer seen by the wider community as a group that represents the holy nature of God, nor even as those who love each other from a pure heart. Instead, the wider culture of unbelievers comes to see Christians as a self-protective group seeking their own interests above all others. Of course, Christians, just like other people, do not like to be confronted with facts that fail to confirm their understanding of reality. The temptation is to start a cycle of self-justification in order to resolve the dissonance between one's beliefs and the new information being received. The challenge is to be lovers of truth even when those truths create dissonance. The dissonance itself between one's current way of thinking and new information is an opportunity to re-examine rather than self-justify.[137] It is imperative that Christians, whose lives are to be characterized by holiness and love, crave the truth of the new birth and the new life made possible through that birth over power or position gained through evil and malicious practices.

1 Peter 2:4–10: Christ the Cornerstone and the Living Stones

[4] Come to him, a living stone, though rejected by mortals yet chosen and precious in God's sight, and

[5] like living stones, let yourselves be built into a spiritual house, to be a holy priesthood, to offer spiritual sacrifices acceptable to God through Jesus Christ.

[6] For it stands in scripture: "See, I am laying in Zion a stone, a cornerstone chosen and precious; and whoever believes in him will not be put to shame."

[7] To you then who believe, he is precious; but for those who do not believe, "The stone that the builders rejected has become the very head of the corner,"

---

[137]   Carol Tavris and Elliot Aronson, *Mistakes Were Made (But Not by Me): Why We Justify Foolish Beliefs, Bad Decisions, and Hurtful Acts*, revised ed. (Boston: Houghton Mifflin Harcourt, 2015).

⁸ and "A stone that makes them stumble, and a rock that makes them fall." They stumble because they disobey the word, as they were destined to do.

⁹ But you are a chosen race, a royal priesthood, a holy nation, God's own people, in order that you may proclaim the mighty acts of him who called you out of darkness into his marvelous light.

¹⁰ Once you were not a people, but now you are God's people; once you had not received mercy, but now you have received mercy.

First Peter **2:4–10** focuses on both Christology, with its emphasis on Christ as the living stone, and on ecclesiology, with its theme of the identity of God's people. This takes place using shared vocabulary ("building," "chosen," "holy," and "stone/stones") and contrasts (belief/disbelief, no mercy/mercy, not a people/God's people). Peter solidifies the identity of the newborn children of God as those who resemble Jesus Christ, the living stone, and who are being built into God's house. First Peter 2:4–10 shares a number of thematic links with what has come before including references to holiness (2:5, 9; 1:2, 15–16), trust/belief (2:6, 7; 1:8), and being chosen (2:4, 6, 9; 1:1). At the same time, this section is its own unit with some significant shifts between 2:1–3 and vv. 4–10. These include a move away from imperative commands to indicative statements, the introduction of new imagery related to stones and building, and the obvious climactic nature of the section. Still, it is not immediately obvious how the language of stones and building in 2:4–10 relates to the theme of new birth and growing in salvation from 2:1–3. Achtemeier traces several possibilities, each of which relies on a particular background in order to enhance understanding of the relationship. One suggestion involves an appeal to the mystery religions that were part of the eastern empire. It is suggested that one liturgical practice of these religions involved a ritual drink of milk followed by worship of a stone.[138] A variety of scholars suggest various Old Testament texts as possible background for the connection. Suggestions include: Deut. 32:18; Gen. 16:2; 30:3; and Joel 3:18.[139] Some posit a typological connection similar to the reference to Christ as the Rock seen in 1 Corinthians 10:4. But the proposal that makes the best sense is to see Psalm 34:6–8, which was directly alluded to in 2:3, as the link forward to

---

[138]   Achtemeier, *1 Peter*, 153.
[139]   Achtemeier, *1 Peter*, 153.

this section as well.[140] The text that begins "O taste and see that the Lord is good" and continues "happy are those who take refuge in him." The word "refuge" is often "associated with God as a rock;" additionally, the phrase "come to him" occurs in Psalm 34:6 in the LXX.[141] All of this together suggests Psalm 34:6–8 as a backdrop for the image of coming to him, the living stone, and as the connecting link between 2:1–3 and 2:4–10.

Peter moves from the quotation of Psalm 34:8 (LXX 33:9) with its focus on tasting the goodness of the Lord, where tasting heightens the reference to milk in v. 2, to a carefully constructed argument about stones and building that is formulated from direct quotations drawn from Psalm 118 (LXX 117:22) and Isaiah 8 and 28. This is followed in vv. 9–10 with a climactic collection of images describing the people of God. Verses 4–10 make use of many Old Testament passages in a short amount of space. In order, 1 Peter cites Isa. 28:16, Ps. 118 (LXX 117):22, Isa. 8:14, Isa. 43:20–21, Exod. 19:6, Hosea 1:6, 9; 2:3, 25. Three main words hold these passages together: "stone" (2:4, 5, 6, 7, 8), "people" (2:9, 10), and "chosen" (2:4, 6, 9). In the New Testament, "[i]n every case, without exception, the *lithos* [stone] image has been applied to Jesus as the Messiah … [T]he messianic/eschatological interpretation begun in pre-Christian Judaism reaches its culmination in its application to Jesus as the Bringer of the Messianic Age."[142] From the early days of the church, the image of Jesus Christ as the stone was a shared Christian tradition found in the Gospels, Acts, Paul (Matt. 21:42–44; Mark 12:6–11; Luke 20:13–18; Acts 4:10–12; Rom. 9:30–33), and 1 Peter. Using these Old Testament quotations Peter will further point to Jesus Christ while reinforcing the identity of the chosen strangers as those who resemble the one who paid the price for their redemption.

A Closer Look: Jewish Interpretation of Old Testament Texts

First-century Jewish interpreters of Scripture used a variety of techniques to understand, communicate, and apply the biblical text, some of which are unfamiliar to twenty-first-century readers. One technique involves the use of catchwords (*gezera*

---

[140] Achtemeier, *1 Peter*, 153; however, he holds this solution lightly.

[141] Achtemeier, *1 Peter*, 153; Beare, *The First Epistle of Peter: The Greek Text with Introduction and Notes*, 93.

[142] John Hall Elliott, *The Elect and the Holy: An Exegetical Examination of I Peter 2:4–10 and the Phrase "Basileion Hierateuma"* (Eugene, OR: Wipf and Stock, 2005), 28.

šawa) to link together texts that might not otherwise seem to be related. In 1 Peter 2:6–8 the catchword is "stone." By linking three Old Testament texts together around a catchword, the author allows Scripture to engage with Scripture. For example, v. 6 begins with Isa. 28:16 and describes the stone that God placed in Zion (referring back to Jesus Christ the living stone of v. 4) and the response of belief. The author then joins another "stone" text, Psalm 118:22 to further describe the stone as one that was rejected by the builders but became the cornerstone. Then, using a simple "and," the author adds one more stone text, Isa. 8:14, to what came before in order to further describe the stone as something that causes stumbling. This technique of joining Old Testament Scripture together, sometimes with additional commentary (as in 1 Peter 2:7a, 8b), happens in other parts of the New Testament as well (e.g., Heb. 4:3–5). This catchword technique can be used in a variety of ways.

There is scholarly consensus that these passages (Isa. 28:16; Psalm 118:22; Isa. 8:14) are joined together around the stone image and that this collection of stone texts is part of the very early Christian interpretation about Jesus, perhaps even originating with Jesus himself. But, scholars have not reached consensus on what form (testimonia, midrash, pesher) this conjoining of stone texts is and exactly how vv. 6–8 relate to vv. 4–5. Some have theorized "that early Christians had collections of proof texts which they used apologetically" and which were known as testimonia.[143] An example at Qumran (4Q175) appears to be a collection of proof texts joined together using a catchword and provides evidence that such collections were created in the first century. Another perspective is that 1 Peter 2:6–10 is a midrash with vv. 4–5 serving as an introduction to the theme that the midrash of vv. 6–10 explores.[144] Midrash is a form of commentary on a text from Scripture. It normally begins with a scriptural text and then provides commentary on that text either by linking it to other scriptural texts or by adding commentary or both.[145] Bauckham's explanation that vv. 4–5 serve as an introduction to the midrash in vv. 6–10 works well to explain the relationship between Jesus the living stone in v. 4 and the stone texts of vv. 6–8, but it does not adequately explain the movement from the use of stones as an image for God's people in v. 5 to the many images applied to them in vv. 9–10, none of which employ stone imagery.[146] However, while 2:6–10 does not seem to be a midrashic commentary on the collection of stone passages in

---

[143] George J. Brooke, "Testimonia," in David Noel Freedman (ed.), *Anchor Bible Dictionary* (New Haven, CT: Yale University Press, 1992), 392.

[144] Richard Bauckham, "James, 1 and 2 Peter, Jude," in *It Is Written: Scripture Citing Scripture*, D. A. Carson and H. G. M. Williamson (eds.), (Cambridge: Cambridge University Press, 1988), 310–11.

[145] Gary G. Porton, "Midrash," in Freedman (ed.), *Anchor Bible Dictionary*, 818.

[146] Sargent, *Written to Serve*, 72.

2:6–8, it does demonstrate a pesher-like quality. Pesher (plural: pesharim) is a form of biblical interpretation that seeks "to extract the desired sense from the biblical citation by indicating the analogy and similarity between the text and the community's situation."[147] In other words, it is a form of interpretation that focuses on the application of the text to the community. This can be seen clearly in 2:7 where Peter connects the community that is being addressed ("you who believe") to one who trusts in him and is not ashamed (v. 6) in contrast to others who disbelieve (v. 7). Meanwhile, Elliott argues that vv. 4–5 arise out of the Scriptural texts that are laid out in vv. 6–10 and that the texts in vv. 6–10 serve as the structure for the thought patterns of vv. 4–5.[148] Scholars have drawn on their understanding of a variety of Jewish interpretive techniques (testimonia, midrash, pesher) to understand 1 Peter 2:6–10 and its relationship to vv. 4–5.

Honor is the most important cultural value of the first century and its flipside, dishonor or shame, is to be avoided if at all possible. Peter's audience already face dishonor because of their status as exiles and aliens, but here both Jesus Christ and the community formed in relationship to him are bestowed honor. This happens both at the level of vocabulary and also at the level of theology. The author repeatedly makes use of words drawn from the register of honor such as "chosen," "valued,"[149] "cornerstone," "head," and "royal." This vocabulary is associated with heightened honor when God is part of the activity. Indeed, it is God who chooses the stone and sees it as valuable. It is God who chooses a people and claims them for God's own. Both Jesus Christ and the community formed around Christ are given high honor and assured that they will not be disgraced or dishonored (v. 6). In contrast, dishonor is attached to those who disobey, disbelieve, and stumble.[150] In this way, Peter reminds his audience of exiles and aliens of the true value of the living stone they resemble and their own status and honor in light of their participation in the community of God's people.

---

[147] Devorah Dimant, "Pesharim," in Freedman (ed.), *Anchor Bible Dictionary*, 250.
[148] Elliott, *The Elect and the Holy*, 48.
[149] Note that *entimos* can have the meaning "honored, respected" as well as "valuable, precious" (BAGD). While it is often translated as "precious," it still belongs to the register of honor.
[150] Campbell, *Honor, Shame, and the Rhetoric of 1 Peter*, 83–87.

First Peter **2:4–5** displays an intricate relationship between the living stone, Jesus Christ (v. 4), and the living stones, the members of the household of God (v. 5). Peter continues to weave together Christology and the formation of the people of God (cf. 1:18–23). The participle ("coming," NRSV: "come") at the beginning of 2:4 coordinates with the main verb of 2:5 and shares the same force (either imperative or indicative) as the main verb, "being built" (*oikodomeisthe*). The NRSV translation of vv. 4–5 takes the imperatival route and translates the participle ("come to him") as an imperative with the passive main verb ("let yourselves be built") having permissive force. However, Dubis notes that there are no clear examples of the middle or passive form of this verb being used as an imperative or a permissive passive as the NRSV has it, and he argues along with other scholars that translating the verb "as a simple passive indicative (with God as the implied agent) best fits the surrounding context."[151] This also impacts the translation of the participle in v. 4 since it does not have imperatival force if the main verb is not an imperative. Dubis provides the following translation, "By coming to him … you yourselves … are also being built into a spiritual house."[152] Other translations read "as you come to him" (ESV, NIV) or "Now you are coming" (CEB) all of which capture the continuous sense of the participle and its identification of activity prior to the main verb. Christians are identified as those who are moving towards the Lord. If we continue to think of the image of new birth and growth, we might even suggest that the newborns have moved from the gift of new birth to the craving for milk (2:2) and continue with active movement towards the one who has called them.

The language of vv. 4–5 establishes the themes and relationships of vv. 4–10., and R. T. France expresses this clearly in the following outline:

A   Christ the stone; verse 4
   B The people and priests of God; verse 5
A1 The stone in the OT [Old Testament]; verses 6–8
   B1 People and priests in the OT; verses 9–10.[153]

---

[151]   Dubis, *1 Peter*, 47–48.
[152]   Dubis, *1 Peter*, 36.
[153]   R. T. France, "First century Bible study: Old Testament motifs in 1 Peter 2:4–10," *Journal of the European Pentecostal Theological Association* 18 (1998): 29; Elliott, *1 Peter*, 408.

In this schema, vv. 6–8, woven together with midrashic commentary, provide scriptural background for Peter's assertions in v. 4, and vv. 9–10 provide support for the claims of v. 5. The one to whom believers are to come is the living stone, Jesus Christ. While the Old Testament does refer to God as a rock or refuge (e.g., 2 Sam 22:2: "The Lord is my rock, my fortress, and my deliverer"), it is best to understand the imagery of Jesus Christ, the living stone, as being derived from the texts of Isaiah and Psalm 118 quoted in vv. 6–8. The depiction of the stone as "living" is a reminder of Christ's resurrection and of the "living hope" that has been given to believers through his resurrection (1:3).[154] This living stone has been examined by and then rejected by humanity who deemed the stone worthless. In so doing, they dishonor both God and God's Messiah. In contrast, before God, Jesus Christ, the living stone, is chosen and precious. The recipients of the letter have been described as "chosen" from the very beginning (1:1); now, they are pointed to the one chosen by God. **Verse 5** begins with a coordinating conjunction "and" that relates the description of Jesus the living stone to the recipients of the letter. Those who believe share in the identity of Jesus. They are like living stones. Achtemeier indicates that because the believers have not yet experienced their own resurrection from death their identity as living stones is derived from Christ's resurrection.[155] They too, like Christ, are chosen by and precious in the sight of God. From the living stones God builds a spiritual house for a holy priesthood that will offer spiritual sacrifices to God through Jesus Christ.

Elliott has argued extensively that "house" (*oikos*) should be understood as referring to the household of the Spirit and should be understood within the familial domain. The word "house" can have a variety of meanings in both the Old and the New Testament. In the Old Testament the word "house" is used to refer to a building, a household, a dynasty (e.g., "the house of David"), and the temple. In the New Testament, "house" is used mainly of dwellings and households. Other Greek words (*naos, hieron*) are usually chosen for "temple." Elliott also argues that household language is prevalent throughout 1 Peter and such language is not limited to words related to "house" but also includes the many references to familial

---

[154] Achtemeier, *1 Peter*, 154.
[155] Achtemeier, *1 Peter*, 155.

relationships within a household context (father, children, brotherly love, milk, the household code of 2:13–3:8, and household steward in 4:10). Elliott rejects the argument that "house" should mean "temple" and that what God is doing here is building a temple for himself constructed from the believers as living stones. Even if the immediate context may support that reading, his argument is that in the greater context of the book and usage in the New Testament, "household" is to be preferred over "temple." The "spiritual house" is the house that is filled with the Holy Spirit.[156]

However, other scholars do understand "house" in 2:5 as a reference to the people of God as God's temple; they note that this is a well-established usage of "house" in both the LXX and classical Greek.[157] In this passage, the verb of building and the architectural vocabulary suggest a connection to an edifice such as a house or a temple.[158] Vocabulary suggesting a temple includes words such as cornerstone, priesthood, and offering sacrifices. And, while "house" is not commonly used for temple in the New Testament, there are examples of it being used in this way.[159] The "spiritual house" of 1 Peter is one that is in the process of being built by God and is not yet complete.[160] More recently, some scholars have wanted to hold together the insights of Elliott that lean towards "household" with the meaning "temple" supported by the context of 1 Peter 2:4–10.[161] Mbuvi notes that understanding *oikos* with this double sense maintains the double sense of the Hebrew word "house" and maintains "the spiritual nature of the household in 1 Peter in contrast to the racial or bloodline brotherhood that characterized Israel."[162] The "spiritual house" that God builds is a "Temple-Community, which may point forward to the priesthood that inhabits the house that God built."[163] The house is for a holy priesthood. God identifies the people of Israel as a priestly nation (see v. 9 below for

---

[156] Elliott, *The Elect and the Holy*, 153; Abson Prédestin Joseph, *A Narratological Reading of 1 Peter* (London: Bloomsbury T&T Clark, 2013), 90.
[157] Selwyn, *First Epistle of St. Peter*, 159–60.
[158] Steven Richard Bechtler, *Following in His Steps: Suffering, Community, and Christology in 1 Peter*, Dissertation Series / Society of Biblical Literature: 162 (Atlanta: Scholars Press, 1998), 140.
[159] One example is found in Luke 11:51, which speaks of Zechariah perishing between the altar and the temple (*oikos*). This is a reference to 2 Chronicles 24:20–21.
[160] Bechtler, *Following in His Steps*, 141.
[161] Mbuvi, *Temple, Exile, and Identity in 1 Peter*, 91.
[162] Mbuvi, *Temple, Exile, and Identity in 1 Peter*, 91.
[163] Mbuvi, *Temple, Exile, and Identity in 1 Peter*, 91.

further comment) and now identifies those who trust God as a holy priesthood.[164] One of the functions of the priesthood both for Israel as a nation and for the church as God's people is to function as representatives for God, offering worship and sacrifices acceptable to God. It is a "holy" priesthood, reflecting the "set aside" nature of those who have been cleansed by the work of Christ (1:2) and who are called to be like their Father in holiness (1:14–16). This priesthood is one that lays aside the evil ways delineated in 2:1 and takes up a way of life embedded in hope, holiness, good conduct, love, and growth in salvation (1:13–2:3). And, continuing the metaphor of temple and priesthood, this priesthood offers spiritual sacrifices. These are no longer the Old Testament sacrifices of animals. Already the Old Testament anticipates an emphasis on right worship and conduct over sacrifice. So, Hosea 6:6a reads, "For I desire steadfast love and not sacrifice, the knowledge of God rather than burnt offerings." The idea of "spiritual sacrifices" is also found in Romans 12:1 ("living sacrifices") where it is associated with doing the will of God. While 1 Peter does not specify the context of these spiritual sacrifices, scholars have made a variety of suggestions including testifying to the good news,[165] a pattern of social conduct offered to God as worship,[166] "dedication of the entire person to God prompted by the Holy Spirit,[167] the Eucharist, which joins the offering of Christ with the offering of believers,[168] and "all behavior that flows from a transformation of the human spirit by the sanctifying work of the Holy Spirit."[169] Whatever the spiritual sacrifices are, they are offered by the collective priesthood and are directed towards God, but they are public words and deeds and can be witnessed by the

---

[164]   During the Reformation, this verse was used to develop the idea of "the priesthood of all believers." This doctrine advocates that all stand equal before God through Christ and are able to offer prayers and worship to God. Ordained clergy serve as representatives of the people rather than having a special status or access. However, this verse is not about individuals and their priestly function (although that could be implied) but is rather about a priesthood, a collective group to which the whole church belongs. In this way, the priesthood is representative of the whole group and functions as a whole.

[165]   Lai, "Holy Spirit," 183.

[166]   Michaels, *1 Peter*, 101.

[167]   Goppelt, *A Commentary on I Peter*, 142. Goppelt adds, "On this basis praise of God, sharing with one's neighbor, winning of persons through mission, and the ministry and martyrdom of the apostle are called offerings."

[168]   Selwyn, *First Epistle of St. Peter*, 162–63.

[169]   Jobes, *1 Peter*, 151.

world. The priesthood of the church is visible to the world. These spiritual sacrifices are offered to God as an act of worship and made possible through Jesus Christ. Peter takes the hearer back to the sprinkled blood of Jesus that points to the new covenant (1:2) and to the precious blood of the lamb which redeemed them (1:19).

Peter introduces the scriptural background in **vv. 6–8** with the formal citation "because it contains in scripture," and then quotes from three passages, making brief comments in between. The quotations begin with Isa. 28:16 and do reflect changes to the LXX text as we know it. The NRSV and the NETS (a recent English translation of the LXX) are laid out below for comparison. The language of "foundations" that is prominent in both the Greek and the Hebrew of Isaiah is missing from 1 Peter. By leaving out the material related to foundations, 1 Peter places emphasis on the stone itself and, as in Isaiah, on the outcome for those who trust in the stone that God has laid.

1 Peter 2:6 (NRSV)	Isaiah 28:16 (NETS)
See, I am laying in Zion a stone a cornerstone chosen and precious	See, I will lay for the foundations of Sion a precious, choice stone a highly valued cornerstone for its foundations
and whoever believes in him will not be put to shame	and the one who believes in him will not be put to shame

The larger Old Testament context in which this verse is found is one of judgment. The people are described as "making a covenant with death" and "taking refuge in lies" (Isa. 28:15), God's response to this is to lay a foundation stone in Zion (28:16) and to make justice and righteousness the standard that will do away with lies (28:17). The people of Israel have built a refuge for themselves but that refuge is built on a foundation of death and lies. In contrast, God's place of refuge is built of living stone that is chosen and precious and thus forms a refuge that is durable and worthy of trust.

The word "behold" is emphatic, an instruction to look, to see, and here it is directed towards seeing what God is doing. God is laying a stone in Zion. Zion is a reference to Jerusalem, and in this context the phrase most likely refers to the founding of the Davidic kingdom.[170] Now, Jesus Christ has

---

[170]   Elliott, *1 Peter*, 424.

become the messianic stone upon which the kingdom of God is founded. This stone is the cornerstone, a large dressed stone used to tie together two walls. It is chosen, implied, by God and precious. Once again, God is portrayed as the builder: the one who chooses and lays the most valuable stone in the right position in order to establish God's kingdom. This same language (chosen, precious) has already been used in 2:4 to describe God's choosing of the one to whom Christians come, Jesus Christ. The identification of the stone with a person is clear in the second half of the quotation as belief or trust is placed "in him." Those who do trust in him will not be put to shame. Dubis notes that this is "the negation of a word in order to affirm or emphasize its opposite; in other words, 'he will definitely not experience shame' is to be equated with 'he will definitely experience honor.'"[171] In a culture where honor and shame were crucial markers of status, those who chose trust in the Lord avoided shame. But, we might ask in whose eyes they avoid shame? In the eyes of the culture around them, they are still strangers and exiles – foreigners to the culture around them, people to be despised. But, in the eyes of God, the one who matters most, they not only do not experience shame because of their choice but definitely experience honor. They are chosen and precious before God and thus find their honor in him rather than in the sight of the world.

Peter follows the quotation of Isa. 28:16 with a brief comment beginning in **v. 7**. The verse begins emphatically with the words "to you" drawing the focus back to the audience. At the end of v. 6 it was clear that those who believe will receive honor and that is drawn out more fully in v. 7. Here, the ESV translation helpfully draws out the connection with v. 6: "So *the honor is for you who believe*" (ESV). The word *timē* can mean either "value" (thus, the NRSV translation "precious") or "honor" (as in the ESV). The Greek word is also nominative and thus the subject of the sentence; although here the NRSV translators understand it as a predicate nominative referring back to Jesus as the stone.[172] However, this imports a meaning to the text that obscures the obvious reference to honor in contrast to the shame of v. 6.[173] In the context of v. 6, it is better to understand *timē* as a reference to the honor believers anticipate as those

---

[171] Dubis, *1 Peter*, 51.
[172] Other English translations also take this position. For example, KVJ, NIV.
[173] Forbes, *1 Peter*, 64; Elliott, *1 Peter*, 427.

who are being built into the house of God. In contrast, "the following scriptures apply"[174] to those who do not believe. The stone, Jesus Christ, becomes a stumbling block. Two quotations are brought together to make the point. In v. 7b Psalm 118:22 (LXX 117:22) lays out the rejection of the stone by the builders. And in v. 8, a quote from Isa. 8:14 is added to draw out the significance of the Psalm. The builders (*oikodomountes*, a word containing the Greek word for "house," *oikos*) reject the stone. Some posit a specific identity of those who reject the stone such as "citizens and magistrates in Rome and in the provinces … who harass Christians in Peter's community and the communities to which he writes."[175] But it is probably best to understand the builders as all those who are enemies of God.[176] Goppelt identifies the builders as "those who want to construct their own world for themselves [and] have rejected Jesus as an inadequate stone for their edifice."[177] The word "rejection" carries with it a sense that the stone has been examined and found wanting, but it is this very stone that has become the "head of the corner." Some scholars have proposed that this refers to the keystone of an arch, the very top stone of a Roman arch that holds the arch in place, but since the next verse speaks of a stumbling stone, it is best understood as the cornerstone.

In **v. 8** Peter joins the quotation from v. 7 (Ps. 118:22) with a quotation from Isaiah 8:14 so that Jesus is now *both* the cornerstone *and* a stumbling stone. For those who believe, Jesus is the foundation of the house that God is building from the living stones he has chosen. But for those who do not believe, Jesus is a stumbling stone and a "rock that makes them fall." "Fall" is not a generic stumbling in life but is rather the specific result of rejecting the living stone, Jesus, who is the precious, chosen cornerstone appointed by God as the foundation of the church, those who trust in him. "The role of the stone in this passage is similar to the role depicted in Isa. 28:16 and Psalm 118:22, functioning as a divisive artifact separating the faithful from those who walk apart from the Lord."[178]

One final set of comments is added by Peter. The reason that they stumble is because "they disobey the word." In 1:23 we have seen that the

---

174 Dubis, *1 Peter*, 36.
175 Michaels, *1 Peter*, 105.
176 Elliott, *1 Peter*, 429.
177 Goppelt, *A Commentary on I Peter*, 146.
178 Egan, *Ecclesiology*, 105.

living word of God is the seed, the source of new birth, and that this word is the good news that was proclaimed to the gathered congregations. To disobey the word is another way to speak of rejecting the good news that was proclaimed. The most difficult part of this verse is the final phrase "as they were destined to do." The implied subject of the passive verb is God. The verse carries two senses. On the one hand, the first two verbs show that they are active participants in rejecting Christ. They stumble. They disobey. On the other hand, the consequence of rejecting the stone, the messianic cornerstone of God's kingdom, is to be rejected from that kingdom. The same God who places (*tithēmi*) a stone in Zion (v. 6), allows those who reject God to be placed (passive verb also from *tithēmi*) or consigned outside the kingdom. The NRSV translation "as they were destined to do" gives the sense that the disobedient are predestined to that choice. However, a better sense of the phrase in the context of 1 Peter is "that those who disobey the word are destined to stumble."[179]

The strong contrast with those who stumble and disobey in v. 8 is immediately apparent in **v. 9** as Peter writes, "but you," and then turns his focus to the identity of the church to which he is writing. He lays out a set of four identity markers drawn from Exod. 19:6 and Isa. 43:20. "The four titles are skillfully placed in a unique sequence – the first and last ("chosen race, people for God's possession") are drawn from Isa. 43:20–21 while the middle two are drawn from Exod. 19:6 ("royal priesthood, holy nation"). This combination not only highlights the intertextual relationship between Isa. 43 and Exod. 19, but relates these two texts to each other theologically."[180] Exodus 19 describes the arrival of the people of Israel at Sinai after their deliverance from enslavement in Egypt. There, God will establish a covenant between God and God's people. This story of God's deliverance of Israel from Egypt and the covenant at Sinai are the foundational identity markers for the people of Israel. In Exodus 19:5–6 God declares that the people of Israel "shall be my treasured possession out of all the peoples. Indeed, the whole earth is mine, but you shall be for me a priestly kingdom and a holy nation." In the context of the covenant that God is making with Israel, the themes of being set apart for the purposes of priestly work and set apart for holy living stand out as marks that should be evidenced by

---

[179]　Forbes, *1 Peter*, 65–66.
[180]　Lai, "Holy Spirit," 150.

those whom God has chosen. While God's election of Israel comes with a purpose that will bring blessings to other nations, that election is born out of the deep love that God has for Abraham and his descendants.[181] The identity markers drawn from Exodus 19 are surrounded on either side by phrases drawn from Isaiah 40, a passage that is part of the new exodus material found in Isaiah.[182] Both in Exodus and in Isaiah, these markers point to God's active choice of God's people and to the set apart nature of those chosen by God. The congregations in Asia Minor are now identified with the language that was applied to God's chosen people, Israel. The church is now "a chosen race, a royal priesthood, a holy nation, God's own people." In 1 Peter, there is no sense of opposition between Israel and Christians such as we see in Paul.

Once again, the audience is marked as "chosen" (cf. 1:1) just as the living stone, Jesus, is "chosen" (2:4, 6) and as God out of love chose the people of Israel from among all the peoples of the earth. The words of this first marker are found in Isaiah 43:20. In this section of Isaiah, which focuses on the return of the people of Israel from exile in Babylon, God promises to provide water in the desert and "to give drink to my chosen people." Now, the people addressed in 1 Peter are marked as the chosen race (*genos*) of God. Horrell notes that here in v. 9 three words related to social identity are used ("race," "nation," and "people").[183] The application of these words to the Christian community is used to describe Christians as an ethnic group that involved, among other things, being a people with a common origin in Jesus Christ and with solidarity with one another, as well as sharing memories and culture that shape their identity.[184] Horrell points out that when the word *genos* is used self-descriptively, it is often "in a context of evident hostility and suffering" similar to the context we see surrounding 1 Peter.[185] In Isaiah, God promised to make provision for his people in the wilderness, so too the chosen race of 1 Peter can trust in God's provision for them as they endure grim circumstances.

---

[181] Lohr, *Chosen and Unchosen*, 90–91.

[182] For further comment on the themes of exodus and new exodus in 1 Peter, see the commentary on 1 Peter 1:24–25.

[183] David G. Horrell, *Becoming Christian: Essays on 1 Peter and the Making of Christian Identity*, Early Christianity in Context (London; New York: Bloomsbury, 2013), 161.

[184] Horrell, *Becoming Christian*, 159.

[185] Horrell, *Becoming Christian*, 161.

The second identity marker for these congregations is "royal priesthood." The emphasis here is not on the priestly role of individual members but rather on their collective status as a priestly group. Similarly, when God identified the people of Israel as a "priestly kingdom," he was not speaking of the role of individuals within Israel but rather of their function as a whole group. The role of Israel as a priesthood is to serve God and to mediate between God and humanity by being a blessing to the nations around them. The church is now identified as a group that mediates between God and the world. The royal priesthood refers "to the Christian community as a body of priests in the service of God their 'king' to whom they now owe their allegiance as his people."[186]

The church is identified with a third marker as a group set apart as a "holy nation." Louw and Nida define *ethnos* as "the largest unit into which the people of the world are divided on the basis of their constituting a sociopolitical community – 'nation, people.'"[187] It is important for us to remember that the nation state as we know it did not arise until the 1600s; rather, first-century people tended to think of themselves as belonging to groups related to their ancestry and to groupings of families bound together into "nations." The behavior of the group that mediates between God and the world must be distinctive from others. Here, the church is marked out as a people group that is characterized by holiness (cf. 1:2, 15–16), which is a reflection of their relationship with the Holy God.

The fourth marker is their identity as "God's own people" (NRSV margin: "a people for his possession"). While this exact phrase does not occur in either Exodus 19 or Isaiah 43, there are approximations to this idea in both places, but the allusion to Isaiah 43:21, where the verbal form of "possession" is used, is especially strong: "to my people whom I have acquired to set forth my excellences" (NETS). This continues the emphasis that those whom God has chosen belong to him.

Each of the four identity markers center around a group of people (NRSV: race, priesthood, nation, people), with an adjective that further clarifies the nature of the group. It is clear that these people are God's people who have been given the same key markers as the people of Israel, indicating their status as the chosen people of God.

---

[186] Achtemeier, *1 Peter*, 164–65.
[187] Louw and Nida

The people of God have a purpose: to "proclaim the mighty acts (*aretas*, plural) of him who called you out of darkness into his marvelous light." The proclamation may be oriented both towards those within the church as a means of encouragement and reminder of God's faithfulness as well as to those outside the church as part of the church's mission and testimony (cf. 3:15). The Greek word *aretē* was used to refer to "goodness or excellence of any sort," and in ethical and moral discussions referred to virtue.[188] BAGD adds that "exhibition of *aretē* invites recognition resulting in renown or glory,"[189] which connects this word to the language of honor so prominent in the first-century world. Thus, many English translations read "proclaim the excellences (or praises) of him who called you . . ." (e.g., NASB, ESV, NIV), and this captures the sense of God's exceeding goodness and of the praise God deserves in light of that goodness. The major opening of the book (1:3) begins with blessing God, and this section ends with proclaiming God's virtues, God's character. But *aretē* has also been used to refer to the manifestations of divine power (e.g., miraculous works).[190] In this interpretation the proclamation of God's people is not simply one of praise but is rather a declaration of what God has actually accomplished in his mighty acts. In the Old Testament, the Psalms praise God by recounting the saving acts of God who delivered Israel from Egypt (e.g., Ps. 105). Still, the character of God and the deeds of God are closely connected. For example, Psalm 106 begins, "Praise the Lord! O give thanks to the Lord, for he is good; for his steadfast love endures forever. Who can utter the mighty doings of the Lord, or declare his praise?" Here, the goodness and love of God are immediately followed by the mighty deeds of God. Now, it is the church who proclaims the *aretas* (virtues, miraculous deeds) of God – both God's mighty deeds and the character that generates them. Peter has already made clear that these mighty deeds include the redemptive work of Jesus Christ made possible in the death and resurrection of the undefiled lamb. At the same time, it is clear that the mighty acts of God do not end with the work of Jesus Christ but include the means by which the church becomes the chosen people of God set apart for the priestly work to which God calls it. God is characterized as one who calls (also in 1:15 "the holy one who calls you"), emphasizing once again the

[188] LSJ
[189] BAGD
[190] BAGD

theme of God's choosing (1:1; 2:4, 6, 9). The church are those who have been called out of the darkness of their former way of life filled with ignorance of God and desires born of their ignorance (1:14). They have been called into God's light, another description of the new life Christians experience through the new birth.

Verse 10 turns to the first two chapters of Hosea to reiterate the movement from darkness to light. The movement from darkness to light in v. 9 is reminiscent of the movement from a group who were not God's people to a group who through God's mercy are now God's people. The book of Hosea depicts a prophet who is instructed by God to marry a prostitute. When Hosea's wife bore her second child, God instructed the prophet to name their daughter "Lo-ruhamah," which means "no mercy" (Hosea 1:6). When her third child was born, God instructed the prophet to name the boy "Lo-ammi [*Not my people*], for you are not my people and I am not your God" (Hosea 1:9). Both of these names were striking judgments against the people of Israel. Those who through God's mercy, God's compassionate love, were brought into covenant relationship with God are now rejected for their failure to fulfill the covenant obligation of loyalty to God alone. However, this abandonment in Hosea is not permanent as the end of Hosea 2 shows God restoring the people of Israel even though they have worshiped other gods. God will "have pity on Not Pitied, and I will say to Not My People, 'You are my people,' and he shall say, 'You are the Lord my God'" (Hosea 2:23, NETS). First Peter alludes to the prophet Hosea while drawing these phrases into a new context where they are applied to the church. Those who were not God's people are now God's people, the church. This is a striking declaration, especially if this is a mixed group of both Jewish and Gentile believers who now find themselves formed together into God's people. It is now the church formed around and through the work of Jesus Christ that has become the chosen race and the holy nation. Similarly, the church, a people who did not know God's mercy when they had not experienced new birth, are now the recipient of God's mercy.

Bridging the Horizons: In the twenty-first century there are countless churches that span every continent, hundreds of languages, and a vast array of forms. Many of these churches came about through division as groups within the church argued with one another over right practice, right doctrine, or even right leadership. Some of these divisions are famous such as the split between eastern and western churches that began in the early centuries of the church and culminated in 1054 CE or the Reformation of the sixteenth century out of which the Protestant churches were born. While these two examples are famous, there are now thousands of denominations around the world. And many of these churches understand themselves as the "real" church and other groups as either false or lesser. While there was some significant movement in the twentieth century towards ecumenism and the resolution of differences (e.g., the agreement between Lutherans and Catholics over the issue of justification), the worldwide church remains divided. This is a stunning contrast to the portrayal of the church in 1 Peter 2:4–10. There, the church is depicted as a unity – the one people of God, the singular chosen race, the collective royal priesthood, and the holy nation. How are we to reconcile the reality of our experience of the church both in our time and over the long history of the church with the unifying call of God and the portrayal of the church in 1 Peter?

It is clear that the church is portrayed as Israel in 1 Peter. Israel is a nation created by God through God's deliverance of the Israelites from Egypt and God's covenant with them at Sinai. We often think of Israel as a unity – all the descendants of Abraham or all the descendants of the family of Jacob (Israel) who went down to Egypt. Yet, the description of the people of Israel who came out of Egypt includes this description: "The Israelites journeyed from Rameses to Succoth … A mixed crowd also went up with them …" (Exod. 12:37–38). "The phrase translated as 'mixed crowd' usually refers to non-Israelites. In the other places that this phrase appears in the Old Testament, it refers to a number of different ethnic groups … A better translation of Exodus 12:38 would be that a large number of different ethnic groups came out of Egypt."[191] In other words, along with children of Jacob other ethnicities followed Moses and Aaron out into the wilderness and to the mountain of Sinai. There, at the covenant initiative of God, they became Israel, the nation born out of God's covenant love and deliverance from slavery in Egypt. Israel would not be the priests of God, the chosen people, the holy nation without God. When Christ appears as the cornerstone of faith, Christ is both the Son of God and a member of Israel. Through the redemptive death of Jesus Christ, a new covenant is made possible in which the church also becomes Israel. We see this portrayed in 1 Peter. The church are those who have been given new birth through the suffering, death,

---

[191] Esau McCaulley, *Reading While Black: African American Biblical Interpretation as an Exercise in Hope* (Downers Grove, IL: IVP Academic, 2020), 102.

and resurrection of Jesus Christ. They have entered into covenant relationship with their Father through the sprinkling of the blood of Jesus. The church is growing in their experience of salvation (2:2) and their response of obedience, and proclaims the wonderful nature and miraculous acts of God. The church takes on both the identity and mission of Israel. Like Israel, the church comes into being through the will of God, is given identity and purpose through the will of God, and is constituted of diverse peoples just as Israel was. And, like Israel, the church is chosen and constituted by God as a unity.

First Peter speaks almost exclusively in hopeful terms. While, it describes the suffering of God's people, especially at the hands of outsiders who do not understand the holy life and good deeds of the church, it does not describe division within the church nor division between Jew and Gentile. And yet, our own experience in the twenty-first century means that we cannot ignore our experience of division in the church in our own time and the many reasons this has come about. Indeed, this is something to lament and a reality worthy of repentance.[192] The place of the church as the elect people of God has too long been used as an excuse to sin against the Jewish people. The church has a long history of abuse in which Jews were killed, tortured, excluded, and persecuted by Christians. Both repentance for division within the church and repentance for treatment of Jewish people outside of the church are needed in the church today. Both of these would be signs, small steps, towards the holy life and brotherly love enjoined by 1 Peter itself. At the same time, we can recognize that God has the capacity to use the divided fragments of the church both to bless those within it and to bless the world. Here, we might identify ways in which different fragments of the church have championed different gifts from God. For example, through the growth of the Pentecostal movement, the gift of the Holy Spirit has become a renewed focus of the worldwide church. Similarly, the rise of evangelicalism has brought a focus on mission and preaching while other parts of the worldwide church have contributed other gifts to the church as a whole.[193] As the people of God, the church's allegiance is to God alone and not to the culture around it nor to a political party outside the church. This new political unit (God's people) is characterized by holiness, by being set apart as a group that through both its trust in God and in God's son Jesus Christ *and* through its conduct makes known its commitment to God and Jesus Christ. This conduct is repeatedly characterized in 1 Peter by love, good deeds, and honorable treatment of all humanity.

---

[192] Ephraim Radner, *Church* (Eugene, OR: Cascade Books, 2017), 123.
[193] Richard J. Foster, *Streams of Living Water: Celebrating the Great Traditions of Christian Faith*, first ed. (San Francisco: Harper, 1998).

1 PETER 2:11–4:11: LIFE AS GOD'S PEOPLE IN EXILE

1 Peter 2:11–3:12: Household Order in the Midst of Suffering

[11] Beloved, I urge you as aliens and exiles to abstain from the desires of the flesh that wage war against the soul.

[12] Conduct yourselves honorably among the Gentiles, so that, though they malign you as evildoers, they may see your honorable deeds and glorify God when he comes to judge.

First Peter **2:11** is the beginning of a new major unit that extends through **4:11**. The shift is marked by a number of features: (1) the use of the direct address, "beloved," which is only used here and then again at 4:12 where it also introduces a new unit; (2) the use of the first person singular, "I urge," which only happens here and in 5:1 where attention is turned to a new topic concerning the role of the elders in the church communities; and (3) the reiteration of the audience's status as "exiles," which we saw previously in 1:1 and to which is now added their status as "aliens."

The large unit of 2:11–4:11 is laid out in two segments. The first segment (2:11–3:12) is a household code containing the following units:

2:11–12 introduction addressed to everyone;
2:13–17 addressed to the whole household;
2:18–25 addressed to slaves;
3:1–6 addressed to wives;
3:7 addressed to husbands; and
3:8–12 conclusion addressing everyone again.

The previous major section encouraged the audience to reject their former way of life and to move into their new identity as the family of God. In 2:11–3:12, the household code provides a guide for the family of God to counter the negative stereotypes associated with Christians, particularly the stereotype of rejecting social order.[194] There has been some debate about whether all of 2:11–3:12 can be properly identified as a household code since 2:11–17 and 3:8–12 are not addressed specifically to members of a household, for example to husbands, wives, or slaves. Those parts of the passage are addressed to the whole congregation and could be understood as being

---

[194] Holloway, *Coping with Prejudice*, 174–75.

more fully related to issues concerning governance.[195] However, since the previous segments of 1 Peter identified God's people using the metaphor of "family," and since the culture of the first century saw that the state and the household were intertwined, it is appropriate to consider the whole segment from 2:11–3:12 as a household code. The second segment, 3:13–4:11, lays out in more detail the situation that the household of God faces in daily life and the responses of God's family to those both outside of and within the family. Although the parts of this segment are closely connected, for the sake of study this second segment can also be broken down into several parts as follows: 3:13–17; 3:18–22; 4:1–6; and 4:7–11. The two major units that make up the larger section (2:11–3:12 and 3:13–4:11) both contain significant instructions for the household of God alongside reflection on the death of Jesus Christ. This continues 1 Peter's practice of interweaving instruction and theology.

After the previous major segment (1:13–2:10), which focused on the identity of the family of God and their responses of hope, holiness, right conduct, love, and longing, Peter now calls them "beloved" (**2:11**) reminding them that he sees them as beloved and that they are loved by God. Yet, he also reiterates their status as "aliens and exiles," which reminds them that their position in the culture is that of outsiders who are not at home in the place in which they reside. Here, these identity markers are introduced with the marker of metaphorical language, the word "as," which points to the idea that those who became part of the household of God became strangers to their former way of life. They may or may not have been literal strangers in the towns and villages they inhabited, but they had become like strangers to the community and its way of life, with which they no longer engaged as they used to do (cf. 4:3).[196] The combination of "aliens and exiles" is found in two locations in the LXX: in Genesis 23:4 where Abraham describes himself as a "stranger and an alien" when seeking a burial place for his wife from the

---

[195]   A short summary is provided in Jennifer G. Bird, *Abuse, Power and Fearful Obedience: Reconsidering 1 Peter's Commands to Wives*, Library of New Testament Studies: 442 (London; New York: T&T Clark International, 2011), 14–20. A longer summary is available in David L. Balch, *Let Wives Be Submissive: The Domestic Code in 1 Peter*, Society of Biblical Literature Monograph Series: 26 (Chico, CA: Scholars Press, 1981), 1–10.

[196]   For further discussion of "aliens and exiles" see the commentary on 1 Peter 1:1.

Hittites; and Psalm 38:12 LXX (Eng. 39:12) where the petitioner asks God to hear his prayer "because I am a sojourner with you, and a visiting stranger, like all my fathers" (NETS). This combination of terms "does not appear in Hellenistic Greek literature except in Jewish or Christian writers."[197] Once again, the author of 1 Peter draws from the Old Testament to describe the identity of the audience; like Abraham and David this audience also knows what it is to be both beloved, chosen, and alien at the same time. While Elliott focuses on the political identification and social status of aliens (*paroikous*), this must be considered within the framework where the phrase "aliens and exiles" is first found in Greek literature, the LXX. The audience, by their identification as followers of Christ, have become alien to the culture and thus are the victims of prejudice. As those who are subject to prejudice from their neighbors, it makes sense to "make every effort not to offend their 'citizen' neighbors."[198] Once again, the minority status of the audience is in view.

Peter strongly urges the household of God to "abstain" or keep away from the desires of the flesh. In 1 Peter, desires (*epithumia*) are always portrayed negatively. In 1:14, desires are associated with ignorance, and the family of God is instructed not to be conformed to those former, ignorant desires. In 2:11 desires are described as "fleshly" (*sarkikos*), which means that they are human or sinful desires in contrast to the type of longing (*epipotheō*) that is oriented towards God (2:2). Again, in 4:2, human desires are seen as something to be put off in favor of living a life in accordance with God's will. And in 4:3 desires are included in a list of activities in which Christians no longer participate. When Peter urges them to abstain from "fleshly desires," he is not simply telling them not to be like their neighbors but rather, "Do not be as *you were*."[199] Thus, "fleshly" refers to the desires of the former life before hearing and responding to the message of hope and new identity in Christ.

In 2:11 the "fleshly desires" are described as "waging war against the soul." The Romans possessed the most effective, well-trained fighting force

---

[197]   Paul J. Achtemeier, "Newborn babes and living stones: Literal and figurative in 1 Peter," in Maurya P. Horgan and Paul J. Kobelski (eds.), *To Touch the Text: Biblical and Related Studies in Honor of Joseph A. Fitzmyer, S.J.* (New York, 1989), 217.

[198]   Holloway, *Coping with Prejudice*, 176.

[199]   Miroslav Volf, "Soft difference: Theological reflections on the relation between church and culture in 1 Peter," *Ex Auditu* 10 (1994): 21.

in the known world. It conquered many types of enemies as the Romans expanded their empire. The Roman armies used techniques such as deploying lines of soldiers who marched in silence towards the enemy. When they had closed in, the Romans would suddenly throw their javelins at the enemy, shout, and rush forward throwing the enemy into disarray. In addition, catapults, siege towers, and other weapons were part of Roman warfare. Those living in Asia Minor may have even seen the Roman legions marching to war on the eastern front of their province. Here, Peter makes use of the metaphor of waging war to describe the force and impact of desires that derive from all that is apart from God. This is the war directed towards the life of the believer.

The NRSV begins **2:12** as a new sentence with the translation "Conduct yourselves." However, in Greek this is a participial phrase (*tēn anastrophē . . . echontes*) that is attached to the previous clause in 2:11; rather than being the beginning of a new sentence, it indicates the means by which they abstain.[200] They abstain by conducting themselves well in their public life. In 1:15 the family of God has already been instructed to be holy in behavior rather than living out the vain behavior inherited from ancestors (1:18). Now, it is clear that this behavior is to be adopted both within the household of God and outside it in the lives that they live among the nations, in other words among those who are not followers of Jesus Christ. Attending to the infinitive ("to abstain") and the means indicated by the participle ("by having good conduct") allows the audience to retain the call for action that Peter urges while also indicating that abstaining from one thing and conducting oneself in a different manner are not two opposite things. Rather, taking up good behavior is the very means of resisting those things that seek to destroy the Christian community. It is important to remember that Peter is encouraging all members of the household of God to conduct themselves well, to walk in holiness and communal love. Such good behavior on the part of the household of God will be recognized as being good by those within God's community and may become the impetus for glory by those outside of God's household.

---

[200] See the discussion at 1 Peter 2:1 about the translation of Greek participles.

A Closer Look: Good Works

In the first century the language of "good works" was often used to refer to the benefactions that wealthy patrons bestowed on cities in order to gain honor and prestige in society. In Asia Minor such gifts often included contributing towards or funding public buildings, with a preference given to religious buildings such as temples, shrines, altars, and statues of gods. Gifts might also support buildings used for entertainment such as theaters, baths, and gymnasiums. Many benefactors preferred gifts that resulted in concrete evidence of their generosity. But other forms of gifts included "distributions of wine, grain, oil, and money which were given to (privileged) citizen groups."[201] In addition, some chose to pay for entertainment for a city. This might include a festival that involved athletics, music, theater, or gladiatorial games. A small number of gifts were made in order to relieve people of debt or taxes or to distribute grain in a time of famine, but these were the least common forms of benefaction.[202] "The vast majority of beneficent contributions were for decoration and entertainment, and even when distributions of grain and wine were made, the largest percentage was given to those on the top of the social hierarchy (not the bottom)."[203] There have been some scholars who have suggested that when Peter encourages the household of God to practice good works, he is encouraging them to take up benefaction as a way of life.[204] However, Williams has shown that while the language of good works is indeed applied to the activity of benefaction, the capacity to fund beneficent gifts was limited to the very rich. Indeed, those who performed good works of this type were the wealthy, and they received honor and affirmation of their status as good and noble people in return for their generosity. Even modest gifts often consisted of the equivalent of a year's wages. Those who could fund such a sum were few and far between.[205] A study of the churches in Asia Minor shows that on the whole few members of the household of God would have the means to provide for a city at the level of public benefaction. In addition, cities did not accept every benefaction that was offered, and there is no guarantee that a benefaction being offered by a despised group would be accepted.[206] So, when Peter enjoins the *whole* congregation, which obviously includes slaves, as well as women married to unbelieving husbands, to engage in

---

[201] Travis B. Williams, *Good Works in 1 Peter: Negotiating Social Conflict and Christian Identity in the Greco-Roman World*, Wissenschaftliche Untersuchungen zum Neuen Testament: 337 (Tübingen: Mohr Siebeck, 2014), 72.

[202] Williams, *Good Works in 1 Peter*, 72.

[203] Williams, *Good Works in 1 Peter*, 72.

[204] Bruce W. Winter, "The public honouring of Christian benefactors: Romans 13:3–4 and 1 Peter 2:14–15," *Journal for the Study of the New Testament* 34 (1988): 87.

[205] Williams, *Good Works in 1 Peter*, 78–79.

[206] Williams, *Good Works in 1 Peter*, 80–81.

good works, it is difficult to imagine that Peter is instructing the whole congregation to engage in public benefaction.[207] The language of good works is indeed derived from the realm of public benefaction, but people of lesser means added to the understanding of good works in the Greco-Roman world. While benefaction is not excluded from Peter's instruction, it is best to look further for our understanding of what constitutes good works.

Both Jews and early Christians valued good works and understood them as important demonstrations of their faith. Jews understood good works as having both a social dimension that contributed to the common good and a vertical dimension in which the good works enhanced their relationship with God. Good works were often associated with keeping the Law of Moses and taking up particular activities such as prayer and fasting and the giving of alms. For example, in the narrative of Tobit 12:7b–8a the angel Raphael tells Tobit, "Do good and evil will not overtake you. Prayer and fasting is good, but better than both is almsgiving with righteousness." During the time of diaspora, observance of the Jewish law accompanied by prayer and fasting and alms giving were important marks of faithful Jewish living.[208]

The New Testament also valued doing good. Jesus himself instructed his disciples to "let your light shine before others, so that they may see your good works and give glory to your Father in heaven" (Matt 5:16). This instruction comes immediately following the beatitudes and right before Jesus' comments that he has not come to abolish the Law of Moses but rather to fulfill it. In the larger context of this passage, good works are associated with both the beatitudes and with the Law of Moses as it is fulfilled through Christ. When good works are taken up in the New Testament epistles they become associated with moral virtue redefined as that which is virtuous in the sight of God. No longer are good works defined by the surrounding community as would have been the case with public benefaction; rather, God is the one who recognizes, approves, and rewards good works in due time (Gal. 6:8).

The letter of 1 Peter is addressed to the family of God in Asia Minor. The people specifically identified and addressed in the book are slaves and women of unbelieving husbands, believing husbands and their wives, and elders and younger members of God's people. The churches across the region of Asia Minor most likely consisted

---

[207] The norm in the Greco-Roman world was for a wife to join herself to her husband's religion. So, if a husband chose to be a Christian it was likely that both his wife and his greater household would also choose the Christian way. Of course, there were households where an unbelieving wife was married to a Christian man (1 Cor. 7:12 is evidence for that), but Peter doesn't address that situation. Because of this norm, it was much more challenging for a wife to be a Christian when her husband wasn't as that could be seen as undermining the husband and/or the family.

[208] Williams, *Good Works in 1 Peter*, 120–21.

mainly of believers drawn from the least and the lowly, with perhaps some members having more resources. While the members most likely did not have the means for public benefaction, they were able to hear the instruction to take up good works as being part of the holy life to which they were called. In the Greco-Roman culture that was prevalent in Asia Minor, good works were the domain of the wealthy who had the resources to be benefactors to the community around them. But in 1 Peter the whole church is identified as having the capacity to engage in good works that reflected their identity as God's people. An activity that was commonly reserved for the elite citizens of the region is redefined as a moral and social activity available to all, even to those despised by the majority culture.

Good works in the hands of God's people had the capacity to be part of "the cautious resistance advocated in the epistle" such as advocating for religious freedom and agency for women and slaves.[209] Many have argued that deeds identified as good works by God's people must also be viewed as good works by those who are not Christian, meaning that what counts as good has to be a set of values shared by both Christians and non-Christians.[210] However, this is only the case if one understands the good works as the proposed solution to the problem of persecution and suffering faced by God's family. It seems, however, that doing good can actually be the cause of suffering. Indeed, when Peter addresses slaves he indicates that their suffering is to be *for doing good*. The household of God receives affirmation and honor in the sight of God and fellow believers, but their good works may be the very thing that bring about malicious speech from the society that identifies them not as those who do good but as "evil doers" (**2:12**). Although, at the time of Christ's return those who speak evil against believers will finally see their good works and glorify God (**2:12**).

Those who do not follow Christ are maligning the audience as evildoers. This is the first use of a word that will recur five times in 1 Peter as either an adjective or a verb.[211] While the etymology of the word *kakopoion* is literally evildoer, the connotation of the word is more like "criminal."[212] This is "the basic charge being leveled at his readers," according to Holloway.[213] The household code that follows will be one means of

---

[209] Williams, *Good Works in 1 Peter*, 265.

[210] As one example, Volf, "Soft difference."

[211] 2:12, 14; 3:13, 17; 4:15; the opposite *agathopoios*, "doing good" and its cognates occur in 2:14, 15, 20; 3:6, 17; 4:19.

[212] BAGD

[213] Holloway, *Coping with Prejudice*, 67.

responding to this charge. Holloway goes on to argue that one of the keys to maintaining Roman peace was the work of getting rid of "bad men," and that being maligned as a bad man was "a truly ominous charge that adduces the governor's imperial mandate and places Christians at odds not only with public opinion but with Roman rule."[214] It is when contending with this challenge – being a member of a despised minority group and suffering accusations of being evil and undermining the order of the empire and the social norms of the locale – that Peter encourages good conduct. The grammatical structure of the Greek sentence (2:11–12) allows us to attend to a second point of emphasis, which is the final outcome of good behavior – glory directed towards God. The Christians of Asia Minor may face daily experiences of being slandered, maligned, and falsely accused of doing wrong. The failure of Christians to participate in expected civic and social conduct, including worship at the shrines of the empire and participation in civic-religious celebrations, leaves them vulnerable to charges of misconduct and social destabilization. But Peter indicates that their good works will be the source out of which flows a type of seeing that results in the nations giving glory to God. Peter makes it clear that the behavior of the nations is not simply a general maligning of Christians; rather, it is the good conduct itself that is maligned. Thus, such things as holiness, hope, brotherly love, and rightly ordered desires may be the very things that are slandered and despised. But Peter urges abstention from destructive desires by means of good conduct *so that* the nations who speak evil things against the household of God may observe (this word, *epipoteuō*, used only once in the New Testament, is used of the kind of looking done by a watchman or overseer[215] and may reflect the intensity of the gaze Christians experienced from those around them) the good works that they are doing and may glorify God in the day of visitation. Once again, Peter draws on the eschatological horizon where a great reversal will take place. It may seem at the time the letter was written that power lies in the hands of those who slander and speak with hatred and contempt about the good behavior of God's household, but in the end the holy behavior, which resembles the one who has given them new birth and brought them salvation, will be the source of exaltation and honor in the form of glory,

[214] Holloway, *Coping with Prejudice*, 68.
[215] LSJ

which involves the praise and exaltation of God. Elliott notes, "Glory, praise, and declarations of honor are what indebted clients owe their powerful and generous patrons. In having this glory and honor of their patrons and benefactors acknowledged by all, clients themselves bathe in and share the honor of their benefactors."[216] The NRSV renders "in the day of visitation" as "when he comes to judge," which captures one aspect of the day of visitation. Like the phrase "the last day," there are two sides to the day of visitation. For those whose good works are finally seen and understood, there is vindication, but for others it is a time of judgment. The phrase "day of visitation" does not appear elsewhere in the New Testament, but it is found in Isaiah 10:3. There it is part of a larger context where it refers to the coming of the one who will judge those who have written laws that kept the needy from receiving justice, and those who have stolen from the poor and plundered widows. The good deeds of the household of God must be understood from within the framework of God's holiness (1 Pet. 1:15–16), meaning that the activities of holiness must be characterized by sincere love for others including the vulnerable and the needy. Indeed, it was the very attention of the household of God to such issues as caring for the poor and the sick that brought them to the attention of the society around them in later centuries.

Bridging the Horizons: Many within the church experience harmful desires (desires that wage war against the flesh) and truly long to overcome them and live in holy and godly ways. We often focus our attention either on searching for a cause behind those desires or working hard to push them away. How might Christians resist the desires that threaten to undo their faith? First Peter suggests another way forward: focusing on good works as a way of fighting the battle against disordered desire. Here, the Christian is reminded that service towards others – feeding the hungry, visiting the sick and imprisoned, and working for life-sustaining programs – serves two functions. First, it helps to reorient the Christian from desires that destroy to actions that give life. Second, these actions serve as a witness to a world that continues to look askance at many Christians and questions their morality, their political aspirations, and their engagement with others. Christians in the twenty-first century should not expect their work for justice and their attention to

---

[216] Elliott, *1 Peter*, 470.

care for the poor to draw applause or recognition from those around them who do not share the same commitments to love and holiness. Part of living as the household of God is to be faithful in good works whether one receives recognition from the world or not. Good works are the obedient response of faith to the salvation offered by God. Like the church in Asia Minor, Christians today also look to God for vindication and continue faithfully in good works out of love for God and one another. At the same time, today's Christians can also long for the day in which good works bring glory to God, whether now or at Christ's return.

[13] For the Lord's sake accept the authority of every human institution, whether of the emperor as supreme,

[14] or of governors, as sent by him to punish those who do wrong and to praise those who do right.

[15] For it is God's will that by doing right you should silence the ignorance of the foolish.

[16] As servants of God, live as free people, yet do not use your freedom as a pretext for evil.

[17] Honor everyone. Love the family of believers. Fear God. Honor the emperor.

First Peter 2:11–12 introduces and frames the larger unit of 2:11–3:12 by reiterating the identity of those addressed, their commitment to doing good, and the purpose of good behavior, which is to bring glory to God. All this takes place in the midst of the suffering they experience due to the slanderous accusations made against them. The first section (2:13–17) of the household code addresses the relationship of the church in Asia Minor to the people with authority over them. The household code serves two purposes at the same time. First, it is a means of addressing the accusation that believers are people who seek to disrupt the peace of the Roman Empire. In response to this malicious talk, they respond to authority with submission when possible. At the same time, the household code is also a subversive mechanism that subtly reminds Christians who is truly in control and to whom they really belong in the midst of suffering and submission.

A Closer Look: Families and Household Codes in the Ancient World

In the Roman Empire the family was the premier unit of social order, and well-ordered families were seen as the building blocks of a stable and secure empire. The household was also the chief unit of economic production, and families usually worked together to secure their survival. The vast majority of families in the first-century world worked in agriculture, but there were also many other types of work (e.g., craftsmanship, building, trade, medicine, law, and entertainment). A tiny percentage of families were extremely powerful and had achieved high status within Roman society. They aimed to retain their status and position through investment, marital alliance, and participation in the economic system of patronage and benefaction. Within this system, the household of Caesar was the most powerful family in the empire. Aristocratic families based in Rome were also very powerful. And locations outside of Rome also had their share of powerful local families, often with connections to Rome.

Patriarchal families were the norm. The well-run Roman family was headed by the oldest living male (in Latin the *paterfamilias*) to whom the rest of the household submitted. The male head of the household determined the business dealings of the family, performed religious rites on behalf of the family, and was legally recognized as being able to enter into contracts and other legal obligations. Households in the first century were a little larger than the nuclear family of twenty-first-century Western culture. The wealthy often lived together in extended family units that might include a mother and father and children, some of their married children, other extended family members, as well as slaves. In addition, freedmen (former slaves who were now free) and clients (those with obligations to the master of the house) were also attached to the household of wealthy patrons with mutual obligations even if they did not live under the same roof.

Within households, slaves had no rights since they were living property and could be used or sold however their masters saw fit. Slaves did not have the right to marry; however, some high-ranking male slaves were allowed to live with a woman as if they were married.[217] Families who were not wealthy also sought to marry and form households. Such households were smaller and might consist of parents and children and any family members in need. The household was the safety net for those in distress in the Roman Empire. Those without families, such as widows and orphans, were particularly vulnerable to abuse and exploitation, as were strangers and temporary residents.

The Romans drew on ethical thinking about the household that dates back to the time of Aristotle. Household codes were a way of describing the different roles and responsibilities of household members. As demonstrated by Aristotle, there was recognition that men and women banded together to form families for mutual

---

[217] Veyne, *The Roman Empire*, 33.

support and survival and in order to raise children. Within this family structure, there were roles that were deemed appropriate for men and others for women. These roles were seen as working together for the benefit and peace of the household. Men were usually seen as being responsible for work that took them further afield from the home, and women were often understood as those who cared for home and children.[218] While each had a role in the family, women were to obey the men in their household. Later authors such as Dio Chrysostom, Seneca, and Dionysius of Halicarnassus continued the idea of the household code with its instructions to the various members therein. The Greek and Roman sources that resonate with the New Testament household codes are usually much longer, however, than the short form we see in the New Testament.

The New Testament has two examples of household codes – Ephesians 5:21–6:9 and Colossians 3:18–4:1 – and each addresses all the expected roles (husband/wife; slave/master; father/children). But the household code found in 1 Peter is unique in that the only pair that is addressed is wives and husbands. And even in that pairing, it is clear that the women who are addressed are not married to the men who are addressed.[219] Thus, reciprocity is not one of the features of the household code in 1 Peter. The New Testament household codes are distinct from the type of household codes we see in the wider Greco-Roman context. In 1 Peter those addressed by the code are addressed directly. In contrast, Greco-Roman sources are addressed to the male head of the household as the person who is ultimately responsible for household management. The direct address to individuals in the household code of 1 Peter indicates the esteem that the author of 1 Peter has both for those he is addressing and for their capacity to heed and follow the advice given. In a world where the privileges of deciding, ruling, and acting accrued to wealthy male heads of households first, Peter privileges those with the least power – slaves and women. This presents a possible contrast between the status of persons within the household of God (perhaps seen as a more private sphere) and the status of persons as viewed by citizens in the public sphere.[220]

---

[218] Aristotle, *Oeconomica* III.I–III, LCL.

[219] Margaret Macdonald's work serves as a reminder that members of the churches who heard these household codes may have multiple overlapping identities. A person may be both husband and master, slave and community member. While this may apply more to the household codes of Ephesians and Colossians, it is worth noting in our study of 1 Peter as well. Margaret Y. MacDonald, "Beyond identification of the topos of household management: Reading the household codes in light of recent methodologies and theoretical perspectives in the study of the New Testament," *NTS* 57 (2011): 73.

[220] Halvor Moxnes, "The beaten body of Christ: Reading and empowering slave bodies in 1 Peter," *Religion & Theology* 21 (2014): 129.

Using sociological analysis, the household code has been understood in two different ways. On the one hand, some have understood it as a means of communicating to the church in Asia Minor that their way of life should be similar to and share the values of the culture around them. This view argues for Christian assimilation in order to avoid unnecessary persecution and provide an opportunity for witness to the surrounding culture. It shows that Christians can be an accepted part of the culture around them.[221] On the other hand, others have argued that the household code is a means of encouraging the Christian community to stand firm in the face of suffering and to live out the values of their Christian faith while dwelling in an antagonistic surrounding culture. For a community that was estranged from the culture around it, the church was a home. The household code encouraged a shared set of values and way of life that was apart from the society around it.[222] Meanwhile, other scholars have argued for a both/and approach in which the church in Asia Minor is both similar to and distinct from the culture in which it is located.[223] David Horrell has argued that a postcolonial approach to 1 Peter may help us to see the way in which the emperor and his government were no longer seen as the savior of the world and the bearer of good news but rather as "the evil power which scatters God's people."[224] In this context, Christians offer "polite resistance." There is no need to draw unnecessary attention and no excuse for conforming to behavior that is any less than holy and loving in the eyes of God.

In **2:13** the household code begins with the imperative "submit" (NRSV: "accept the authority of"), which is directed to the whole audience. Christians were maligned as bad actors who sought to undermine the peace of the Roman Empire, so the imperative to submit promotes the Christian group as one that is not politically or socially subversive.[225] Many translations (NRSV, ESV, and CEB) have chosen to use the phrase "every human institution" for the focus of the believers' submission. However, Christians are to submit to *ktisis*, which can be translated as "every human creature" (author's translation and Douay Rheims Bible). *Ktisis* regularly refers to either creation or created beings – "creatures."[226] Older

---

[221] Balch, *Let Wives Be Submissive*.
[222] Elliott, *A Home for the Homeless*.
[223] For example, Bechtler, *Following in His Steps*; Volf, "Soft difference."
[224] Horrell, "Between conformity and resistance," 142.
[225] Holloway, *Coping with Prejudice*, 179.
[226] While the gloss "institution" is provided by the leading New Testament lexicon, BAGD, no strong supporting evidence for this reading is supplied.

commentators support the reading "institution" by arguing that institutional government and systems are in view here,[227] but more recent readings have attended to the created nature of those to whom the readers submit.[228] In **v. 14** those to whom submission is directed are further identified as the king/emperor or governors rather than systems such as the law. Williams points out that "the use of *ktisis* in 1 Pet. 2, 13 was intended to communicate a subtle yet calculated critique of the emperor by emphasizing his human nature (or creatureliness)."[229] This is in contrast to the divine status often associated with the emperor in light of his exalted status as a benefactor.[230] Indeed, the text goes on to assert that submission to the emperor is done "for the Lord," and this is also a reminder to this minority group, Christians, that ultimately the Lord and Father to whom they belong is in control in a world where by all appearances Caesar reigns supreme. First Peter also acknowledges the hierarchical structure of the Roman Empire. Caesar, the emperor, had authority over the whole empire, and he appointed governors as his representatives in provinces throughout the empire. In the view of the Roman Empire, the purpose of governors was to exercise power to maintain order where they were sent. In a society where honor was the highest value, rulers made use of both praise and discipline to secure the peace. Those who committed crimes were punished. Here, we must remember that crimes in the first century might include such things as murder and stealing but also included sedition, treason, and undermining the emperor. Punishing wrongdoing refers to the judicial function of sentencing criminals.[231] Similarly, doing good deeds includes proper moral action, which may include exercising religious-civic responsibilities as expected. Praising those who did good and punishing those who did wrong was an expected role of those who governed. Socrates commented that guardians of the law are selected "to praise the one who acts lawfully, and to punish the one who acts contrary to the laws."[232] These expectations of the proper role of those who

---

[227] Selwyn, *First Epistle of St. Peter*, 172.

[228] Achtemeier, *1 Peter*, 182; Elliott, *1 Peter*, 489.

[229] Travis B. Williams, "The divinity and humanity of Caesar in 1 Peter 2,3: Early Christian resistance to the emperor and his cult," *Zeitschrift für die neutestamentliche Wissenschaft und die Kunde der Älteren Kirche* 105:1 (2014): 145.

[230] Williams, "The divinity and humanity of Caesar in 1 Peter 2,3," 145.

[231] Bechtler, *Following in His Steps*, 90.

[232] Quoted in Elliott, *1 Peter*, 492 and found in Xenophon (Oec. 9.14).

governed continued into the age of the Roman Empire even though such expectations often went unfulfilled as governors used their considerable power both to keep the peace, even if that necessitated military force, and to enrich themselves. In the context of 1 Peter 2:11–12, it is clear that Christians are being accused of engaging in criminal behavior simply by being Christians. In other words, in the eyes of those outside the faith, these are people worthy of being duly punished by those in power. In contrast, Peter encourages his audience to maintain good conduct so that those around can see that they are people who do good; through good conduct they show that they are people worthy of praise by those in power.[233]

Verse 15 gives further reason that the readers are to engage in good behavior. Already we have seen that good behavior will cause the nations to glorify God (v. 12). Now, we see that doing right is God's will, a reminder that the instructions within the household code are to be understood in relationship to God (i.e., "for the Lord's sake" in v. 13). In this way (*houtōs*), through good works, Christians silence foolish ignorance. The word "silence" here could be more literally translated as "muzzle." The good works of Christians are meant to have a restraining impact on the ignorance of foolish people. "Foolishness" and "fool" are rarely used in the New Testament but are prominent in Jewish wisdom literature, particularly the book of Proverbs (cf. Prov. 12:15, 16, 23, and others) where they are often contrasted with the knowledge and activity of the wise. In 1 Peter foolish people are silenced by an encounter with that which is good and right.

In the Greek text, vv. 13–16 form one long sentence. The imperative "submit" (v. 13) is explored in multiple ways. First, those to whom one submits are indicated (the emperor and his governors). Then, the mode of submission is explored – a life of good works. Now, the true identity of believers is added to the mix. Those who submit are not slaves of the emperor or of any other human master. Rather, they are free people who ultimately belong to God and are God's slaves (**v. 16**). Elliott notes: "The notion of being both free and slaves of God expresses one of the great paradoxes of human life, as Philo also has noted: 'For in truth he who has God alone for his leader, he alone is free' (*Prob.* 20)."[234] No matter what

---

[233] Holloway, *Coping with Prejudice*, 181.
[234] Elliott, *1 Peter*, 497.

their status in the world (citizen, exile, sojourner, free, freedman, slave), ultimately every reader who has been ransomed from their former life with the sprinkled blood of Jesus Christ (1:2, 18) now belongs fully and completely to God. The freedom that they have obtained as the people of God allows them to submit to human governance as long as it is not at odds with God's will. The freedom they have is not to be misused as a cover for evil. One suggestion is that "freedom" refers to using freedom to foment revolt or subversive activity against the government.[235] But a group with the minority status of the church in Asia Minor was highly unlikely to foment revolt.[236] A more likely view is suggested by Achtemeier who argues that Christians might view all laws as subordinate to Christ and thus as inapplicable to them. In this way, Christians might use their status in Christ in ways that create upheaval in the society around them when this is not necessary.[237]

The section (2:13–17) concludes with four imperatival instructions arranged in a small chiasm.

A. <u>Honor</u> everyone
    B. Love the family of believers
    B¹ Fear God
A² <u>Honor</u> the emperor

The first imperative to honor everyone treats all people with equal respect. All human beings are worthy of being treated as people of worth. In the cultures of the first century this was a radical concept. Honor and status were highly valued and derived from such things as one's familial relationships (e.g., people of the family of Caesar and of other leaders in the empire had higher status and thus were seen as being worthy of higher honor), the performance of one's religious and civic duties, one's capacity to be a benefactor to the community, and one's performance in the public square, including such things as the ability to engage in and win debates. To suggest that everyone – women, children, slaves, freedmen, senators, equestrians, travelers, and tradespeople – was equally worthy of honor

---

[235] Bo Reicke, *The Epistles of James, Peter, and Jude*, Anchor Bible Commentary (Garden City, NY: Doubleday, 1964), 96.

[236] Reinhard Feldmeier, *The First Letter of Peter: A Commentary on the Greek Text* (Waco, TX: Baylor University Press, 2008), 162.

[237] Achtemeier, *1 Peter*, 186.

was a potentially radical concept. As Peter advises a minority group of Christians seeking to live out their faith as "aliens and exiles" in Asia Minor, he instructs them to give respect to all – both those outside and those within their fellowship.

In the second and third instructions, attention is turned inward to the "family of believers." In 1 Peter 1:22 the instruction is given to love fellow Christians with a pure heart. That instruction is reiterated here. Loving others is one of the signs of having been reborn (1:3, 23). "Fear God." Fear is often the result of a difference in power between the one who experiences fear and the one who is feared.[238] Fear directed towards God is a reminder that God has power over believers. In chapter 1, God is the source of inheritance, salvation, glory, and redemption (1:3–17). These gifts are bestowed out of God's mercy (1:3). But the right response to God's character is an acknowledgment by believers of "God's power over their flourishing."[239] Currently, Christians are often reluctant to use the word fear to describe relationship with God preferring "awe" or "reverence." However, backing away from the word fear also pushes us away from our understanding that God is indeed a judge and one whose justice and judgment is severe and dreadful. However, fear should not paralyze the believer. Rather, fear of God should lead to action, and in 1 Peter that is conformity to God's holy character as demonstrated in good works, which reveal one's agreement with God's character and demands.

The section ends with the command to honor the emperor. When this instruction is taken in the context of both **v. 17** and vv. 13–17, it serves as a reminder that on the one hand the emperor is due honor, while on the other hand the emperor is also human, a creature rather than a god. Everyone was expected to honor the emperor. How was an emperor given honor in the first century? Warren Carter argues that this depends on the status of the one giving honor and their resources. Elites might honor the emperor by paying for festivals, paying for part or all of a new building (or temple), and paying for sacrifices.[240] Other citizens with less money

---

[238] Hockey, *The Role of Emotion in 1 Peter*, 189.

[239] Hockey, *The Role of Emotion in 1 Peter*, 189.

[240] Warren Carter, "Going all the way?: Honoring the emperor and sacrificing wives and slaves in 1 Peter 2.13–3.6," in Amy-Jill Levine and Maria Mayo Robbins (eds.), *A Feminist Companion to the Catholic Epistles and Hebrews* (London: T&T Clark International, 2004), 20.

would be expected to honor the emperor by participating in or watching processions and attending feasts. Sometimes noncitizens were also invited to watch such processions and attend feasts.[241] In the first century, religion was intertwined with the government and honoring the emperor may have included aspects of participation in the celebrations and sacrifices sponsored on behalf of the imperial cult. At the same time, this minority group of "exiles and aliens" is reminded that all people are to be honored. In this way, the emperor is just one person among all the people of the world. And v. 13 reminds readers that while they are to submit "to every human creature," (rather than "institution") the emperor is just that, a human creature – one made by God. Any act of submission on the part of the believer is always for the Lord's sake because the believer knows to whom they truly belong. Warren Carter argues that "honoring the emperor" meant participating in the public religious duties of the day. Doing so was a way of honoring the emperor and showing that Christians were not a threat to society. For those who were weak in the eyes of society (slaves, women, and perhaps the men addressed by 1 Peter), such outward conformity does not necessarily mean that the group had inward conformity. Indeed, he goes on to argue that participation in public religion for minority groups was not an affirmation of that public religion. Instead, the internal identity of the person and the group mattered more than the external association with the public celebrations of the cult.[242] This approach focuses on the *internal* resistance and identity of a minority community, though other scholars have pushed back arguing that the community did suffer and therefore must not have been participating in cultural activities in ways that made it invisible.

Bridging the Horizons: It can be challenging to know how to bridge the divide between the political reality of the Roman Empire and the Western democracies of today. Caesar had mostly unchecked power and appointed those who would do his will to rule in the provinces beyond Rome. Rebellions were ruthlessly suppressed and the "peace" of the Roman Empire was maintained through the strategic

---

[241] Carter, "Going all the way?," 21.
[242] Carter, "Going all the way?"

deployment of the Roman legions. In this context, Peter describes those who govern as using an ideal agreed upon by most people in both the ancient world and the world today, an ideal in which wrongdoing is punished and those who do right are praised. Whether one should submit to a government that is doing the very opposite (e.g., praising evil and punishing good) has been a disputed topic. There are many examples of churches and Christians who have chosen to submit to such governments while maintaining their call to worship and doing good in the community. However, since the Reformation the description of the ideal government has also been used to argue that Christians are not obligated to submit to the governance of a tyrant or to those who praise evil and punish good.[243] In this view, Christians are ultimately responsible to God and only secondarily to those in power, especially when leaders abuse their power. As government changed from monarchies to democracies there was greater opportunity for a multiplicity of voices. However, there are repeated examples of those in power seeking to retain and maintain power by excluding voices that might undermine their position. In the United States, we might consider the long struggle for equal voting rights first for men without land, then for black men, then for women of all races. Over and over again rights were won for formerly excluded groups by arguing, writing, and ultimately protesting against the injustice and exclusion of the state. Christians have frequently been leaders in these efforts to bring about justice and inclusion for those suffering exclusion and oppression. Some Christian leaders have broken the law of the land in order to pursue what they understood to be the law and call of God. In the United States, the civil rights movement and the civil disobedience led by Dr. Martin Luther King Jr and others was an example of refusal to submit to unjust laws. Similarly, refusal to abide by the rules of apartheid in South Africa is another example of resistance to injustice. And, in Nazi Germany and the countries it occupied some Christians resisted the genocidal practices towards Jews and the concentration of authoritarian power in one man. Corrie ten Boom and Dietrich Bonhoeffer were both examples of this resistance and both paid deeply for their opposition to evil government. Looking back on history, it becomes easier to identify those who stood up for justice against the injustice of governing powers. But, at the time that these events unfold, it is often deeply challenging to resist the injustice of the government. Indeed, we note that self-identified Christians have been found on both sides of the law: those who marched for civil rights and those who enforced either the status quo or the laws of the land; those who rescued Jews and the

---

[243] Peter Scott and William T. Cavanaugh (eds.), *The Blackwell Companion to Political Theology*, Blackwell Companions to Religion (Malden, MA: Blackwell, 2004), 26.

many German churches who either supported the Nazi regime or remained silent in order to continue with worship as they knew it. Submission to authority cannot become the excuse that allows the church to escape its responsibility to those experiencing injustice at the hands of those in power. This is especially true in countries where Christians or Christian structures remain pervasive. Here, it is important to be reminded of the minority status of Christians in the first century and the limited options available to them. Peter cannot advocate for rebellion or resistance without threatening the very existence of this scattered community of exiles. But what he does do is to make absolutely clear two important realities: First, ultimately all Christians belong first and foremost to God. Christians belong to God and as such act first and foremost as God's agents for the good of the society in which they live. Second, government officials are only human. In the first century, the emperors were identified as gods and worshiped as such. But Peter makes clear that they stand on the same level as all other humans and are due the same respect – neither more nor less. These two realities are foundational to the call upon the church to do good works and to exercise good behavior. This may manifest itself in one form in a culture where Christians are a persecuted minority and in quite different forms in cultures that understand themselves to be majority Christian cultures. When Christians are the minority and face persecution for their beliefs and actions, the reality of polite resistance looks significantly different. But when Christians are the majority or when a nation expects in some vague way the implementation of Christian values, then the instruction to submit to the government should not be used as an excuse to further injustice. Now, in Western democracies, and in the twenty-first century, the people can and must exercise their power to hold government accountable for the way in which it treats people. One of the great mistakes of the church has been to act out of the fear of losing power and influence rather than acting out of a deep love for one another and for the world around (even those who might ridicule or persecute Christians, even as Christians were persecuted in the first century). Now, as we move into the twenty-first century and a post-Christian society, Christians may be reminded of the call placed upon them to demonstrate to whom they belong through their good works and good behavior. All Christians may find value in taking up the idea of polite resistance to the culture surrounding them. Rather than seeking to entrench our values and worldview through power, we might winsomely move towards the work of justice by elevating the least among us to places of honor, by treating all with respect, and by living out our love for one another and our fear of God in practical ways. In this manner, Western Christians may learn from the lives of minority Christians in locations around the world who must live out their identity as God's people in ways that offer both invitation and resistance to the culture around them.

[18] Slaves, accept the authority of your masters with all deference, not only those who are kind and gentle but also those who are harsh.

[19] For it is a credit to you if, being aware of God, you endure pain while suffering unjustly.

[20] If you endure when you are beaten for doing wrong, what credit is that? But if you endure when you do right and suffer for it, you have God's approval.

[21] For to this you have been called, because Christ also suffered for you, leaving you an example, so that you should follow in his steps.

[22] "He committed no sin, and no deceit was found in his mouth."

[23] When he was abused, he did not return abuse; when he suffered, he did not threaten; but he entrusted himself to the one who judges justly.

[24] He himself bore our sins in his body on the cross, so that, free from sins, we might live for righteousness; by his wounds you have been healed.

[25] For you were going astray like sheep, but now you have returned to the shepherd and guardian of your souls.

In 2:11–17, Peter identifies his audience as "aliens" and "exiles." Each of these identity markers places the recipients of the letter on the margins of Roman society. At the same time the address "beloved" and the identification of the audience as "slaves of God" reminds them that they are God's and their ultimate allegiance is to God. In this context, Peter addresses slaves directly using the plural with the article as the vocative "slaves" (*oiketai*, household slaves) in 2:18–25.[244]

A Closer Look: Slavery in the Roman Empire

Slavery was a reality of the Roman Empire. Estimates regarding the percentage of slaves in the Roman Empire range from 16 to 20 percent of the total population.[245] There was a higher percentage of slaves on the Italian peninsula but slavery was a reality throughout the empire, including within the provinces of Asia Minor. Slaves were either born into bondage or became slaves by being captured in war, kidnapped, or sold to pay off their own debts or the debts of their relatives. Many slaves in the Roman Empire lived their whole life as slaves but some, especially those in cities and urban households, obtained their freedom after a period of enslavement. Masters used both punishment and promises of manumission as ways to strengthen

---

[244] Forbes, *1 Peter*, 86.
[245] William V. Harris, "Toward a study of the Roman slave trade," in J. H. D'Arms and E. C. Kopff (eds.), *The Seaborne Commerce of Ancient Rome: Studies in Archaeology and History*, Memoirs of the American Academy in Rome: 36 (Rome: American Academy in Rome, 1980), 118.

their social control of slaves. Both the fear of punishment and the hope of release provided incentives for good behavior. Manumitted slaves often continued to have a relationship with their former master as a freedman or freedwoman who owed honor and allegiance to the family that had freed them. While they might obtain release, they did not escape the stigma of having been slaves. Both slaves and former slaves were classes of people who were despised and shamed by those with higher status and honor. Some slaves, especially in the household of Caesar, had enormous responsibility and oversaw important aspects of the running of the empire. In fact, a few of these slaves even owned slaves of their own. Yet even these high-level slaves did not obtain honor from those of the upper classes with high status.

Slaves were used in a variety of different contexts. There were slaves who served on rural farms and plantations and slaves who worked in the cities. There were also slaves used in hard labor in mines or rowing ships. And there were slaves who were owned by the government and served in temples and other public locations. Conditions in the mines and ships were brutal and inescapable and slaves in these contexts often died quickly. Slaves were also used in farming on rural estates where they tended animals, did agricultural work, and where some even managed other slaves as overseers. Urban slaves might work in a large household, in the city's marketplace or temples, or doing the work of the emperor. Household slaves would cook, clean, provide personal care for the master or mistress (e.g., as hairdresser, attendant, room servant, messenger, bodyguard), and help with the needs of the household (as doctor, accountant, secretary, and tutor). In the marketplace, slaves ran small shops, eateries, and other services. While slaves might be allowed to keep some of the money that they earned, this was at the discretion of their master. Ultimately, the slave and all the profits generated by the slave were the property of the master. Slaves were ubiquitous both in homes and in public spaces.

While the ancients spoke of slaves as "living tools,"[246] more recent comparative and sociological studies attend to the power dynamics between master and slave. Orlando Patterson has shown that across many cultures, the enslaved experienced "social death." The slave had no rights nor any claims to legitimization in the eyes of others. As such, the slave "could have no honor because he had no power and no independent social existence, hence no public worth. He had no name of his own to defend. He could only defend his master's worth and his master's name."[247] Masters gained honor and status by owning slaves while their slaves were dishonored by their position in bondage. Despite their lowly status, slaves did have choices that they could make. "He might, in relative terms, be powerless; but

---

[246] Aristotle, *Pol.* I.II, LCL.
[247] Orlando Patterson, *Slavery and Social Death: A Comparative Study* (Cambridge, MA: Harvard University Press, 1982), 10–11.

he always had *some* choice. He might react psychologically, play the slave, act dumb, exasperate. He might lie or steal. He might run away. He might injure or kill others, including his own master. Or he might engage in armed revolt. Barring all these, he might destroy his master's property by destroying himself."[248] Slaves made choices about how to behave both when the master was present and when the master was absent. They also, like many minority groups, probably made use of a "hidden transcript." A hidden transcript "reveals what the subordinated people really think, as opposed to the 'public transcript' that reflects the views of those in power. This hidden way of speaking expresses what the subordinated cannot say explicitly in public because it would constitute open confrontation with those in power and so bring them punishment."[249] Our study of 1 Peter looks at the way a hidden transcript may have functioned in the life of Christian slaves. Aristotle noted that three things make up the life of a slave: "work, punishment, and food" (*Oec.* Book 1.4, lines 35–36). In this context, where there is little choice, no self-determination, and the brutal reality of being owned by another, Peter addresses slaves.

That Peter would speak to slaves is itself noteworthy. It is a reminder that the lowliest members of the Christian communities were viewed as people with the capacity for choice and decision-making. Peter's instruction to submit (NRSV: "accept the authority of your masters") reflects the reality of the first-century context. Slaves who were rebellious faced certain punishment from a master who wielded the power of life and death. Peter's minority audience is in no position to stage a revolt against the status quo. Instead, Peter hints at a hidden transcript that drives the behavior of slaves who belong to Christ. Those with privilege expect submission to the emperor or to masters. This is the way things are. The inferior submits to the superior. The ignoble submit to the noble. Those who are degraded submit to those who are honorable. But in Peter's discourse just as the whole assembly of exiles and aliens that makes up the church is to submit to the emperor and his governors "for the Lord's sake" and not because of the power of those rulers (v. 13), so too slaves are to submit with an attitude

---

[248]   Patterson, *Slavery and Social Death*, 173.

[249]   In his comments on the household code in Colossians Jerry L. Sumney, *Colossians: A Commentary*, first ed., The New Testament Library (Louisville, KY: Westminster John Knox Press, 2008), 236–37.

of reverence towards God (v. 18).[250] The hidden transcript comes into view with awareness that this segment of 1 Peter is dominated by vocabulary and phrases that makes it abundantly clear that the choice a slave makes to submit to their master is a choice that comes out of a narrative about their new identity in Jesus Christ. They are no longer simply slaves, living tools with limited capacities. Rather, they are the newborn children of God who are looking forward to their inheritance and who are confidant in their status as those who are redeemed and made holy like their true Father, the merciful and just God. As children of God, their submission is not self-serving nor is it the submission of the inferior slave to the greater master. Instead, their identity as the beloved children of God provides them with a hidden reason known to them and the community of God's faithful people to submit to those in the world with authority over them. Peter specifically notes that such submission is to all types of masters – both those who are good and those who are crooked (NRSV: harsh). In **vv. 18–21**, the hidden transcript of their true identity as God's children is repeatedly invoked. They act out of reverence towards God (v. 18) and experience favor (the Greek word for grace, *charis*) (v. 19). They have an awareness of God (v. 19) and have God's favor/grace (v. 20). The vocabulary of reverence and grace provides the language that shapes their identity as recipients of God's divine favor. In addition, they are enabled to follow in the footsteps of their true patron, Jesus Christ, who also suffered. When these phrases are read from the position of a minority group such as those addressed in 1 Peter, they point once again to the true identity of the group as God's chosen faithful children and provide strength for the reality that they face. However, it is important to be aware that when these phrases and instructions are read from a position of power and privilege, they can also be read in such a way that obedience to the master is no longer a form of faithfulness to the Lord and resistance to the ways of the world but rather a way of reinforcing the status quo submission of slaves to masters. In this second type of reading the focus is on assimilation – the slave who defers, who acts rightly and endures, who supports the status quo functioning of power and

---

[250] The NRSV translates *en panti phobō* (literally, "with all fear/reverence") as "with deference" implying that they defer to their masters, but this is already made clear by the instruction to "submit." In v. 17, "fear/reverence" is directed towards God and should be understood as being directed in that manner here.

oppression in the Roman Empire. In this reading, such a slave has God's approval. But in a book written by a minority to minorities, it seems a stronger argument to affirm that hidden transcripts are used to strengthen the resolve of those who have no way out of their suffering. Those in power who have read the book in such a way as to affirm their own position and the submission of those with lesser power are reading against the grain of the minority context.[251] They are also reading against the exemplary nature of the slaves (2:18–25) and wives (3:1–6), for these two groups show those who, in the eyes of the wider culture may have some greater freedoms, how to live as God's beloved children amid persecution and suffering. Finally, they are reading against the grain of the exemplary nature of Christ himself who demonstrates a sinless way of life in the midst of unjust suffering. The suffering of Christ is not a tool to tell others that they too must suffer but is rather an example for the whole congregation who experience suffering on account of their faith.

Looking at the chiastic structure of vv. 19–21a will give us a stronger sense of Peter's direction in these verses.

A v. 19a – this is *charis* (favor, grace, thankfulness)
   B v. 19b – <u>if</u> through awareness of God anyone <u>endures</u> (*upopherei*) sorrows while <u>suffering</u> (*paschōn*) unjustly
      C v. 20a – for what sort of fame is it if you sin and endure (*upomeneite*) being beaten?
   B¹ v. 20b – But <u>if</u> you do good and <u>endure</u> (*upomeneite*) <u>suffering</u> (*paschontes*),
A¹ v. 20c – this is *charis* (favor, grace, thankfulness) before God.[252]

This passage begins and ends with the phrase "this [is] *charis*." The Greek phrase "*touto charis*" (*touto* ("this"), *charis*, translated as "grace" elsewhere in 1 Peter; e.g., 1:2, 10, 13) has been translated into English in a wide variety of ways in these two verses. In the following translations,

---

[251] Achtemeier, *1 Peter*, 196.

[252] Author's translation. See also the somewhat different proposal in Campbell, *Honor, Shame, and the Rhetoric of 1 Peter*, 129–30 Campbell notes the changes in vocabulary and suggests they are synonyms used for literary effect. The NRSV obscures some of the Greek vocabulary in this section. *Charis* is translated as "credit" in v. 19 and "approval" in v. 20, and *kleos* in v. 20 is translated as "credit" as if it is a synonym of *charis*. It is more properly related to the domain of fame or glory (BAGD).

I have put brackets around the words added by translators. NRSV: "it [is] a credit [to you];" NIV, CEB: "it [is] commendable;" NET: "this [finds God's] favor" (similarly, NASB); NLT: "[God is] pleased [with you];" and ESV: "this [is] a gracious [thing]." The majority of these translations focus on the idea of "a human action which secures a favorable response from God."[253] The exception is the ESV, which focuses on the beauty or goodness of *charis*, which is another definition. In the first century, the word *charis* was often used in the context of gift giving. It could be used to describe both what was given (a benefit or beneficence) and to describe the obligations of thankfulness and reciprocity that it created.[254] Williams argues that the phrase *touto charis* is definitional and that the author of 1 Peter is redefining grace for his audience. They have received grace (benefits) from God in the form of new birth, new identity, and salvation. Now, they have the opportunity to return that grace (reciprocity) by enduring suffering faithfully. In so doing, the very thing that would have been a source of shame in the eyes of their master becomes a source of favor (commendation, approval, credit) in God's perspective.[255]

Peter uses three if/then statements in vv. 19–20. The first one is arranged with the "then" (apodosis) in front of the "if" (protasis) so that the focus is drawn towards the favor experienced by the one who suffers unjustly. The phrase "this is favor" will be repeated and expanded at the end of the chiasm to make it clear that the one who suffers unjustly is the object of divine favor. In the center of the chiasm is Peter's question that shows that no fame, glory, or acclaim comes from suffering for wrongdoing. In other words, those who do wrong have no status either in the eyes of their masters or in the eyes of God. The verb here is "sinning" (*amartanontes*, NRSV "wrongdoing") and can refer to either doing what is wrong in the eyes of one's master[256] or to doing what is wrong in the eyes of God.[257] In the context of v. 20, it is clear that a slave's actions before God are under consideration ("you have God's approval"). In other words, it is God who

---

253 Williams, "Reciprocity and suffering in 1 Peter 2,19–20," 424.
254 Williams, "Reciprocity and suffering in 1 Peter 2,19–20," 429; John M. G. Barclay, *Paul and the Gift* (Grand Rapids, MI: Eerdmans, 2015), 26–32.
255 Williams, "Reciprocity and suffering in 1 Peter 2,19–20," 436–37.
256 This is the primary view given by Elliott, *1 Peter*, 521.
257 Michaels, *1 Peter*, 141 argues that "'sin'" is a term better suited to offenses against God or the Christian community than to misconduct in the slave-master relationship."

determines what is considered sin/wrongdoing and what is considered good behavior. It is quite possible that slaves who follow God's will and do good might suffer for it. Achtemeier writes, "even when they did the good by following God's will, it might have necessarily involved disobedience to a non-Christian master, and punishment would then ensue."[258] It is those who suffer unjustly for doing good who receive God's favor. There is an interplay between the person who suffers with an awareness or consciousness of God (v. 19) and the reception of God's favor (v. 20). Both the one who suffers and the God who shows favor are acutely aware of the other and of the injustice of the suffering that is experienced. In an honor/shame society, where gaining honor was very difficult for slaves, being beaten was shameful. For those engaged in wrongdoing, social values assumed that being beaten was both shameful and deserved. On the other hand, those who suffer for doing good find favor in the eyes of God. Here, slaves who do right gain honor in the sight of the one whose opinion truly matters, God. There are a variety of courts of opinion for these slaves. Society, the master, and the master's household form one court of opinion that judges the worth and activity of the slave. But the more important court of opinion is God. And an additional court of opinion is the wider group of Christians. Here, those who are low on the social hierarchy find their value in the eyes of God as they choose to do what is good and right in God's eyes. Additionally, they are lifted up by the author of 1 Peter before the congregation as an example of people who are shown favor by God. Verses 19–20 are a concrete example of the prominent theme in 1 Peter of right behavior or good conduct even when faced with oppressive circumstances. Those who are part of the household of God are instructed to practice right behavior in ways that are visible to those in the world around them. If they endure suffering, such suffering should come about not because of sin or wrongdoing but on account of their good behavior that stems from their identity as God's people. A slave, by nature of who they are, cannot escape the gaze and control of their master. Yet these very people who are seen by those around them as having low status serve as the example par excellence for anyone (*tis*) who suffers on account of injustice. In this way they come to experience honor in the sight of God. Those who

---

[258] Achtemeier, *1 Peter*, 197.

face the real possibility of being beaten for failing to satisfy the demands of the master become an example of those who do good as a response to their awareness of all that God has done on their behalf.

Finally, we should note that in v. 19 Peter uses the verb *pascho* (suffer) for the first time. This is a word that will recur twelve times in the remainder of 1 Peter. The theme of suffering that runs through the book of 1 Peter is introduced as early as 1:6 where we see the verb for "pain" used to describe suffering in this life. The cognate noun (*lupe*, "pain") is used in 2:19 where it is combined with suffering (NRSV: you endure pain while suffering unjustly). This theme of suffering expands as we move further into the book and will come to a crescendo in 1 Peter 4:12–19.

These slaves, like the rest of God's household, are called (2:21). "You were called to this (*touto*)." What does "this" refer to? Most likely it refers back to the whole context of vv. 19–20: namely, the calling to have right conduct and to endure in the face of suffering unjustly. Suffering may result from this call upon their lives, but this does not negate the call to bear up under the suffering. We might note at this point that there are a variety of types of suffering that those who endure may experience. In v. 19 the text uses the plural (*lupas*, "afflictions," "griefs," or "sorrows") to indicate a variety of pains that may be part of suffering. Such suffering is not for the sake of suffering nor does the text demand that suffering be sought out. Rather suffering comes about because of one's choice to do good in the sight of God. "Doing good" (*agathopoiountes*) is the same activity that governors are sent to praise (v. 14) and that God uses to muzzle foolish people (v. 15). The slaves addressed in v. 18 are equated with those who should be recognized by the emperor and his governors as "doing good" (v. 14), and they are identified as those who have freedom in God (v. 16). They, like the rest of the church, can exercise their identity as God's slaves (v. 16) by doing good. In this way, 1 Peter treats slaves as having fully human capacities to choose, to act, and to enter into relationships with God and others.

The slaves and the whole congregation listening to the instructions addressed to slaves have as their example, Christ, the one anointed and chosen by God as "the agent of final divine deliverance."[259] The anointed

---

[259] Andrew Chester, *Messiah and Exaltation: Jewish Messianic and Visionary Traditions and New Testament Christology*, Wissenschaftliche Untersuchungen zum Neuen Testament: 207 (Tübingen: Mohr Siebeck, 2007), 4.

one suffers for the least, the slaves, the aliens, the exiles. He suffers for "you" (*humōn*). Through his body a way is made into the family of God. This is the one who suffered on their behalf. Peter points his audience to the cross, but instead of focusing on the death of Jesus Christ, he highlights Christ's suffering. The Gospels show that he was beaten (Luke 22:63), scourged (Matt 27:26), mocked and humiliated (Mark 15:16–20) before being shamefully crucified naked on a cross (Mark 15:24). Peter will go on to talk explicitly about the cross in v. 24, but the suffering of Christ is more than the suffering he endured on the cross. Michaels talks about all the suffering involved in the whole of Christ's passion,[260] but Jesus Christ also endured suffering throughout his life as he chose to walk in accordance with the Father's will. There were crowds who wanted to kill him (Luke 4:28–30). There were followers who fell away as his journey took him closer and closer to conflict with the religious leaders and governing powers of his day (John 6:66). He experienced suffering as he prayed and contemplated the steps that lay before him (Matt 26:38). And finally, Christ's closest friends abandoned him, leaving him to be imprisoned and tortured before being crucified on a cross. Jesus Christ was "a man of sorrows" (Is. 53:3). John Stott writes that Christ "entered our world of flesh and blood, tears and death. He suffered for us. Our sufferings become more manageable in light of his. There is still a question mark against human suffering, but over it we boldly stamp another mark, the cross that symbolizes divine suffering."[261] Peter points to Christ's suffering as a reminder that the suffering that slaves might endure for the sake of doing right in the sight of God had already been endured by their Lord, Jesus Christ himself. Indeed, Christ endured such suffering *on their behalf.* Christ lived rightly and was innocent of wrongdoing. He did not deserve to suffer, but his suffering was for them, as Peter will go on to show in the verses that follow. Like the slaves addressed in 1 Peter who may have endured beating, so too Christ endured beating (Luke 22:63). Peter highlights Christ as an example to imitate with the word *hupogrammon*, meaning model or pattern. *Hupogrammon* is derived from the type of pattern that was used to help people learn to write. The repetition of

---

[260] J. Ramsey Michaels, "St. Peter's passion: The passion narrative in 1 Peter," *WW* 24 (2004): 391.

[261] John R. W. Stott, *The Cross of Christ* (Downers Grove, IL: IVP, 1986), 336.

tracing over the letters/pattern laid down eventually produced, with practice, the ability to write. Christ's suffering is a model for those who suffer on account of doing right in the sight of God. They follow in the footsteps of Christ. They go where he has already led.

In **vv. 22–24**, the Christ, his suffering and death, and its effects are described more fully. Each verse begins with the relative pronoun "who" and describes more about Jesus Christ's actions. Verses **22–23** lay out the manner in which he endures unjust suffering at the hands of those who had indiscriminate power over his body. This provides the example promised in v. 21. Verse **24** portrays Christ's suffering on the cross, and its impact on believers. Peter will explore the exemplary suffering of Christ and its results by weaving together material from Isaiah 53:4–12 and the life and death of Christ. There has been a great deal of discussion about the form of vv. 21–25. Since the 1950s a variety of scholars have argued that some or all of vv. 21–25 is hymnic in nature.[262] Other scholars have suggested that these verses were composed by the author and that their obvious reflection on and interpretation of the prophet Isaiah is a sufficient explanation of their form.[263] More recently, David Horrell has argued that these verses are an example of history scripturalized; in other words, they are an example of the passion account being remembered through the lens of Scripture.[264] This passage is the most extensive reflection on Isa. 53 in the New Testament.[265]

Isaiah 52:13–53:12 presents the Song of the Suffering Servant, a figure who was already introduced in Isaiah 42:1–9; 49:1–6; and 50:4–9. These references to the Servant occur in the larger unit of Isaiah 40–55, which focuses on God's comforting words to the Israelites, who are suffering in exile, and on God's promise to make a way for them out of exile and back to their home in Jerusalem. The Servant is part of the means

---

[262] Scholars who hold this view include Windish, Bultmann, Kelly, Hengel, and others. See Sharon Clark Pearson, *The Christological and Rhetorical Properties of 1 Peter*, Studies in Bible and Early Christianity: 45 (Lewiston, NY: E. Mellen Press, 2001), 117–19.

[263] Elliott, *1 Peter*, 548; Michaels, *1 Peter*, 137.

[264] David G. Horrell, "Jesus remembered in 1 Peter? Early Jesus traditions, Isaiah 53, and 1 Peter 2.21–25," in Alicia J. Batten and John S. Kloppenberg (eds.), *James, 1 & 2 Peter, and Early Jesus Traditions* (New York: Bloomsbury, 2014), 143–45.

[265] Isaiah 53 is cited extensively in the New Testament. For example, it appears in Matt 8:17, Luke 22:37, John 12:38, Romans 10:16; 15:21, and Acts 8:32–33. The text is alluded to elsewhere in the New Testament as well.

by which God will rescue Israel. The song begins and ends with God's exaltation of the Servant, but the middle portions of the song focus on the Servant's humiliation and suffering. The Servant's appearance was marred (Isa. 52:14); he was despised and rejected (Isa. 53:3); he was struck down and afflicted (Isa. 53:4); he was oppressed (Isa. 53:7). When Peter quotes from Isaiah 53, these backgrounds – the broad background of God's comfort and promises to Israel and the narrower background of the suffering servant – inform what is heard in the quotations and allusions from Isaiah. But this is not simply a quotation or allusion to Isaiah, rather, it is an interpretation of Isaiah in light of the suffering and death of the Messiah, Christ.[266] These are the sufferings that the prophets of 1:10–12 anticipated for the Christ.

Verse 22 begins with a direct quotation from the LXX of the final line of Isaiah 53:9 with just one change. In Isaiah 53:9 the word "lawlessness" is used; Peter replaces this with the word "sin." Sin and lawlessness are both used in Isaiah 53 to describe a people who have strayed from the path of faithfulness to God. Peter has already used "sinning" in his description of the slaves circumstances (v. 20), and he now uses "sin" both to describe Jesus as one who had no sin and to refer to the sin of humanity in v. 24. When Jesus suffered he did not sin. The whole of the New Testament points to an understanding of Jesus in which he was fully human and yet without sin (e.g., 2 Cor. 5:21; Heb. 4:15; 1 John 3:5). Continuing the quote from Isaiah, Peter adds "no deceit was found in his mouth." Deceit involves treachery, betrayal, trickery, and taking advantage of others through cunning (BAGD). The community in Asia Minor has already been instructed to lay aside this behavior (2:1). And now it is clear that this behavior is antithetical to the life of Jesus and is not to be found even in his unjust suffering. Jesus sets the example for the community of a life without deceit even in the midst of suffering.

Verses 23–25 contain allusions to Isaiah 53 rather than direct quotations. The direct quotation in 1 Peter 2:22 serves to call to mind the whole passage about the suffering servant. It is now alluded to generously in the remaining verses of 1 Peter 2 either using catchwords such as "sin," "bear," "bruise," "healing," and "sheep" that resonate in the mind of the hearer who is familiar with this passage, or bringing to mind the images of Isa. 53.

---

[266] Schutter argues that the "handling of Is. 53 indicate[s] the presence of a pesher-like hermeneutic," Schutter, *Hermeneutic*, 143.

Unlike 1 Peter 2:22, v. 23 does not contain any words that are derived directly from Isaiah 53; however, it draws on the image of Isaiah 53:7, "And he, because he has been ill-treated, does not open his mouth; like a sheep he was led to the slaughter, and as a lamb is silent before the one shearing it, so he does not open his mouth" (NETS). While 1 Peter may allude to this image, note that Peter does not portray Christ as silent. Instead, Peter portrays Christ as a person who has experienced intense insult and verbal abuse but who does not respond in kind. We know that Jesus spoke, but it is clear that he did not threaten those who accused him falsely (cf., Mark 14:62), and when they hurled insults at him (e.g., Mark 15:18, 29), he did not reply in kind. Michaels notes, in contrast, other Jewish martyrs who call down retribution on those who persecute them.[267] The last and seventh son of the Maccabean martyrs says:

"But you, unholy wretch, you most defiled of all mortals, do not be elated in vain and puffed up by uncertain hopes, when you raise your hand against the children of heaven. You have not yet escaped the judgment of the almighty, all-seeing God. For our brothers after enduring a brief suffering have drunk of ever-flowing life, under God's covenant; but you, by the judgment of God, will receive just punishment for your arrogance" (2 Mac 7:34–36 NRSV).

In contrast Jesus will say from the cross, "Father, forgive them; for they do not know what they are doing" (Luke 23:34). And the Lord will promise the criminal on the cross beside him "Truly I tell you, today you will be with me in Paradise" (Luke 23:43). Even in suffering, Jesus' speech was filled with truth and grace. It was not mean or bitter or abusive. Similarly, when Christ suffered, he did not respond by threatening others. Indeed, when he was arrested in the garden and his followers responded with the sword, he instructed them to put their swords away. This was not because he lacked power (note Matt 26:53 and the reference to legions at his command) but because this was his calling, the cup that lay before him. And so he faces those who threaten him. For the slaves who are addressed in this section of the text, Christ sets an example of a person who suffers injustice but does not respond with either violence or threatening speech. This type of response for those who are enslaved is sensible as a verbally abusive or threatening response to injustice would only rile up the slave master and

---

[267] Michaels, "St. Peter's passion," 391.

most likely intensify punishment for the slave. But 1 Peter does not appeal to the sensibility of such action but to the identity of the slaves as followers of Jesus enabled to hear and follow the call of God and to do so with awareness of God and God's favorable disposition towards them. Thus, this minority gain their identity in the face of injustice and are challenged to live into it by following the example of Christ.

Instead of responding with violence, threats, or abuse, Christ "entrusted to the one who judges justly." The word for "entrusted" (*paredidou*) means "handed over." In Isaiah 53:6 the same verb is used in the phrase "the Lord gave him over (*paredōken*) to our sins" (NETS). But in 1 Peter it is Christ who hands over/entrusts to the one who judges justly. The text does not provide an object that indicates what is entrusted to God. Some commentators indicate that Jesus entrusts himself to God and in this way lays responsibility for his life and future in the hands of God.[268] Others suggest that what we should see here is that Jesus entrusts his enemies to God. In the previous two clauses, Jesus refuses to retaliate against his enemies who mistreat him. Continuing with that same object (enemies), Jesus trusts that the one who rightly judges the whole world will judge those who threaten him.[269] But the focus of the text is not on the object of what was entrusted but rather on God as the righteous judge. There is perhaps here an echo of the traditional instruction to leave judgment in the hands of God. Romans 12:19 develops this idea with the saying, "Beloved, never avenge yourselves, but leave room for the wrath of God; for it is written, 'Vengeance is mine, I will repay, says the Lord.'" God's role as a righteous judge is well attested throughout the Old Testament (e.g., Isa. 33:22; Ps. 7:11; Zeph. 3:5). In contrast to those who are causing suffering to Christ and insulting him, there is one whose judgment is right and true, and Christ can trust the just judge with his very life and with the outcome his enemies experience as well. This just judge is so reliable that Christ can release himself and the future of his enemies into his care. This is the example Jesus leaves for the slave who has no control over his own body or over those who would judge him, the slave, harshly and unjustly. Like Christ, slaves can entrust themselves to God, the true and righteous judge, and they can trust that the just judge holds the future of their enemies in his care as well. Those enemies

---

[268] Achtemeier, *1 Peter*, 201.
[269] Michaels, "St. Peter's passion," 392.

may come to experience reconciliation with God just as other enemies of God have been brought into right relationship with God (cf. Rom. 5:10) or they may experience the judgment of God, but whatever happens to them will be in God's time and control. Christ's willingness to trust the just judge does not mean that he escapes suffering or death. In the next part of the sentence (v. 24), our attention moves from Christ's non-retaliation against abuse and suffering to his death on the cross.

Verse 24 is the final part of the sentence that began at v. 21. Once again, Peter alludes to Isaiah 53, this time drawing on the phrases "he bore our sins" (Isa. 53:4a, 12) and "by his wound you are healed" (Isa. 53:5d). Now, Jesus is described as the one who bore our sins in his body on the cross (*xulon*, meaning wood or tree, here "cross"). While Isa. 53 portrays the suffering servant as bearing the sins of Israel, Peter adds the phrase "in his body on the cross" and in this way connects Isaiah with the location and means of Christ's bearing of sin. Peter thus makes the suffering of Christ even more concrete as he draws attention to the crucifixion. He not only endured abuse and suffering but also the reality of sin. His innocence in the face of capital punishment now adds to the suffering he bears under "our sins." Then, Peter points to Christ's death on a cross. This is a real, physical death experienced in a real human body. There is no hint here that Christ escaped real, physical bodily suffering and death. The death of Jesus Christ on a cross was a central proclamation of the church from the earliest days (cf. 1 Cor. 2:2; Acts 2:23). Crucifixion was a public, humiliating, torturous, and shameful death usually reserved for slaves and non-Roman citizens.[270] The Old Testament itself indicates that "anyone hung on a tree is under God's curse" (Deut. 21:23). In a culture where honor was the highest value, the crucifixion was a source of shame and humiliation. But this is the manner by which God addresses sin. Christ experienced the death of the most devalued among society and even when experiencing that he did not sin (2:22). Additionally his death became an offering for "our" sin. The author moves from "you" in v. 21 where he addresses the slaves along with the wider audience listening in and now indicates that Christ's bearing of sin on the cross is for "us," the whole church and the writer himself. But the sins of humanity do not simply disappear. Rather, they are born by

---

[270] Martin Hengel, *Crucifixion in the Ancient World and the Folly of the Message of the Cross* (Philadelphia: Fortress Press, 1977), 22–32.

Christ, the chosen and anointed king, in his body. He takes them upon himself on the tree and carries them in our place.[271]

The result of Christ's death upon the cross is that those who have become part of the people of God might become holy. In 1 Peter sin is repeatedly associated with Christ's suffering and atonement. Sin is described as something that is dead (2:24) or something to be finished with (4:1).[272] But Peter does not linger on sin as a problem in the community that he is writing to. Rather, the focus is on living rightly, doing that which is good in the sight of God even when the culture mocks, persecutes, oppresses, or beats those who do so. Such righteous living is not mustered out of the self but enabled by the sacrifice of the king on the cross. Through Christ, God's household is enabled to live a life of righteousness, a life defined by their right relationship with God and with the household of faith.

The final description of Christ points to the healing provided through his wound (*mōlōpi*, singular, "wound" or "bruise") with an allusion to Isaiah 53:5. The suffering servant is described as one who has been wounded and weakened by the sins of the people, but ultimately his bruise becomes a source of healing for his people. Troy Martin notes that modern people see sores as disgusting, especially if they ooze or drain pus and that it is hard to understand how a sore or wound can be seen as a source of healing. He then goes on to argue that attention to the medical thinking of the first century helps us better understand the meaning of Peter's assertion that "we are healed by Christ's sore."[273] Peter chose a broad term that "refers to any non-running sore produced by the body as a result of trauma."[274] In ancient medicine, "The function of a sore in drawing harmful substances to itself to facilitate the health of the surrounding

---

[271]   Verse 21 reads "Christ suffered for you" (*huper humōn*). While there is some debate over whether the preposition "*huper*" ("for," "on behalf of") indicates substitution, its usage in both the New Testament and broader Koine Greek indicate that substitution is certainly part of the range of meaning for this preposition. Stanley E. Porter, *Idioms of the Greek New Testament*, Biblical Languages: Greek: 2 (Sheffield: Sheffield Academic Press, 1992), 176–77.

[272]   See the commentary on 1 Peter 4:1 for a discussion of the difficulties associated with this phrase.

[273]   Troy W. Martin, "Christ's healing sore: A medical reading of 1 Peter 2:24" (Presentation to the Society of Biblical Literature, Boston, November 2017), 1.

[274]   Martin, "Christ's healing sore."

tissue ... is an essential feature of the source domain of Peter's metaphor of Christ's healing sore."[275] In other words, a bruise is a mechanism for healing because it draws the trauma endured to itself, encapsulates it, and then heals it. Many authors who have explored this phrase have focused on the trauma that Christ endured either when he was beaten or pierced, but the word bruise (*mōlōpi*) that is used here can be understood more fully in light of the medical thinking of the day. Thus, the traumatic suffering that Christ endured made his body a bruise that draws to itself all the trauma (the "dis-ease") caused by sin – both the sins done to Christians and the sins committed by Christians – to create health for the household of God. Slaves whose bodies have born unjust beatings are made well through the bruise that Christ endured because that bruise draws to itself the sinful injustice they have endured.[276] It is perhaps significant that when Peter turns his attention to healing, he returns to the second person "you" when addressing slaves. As those perhaps most in need of healing from the sins of others, they are offered healing only available through Christ's body, which was bruised for them. Of course, the rest of the church continues to listen in as Peter offers healing to slaves who have suffered unjustly.

Peter wraps up 2:21–25 with a final allusion to Isaiah 53:6: "All we like sheep have gone astray" (NETS). The first part of the sentence draws from the imagery in Isaiah 53 of Israelites as wandering sheep. The second part introduces the language of "returning" (*epestraphēte*),[277] "shepherd," and "guardian," none of which are found in Isaiah 53. The lack of connection with Isaiah 53 has led scholars to explore other possible backgrounds for the second half of the verse. Isaiah 6:10 has language that connects "turning" and "healing." Another suggestion is Ezekiel 34 with its portrayal

---

[275] Martin, "Christ's healing sore," 6.

[276] Martin, "Christ's healing sore," 7.

[277] The verb is passive in form but most English versions translate it as active (e.g., NRSV, "you have returned"). The KJV is an exception ("you are returned") as is the GNB ("you were brought back"). Most scholars, whether they take the verb as active or as passive, understand "turned" or "returned" to be a reference to conversion. So, Forbes, *1 Peter*, 93–94; Achtemeier, *1 Peter*, 204. However, Elliott argues for a more complex metaphor of salvation: Elliott, *1 Peter*, 538. In 1 Peter, salvation is both a present experience and future expectation. Finally, Liebengood argues that the passive verb should be understood in the context of restoration and return from exile: Kelly D. Liebengood, *The Eschatology of 1 Peter: Considering the Influence of Zechariah 9–14*, Society for New Testament Studies Monograph Series: 157 (New York: Cambridge University Press, 2014), 86–87 with reference to Jobes, *1 Peter*, 198.

of God as the true shepherd of Israel; God rescues his people from the false shepherds who have decimated the flock. The language of "sheep," "straying," "return," and "oversight" are all present in Ezekiel 34. An even more recent suggestion has pointed to Zechariah 9–14 as another possible background for this passage.[278] There are no clear allusions to Zechariah in 1 Peter or in this passage. However, Zechariah, in vv. 9–14, is widely acknowledged as reworking the messages of earlier prophets for his own time, including the prophetic messages of Isaiah and Ezekiel.[279] In addition, Zechariah provides background for the passion narratives and Liebengood interprets Zechariah 9–14 as presenting the same narrative as 1 Peter 2:21–25, a narrative in which the king arrives, suffers, and dies, followed by a scattering of Israelites prior to their regathering to worship God.[280] In light of this, Liebengood argues that the image of 1 Peter 2:25 is of a suffering people whom God has returned to their shepherd.[281] The suffering of the king and the suffering of the scattered people are both part of the unfolding eschatological reality. Despite the lack of direct allusion to Zechariah, the possibility that Zechariah lies behind portions of 1 Peter is intriguing, especially in light of its use in Mark's gospel (like 1 Peter, a text associated with Peter).[282] Because Zechariah is a reworking of other prophetic voices and because it was deeply associated with the passion narrative, it is possible that early Christians may have heard the references to Isaiah and Ezekiel along with an echo of Zechariah's interpretation of those prophets, especially in light of the connection to the passion in 1 Peter 2:21–25. Indeed, the metaphors that are used in the second half of the passage are found in multiple texts in the Old Testament. God is the shepherd of Israel (Ps. 77:20; 78:52; 80:1; Isa. 40:11; Ezek. 34:12) and promises to set up a Davidic shepherd over God's people (Ezek. 34:23). God's people are sheep who are described as wandering or straying, which is another common Old Testament motif (Isa. 13:14; 53:6; Jer. 23:1; 50:6). As Peter draws this section describing the suffering and death of Christ to a close, it

---

[278] Liebengood, *The Eschatology of 1 Peter*.

[279] George L. Klein, *Zechariah*, Accordance electronic ed. E. Ray Clendenen and Kenneth A. Mathews, *The New American Commentary: An Exegetical and Theological Exposition of Holy Scripture*: 21B (Nashville, TN: Broadman & Holman, 2007), 54.

[280] Liebengood, *The Eschatology of 1 Peter*, 50.

[281] Liebengood, *The Eschatology of 1 Peter*, 102.

[282] Christopher A. Beetham, "The eschatology of 1 Peter: Considering the influence of Zechariah 9–14," *JETS* 58:1 (2015): 199.

is possible that he draws on a mixture of images from multiple prophetic sources. While Ezekiel 34 may be the most likely, other potential backgrounds echo in this text as well.

In their former life the people of God in Asia Minor *were* like straying sheep. First Peter has already characterized their former life as consisting of ignorant desires (1:14) and the vain behavior of their ancestors (1:17). In contrast, they have been turned away from these things to a new covenant relationship with God that is embodied in their holy life and love as participants in the community of God's people. The new birth that they received was a gift from God as is their experience of being called (2:21) and healing (2:24). Instead of wandering, they have returned to their shepherd and guardian. The turn to the shepherd has already happened ("now") and characterizes the new life that they live. This metaphorical description of the shepherd relies on Ezekiel 34 and its description of sheep that are scattered because they lack a caring shepherd (34:5–6). Then, Ezekiel describes God as the shepherd who seeks out the sheep and rescues them. God describes himself saying, "I myself will be the shepherd of my sheep, and I will make them lie down, says the Lord GOD. I will seek the lost, and I will bring back the strayed, and I will bind up the injured, and I will strengthen the weak, but the fat and the strong I will destroy. I will feed them with justice" (34:15–16).[283] The same shepherding metaphor is applied to Jesus (e.g., John 10:11; Heb. 13:20) the true Lord and anointed king ("Christ"), and it most likely refers to Jesus Christ here in 1 Peter. Thus, the one who provides care and oversight to the people of God is also the one who sets an example of what it looks like to live without sin in the midst of unjust suffering. The one who is the guardian of their lives is also the one who bears sins on behalf of them. Thus, the shepherd and guardian leads from a position in which he knows and understands suffering. In the midst of the struggle to live rightly before God, the Christian slaves (and all the other members of God's household) have turned to the one who sets an example for them, bears their sins for them, and cares for their very life (NRSV: "souls" here should be understood as referring to the whole self and not simply a spiritual part of the body).

---

[283]   In Ezekiel 34, "the fat and the strong" refers to the leaders of Israel who abused those under their care in order to care for themselves. These are the leaders who will receive justice when God leads the people.

Bridging the Horizons: Christ's example stands at the very center of the household code, and it is just as relevant today as it was to the churches of Asia Minor millennia ago. For those who live comfortably in the Western world, it is important to remember that this book is addressed to God's chosen who are residing as exiles and aliens in their society. And this portion of the text is addressed to slaves, a slave being someone with limited capacity in the eyes of their master and the world. Christ calls the lowest members of society to a life of following his example. In this way, Peter draws the attention of the whole Christian community and of the slaves themselves to their agency, their ability to follow Christ even when faced by the most challenging of circumstances. What is the example that Christ left? First, he left the example of not committing sin. This is the life of holiness to which all of Peter's readers have been called. This life of holiness encompasses the good way of life that the whole church is instructed to take up (2:12, 15). Second, Christ left an example of non-retaliation. He did not return abuse for abuse or threaten those who caused his suffering. Sometimes, this has been taken to mean a life of passivity, of taking whatever comes and just accepting it and getting on with life. However, 1 Peter does not envision a life for believers of passively accepting evil. Instead, Christians are to refuse to respond to evil on evil's own terms or with the mechanisms of evil.[284] Rather than retaliation, the church is to respond to evil without sin and without threats and abuse. First Peter has already laid out how the church is to respond to evil from outsiders. They are to continue to do good, to pursue holiness, and to love one another. At the end of the household code, 1 Peter will advocate returning a blessing when encountering abuse. The church has sometimes failed to remember its minority status and has instead sought to grasp power through the ways of this world. But Christ demonstrates that instead of grasping for power, it is enough to live as God calls and to then entrust the outcome of that life to God, for God is the one who judges all things rightly. Perhaps the challenge of this text for some Christians today lies in having a different vision. Some Christians have forgotten what it is like to see themselves from the margins and the edges, from the perspective of those without power. Here, attention to Christians who live on the margins and to the challenges they face in living out Christ's call on their life may be instructive for the whole church. In the United States, portions of the African-American church have been examples of Christians who have pursued faith and good works and nonviolent advocacy in the face of suffering. Throughout the world, there are Christians who have continued in faithfulness and doing good despite persecution on account of their faith. Such examples call the whole church to faithfulness and good works in the face of opposition to the faith.

---

[284] Walter Wink, *The Powers That Be: Theology for a New Millennium*, A Galilee Book (New York: Doubleday, 1999), 98–111.

¹ Wives, in the same way, accept the authority of your husbands, so that, even if some of them do not obey the word, they may be won over without a word by their wives' conduct,

² when they see the purity and reverence of your lives.

³ Do not adorn yourselves outwardly by braiding your hair, and by wearing gold ornaments or fine clothing;

⁴ rather, let your adornment be the inner self with the lasting beauty of a gentle and quiet spirit, which is very precious in God's sight.

⁵ It was in this way long ago that the holy women who hoped in God used to adorn themselves by accepting the authority of their husbands.

⁶ Thus Sarah obeyed Abraham and called him lord. You have become her daughters as long as you do what is good and never let fears alarm you.

First Peter 2:21–25 with its focus on Christ as example – bearer of sins, healer, and shepherd – forms the center of the household code. Chapter 3 begins in Greek with "in the same way" and highlights the shared experience of the wives and slaves as followers of the suffering Christ who cares for them. Peter addressed the slaves directly and by doing so highlighted their capacity as members of the household of God and human beings whose worth is found in their relationship with God. So too, Peter now addresses wives. Like everyone else who has been addressed – the whole household of God (2:13) and slaves (2:18) – wives are also instructed to practice submission, in this case by accepting the authority that their husbands have over them. This acceptance of their husbands' authority has a goal: winning their husbands to a relationship with Jesus Christ.

The particular situation that Peter is addressing appears to be marriages between believing wives and unbelieving husbands. The verb *apeitheō*, meaning disobey or disbelieve, describes the husband (3:1). In 1 Peter 2:8 the phrase "disobey the word" was used to describe those who stumbled over and rejected Jesus Christ as the cornerstone. And even earlier (1:23–25), the "word" is associated with the source of new birth through the living God and with the good news message that has been proclaimed. Those who disobey the word are those who reject the message about Christ and may perhaps be actively opposed to that message.[285] First Peter has already contrasted those who obey (1:22) with those who disobey. Those who obey have heard (e.g., believed and responded to) the message and it

---

[285] Achtemeier, *1 Peter*, 210.

has permeated their actions. These wives find themselves living with husbands who may have heard the message but have not been won over to faithful obedience to Jesus Christ.

Like the rest of the household code (2:11–3:12), 3:1–6 continues to be about good behavior as members of God's household, including good behavior towards those outside of the household whether harsh masters (2:18) or unbelieving husbands (3:1). The whole community is to conduct themselves well in a way that can be observed by those around them (2:12, 15). The behavior (*anastrophēs*) of the wives is a subset of the behavior (*anastrophēn*, 2:12) of the whole church. In 3:1 the purpose of the wives' good conduct is that the husbands may be won to faith through the conduct of their wives. In other words, the gospel message is proclaimed by believing wives through their embodied actions. Peter does not advocate more words as an approach to those in intimate relationships who have already heard the message of the gospel; instead, the witness of a life of obedience to the Lord combined with an attitude of respect towards one's disbelieving husband has more potential to win these husbands to the Lord. Such an embodied witness, combined with reverence towards God, is visible to a husband as a life of holiness (3:2), a life the whole household of God is called to embody. Although the object of the wives' reverence is not explicit, elsewhere in 1 Peter "reverence" or "fear"[286] is used both in contexts about God (1:17; 2:17) and people (e.g., 2:18). But the believers' first orientation throughout 1 Peter is reverence towards God.[287] In 1 Peter 2:12 the same word for seeing (*epopteuō*) is used: when those who speak of believers as evildoers or criminals see the good deeds of Christians, they will glorify God when Christ returns. The good deeds of both the household of God and, more particularly, of the wives addressed here are actions that can be closely watched and observed. Batten writes, "Mediterranean collectivist societies were strongly ocular, people had little privacy, and sources indicate general anxiety about how one was observed in public.

---

[286] *Phobos* is often translated as "fear" when the object is people and "reverence" when the object is God. It is worth remembering that when the object is God it may be appropriate to translate the word as "reverent fear" in order to retain the sense of trembling with awe before God's presence.

[287] Peter H. Davids, "A silent witness in marriage: 1 Peter 3:1–7," in Ronald W Pierce, Rebecca Merrill Groothuis, and Gordan D. Fee (eds.), *Discovering Biblical Equality: Complementarity without Hierarchy* (Leicester: IVP, 2004), 229.

A person's identity depended upon how he or she was perceived by the group."[288] Both the wives and the whole household of God may win over some who are watching but others will only come to understand what they have seen when the Lord returns. Meanwhile, those who witness through their holy and good conduct must rest secure in their identity as God's chosen and beloved people, so that they can maintain that identity while living acceptably in God's sight.

Just as it is important to note that Peter directly addresses the slaves who are members of God's household (2:18), so, too, it is noteworthy that the wives are also addressed directly. In Greco-Roman household codes, wives are written about rather than spoken to. And, once again, as with the slaves, there is also a hidden script that is part of this segment for wives. A woman living in a household where her choice to follow Jesus Christ puts her at odds with her husband's religious observances and thus at odds with her husband's household leadership needs to know that her behavior is approved by the Lord. Peter identifies her way of life as one that is "precious before God" (v. 4) and modeled after the ancient women who "hoped in the Lord" (v. 5). As a Christian woman, she may win her husband through her behavior, but her approval and the reasons for the life she lives come from the God who has given her new birth and hope for an eternal inheritance. The hidden transcript provides a meaning for a wife's action, so that her behavior is based on her commitment to the Lord and not solely on her acceptance of a husband's authority or on conformity to societal norms.

Verses 3–4 contrast outward adornment with the inner person. Statues and coins from Asia Minor depict wealthy women with intricately braided hair.[289] The hairdos referred to in 1 Peter involve an elaborate hairstyle that may have included "accessories such as hair pins, clasps, bands, or cords into the styling of the hair but more likely blends foreign hair from animals or humans into a woman's natural hair. Whatever its precise appearance, this hairstyle probably requires a fair amount of time to style and careful, attentive maintenance afterward. Finally, it can be used competitively

---

[288] Alicia J. Batten, "Neither gold nor braided hair (1 Timothy 2.9; 1 Peter 3.3): Adornment, gender and honour in antiquity," *NTS* 55 (2009): 488.

[289] Troy W. Martin, "Dating First Peter to a hairdo (1 Pet 3:3)," *Early Christianity* 9:3 (2018): 314.

among women."[290] Peter, like Greco-Roman moralists, encourages modest hairstyles over the fancy coiffeurs of the upper classes; although, while Peter discourages the status-oriented fancy hairdos of the upper classes, he does not provide a description of an acceptable hairdo. In other words, a wide variety of styles may have been acceptable in the church as long as these were not the types of elaborate hairstyles described above. In the same way, wearing gold or fine clothes were both outward signs of wealth and privilege. While the vast majority of early Christian converts came from groups who had low status and limited resources, there were also converts from among those with wealth and position who would have the means to adorn themselves with expensive items. Instructions for women to dress and act modestly were well within the norms of both Jewish and Gentile culture. Peter's advice to wives is that the heart, the inner person, is the most precious and lasting adornment. The qualities of the inward person that are commended are gentleness and quietness of spirit. Gentleness "pertains to not being overly impressed with a sense of one's own importance" and can include the sense of being humble or meek as well as gentle.[291] In Matthew, Jesus proclaims a blessing on the meek ("gentle," Matt 5:5). And Jesus himself is identified as a person who is gentle when he says, "Take my yoke upon you and learn from me; for I am gentle and humble in heart" (Matt 11:29). And finally when Jesus rides into Jerusalem this is seen as the fulfillment of the prophecy in Zechariah 9:9 which declares that the king will come as one "gentle, and mounted on a donkey" (Matt 21:5, NASB). The wife of a disbelieving husband takes up an attitude of the heart that Jesus blesses and demonstrates even as he makes his way through Jerusalem towards the cross. The second quality that describes the inner person is a "quiet" spirit. Here, quietness refers to calm and tranquility. The inner person characterized by these qualities is imperishable, in contrast to outward adornment, which is temporary. Again, Peter employs the word "imperishable." Previously (1:4, 23) he used it to refer to the inheritance of believers and to God's word. This time he uses it in reference to the inner qualities of the heart, which are likewise indestructible. These characteristics are precious before God. Ultimately, it is the Lord who approves the heart and before whom a wife must seek approval.

[290]　Martin, "Dating First Peter to a hairdo (1 Pet 3:3)," 304.
[291]　BAGD

A Closer Look: Wives in the Ancient Household

Wives were part of a wide variety of households in the ancient world; these households varied in the social and economic opportunities they afforded a woman. Marriage was limited to the free born and those who had been freed from slavery. So, while female slaves might form relationships, these were not viewed as households by society. Indeed, slaves remained attached to their owners and those who served families were part of the larger household of the master. The wives addressed in 1 Peter were among those who were free and able to enter into marriages. Marriages in the Jewish community usually involved a marriage contract that at bare minimum indicated the names of those to be married, the dowry brought to the marriage, a stipulation to return the dowry in the event of divorce, and witnesses.[292] Other groups of people also used marriage contracts, especially if the wife came to the marriage with a dowry. However, those who lived together with the intention of being husband and wife were also considered married.[293] The household depended on sharing labor and responsibility among the members in order for the family to flourish. In Aristotle's *Economics* the philosopher notes that the man and the wife are distinguished from each other in terms of their powers, but they share a common life and a common purpose to raise children and secure a livelihood (*Oec.* I.3.1343.20–28). The household reflected the hierarchical nature of the society of which it was a part. First came the husband, then the wife, then sons followed by daughters, and finally freedmen and women, followed by slaves.

Women were part of a culture that valued honor and honorable behavior and that intensely avoided shame and any reduction in honor. Women's honor was derived from multiple sources. A woman's family could be a source of honor. Those who were well born or members of the higher strata of society obtained honor through their family association. Similarly, a woman obtained honor through association with her husband and his honorable status. A woman also obtained honor for herself and her family through her actions. A wife who cared for her home, saw to the needs of her husband, and attended to her children was considered honorable. Another source of honor was a woman's behavior in the eyes of the society around her. Those who acted quietly and with modesty and compliance were considered honorable but shame could easily accrue to a woman who was seen as being sexually available, shameless, or striving for a position to which she was not entitled. Honor is always in the eye of the beholder. While this is true for both men and women, women, perhaps, bore the brunt of this as they found their roles and identity

---

[292] David Instone Brewer, "1 Corinthians 7 in the light of the Graeco-Roman marriage and divorce papyri," *Tyndale Bulletin* 52:1 (2001): 103.

[293] Brewer, "1 Corinthians 7 in the light of the Graeco-Roman marriage and divorce papyri," 104.

circumscribed by the men in their lives (fathers, husbands, and sons) who benefited from the honorable status of their daughter, wife, or mother. Knowing how to dress in a manner that reflected one's station in life was also a source of honor. Those who tried to flaunt their position with clothes that were too fine or jewelry that was too costly ended up shaming themselves and their families. Alicia Batten notes that clothing in the ancient world denotes status by the material that it was made from, its ornamentation, and its quality.[294] Thus, even the wives of the earliest emperors were often depicted with modest hairdos and no jewelry in official portraits.[295] Later portraits of imperial wives beginning around the time of Titus (79 CE) depicted them in elaborate hairdos and clothing.[296] But generally, women were expected to dress modestly. Those who wore see-through clothing or who adorned themselves lavishly were viewed as suggesting sexual availability and thus shamefulness.[297] Jewelry too could be both a source of honor or shame. On the one hand, wearing jewelry to advertise one's wealth, station, or resources was dishonorable as it was a failure to embody the Roman ideals of modesty and humility. On the other hand, wearing jewelry at appropriate times was a way for a wife to bring honor to her family by making her appearance a source of praise (e.g., honor) for her husband.[298] Finally, owning jewelry was a source of financial freedom for a woman as it seems that the jewelry belonged to her and could be disposed of as needed to meet her own needs or the needs of family members. Choices about clothing and jewelry were just as fraught in the ancient world as they can be in the modern world. But it helps to remember that while the choices a wife made in the ancient world were about her appearance they were also very much about how she was perceived in the eyes of others and the honor that perception would bring to her family.

Honor and shame is only one lens through which the ancient household and the relationship between husbands and wives may be understood. Other lenses that shape our understanding of women and their roles in ancient households are connected to age and socioeconomic status (a widow, for example, might be the head of a household and have significant ability to deploy resources to achieve household flourishing). Similarly, a woman's status could impact her contribution to the household. Women who were citizens or freeborn could work, although women from the elite did not do so, as work was seen as the lot of the lower

---

[294] Batten, "Neither gold," 489.
[295] Batten, "Neither gold," 496.
[296] Martin, "Dating First Peter to a hairdo (1 Pet 3:3)," 313.
[297] Davids, "A silent witness," 230.
[298] Batten, "Neither gold," 495.

classes.[299] From literary texts, epitaphs on tombstones, and ancient inscriptions, it is clear that wives came from a variety of social locations, worked and supported themselves and their households in a variety of ways, and were not limited to a singular experience of life and/or marriage.

Yet, culturally, there were certain expectations about the relationship between a husband and wife and the general running of the household. A woman who was free born or a Roman citizen was raised with the expectation that she would marry and move from her father's household to her husband's. Marriage often took place at a young age. Women usually married in their mid to late teens. Usually, she married a man who was older than herself. Sometimes, the marriage might be with a significantly older man who was already a widower or divorced. A husband expected his wife to be docile, able to run a household, and to present herself through her appearance and behavior as a credit to him and his household. Xenophon describes a conversation in which a husband obtains a wife when she is 15 years old and trains her. She is portrayed as one who works to better the circumstances of the whole household.[300] First Peter is actually interesting because the ancients would have understood that a wife should receive instruction first and foremost from her husband. However, in this book Peter, a marginalized Jew and an apostle of Jesus Christ, offers advice to both slaves and wives thus taking the role usually reserved for the master or husband. Yet, his instruction is to submit to or show respect towards masters or husbands, thus affirming their authority.[301] In this way, Peter affirms both the human capacity of slaves and wives to hear and respond to instruction and the authority of those in charge of households. "Peter both upholds and subverts the social order."[302]

A wife was to do all that she could to support, encourage, and uphold her husband and promote his status in the community. To that end, Plutarch observed that "a wife ought not to make friends of her own, but to enjoy her husband's friends in common with him. The gods are the first and most important friends. Wherefore it is becoming for a wife to worship and to know only the gods that her husband believes in, and to shut the front door right upon all queer rituals and outlandish superstitions."[303] That the wives addressed in 1 Peter each worshiped a god other than that of her husband made her potentially suspect, especially since all sorts of calamities and troubles might be associated with failure to appease the gods

---

[299]   Katherine Bain, *Women's Socioeconomic Status and Religious Leadership in Asia Minor: In the First Two Centuries C.E.*, Emerging Scholars (Minneapolis, MN: Fortress Press, 2014), 45.

[300]   Xenophon, *Oec*, VII.4–43, trans. E. C. Marchant and O. J. Todd, LCL.

[301]   Jobes, *1 Peter*, 204.

[302]   Jobes, *1 Peter*, 204.

[303]   Plutarch, Advice to Bride and Groom 19, *Moralia*, 140D (LCL).

or engage in proper religious duties. Some have suggested that maintaining modest dress and gentle ways of being would have protected the wives of 1 Peter from the possibility that they were seen by their husbands as engaging in a lover's tryst rather than going out to worship.[304]

Similarly, Michaels can rightly note that "there is nothing distinctly *feminine* about a 'humble and quiet spirit,'" since these were qualities that all Christians were to share (*1 Clem.* 13:4; *Barn.* 19:4).[305] At the same time, it is clear that quietness or even silence was especially expected of women.[306] Thus, Sophocles can write, "For a woman, silence is a decoration," and Sirach can say, "A silent and loving woman is a gift of the Lord" (26:14).[307] Christians broadly and Christian wives in particular were encouraged to practice humility and quietness as a way of life.

Peter concludes his instructions to wives by turning to the holy wives of old, particularly Sarah, as examples that support the call to submission, quietness, and gentleness in 3:1–4. We might ask who Peter is referring to with the designation "holy women." Let us pause to note that all the major English translations read "holy women" here, but the word (*gunaikes*) is identical in both form and meaning to the "wives" of 3:1. The designation of holy wives/women does not occur elsewhere in the Old or New Testament. Commentators, based on the discussion of Sarah in the next verse, point to the matriarchs of Israel as the women referred to as holy wives. Most likely these would include Sarah, Rachel, Rebecca, and Leah. However, it is important to note that in the Old Testament these women are not referred to as submitting to their husbands or having a submissive attitude. Indeed, a study of these four wives shows that each one acts in ways that secure their vision of the future. For example, Rebecca helps Jacob obtain a blessing from his father at the expense of his older twin, Esau. Rachel and Leah engage in various kinds of deals to secure the right to sleep with Jacob and bear his children. These women are not known for their meekness. But Peter goes on to hold up the wives' hope in God and their submission to their husbands as their "adornment." While the stories from the Old Testament do not focus on the submissive nature of the

[304] Jobes, *1 Peter*, 205.

[305] Michaels, *1 Peter*, 162.

[306] David G. Horrell, "Fear, hope, and doing good: Wives as a paradigm of mission in 1 Peter," *Estudios Bíblicos* 73:3 (2015): 415.

[307] Sophocles is quoted in Achtemeier, *1 Peter*, 214.

matriarchs nor on their virtues as women, other first-century writers did focus on the virtues of the matriarchs. For example, Philo allegorizes the matriarchs when he writes, "Sarah is princess and guide, Rebecca is perseverance in what is good; Leah again is virtue" (*Cher* 40.41). The allegorized virtues of the matriarchs serve as examples for Philo's audience. Peter too uses the holy wives as an example for his audience. Just as the wives of vv. 3–4 were not to focus on outward adornment but were instead to focus on the inner person, now Peter draws a similar conclusion about the holy wives of long ago.

Peter's allusion to Sarah brings to mind both the story of Sarah from Genesis as well as interpretations of that story with which the audience may have been familiar. The basic outline of the story begins with Sarah's marriage to Abraham followed immediately by her inability to have children (Gen. 11:29–30). The middle of the story continues with her journey alongside Abraham to Canaan and then Abraham's request that she call herself his sister. The result of this is that Pharaoh takes her as one of his wives. When Abraham's deceit becomes apparent, Sarah is released. Abraham and Sarah leave Egypt and return to Canaan. Even when God's promise of descendants is reiterated, she remains barren. So, she gives her slave Hagar to Abraham and Ishmael is born from this union. Sarah torments her slave because she is jealous of the child. Once again, God promises to give Abraham and Sarah a child even though they are old. And Sarah laughs. She says to herself, "It has not yet happened to me up to the present, and my lord is rather old" (Gen. 18:12, NETS). But after one more incident of being taken into the harem of a foreign ruler, Abimelech, Sarah becomes pregnant and gives birth to Isaac. Sarah dislikes the way Ishmael treats Isaac and sends Ishmael and Hagar away. And then Sarah dies at the age of 127 when Isaac would have been about 35 years old.

The challenges for interpreters of 1 Peter are numerous. First, Peter seems to indicate that Sarah's choice to refer to Abraham as "my lord" is an act of submission. However, Genesis 18:12 is the only time in the biblical text that Sarah refers to Abraham in this way, and this is not in a context of submission. This makes it challenging to see the narrative of the promise of Isaac as the context for the reference in 1 Peter. Second, Sarah does submit to Abraham by allowing him to call her his sister (a kind of half-truth according to Genesis 20:12), but this submission puts not only her life in danger but also endangers the promise God made to Abraham. After all, if

Sarah gives birth to a son after being kept in the harem of a foreign ruler, whose son would it be? And the text is clear that Abraham has been asking Sarah to identify herself as his sister wherever they went (Gen. 20:13). Sarah's experiences come about because of her husband, his fear, and his desire for self-preservation (Gen. 12:11–12; 20:11).[308] This is often the text that interpreters point to as the place where Sarah submits to or obeys Abraham. Only a few interpreters point out that Abraham is not the paragon of virtue in this text and is, in fact, disobeying God's instruction to "go to the land that I will show you." He is instead going to the land of Egypt and can, therefore, be characterized as one who is disobedient to the word at this point in his life. However, pointing to these sister–wife episodes as the place where Sarah obeyed Abraham can become a way of enshrining submission to abusive and endangering husbands. Third, we must be aware as contemporary readers that there is a difference between what the text might have meant for the first readers who *may* have heard this example as a word of encouragement and the way in which the text has become canonized as *the* way for all Christian women to live within their marriages. The text has been read in ways that endanger the lives of some Christian women, who remain in abusive situations because of the way the text has been interpreted. And, often there has not been enough push back within commentaries to highlight the way in which the meaning of this text has become inscribed in a way that endangers women.

How shall we move forward in interpreting this text? First, we will attend to what the text may have meant in its first-century context in light of what we know about the readers of the text and its author. Second, we will consider the way in which canonization has concretized the meaning of the text in ways that may need to be reconsidered.

Philo, another first-century Jewish author, repeatedly describes Sarah as a person of virtue (e.g., *Leg.* 3.244, *Cher.* 40.41) and indeed indicates that Abraham listened to her and followed her advice. Philo does not present Sarah in the same way as Peter does, and it is clear that the story of Sarah has been adapted for the purposes of the individual authors, whether Philo or Peter, and for the audiences that they address. Philo pursues an allegorizing interpretation of Sarah as a woman of virtue in his overall project of

---

[308] Paul Borgman, *Genesis: The Story We Haven't Heard* (Downers Grove, IL: InterVarsity Press, 2001).

interpreting Genesis as an ethical text with moral guidance for his audience. Similarly, Peter presents an interpretation of Sarah as a person who is idealized as a woman worthy of being emulated. Both authors identify a woman who is respected by those who are addressed and whom the audience would most likely consider worthy of following. Neither author presents the whole story of Sarah nor do they highlight aspects of Sarah's story that do not fit the idealized portrait of Sarah that they present. Both authors present an idealized picture of a wife – a woman of virtue in one case (Philo); a woman of gentleness, quiet spirit, and submission in the other (1 Peter). And both idealized portraits are presented in a particular context. In 1 Peter, women who have courageously chosen a dangerous path, conversion to a foreign minority religion that their husbands have not chosen, are reminded that Sarah also faced danger when she obeyed her husband. This is one piece of encouragement given by Peter about evangelizing and living with an unbelieving husband. In the first century, this text may have encouraged women to take heart when facing situations that made them afraid and to continue in faith with courage. But this is not the only description of or advice about wives, marriage, or wives' behavior in the New Testament. In other words, our interpretation of 1 Peter 3:6 need not be prescriptive for every marriage and every situation that a Christian wife may encounter.

The wives of 1 Peter 3:1 are described as those who have become the children of Sarah. Abraham and Sarah are both referenced as the parents of God's chosen people, and here we can see that the wives have become members of God's covenant people as followers of Jesus.[309] The participles that follow are often translated as circumstantial participles that tie the behavior of the wives to their identity as Sarah's daughters. In other words, when or if a wife does right and is unafraid, then she is Sarah's daughter. But throughout 1 Peter we see that rebirth and covenant status come first and that holiness and right behavior flow out of that new identity.[310] A translation that fits the use of participles elsewhere in the household code and that shows clearly the relationship between the inclusion of the wives in God's chosen people and their behavior can make use of the imperative, "you have become Sarah's children, so do good and do not give

---

[309] Greg W. Forbes, "Children of Sarah: Interpreting 1 Peter 3:6b," *BBR* 15 (2005): 104.
[310] Forbes, "Children" following Michaels, *1 Peter*.

way to fear!"[311] The right behavior and lack of fear on the part of these wives comes from their covenant status as newborn women who have an inheritance kept for them by God. This identity as the covenant daughters of Sarah enables them to live a new life in the face of opposition, whether that comes from their husbands or the larger world around them.

This word *agathopoiousai* , meaning "doing right," is first used in 2:15 where Peter writes, "For it is God's will that by doing right you should silence the ignorance of the foolish." Good behavior is identified by Peter as a way of bringing glory to God in the sight of the nations (2:12) but also as a way of silencing those who do not know the ways of God. This verb is used in the situation faced by slaves when they choose right behavior before God and experience suffering because of it (2:20). Now, women are also instructed to choose right behavior. While we might be tempted to limit right behavior to silence, gentleness, and submissiveness, such a reading would indicate that wives are only addressed in this part of 1 Peter. Elsewhere in the book all Christians are instructed in right behavior that is courageously hopeful, loving, holy, and honoring in the face of a culture that disobeys and disregards God. Doing right can be bold action understood both as a way of glorifying God and of silencing critics. Not only are Sarah's daughters to do right, but they are also told not to be afraid (*phobos*) of anything that causes terror (*pto/hsin*) or alarm.[312]

Bridging the Horizons: While the text of 1 Peter 3:1–6 may have inspired courage in the face of fear for wives in the first audience, the text of 1 Peter 3:1–6 has also been used by men with power in ways that have endangered women and reduced their voice both within their own families and within the church. From the early days of Christian interpretation, texts such as 1 Peter 3:1–6 have been read in ways that advised women to stay in abusive relationships. Often the agency that exists in 1 Peter 3:1–6 in which a wife chooses to submit to a nonbelieving husband for the purpose of winning him to faith is neglected. Another aspect of the text that has been overlooked in the history of interpretation is the minority context of the wives of 1 Peter 3:1–6. There was a certain danger for a Christian woman married to a nonbelieving husband in a situation where persecution was a real possibility. The

---

[311] Forbes, "Children," 106.

[312] For further discussion of the emotions see the Closer Look section on emotion.

husband who wanted to be rid of his wife could use her Christianity against her, accusing her of being a "bad person" trying to undermine the household and the state. Instead, male interpreters use the Bible to tell women what they ought to do and remove their agency in the situation. For example, Basil the Great (329–379 CE) interprets several texts together when discussing whether a woman can seek divorce. He says: "If she was beaten and did not bear with the blows, she ought rather to have endured than be separated from her mate … a wife has been commanded not to separate even from an unbelieving husband" (LCL 246:36). The ancient interpreter most sympathetic to women's issues, John Chrysostom (349–407 CE), still understood that legally men were allowed to beat their wives and that domestic abuse was not a legally acceptable reason for divorce during his time.[313] He shamed men who beat their wives and showed sympathy towards women who endured such abuse.[314] Despite his attention to the issue of domestic violence in his congregation, Chrysostom still held the position that in marriage husbands ruled and wives submitted. Again, the nuance of female agency is not attended to. While Chrysostom does not explicitly state that a woman may leave her husband over abuse, he does seem to indirectly permit it.[315] This pattern of using the biblical text to indicate that a woman must submit to and obey her husband is repeated down through the centuries. So, while 1 Peter 3:1–6 may have originally been intended as a word of encouragement for women in difficult situations, it sometimes became a means (often used by men) of controlling women and their relationships in ways that could be harmful to women's health and well-being. Contemporary scholars usually reject readings of this passage that would encourage a woman to stay in an abusive relationship. Karen Jobes notes that, "Because even Greco-Roman statutes did not sanction spousal abuse, a woman who endured domestic violence would not necessarily have been considered a virtuous wife."[316] And she also notes that the household code of 1 Peter is designed to both encourage a distinctive way of life as the household of God and to live within societal norms to the extent possible. She argues that since our own societal norms have changed, what submission looks like in our contemporary culture is also open to change. Peter did not describe exactly what submission looks like for wives and Jobes suggests this has to be worked out within the confines of individual cultures.[317] Finally, Dennis Edwards reminds us

---

[313] Joy A. Schroeder, "John Chrysostom's critique of spousal violence: Full text finder results," *JECS* 12.4 (2004): 414.
[314] Schroeder, "Spousal violence," 420–21.
[315] Schroeder, "Spousal violence," 436.
[316] With reference to David deSilva, Jobes, *1 Peter*, 206.
[317] Jobes, *1 Peter*, 212.

that submission is not a way of life solely for women but is rather "offered as a strategic way of life for all men and women. In so doing they could glorify God and simultaneously minimize the conflict that they might face, particularly from those who were above them in the social hierarchy."[318] Indeed, David Horrell argues that the wives of 3:1–6 provide a pattern of mission for the church. "The author of 1 Peter promotes a mode of missionary engagement that is essentially the quiet and gentle living of a good way of life. Verbal witness is to be given when requested or required."[319] Even an early church father like Tertullian could see that a wife could be a conduit for God's work in her unbelieving husband. The husband might not appear to have a problem with Christian theology but instead might be troubled by "the distinctive religious observances of [Christians'] daily life, these practices of ours, our way of life."[320] By living in love and holiness with quietness and humility, the wife may win her unbelieving husband to the Lord. Far from being a doormat, a wife of 3:1–6 is an agent who sets the missional example for the church in Asia Minor, and the church today can continue to learn from her example.

[7] Husbands, in the same way, show consideration for your wives in your life together, paying honor to the woman as the weaker sex, since they too are also heirs of the gracious gift of life – so that nothing may hinder your prayers.

First Peter **3:7** is a single verse addressed to husbands.[321] The direct address to husbands uses the same form as the address to slaves and wives and is followed by the words "in the same way," which also appeared in 3:1. This is a continuation of Peter's instructions to particular groups within the household of God. The main verb for this whole section (2:13–3:7) is the imperative "submit," which appeared back in 2:13. This verb is reiterated as a participle addressed to slaves (2:18) and wives (3:1).[322] Now, the instructions to husbands are introduced in the context of that direct address to slaves and wives. Peter places husbands alongside slaves and wives, all of

---

[318]   Dennis R. Edwards, *1 Peter*, Tremper Longman and Scot McKnight (eds.), Story of God Bible Commentary, New Testament Series: 17 (Grand Rapids, MI: Zondervan, 2017), 128.

[319]   Horrell, "Fear, hope, and doing good," 409; See also Alan Kreider, *The Patient Ferment of the Early Church: The Improbable Rise of Christianity in the Roman Empire* (Grand Rapids, MI: Baker Academic, 2016).

[320]   Quoted in Kreider, *The Patient Ferment of the Early Church*, 89.

[321]   In English, this verse may at first seem straightforward, but a careful study of the Greek reveals a number of grammatical challenges and unusual word choices that make the interpretation more complex than anticipated. Good overviews are provided by Dubis, *1 Peter*, 93–97; Forbes, *1 Peter*, 103–5.

[322]   The participles carry imperatival force that is derived from the main participle in 2:13.

whom are part of the larger audience instructed to submit in 2:12. The instructions have moved from those with the lowest status (slaves), to those with higher status (wives), to those of highest status (husbands). However, it is important to note that these husbands are still part of a minority group described as aliens and exiles. It would be tempting for them to assert their power within their familial relationships as a way of securing their sense of position in a situation where they experience suffering and rejection in wider society on account of their faith. But instead they are instructed to live with their wives in ways that are not domineering but rather honoring of their partner. Michal Dinkler argues that Peter does not tell husbands to submit because a husband is the head of the household and there is no one above him within the household.[323] Here the husbands are instructed to live together with their wives in a way that honors them as fellow recipients of the good news. It was also not uncommon for the pagan moralists of Peter's day to assert that treating one's wife with honor was more likely to result in a harmonious marriage than if one treated one's wife with disrespect and violence.[324] Honor was the most important social value of the first century and one that the husband shared with his wife.

There is some debate about the circumstances these husbands are experiencing. The majority of scholars suggest that the husband is sharing life with a wife who is also a follower of Jesus Christ. They understand the phrase "heirs of the gracious gift of life" to refer to the wife's shared conversion to Christianity.[325] In this view, both the husbands and the wives have experienced new birth and both inherit the gifts that God has reserved for them. As such, a husband is to treat his wife with honor even though she is "the weaker vessel." However, several recent scholars have suggested that a husband addressed here may, like a wife of 3:1–6, be married to a nonbelieving partner.[326] Nugent argues that, in the larger context of the groups addressed, understanding the situation of the husbands addressed here as each being married to an unbeliever continues the theme of

---

[323] Michal Beth Dinkler, "Sarah's submission: Peter's analogy in 1 Peter 3:5–6," *Priscilla Papers* 21 (2007): 11.

[324] Schroeder, "Spousal violence," 424–25.

[325] Achtemeier, *1 Peter*, 218; Elliott, *1 Peter*, 579; Goppelt, *A Commentary on I Peter*, 228; Michaels, *1 Peter*, 270.

[326] John C. Nugent, "The 'weaker sex' or a weak translation?: Strengthening our interpretation of 1 Peter 3:7," *Priscilla Papers* 32:3 (2018): 9; Jobes, *1 Peter*, 207–8.

challenging circumstances described in the previous sections, where Peter addresses slaves who live well before crooked masters and wives who conduct themselves well in relationship to unbelieving husbands.[327] He takes the phrase "grace of life" ("gracious gift of life" in the NRSV) to mean "the gift of life," referring to the reality that wives, like their husbands, receive life itself as a gift from God.[328] Jobes also notes that *hōs kai* ("since ... also" in the NRSV) can be translated as meaning "as even," meaning a wife is to be treated as even a coheir. "This would then indicate that the husband is to treat his wife as if she were a sister in Christ."[329] In this view, the husband is not to coerce his wife into accepting his religious orientation but is instead to treat her with honor and with the understanding that she too may come to join the company of believers. Whether or not a man's wife is a believer, the husband is to live together with her in an understanding way, showing her consideration and knowing that she is a "weaker vessel." "Vessel" here is probably best understood as referring to the human body. Both men and women could be described as vessels, but the woman is the "weaker" vessel.[330]

There is some debate about what "weaker vessel" means. In the ancient world some argued that women were morally or intellectually weaker.[331] Some commentators have suggested that the phrase refers to "the socially weaker position."[332] Many commentators point to the general reality that many women are not as physically strong as many men.[333] Aristotle points to the way in which differences between the strength of the sexes contributes to different roles within the family when he writes, "For nature has made the one sex stronger, the other weaker, that the latter through fear may be the more cautious while the former by its courage is better able to ward off attacks; and that the one may acquire possessions outside the house, the other preserve those within."[334] The reference to a weaker vessel

---

[327]   Nugent, "The 'weaker sex' or a weak translation?," 9.
[328]   Nugent, "The 'weaker sex' or a weak translation?," 9. Other commentators note this meaning of "life" but then connect it with salvation: Achtemeier, *1 Peter*, 218; Goppelt, *A Commentary on I Peter*, 228.
[329]   Jobes, *1 Peter*, 208.
[330]   Dubis, *1 Peter*, 94.
[331]   Craig S. Keener, *1 Peter: A Commentary* (Grand Rapids, MI: Baker, 2021), 248.
[332]   Keener, *1 Peter*, 245.
[333]   Achtemeier, *1 Peter*, 217; Jobes, *1 Peter*, 209.
[334]   Aristotle, *Oec.* I.3, lines 30–34, trans. E. S. Forster (Oxford: Clarendon Press, 1920).

is most likely a reference to the fact that many women are physically weaker than most men. Finally, Peter concludes his instruction to husbands by reminding them that their actions have consequences. A husband's prayers will be hindered if he fails to treat his wife with honor and as a coheir of the gift of life. The efficacy of the husband's prayers is tied directly to his treatment of and attitude towards his wife.

Bridging the Horizons: The picture that 1 Peter paints of the relationship between a husband and a wife is one in which the husband gives consideration and honor to his wife. The husband recognizes the wife as a full recipient of the same kind of grace that he himself has received and he values her as a person fully able to receive the same kind of gift from God. He also recognizes that the way he treats his wife has repercussions for his relationship with God. The text of 1 Peter gives no grounds for behavior that dominates, controls, or coerces wives. In a culture that expected a husband to be in control and that expected wives to take up the religion of their husband, Peter puts forward a way of life based on knowledge, care, respect, and honor. This is just as culturally subversive as the instructions to slaves and wives to ground their lives in God's approval rather than obedience to a master or husband. Scot McKnight in his comments on the contemporary significance of this passage notes that there is absolutely no room for violence against women, whether that is physical violence or whether that is the violence of psychological abuse.[335] Instead, the call to treat one's spouse with honor, care, and respect is just as relevant today as centuries ago. And indeed the work of knowing and understanding one's wife is a lifelong endeavor. This way of living in relationship with one's wife is not only beneficial to the marriage relationship, but is also a testimony to the larger society as a husband lives in consistent consideration of his wife, lifting her up and honoring her before others. Finally, this way of living continues to be part of the spiritual relationship between a husband and God. A husband is enabled through the new life that God has given him to live with brotherly love, holiness, and respect towards his wife. The new life also enables him to be in prayerful conversation with the Holy God who has called him to this particular form of Christian life in intimate relationship with another.

[8] Finally, all of you, have unity of spirit, sympathy, love for one another, a tender heart, and a humble mind.

---

[335] Scot McKnight, *1 Peter: The NIV Application Commentary from Biblical Text to Contemporary Life*, The NIV Application Commentary (Grand Rapids, MI: Zondervan, 1996), 194.

⁹ Do not repay evil for evil or abuse for abuse; but, on the contrary, repay with a blessing. It is for this that you were called– that you might inherit a blessing.

¹⁰ For "Those who desire life and desire to see good days, let them keep their tongues from evil and their lips from speaking deceit;

¹¹ let them turn away from evil and do good; let them seek peace and pursue it.

¹² For the eyes of the Lord are on the righteous, and his ears are open to their prayer. But the face of the Lord is against those who do evil."

In **3:8** Peter begins the conclusion of the household code with the word, "finally." Like the beginning of the code, this section is addressed to everyone, "all of you." Of the five descriptions used for the character of the household, four appear only here in the New Testament and one ("a tender heart") is used here and in Ephesians 4:32. While these descriptions are rare in the New Testament, similar ideas occur in the teaching sections of the Pauline epistles. First, Christians are to have a unity of spirit and act in ways that promote unified purpose within the community (see 1 Cor. 1:10; Phil. 1:27 for examples of this call to unity). Second, they are to be sympathetic by showing understanding to one another (Hebrews 10:34 shows a community acting with sympathy towards those who were imprisoned because of their faith). Third, they are to have mutual affection for one another, a familial type of love for each other (familial love is featured in Romans 12:10 and 1 Thessalonians 4:9). Fourth, they are to be tenderhearted in their care for each other (in Ephesians 4:32 such a tenderhearted attitude is connected to forgiving as God forgave them). And finally, they are to have a humble attitude. Humility does not exalt itself over another and is a characteristic of Christian community. (Humility is often contrasted with pride or arrogance and Christians are instructed to be humble: Romans 12:16.) First Peter 5:5 also instructs the members of the community to practice humility towards one another. Elliott suggests that the words describing the attitude and behavior of the community are arranged in a chiastic structure:

Like-minded
   Compassionate, sharing feelings
      Loving brothers and sisters
   Compassionate, good feelings
Humble-minded[336]

---

[336] Elliott, *1 Peter*, 603.

Elliott argues that the outer two elements of the chiasm relate to the way of thinking that should characterize God's household, the middle pair relates to the feelings the household should have towards one another, and the central element – the focus of the chiasm – centers around the familial love of the household. This echoes the emphasis on love that was seen in the center of the instructions in 2:17: honor everyone, love the family of brothers and sisters, fear God, honor the emperor. It also reminds the reader of the instruction to love one another in 1:22. At the center of God's community is love.

In **3:9** it seems that attention shifts to those outside the community since in 1 Peter the focus has not been on evil or abuse within the Christian community but rather on the external threats faced by Christians. So, the emphasis shifts from a focus on loving the communal family of God (v. 8) to non-retaliation against those who seek to do evil to God's family (v.9). In 2:23 Jesus is set forth as an example of non-retaliation for slaves; here that same attitude of non-retaliation is to characterize the whole community when they experience evil or abuse. Instead of retaliating against those who seek to harm them, the community is instructed to "repay with blessing." This echoes the words of Jesus, "bless those who curse you, pray for those who abuse you" (Luke 6:28), as well as the advice of Paul who also writes, "Bless those who persecute you" (Rom. 12:14). The contrast between abusive speech (*loidoria*) and blessing is especially stark. Instead of returning insult for insult or slander for slander, Christians are to respond to abusive speech with speech that brings the blessing of God to bear on the situation. "To bless" can simply mean to speak well of another, and would indeed be a way of introducing peace into an abusive situation. But in the context of the biblical text, blessing can refer to the blessing that comes from God through human beings to those around them. Elliott reminds us that the Christian community, a minority group, was unlikely to win a war of words in the public square in a way that would reflect favorably on it.[337] Instead, the community may, by speaking in ways that bless even those who are hostile towards them, invite further consideration by those who seek to oppress them. The same phrase that occurred in the address to slaves, "it is for this that you were called," (2:21) is repeated here

---

[337]   Elliott, *1 Peter*, 608.

in 3:9 and also points backwards. It is God's calling to repay evil with blessing, and the reminder the community receives is that God blesses those who bless others. The NLT captures this well: "Instead, pay them back with a blessing. That is what God has called you to do, and he will bless you for it." The text speaks of this blessing as an inheritance, which connects it back to the inheritance that is part of their new birth (1:3–4). "[I]nheritance is a blessing – God's final bestowal of eternal well-being on his people at the last day."[338] One suggestion that has been offered is that 1 Peter alludes to characters who have been called to bless others in difficult circumstances. The household code begins with an unusual pairing of "alien and exile," which is found in the Abraham story (1 Pet. 2:12; Gen. 23:4) and draws to a close with a focus on blessing those who seek to abuse or do evil to one. Similarly, Abraham was also called to a life of blessing those around him so that "in you all the families of the earth shall be blessed" (Gen. 12:3). Perhaps "[i]ndirectly then, Abraham appears in 1 Peter as a prototypical exemplar of the elect-sojourning life of blessing to which the church has been called."[339]

The household code concludes in **3:10–12** with a quotation from Psalm 34 (Ps. 33, LXX). This Psalm begins with an ascription: "Of David, when he feigned madness before Abimelech, so that he drove him out, and he went away." This links the Psalm to the narrative of a time when David's life was in danger. Samuel had already anointed David as king, but he had not yet come into possession of the throne. In fact, this Psalm is attributed to a time when he fled from King Saul who sought to destroy him. David now finds himself, a stranger in the presence of a foreign power, in the company of a Philistine king who also considers killing him (1 Sam 20:10–15). This narrative of David's flight for his life and his status as a sojourner, a foreigner, an exile in the presence of another ruler forms the narrative frame of Psalm 34. We can also consider the larger story of David's sojourn when he had the opportunity to kill Saul, but chose not to take advantage of the situation. In fact Saul says to him, "You are more

---

[338] Fika van Rensburg, "No retaliation! An ethical analysis of the exhortation in 1 Peter 3:9 not to repay evil with evil," in John T. Fitzgerald, Fika J. van Rensburg, and Herrie F. van Rooy (eds.), *Animosity, the Bible, and Us: Some European, North American, and South African Perspectives*, (Atlanta: Society of Biblical Literature, 2009), 229.

[339] David M. Shaw, "Called to bless: Considering an under-appreciated aspect of 'doing good' in 1 Peter 3:8–17," *BTB* 50:3 (2020): 165.

righteous than I; for you have repaid me good, whereas I have repaid you evil" (1 Sam 24:17). In other words, David himself is an example of a righteous person refraining from returning evil for evil and in fact blessing his enemy even in a challenging situation.[340]

Before considering the quotation itself in 1 Peter, it is important to be aware of the whole of Psalm 34. The Psalm begins with an extended section of praise for God's salvation and deliverance in the face of trouble (vv. 1–10) before moving into a section of instruction from which our quotation is drawn (vv. 11–14) and finishing with teaching about God's concern for the righteous (vv. 15–22). First Peter shares similar motifs with both the David narrative and the themes explored in Psalm 34. Like David, the audience of 1 Peter is also experiencing trouble and alienation. They too find themselves a minority presence in their land and troubled by those around them. As David in the Psalm, they too have experienced God's salvation and are being reminded of God's care for the righteous. The Psalmist testifies to God's deliverance (vv. 4–6), just as the audience of 1 Peter testifies about moving out of darkness and into God's light (2:9). And they too are receiving instruction about the particular way of life that is expected of those who have received the Lord's salvation.

The quotation in **1 Peter 3:10** is connected with what came before by "for," showing that it is meant to relate to and provide a reason for the instructions that were given about caring for one another, not retaliating to evildoing, and being people of blessing. There is some variation between the text of the Psalm in the LXX and the quotation in 1 Peter, but these do not substantially change the meaning of the text.[341] Developing an idea put forward by Richard Bauckham, Christensen presents the following chiastic structure that shows the relationship between 3:8–9 and 3:10–12:

---

[340] Shaw, "Called to bless," 168.

[341] There is some debate over the changes in the text. Recently, it has been argued that the differences reflect the developing manuscript tradition of the Old Greek Psalms. Patrick T. Egan, "Did Peter change scripture? The manuscript tradition of Greek Psalms 33–34 and 1 Peter 3:10–12," in Siegfried Kreuzer, Martin Meiser, and Marcus Sigismund (eds.), *Die Septuaginta: Entstehung, Sprache, Geschichte: 3. Internationale Fachtagung Veranstaltet von Septuaginta Deutsch (LXX.D), Wuppertal 22.-25. Juli 2010* (Tübingen: Mohr Siebeck, 2012), 505–28. Many others have argued that Peter changes the text to suit the context of the letter he is writing. For example, Karen H. Jobes, "Got milk?: Septuagint Psalm 33 and the interpretation of 1 Peter 2:1–3," *WTJ* 64 (2002): 1–14.

A: 3:8 Exhortation towards peaceful living
   B: 3:9a Manner of living, turning from evil
      C: 3:9b Manner of living, blessing with speech
         D: 3:9c Theological motivation, inheriting the blessing
            D^1: 3:10a Theological motivation, "to love life and see good days"
         C^1: 10b Manner of living, not retaliating with speech
   B^1: 11a Manner of living, turning from evil
A^1: 11 b Exhortation towards peaceful living

Christensen then sees v. 12 as a summary of the entire argument "with the reminder that the risen Lord is an ever-present advocate of the righteous, but likewise an opponent to those who do not head the exhortations that preceded."[342] This structure shows the relationship between vv. 8–9 and the quotation from Psalm 34. Each item that is laid out in vv. 8–9 corresponds with part of the quotation in vv. 10–11. Christensen will go on to argue that when the Psalm is seen through the lens of the crucified and risen Lord, then it can be understood that it both calls to mind the action of Christ, who did not return abuse for abuse, and draws the readers into the story of God's care for and redemption of David and Israel in their time of distress.

The five imperatives of the Psalm sum up the ethical behavior of the household of God. Members of the household are to keep their mouths from speaking evil (the opposite of blessing) and their lips from deceit. The community has already been instructed to lay aside deceit in 2:1. And Jesus sets the example of living a life without deceit in 2:22. The parallelism with the Psalm points to a general command to avoid speech that mocks, abuses, oppresses, or attacks others. Believers are to turn away from evil and instead do good. Here, the example of slaves who suffer for righteousness comes to the forefront, as do earlier instructions to pursue good and right behavior (2:12, 15). Believers are also to seek and pursue peace. Peace with others and with God is a common aspect of the Christian life (John 14:27; Acts 10:36; Rom. 2:10; 5:1; 14:19). They are not only to seek peace, but they are to strive to attain that peace both in this life and with the hope of experiencing the fullness of God's peace in the life to come. However, such

---

[342] Sean M. Christensen, "Solidarity in suffering and glory: The unifying role of psalm 34 in 1 Peter 3:10–12," *JETS* 58 (2015): 341.

peace cannot be obtained by "going all the way" in fitting into the culture.[343] The five imperatives summarize the activities of those who are seeking "the good life." We should not see this "good life" as being relegated solely to the eschatological future. God's blessing is real and present in the life lived now. At the same time, these activities do not guarantee a life free from suffering. God is present in the midst of suffering. God enables that suffering to be redeemed. And God invites those who suffer to continue to choose the life of resistance to evil, turning towards the good, and seeking peace. At the same time, readers should also anticipate the future blessing, the inheritance, which is theirs in the life to come.

In v. 12 the Psalm taps into a common ancient ethical understanding of the two ways: the way of righteousness, of doing right, and the way of evil, wickedness, or wrongdoing. God sees all people and the way that they have chosen. God's ears are open to those who have chosen to do right and God is against those who choose evil. This reinforces the exhortation of Peter (both in the last few verses [vv. 8–12] and throughout the household code) to choose to live rightly in the face of suffering and to choose to repay suffering with blessing. Ultimately, the court of opinion that truly matters is the court that unfolds before the eyes of God. Attention to God's favor can provide the courage to continue to choose the way of righteousness over the way of evil.

Bridging the Horizons: This "Bridging the Horizons" section takes time to reflect on the whole household code and how it might inform our contemporary thinking. As we try to reach across time to understand the household code of 1 Peter and its relevance for today, twenty-first-century readers in the West must remember that there are significant differences between life in the first century and life in the twenty-first century. Although in some countries Christians remain a minority group who experience persecution from the dominant majority and/or the government, Western Christians do not live in the Roman Empire but in democratic republics where they have the power and freedom to impact both society and the legal structures of society. Indeed, groups of Christians have influenced the political situation in North America for centuries. Second, Christianity is not a minority

---

[343] Contra, Carter, "Going all the way?"

religion in North America. In fact, even though the influence of Christianity is waning, many structures and ways of life still reflect the dominance of Christian thought and expectations. Christians in North America are not a tiny minority outpost in a hostile world run by an emperor. Third, neither the church nor the culture advocates owning slaves and slavery is illegal. While struggles related to racism and the legacy of slavery persist, the conversation is different than it would be if slavery were still legal. Fourth, women have equal authority with men to vote, run their affairs, make decisions about their personal lives, and earn a living. A woman does not have to depend on a man or get married in order to live. Other differences between our cultures are more subtle but equally powerful. For example, North Americans tend to think in terms of right and wrong, while the ancient world thought in terms of honor and shame. And North Americans tend to think in terms of the individual rather than the group. All of these differences challenge us as we think about the meaning of the household code in the contemporary context.

In addition, we must acknowledge that down through the centuries certain readings of the household code in 1 Peter have been used by those with power and authority to retain their status at the expense of others. In the past, Christian slaveholders used 1 Peter 2:18–25 to justify their holding of slaves. In the contemporary Western world, pastors and other spiritual leaders have made use of 1 Peter 3:1–6 to advise women to remain with men who abuse them. Here, it is important to remind ourselves that those addressed by 1 Peter were a minority group living in a situation where they lacked power and where society was aligned against them. And we remember that 1 Peter was written from one minority (Peter) to another minority (God's household in Asia Minor). When those in power use the book to tell those who are minorities, those who are oppressed, or those who are endangered what to do, they have removed the book from its minority context and interpreted it as a person of power and authority in a way that removes agency from the oppressed. That agency is the very agency that Peter gives when he places slaves first in the list of those specifically addressed, the very agency that Peter gives when he places the power to accept the authority of others in the hands of women and slaves or in the hands of aliens and exiles. Attention to the power and position of the interpreter and the differing situation between our century and the first century are necessary in the effort to avoid misappropriating 1 Peter in our own time.

Next, it is also important to note that while women have gained freedom, slavery has been abolished in much of the world, and democracy instead of kingship has taken root in the Western world, inequality, slavery, and a lack of democracy all still exist as contemporary challenges in many places. Slavery in various forms still exists around the world, including within Western democracies.[344] Thinking of women as "less than" rather than as full agents capable of being effective missional agents continues to be a problem. And domestic violence and the misuse of power plagues marriages both inside and outside the church today. The way in which we take up these challenges has much to say about the God we worship and the Christian assembly in which we participate. In Peter's day, it was very clear that the government was run by an emperor who had no consideration for the Father, Son, and Holy Spirit and the beliefs and practices of a miniscule minority in a provincial setting. It was also clear that undue attention drawn to a small group of people proclaiming a new and different lord could be a disaster for the young church. But in our own day, Christians who submit to the government without question divest themselves of some aspects of power that are in the hands of the people. While some Christian groups such as the Amish and Mennonites do divest themselves of this power and choose to live a life set apart from the common operation of secular government, most Christians retain and use the political power that exists within democracies. However, Christians must carefully evaluate the policies and laws of the government and the candidates that they vote for in light of gospel emphases on justice, liberation, life, and hope. Those laws and policies that bring about oppression or that evidence disregard for any form of life can be challenged by Christians in the public square. Christian participation in the public conversation about governance in Western democracies has the potential to bring about life and justice for both Christians and non-Christians in society.

One example of this can be seen in the abolition of slavery. Many Christians in both Europe and the Americas were involved in the movement to abolish slavery, and they used their voices and political power to advocate for those whose voice was muted and whose political power was nonexistent. At the same time, even though slavery has technically been abolished in most countries today, forms of slavery still exist throughout the world. There are estimates that thirty-five to forty million people are living in slavery today.[345] It is important for Christians who have a voice and who have access to political power to advocate for policies that will end all forms of slavery throughout the world. It would be a misreading of 1 Peter for those with power to encourage those who are enslaved to bear their suffering patiently. In the Western context, Christians are no longer a minority group in a minority

---

[344] For one contemporary story of slavery in America see Alex Tizon, "My family's slave," *The Atlantic*, June 2017, www.theatlantic.com/magazine/archive/2017/06/lolas-story/524490/. Additionally, human trafficking remains widespread around the world.
[345] Global Slavery Index, "2018/Findings: Highlights," n.d. www.globalslaveryindex.org/2018/findings/highlights/

world,[346] and as such we must use our voices to advocate for the release of those who are enslaved and for right behavior by governments and by those who oppress others towards those who are enslaved. The difference in our situation means that how we understand and take up the call for "right behavior" has changed from the understanding and actions of millennia ago. At the same time, we demonstrate by our righteous activity on behalf of others the very things commanded in the household code: right behavior, turning away from evil, and seeking peace.

Similarly, while Peter gave advice to wives living with husbands who were not followers of Jesus, that advice and its depictions of the relationship between a husband and wife is only one part of the broader picture of life as a Christ-follower. It is important to recognize the evangelistic impact that a woman can have in her relationship with a man who is not a follower of Jesus. And just as all Christians are encouraged to act in upright and honorable ways that bring glory to God, so too Christian wives should act in that way. We, like the women of 1 Peter, find ourselves called to witness, through our actions, to those who do not believe. We, like the women of 1 Peter, do not find our primary value in outward displays of our wealth and status. Instead, inner character and gentleness become one means of winning to faith those who have not yet chosen the way of Jesus. This is, however, not the only role for women; women are equally members of the household of God and like the whole household of God are called to a life characterized by holiness, love, and growth in good works.

Peter advises husbands to live with their wives in a way that honors them as fellow heirs of the good news. They should be viewed as equally worthy to participate in all the activities of church, society, and home. In addition, the husbands set an example for the whole community about how they are to treat others – with honor, as fellow coheirs. Living in this way is a catalyst for one's prayers.

There are three aspects of living the Christian life that we can attend to from the three specific groups who are addressed. The slaves, the very lowest of society, have a calling from God to live rightly in a way that wins God's gracious favor. The wives, those whose husbands have significant control over their lives, are encouraged to live and act with such a disposition that their husbands may be won over to the

---

[346] Christianity is declining in the West, but Christians do not need to fear a return to minority status. The temptation is to retain power at all costs, but this was never the instruction of 1 Peter. Instead, the instruction in circumstances where one is the minority is to live a life of good works, to witness to others with gentleness and patience, and to display the work of God in the way the community of God's people live together.

gospel message, and husbands are encouraged to treat their wives with the honor that is due to one who shares an inheritance. These three ways of life are not solely for the groups that are addressed but are intended to characterize the lives of the whole household of God. This is a challenge for individuals who often look to the church not as a household to which they belong with all of its thick kinship ties but rather as an institution that should benefit the growth of the individual. The whole church is to live together in ways that win the favor of God, that speak through action into the lives of those who resist the message of God, and to treat fellow believers with honor and respect. And all are to have lives that are characterized by unity of purpose, compassion, love, and fear of God. These values of the household of God remain the same down through the ages and can be a guide both for the life of God's community and for the community's engagement with the world around them. The challenge in our century is to understand and participate in the household of God as the family formed by God for the purpose of worship, witness, and mutual affection and care.

1 Peter 3:13–4:6: Suffering for Righteousness

¹³ Now who will harm you if you are eager to do what is good?

¹⁴ But even if you do suffer for doing what is right, you are blessed. Do not fear what they fear, and do not be intimidated,

¹⁵ but in your hearts sanctify Christ as Lord. Always be ready to make your defense to anyone who demands from you an accounting for the hope that is in you;

¹⁶ yet do it with gentleness and reverence. Keep your conscience clear, so that, when you are maligned, those who abuse you for your good conduct in Christ may be put to shame.

¹⁷ For it is better to suffer for doing good, if suffering should be God's will, than to suffer for doing evil.

With the passage 3:13–4:6, we move into the second section (3:13–4:11) of the major unit that extends from 2:11–4:11. Verse 13 begins with *kai*, here with the meaning "then," "so then," or "now," which shows that while a new subunit is unfolding, it is directly connected to what has come before. Barth Campbell argues that this section answers objections that the recipients of the letter may have to the instructions in 2:11–3:12.[347] Peter has

---

[347] Campbell, *Honor, Shame, and the Rhetoric of 1 Peter*, 172.

instructed his audience to persevere in good conduct and has instructed slaves, wives, and husbands to act with awareness of God when engaging those outside of the faith. Such an audience might rightly reply, "But wait! Our lives are going to be in danger if we live the way that you are asking!"[348] This is the implied objection to which this section responds. Immediately before this section, Peter has quoted Psalm 34 to put emphasis on doing good in the sight of God who sees the good behavior of the righteous. Now, Peter asks "who will harm you for doing good?" and then goes on to indicate that they do not need to be afraid of suffering. First Peter 2:21–25 and 3:6 already present suffering as something that need not be feared, but in 3:13–17, the discussion of evil, abuse, and suffering for right behavior becomes more focused. Suffering has already been addressed in 1 Peter, both in the opening statement about the identity and situation of the audience (1:3–12) and in the household code (2:11–3:12) where the suffering of slaves and where the example of Christ enduring suffering formed the central theological and ethical instruction for the whole household code. Now, the question of suffering as a consequence of doing right rises to the fore. In this section, the author continues to ground ethical behavior in theological reflection. First Peter 3:13–17 revisits a number of themes that have already been explored including suffering for doing right (2:12, 20), having a good conscience (2:19, *suneidesin*, NRSV "being aware"), being gentle in one's speech and actions (3:4), and not being afraid (3:6). Some of these instructions were first laid out for specific groups such as slaves and wives, but now they are reiterated for the whole household of God. Suffering on account of good behavior in the sight of God is not restricted to any one group.

First Peter 3:13 opens with a question. "Who will harm you if you are eager to do what is good?" The obvious answer is "no one." In other words, the expectation is that when Christians do what is right, this will be rewarded and not punished. This fits with the cultural expectations already laid out in 1 Peter. For example, Peter indicates that the role of the emperor and his subordinates is to "punish those who do wrong" and to "praise those who do right" (2:14). It is human to expect that when one does what is right and good, one will not experience injury or harm as a consequence.

---

[348] Campbell, *Honor, Shame, and the Rhetoric of 1 Peter*, 172.

Yet, it is already clear from 2:18–20 that those who do good may experience unjust punishment and physical harm. It is already clear that there are those outside the community of faith who malign, mock, abuse, and mistreat Christians. We can hear the slave or the married woman who replies to the question "who will harm you" with the answer "my crooked master" or "my unbelieving husband," and it is clear that they are not the only members of God's household who may suffer on account of their faith in God. Doing good can be the trigger for injustice and abuse in some situations. In light of this, commentators have made two suggestions about the type of harm Christians may experience. Some suggest that the reference is to the ultimate harm of destroying the Christian's intimate relationship with God through Jesus Christ and their experience of final salvation. They argue that while members of God's household may experience physical suffering, no one can destroy the inner relationship between the believer and God that will be consummated in union with God.[349] This explanation enables us to understand how Christians may experience suffering while still escaping ultimate harm. In Matthew 10:28, for example, Jesus warns his disciples not to fear those who can kill the body but who have no power over the soul, the ongoing life of the believer. Other commentators suggest that this question refers to physical harm but is used here in a proverbial sense drawing from wisdom literature as a means of encouraging the Christian audience.[350] The word "harm" (*kakoō*) of v. 13 echoes the "evil" (*kaka*) of v. 12 just as being eager to do good in v. 13 echoes the "do good" of v. 11. The quotation of Psalm 34 makes it clear that the actions of both those who are righteous and those who do evil do not escape the gaze of God. At the same time, harm is associated with physical harm elsewhere in the New Testament (Acts 7:6, 19; 12:1; 14:2; 18:10). There is a sense in which there is both real persecution that causes suffering and harm and a reality that ultimately the relationship between the church and God cannot be destroyed. It is important to note that the "you" in the question "who will harm you?" is plural signifying the church rather than the individual. The close connection to v. 14 shows that it cannot be a blanket statement that ensures that individual Christians will

---

[349] Feldmeier, *The First Letter of Peter*, 192; Elliott, *1 Peter*, 619; Achtemeier, *1 Peter*, 230; Green, *1 Peter*, 115.
[350] Goppelt, *A Commentary on I Peter*, 240; Jobes, *1 Peter*, 227.

never suffer or experience evil when they practice good behavior, but ultimately the church will not be destroyed.

It remains clear that the household of God is to be zealous (NRSV "eager") to do good. The quotation from Psalm 34 identifies good as both the cessation of speaking evil and deceit and the active pursuit of peace (3:10–11). And it is clear that while some things may be considered good in the eyes of the culture around them, the most important judge of what is good is God. God's eyes are on the righteous and on those who do evil (3:12), and both the slaves and the women of 2:18–3:6 know that their behavior is good because it is approved by God (2:20; 3:2), even if it is behavior that others may deem culturally appropriate. Zeal for doing good speaks to an earnest commitment, a deep intense pursuit of doing good (cf. Titus 2:14). Elsewhere in the New Testament Paul uses the word to describe his focused pursuit of God (e.g., Acts 21:20; Gal. 1:14). As elsewhere in 1 Peter, the focus is on pursuing good despite how those outside the Christian community might judge that pursuit.

The opening word of **v. 14**, "but," introduces a qualification to the question "who will harm you?" While suffering may not be expected, it is certainly a possibility, one already known by the community to which 1 Peter is addressed. The NRSV translation reads: "*But* even if you do suffer for doing what is right . . .". Once again, the focus is on suffering because of doing good. Here, the word *dikaiosunē* is translated as "doing what is right," but it can also be read as "righteous." This echoes 3:12, "the eyes of the Lord are on the righteous." Suffering for righteous behavior does not go unnoticed by God.

In form, v. 14 is a short beatitude: "But even if you do suffer for doing right, you are blessed." The Greek verb is optative, a mood expressing a hypothetical possibility. Those who heard this letter may or may not have experienced suffering. The community is scattered across Asia Minor and different communities may have encountered different experiences of suffering.[351] Indeed, some may not have suffered at all for their faith. But, the author indicates that if it should come to pass that they do experience suffering because they have chosen the right behavior that stems from their new birth and their new life as the holy children of God, then they receive

---

[351] Achtemeier, *1 Peter*, 231.

God's favor, God's blessing. This beatitude is reminiscent of Jesus' saying in Matthew 5:10, "Blessed are those who are persecuted on account of righteousness." The saying in Matthew and this one in 1 Peter share the language of blessing and righteousness although they use different verbs: being persecuted and suffering. The suffering the church experiences stems from those who do evil (v. 12). Both Jesus and Peter indicate that doing right can bring about persecution and that those who experience such persecution should remember that in God's court of opinion, they are blessed.

The second half of v. 14 begins a long sentence that concludes at the end of v. 16. It begins by instructing the audience not to be afraid (14b) but rather to set apart Christ as holy in their hearts (15a). This is followed by reminding them to be ready to present a defense of their hope to those who ask (15b) but to do it with gentleness and reverence (16a) for the purpose of shaming those who mock their good behavior (16b). The married women of 1 Peter 3:6 were instructed to do what is good and right without fear. Now, that instruction is extended to the whole community. Do not be afraid. There are two ways to understand what it is that they are not to fear. The NRSV puts it this way: "Do not fear what they fear." In other words, do not be concerned about the things that make your enemies afraid. In the ancient context, this might include the fear that non-Christians felt when Christians failed to conform to social expectations about the worship and appeasement of the gods and participation in other social rituals. The translation of the NRSV would focus on not being afraid of the things that non-Christians fear. The second way to understand this can be found in other translations such as the ESV, "Do not fear them," or NIV, "Do not fear their threats." In this reading, the household of God is not to fear their enemies, those who would harm them. The grammar of the Greek text is indeterminate and either reading is grammatically acceptable. However, Forbes argues that 1 Peter is not concerned with the fears of unbelievers, so, based on the context of the whole book, the first reading should be rejected in favor of the second, which accords with the concern God has for God's household.[352] God's household is not to become unsettled or intimidated or disturbed by the threats that people make against them.

---

[352] Forbes, *1 Peter*, 115.

Instead of being troubled, in their hearts they are to sanctify Christ as Lord (v. 15a). The heart refers to "the seat of the instinctive and affective life, where fear would reside, if it were present."[353] God is honored and worshiped when the members of God's household have God at the center of their being. First Peter 2:5 identifies the household as the living stones who become God's temple and God's priesthood, and who offer God sacrifices. The instruction to sanctify Christ also reflects 1 Peter's ongoing concern with holiness (e.g., 1:12, 15, 16; 2:5, 9; 3:5). Throughout the letter the holiness of God and God's community results in good behavior that has God's favor. Here Peter's concern is that his audience will have Christ, the anointed, the Messiah, at the center of their lives. In a world where Caesar is lord, they are to hold firmly to Christ as their Lord. Instead of fear, they will identify Christ as their Lord, their master. They recognize that Christ is set apart and is worthy to be worshiped or revered.

The end of v. 14 and the beginning of v. 15 draw on Isaiah 8:12–13 LXX, "do not fear what it fears, neither be troubled. Sanctify the Lord himself" (NETS). Isaiah 8 is already familiar to the readers of 1 Peter since it was quoted in 1 Peter 2:8. The wider context of Isaiah 8 describes the coming military victory of the Assyrian empire against Syria and Damascus, the close neighbors of Israel and Judah. While it would be tempting for Judah rejoice at the destruction of their enemies, Syria and Damascus, Judah has reason to be afraid of this great military power that has brought death and destruction to many. By siding with the great empire of the day, Assyria, they rejected the Lord.[354] Now, the Lord indicates that Judah will also be destroyed. The Lord, however, instructs them not to be afraid (Isa. 8:12) but rather to regard the Lord as holy (Isa. 8:13). Instead of being afraid, they are to come to the Lord and find their sanctuary in him (Isa. 8:14). Isaiah continues with the observation that the Lord will be either a source of sanctuary or a source of stumbling – a rock that they stumble over (Isa. 8:14). First Peter 2:6–8 has already laid out this same choice: there are those who will disbelieve and disobey, and they will find the Lord to be a rock that causes offense. But others will come to the Lord as living stones

[353] Selwyn, *First Epistle of St. Peter*, 193.
[354] Gary V. Smith, *Isaiah 1–39*, ed. E. Ray Clendenen and Kenneth A. Mathews, Accordance electronic., vol. 15A of *The New American Commentary* (Nashville, TN: Broadman & Holman, 2007), 225.

to be built into his sanctuary (1 Pet. 2:4–5). Now, this same passage (Isa. 8) is brought into the argument to remind God's household that there is no need to be afraid of their enemies, but instead they are to choose with their whole hearts to recognize Christ as holy.

To facilitate understanding, the NRSV begins a new sentence in the middle of v. 15 although the Greek is a continuation of what came before. "Always be ready to make your defense to anyone who demands from you an accounting for the hope that is in you" (3:15b). God's people are to be ready to respond to those who ask about their faith, here described as "hope." It would make sense for society to judge those experiencing suffering on account of persecution as hopeless. After all, they bore shame in the eyes of the majority culture around them. But instead, they exhibited hope. Hope is a characteristic of the new birth they received from God and is based on the resurrection of Jesus Christ (1:3), which orients them both to their present life and to their future expectation of final salvation and inheritance (1:4). Christians place their faith and hope in God (1:21) because God raised Jesus Christ from death, demonstrating God's faithfulness and ability to guard those who suffer and give them the promised inheritance. This is the hope to which they must be ready to witness. Being ready implies preparation for and anticipation of such an occasion or opportunity. The Christians have already been instructed to be prepared and to be calm in their demeanor (1:13), and this same attitude will be discussed in 4:7. So while the wording is different here, the idea of being ready runs throughout the book. The word "defense" (*apologia*) was frequently used as a legal term when a person's defense was presented in court or before a group of people who could pass judgment.[355] Here, Christians are to be ready to present a reasoned argument in support of their faith to those who ask or demand such an account. It is possible, indeed even likely, that the Christians in Asia Minor could have been dragged into court where they would have had to choose between defending their position or repudiating their faith in Jesus Christ.[356] A defense offered in court before the governor or his representatives might point both to the hope found in Jesus Christ as well as to the good behavior of those accused.[357] But defending one's faith

---

[355] BAGD
[356] Williams, *Persecution in 1 Peter*, 179.
[357] Holloway, *Coping with Prejudice*, 202.

was also a part of encounters in the marketplace and wider society. Throughout 1 Peter the focus has been on good behavior but here we have a reference to a verbal defense. Horrell notes, "Giving verbal testimony is an unusual, 'extraordinary' mode of mission that is adopted when required by the enquiries of others, particularly in courtroom settings, though not exclusively there. The focus on situations where the Christians are being falsely maligned and accused . . . suggests that the author's main hope is for an end to such negative stereotyping and the forms of suffering to which it may lead."[358] Jewish tradition expressed this defense this way, "R. Eleazar said: Be alert to study the Law and know how to make answer to an unbeliever" (Avot 2:14). Christians are to be prepared to give a defense when asked. It is possible that some outsiders might be won over to the faith by such a defense, but 1 Peter does not focus on this outcome. It is also possible that those outside the faith will not truly see and understand until the day that Christ returns (2:12).

"But" in **v. 16** introduces a clarifying comment on what has come before. Their reasonable and logical defense is to be presented with two particular characteristics – gentleness and reverence (*phobou*, meaning fear/reverence). The requirement to adopt these two qualities has already been addressed to the wives seeking to win their unbelieving husbands to faith (3:1–16). The use of these same qualities in relationship to the whole church provides further evidence that the wives addressed in 3:1 are both spoken to and also serve as a missional paradigm for the whole community. The whole community is to speak with gentleness and reverence on behalf of the hope that orients their lives. David deSilva argues that the meaning of gentleness can be understood as "proper restraint of anger or power, out of consideration for the other person, thus 'forbearance' may capture its essential meaning."[359] Peter has already told them that they do not need to be afraid (v. 15), so the attitude here, as elsewhere in 1 Peter, is one of reverence towards God as they recount the life and hope they have received from God. Once again the NRSV begins a new sentence in the middle of v. 16, translating the participle (*echontes*, having) as an imperative. Many commentators argue that, rather than functioning as an imperative,

---

[358]   Horrell, "Fear, hope, and doing good," 429.
[359]   David deSilva, *Global Readings: A Sri Lankan Commentary on Paul's Letter to the Galatians* (Eugene, OR: Cascade Books, 2011), 271.

"having a good conscience" describes a circumstance that accompanies the attitudes of gentleness and reverence previously described,[360] but Forbes makes a good argument that this participle describes the result of being gentle and having reverence. In other words, be gentle and reverent in your response *so that* you can have a good conscience.[361] Here, a good conscience is used in the typical New Testament sense of having good moral awareness. The purpose of this whole sentence, which began at 14b, is now made clear at the end of v. 16: "So that, when you are maligned, those who abuse you for your good conduct in Christ may be put to shame." "When you are maligned" is the same phrase that opens 1 Peter 2:12. The experience of God's household in Asia Minor is one shaped by slander, defamation, and verbal abuse, all of which could be either informal or lead to formal accusation in a court setting. They should not be surprised by it. The word "abuse" (*epēreazontes*) only happens in one other New Testament passage (this is not the same word that is translated as "abuse" [*loidoroumenos*] in 2:23). The word for "abuse" in 3:16 also occurs in Luke 6:28, which is part of Jesus' sermon on the plain. There he proclaims, "Bless those who curse you, pray for those who abuse you." As in this passage and throughout 1 Peter, those who suffer for their faith are encouraged to respond with gentleness and reverence towards God. The words from Luke's gospel provide a concrete example of what that might look like. Jesus' response of blessing those who curse and praying for those who abuse might also be brought to mind by the use of this unusual word. This abuse is specifically related to the good behavior of members of the community as Christians. This theme of good behavior (1:15, 18; 2:12; 3:1) and good works (1:17; 2:12) continues throughout 1 Peter. The response of Christians to those who malign them has the potential to bring shame upon those carrying out the mistreatment. This echoes the silencing of "the ignorance of the foolish" (2:15). In a culture where honor and shame are the driving cultural values such shame is a force to be reckoned with. With their readiness to defend the faith in a logical and winsome manner in both word and deed, Christians can receive honor in the eyes of God and bring shame on those who mistreated them.

---

[360] Achtemeier, *1 Peter*, 235.
[361] Forbes, *1 Peter*, 117.

In **3:17** Peter once again reiterates that it is better to suffer for doing good rather than evil (see 1 Pet. 2:20; 3:14). But here, he adds the phrase "if it is the will of God." The verb that is used here (*theloi*, meaning will/wish) is in the optative (the mood of possibility), which the NRSV translates as "if suffering should be God's will." In other words, the reality is that they may experience suffering on account of their faith. The text is not talking about the general suffering that is part of the human condition (e.g., sickness, death, tragic accidents) but about suffering that comes about as a direct result of doing good in response to faith. God's will does not involve every kind of suffering; rather it is suffering for doing what is good and right in God's sight. "The qualification, *if this should be God's will*, refers to suffering *for doing what is right* and not simply suffering per se. The point is not that God wills suffering but that *God wills doing what is right* rather than doing what is wrong ... even if and when this results in suffering."[362] In a context where suffering on account of one's beliefs may lead to dishonor in the eyes of wider society, especially when such beliefs contradict widespread social agreement (see commentary on 1 Peter 4:3–4), Peter affirms that those who suffer for doing right are within the will of God and can expect to find honor in God's eyes. It is clear that various types of suffering are being experienced (e.g., 1:6; 2:12, 19–20; 3:6, 9). And, in the material that follows in 1 Peter 4, suffering because of one's faith becomes an even stronger theme. However, this letter was written to be heard, read, and distributed across a large region, and it is possible that not all of the Christians to whom it was originally addressed experienced suffering, the same level of suffering, or were experiencing suffering at the time it was written and/or received. First Peter can indicate that churches can both expect that doing good will not bring about harm and at the same time recognize that doing good can indeed bring about various kinds of suffering. In this context, those who experience suffering are still within the will of God, just as the slaves and married women of 2:18–3:6 are also within the will of God. From this point, Peter turns immediately to the suffering of Jesus, just as he did after discussing the suffering of the slaves in 2:18–20.

---

[362] Elliott, *1 Peter*, 635, emphasis in the original.

Bridging the Horizons: First Peter's vision of mission is directly tied to the good conduct of the church. Throughout 1 Peter the recipients of the letter are addressed as a group, and 3:13–17 is not an exception. The focus from the beginning to the end of 3:13–17 is on doing good. They are to be eager to do good (3:13); they are to do good so that those who malign them are ashamed (3:16), and if they suffer it should be for doing good (3:17). It is with the repeated instruction to do good that the church is told to be ready with a verbal defense for the hope that informs their lives. Before the church can focus on the message of the good news about Jesus Christ, it must first focus on its behavior. In David Kinnamon's book *Unchristian*, polls reveal how the younger generation in the United States views Christians. They are seen as hypocritical, antigay, judgmental, too political, and only interested in notching up a conversion.[363] The old adage "actions speak louder than words" still applies. The way the church is viewed by outsiders has also been affected by the myriad scandals that have rocked the church across denominations. Reports of widespread abuse of children and the subsequent coverup by authorities in the Catholic church is only one scandal among many.[364] Within various branches of the evangelical church, prominent leaders, pastors, and theologians have misused their positions to abuse women. And the list could go on. In addition to sexual scandal, the white evangelical church has mainly become associated with one political party, so that in the minds of those outside the faith who do not align with that party, it seems that if you are a white evangelical Christian you must also have one particular political persuasion.[365] At the same time, outsiders see hypocrisy on the part of evangelical Christians who demanded a certain sexual ethic and then excuse the behavior of elected officials. All of these scandals, attitudes, and political behaviors make it very challenging for the church to be known for doing good by those outside the faith. One of the challenges for our time is engaging in bold actions that are understood as good by those who are not part of the faith. On the one hand, the church has a long history of spearheading relief efforts after natural disasters, of assisting people living on the streets or experiencing hunger, and of engaging in poverty relief. On the other hand, the actual experiences of people of the local church as a source of "doing good"

---

[363] David Kinnaman and Gabe Lyons, *Unchristian: What a New Generation Really Thinks about Christianity – and Why It Matters* (Grand Rapids, MI: Baker Books, 2007).

[364] Matt Carroll, Sacha Pfeiffer, and Michael Rezendes, "Church allowed abuse by priest for years," *Boston Globe*, January 6, 2002. www.bostonglobe.com/news/special-reports/2002/01/06/church-allowed-abuse-priest-for-years/cSHfGkTIrAT25qKGvBuDNM/story.html, accessed 3/11/2021.

[365] David French, "The cultural consequences of very, very Republican Christianity," The French Press, November 15, 2020. https://frenchpress.thedispatch.com/p/the-cultural-consequences-of-very, accessed 3/11/2021.

may be limited. Recently, some churches in the United States have taken up the bold, creative, and eye-catching action of paying off medical debt for strangers in their community.[366] Many of these churches made a connection between their experience of having the debt of sin removed and their choice to pay off debt for outsiders. Churches today have the challenge of continuing to think creatively about ways that they can engage in good behavior that serves as a witness to their communities. Such good behavior can include both the moral imperatives of 1 Peter to pursue holiness, brotherly love, and respect for all humans as well as bold good works that are visible to the larger society. First Peter makes it clear that when outsiders see the good works that are done by the church they will be put to shame (3:16) and will come to glorify God (whether through their own conversion or in recognition of who God is at the last day, 2:12). It is in the context of living well – living with integrity (part of holiness), with care for others (part of brotherly love), and honoring all those one encounters – that the opportunity may arise to offer a defense of the faith. The first activity of the church's mission is not preaching but rather action, and then in the context of right action there is an opportunity to explain to those who ask the reason for the life Christians live. First Peter invites Christians to think about mission broadly as both deeds and words.

[18] For Christ also suffered for sins once for all, the righteous for the unrighteous, in order to bring you to God. He was put to death in the flesh, but made alive in the spirit,

[19] in which also he went and made a proclamation to the spirits in prison,

[20] who in former times did not obey, when God waited patiently in the days of Noah, during the building of the ark, in which a few, that is, eight persons, were saved through water.

[21] And baptism, which this prefigured, now saves you – not as a removal of dirt from the body, but as an appeal to God for a good conscience, through the resurrection of Jesus Christ,

[22] who has gone into heaven and is at the right hand of God, with angels, authorities, and powers made subject to him.

Although the commentary begins a new section of study with these verses, these verses are directly linked with what came before and are part of the larger unit that began in 2:11. This section exhibits a change in form as the

---

[366] Elizabeth Bruenig, "Churches step in where politicians will not," *New York Times*, November 27, 2020. www.nytimes.com/2020/11/27/opinion/covid-medical-debt-church-charity.html, accessed 3/11/2021. These churches made use of an organization called RIP Medical Debt (https://ripmedicaldebt.org).

author moves away from the household code and instead focuses on suffering within the context of the broader society. The structure of 3:13–22 is similar to that of 2:18–25. There, a problem, suffering for doing right as a slave (2:18–20), is presented and then a theological observation about Christ provides encouragement and instruction (do not sin in response to suffering but continue to live rightly) related to that problem (2:21–25). Similarly, 1 Peter presents the problem of suffering for doing right in 3:13–17 and then turns to theological observations about Christ (3:18–22).[367] The interpretation of 3:18–22 must both expound the meaning of these verses and show how that interpretation fits the larger context in which the audience faces suffering because of their ongoing commitment to faith in Jesus Christ and to doing what is right in both word and deed. These verses remind the audience of the death, resurrection, ascension, and reign of Christ and provide a vision of the one on whose behalf they suffer. The passage 2:21–25 formed a hinge between the instructions to slaves and the instructions to wives married to unbelievers. Similarly, 3:18–22 forms a hinge between 3:13–17 and 4:1–6, and all three units in this section (3:13–17, 18–22; 4:1–6) connect to the theme of suffering.

This section, 3:18–22, is one long, complex sentence in Greek. The NRSV translators have broken it into three shorter sentences to enhance the readability of the translation. But the commentary will trace the relationship between the phrases of this long sentence following the Greek text. In addition, these verses present some of the most exegetically challenging questions in the whole of the New Testament. There are questions about the text itself (text criticism), about the meaning of particular words, about how particular grammatical constructions should be interpreted, about the activities that Jesus is engaged in, and about the overall purpose of the passage. But in the end, this passage presents a narrative about the work of Christ and its relevance for communities who are suffering because of their faith. Finally, there has been a long debate about whether this passage is describing the activity of Christ between his death and resurrection. There

---

[367] Wayne Grudem argues that the context of 3:18–22 is evangelism. While 3:15 does indicate that Christians should be willing to give a defense of their faith, the focus of 3:13–17 is not evangelism, nor does the book of 1 Peter seem overly concerned about evangelism, although it is suggested at places such as 3:1–2. Wayne A. Grudem, "He did not descend into hell: A plea for following scripture instead of the Apostles' Creed," *JETS* 34:1 (1991): 103–13.

is a long theological tradition, known as the *descensus*, which holds that Christ descended to hell or to the dead during the period between his death and resurrection. This assertion may be related to Ephesians 4:9 and is also found in the Apostle's Creed. Whether this text, especially 1 Peter 3:18–20, relates to that doctrine is debated. Many scholars both ancient and modern have come to the conclusion that 1 Peter 3:18–20 is not related to the idea that Christ descended to the dead.[368] At the same time other scholars both modern and ancient maintain that this text is related to that doctrine.[369] This commentary argues for the position that this passage in 1 Peter is unrelated to the doctrine of Christ's descent to hell or to the dead.

Verse 18 connects to what came before with an explanatory "for" (*hoti*). This is the same structure we have already seen in 2:21b where 2:18–21a is joined to 21b–25 with "for" (*hoti*). What appears in 2:21b–25 is a carefully constructed, deeply theological reflection on the suffering of Christ and its significance for slaves (and, likewise, for the whole community of Christians). Here, the deeply theological assertions of 3:18–22 are similarly joined to what has come before. Christians who suffer for their faith are not alone in their suffering. Christ, the anointed king, also suffered. This was true both in his life, where his message was rejected by crowds and family alike and ultimately by his disciples, and in the mocking, beating, and public humiliation he endured on the way to death on the cross.[370] Peter indicates that Christ's suffering happened once for all time (*hapax*)

---

[368] William Joseph Dalton, *Christ's Proclamation to the Spirits: A Study of 1 Peter 3:18–4:6*, Analecta Biblica (Rome: Pontifical Biblical Institute, 1989), 8.

[369] Bo Reicke, *The Disobedient Spirits and Christian Baptism: A Study of I Peter III. 19 and Its Context* (Eugene, OR: Wipf & Stock, 2005), 115–16.

[370] At this point, there are a variety of textual variants in the manuscript tradition. The major issues in this verse include: (1) The word "suffered" (*epathen*) is replaced with "died" (*apethaven*) in some manuscripts and (2) quite a few manuscripts also add longer phrases such as "on your behalf" (*huper humon*) to this verse. The longer phrases should be rejected as later scribal editions. However, the evidence indicating whether "suffered" or "died" should be preferred is fairly evenly divided. In light of this, some English translations read "died" (NASB, RSV). However, it is unlikely that scribes would change a reading from "died" to "suffered" since "died" reflects conformity to the Christian tradition. Instead, it is more likely that the text was changed from "suffered" to "died" to conform to the wider tradition (e.g., Christ died for us or Christ died for our sins, Rom. 5:8; 1 Cor. 15:3). In addition, "suffered" is a word used repeatedly in 1 Peter and in the immediate context. "Suffering," as the NRSV, ESV, NIV, and others read, should be retained as the more difficult and shorter reading which fits the context of the passage. Bruce M. Metzger, Deutsche Bibelgesellschaft, and United Bible Societies, *A Textual Commentary on the Greek New Testament: A Companion Volume to the United Bible*

and that it was "for sins." The New Testament supports the understanding that Christ's atonement addressed sin (e.g., Matt 1:21; 26:28; 1 Cor. 15:3). Similar to the book of Hebrews, which also focuses on the once-for-all nature of Christ's work to address the problem of sin, 1 Peter also addresses the problem of sin. In Hebrews 9:26b the writer indicates, "he [Jesus] has appeared once for all at the end of the age to remove sin by the sacrifice of himself." Christ's suffering was limited and does not extend throughout time. In addition, his suffering was effective in dealing with sin. This echoes 1 Peter 2:24: "He himself bore our sins in his body on the cross." Christ's bearing of sin elsewhere in 1 Peter enables Christ's followers to live rightly and here we can infer that Christ's bearing of sins (including the sins done to Christians) enables Christians to live rightly in the face of suffering.

Christ is described as "the righteous" one, the one who does what is right in the sight of God. Being "righteous" is an important concept in both Greco-Roman and Jewish culture. In the Greco-Roman culture, a righteous person was one who performed his personal and religious duties and acted in ways that upheld and benefited society.[371] Within Judaism, being righteous referred to right relationships with God and others.[372] Christ was a person without sin and thus was in perfectly right and holy relationship with both God and others – the ideal righteous person. He suffered on behalf of those who are unrighteous. The suffering he endured was not for people who were good or deserving but for all humanity, including those characterized as crooked and pursuing that which is not right. Those who have been reborn ("you") already know the purpose of Christ's suffering: to be brought into God's presence, to be made part of God's family, to be designated as God's heir. While the word (*prosagō*) has the simple meaning to bring someone or something to someone, it is used repeatedly in Leviticus to describe bringing an offering to God (Lev. 3:7, 12; 4:3, 14, and many others). That sacrificial overtone is present in this text, so that we understand that Christ's suffering on behalf of our sin is a sacrifice and that

Societies' *Greek New Testament (Fourth Revised Edition)* (Stuttgart; USA: Deutsche Bibelgesellschaft; United Bible Societies, 1994), 622–23.
[371]   BAGD
[372]   BAGD

sacrifice enables those who have sinned to be cleansed and reborn and brought into God's presence.

Verse 18 ends with a beautifully balanced comparative clause in which the emphasis falls on the final part of the clause ("made alive"). The clause contains two passive participles, and each one is followed by nouns in the dative case.[373] The NRSV begins a new sentence here and accurately shows that these two phrases further describe Christ. A more literal translation from the Greek reads "Although on the one hand, he was put to death in the flesh, on the other hand, he was made alive in the spirit." How this whole phrase is understood will impact the meaning of v. 19 and the following materials. There is a growing consensus that the meaning of "put to death" and "made alive" refers to the death and resurrection of Christ. The verb "put to death" is used in the Gospels to describe those who sought to end Christ's life (Matt 26:59; 27:1; Mark 14:55). And "made alive" is consistently used to describe giving life or resurrection (especially 1 Cor. 15:22, 36). This is the only time in the New Testament that "made alive" is applied to Christ, but it is synonymous with the New Testament emphasis on bodily resurrection that comes about through the power of God. Here, the passive verb is a reminder that Jesus Christ does not resurrect himself but is resurrected by God (cf., Acts 2:32). Donelson, in discussing the verb's relationship to the resurrection, states that "the claim is that Jesus is 'made alive,' not that his spirit somehow survives the death of his flesh."[374]

The challenge comes from the datives "in the flesh" and "in the spirit." There are three common proposals about the meaning of these phrases, and these three proposals correspond to three grammatically possible uses of the dative. Here, it is important to be aware that because the phrases

---

[373] The inclusion of traditional elements (e.g., the death, resurrection, and ascension of Jesus, vv. 18, 22) and the use of particular forms such as the balanced phrases of "the just for the unjust" and "put to death … made alive" have suggested the possible use of either a whole creed or fragments of creeds or hymns in this portion of 1 Peter. In addition, vv. 19–21 present material from other traditional domains related to Israelite understanding of Genesis 6–8 and early Christian understanding of baptism Elliott, *1 Peter*, 705; Goppelt, *A Commentary on I Peter*, 249. Elliott, in particular, provides a detailed overview of these issues related to possible sources. These materials have been woven together in a way that is unique to 1 Peter. It is the very weaving together of different traditional elements that creates some of the difficulty in understanding 3:18–22.

[374] Donelson, *I & II Peter and Jude*, 111.

"put to death" and "made alive" are grammatically parallel most scholars have worked from the idea that the use of the dative must also be parallel;[375] although, there are some scholars who argue for two different interpretations of the datives at this point.[376] The first view can be characterized as an instrumental view of the dative. In this view, "in the flesh" refers to those human agents who put Jesus to death and "in the spirit" refers to the Holy Spirit as the agent of resurrection.[377] While the understanding of instrument or agency makes very good sense in reference to "in the spirit," and can flow well into the rest of the sentence, which continues in v. 19, the understanding of "flesh" as referring to the human agents of the crucifixion or to the instrument of Christ's death does not have equal support.[378]

The second and third view can be dealt with together as they generally lean towards the same meaning.[379] The second view argues that the datives are locative or datives of sphere and the third view argues that these are datives of respect or reference. In the second view, "in the flesh" refers to the sphere or realm of Christ's earthly life and "in the spirit" refers to the spiritual realm in which Christ's glorified body lives after his resurrection. Goppelt writes, "Jesus was killed insofar as he belonged to 'the flesh,' to mortal human existence, and 'made alive,' raised, insofar as he belonged to the Spirit."[380] It is not that there is a distinction between Christ's body and soul, which is a Greek concept, but that Christ's life in the flesh came to an end and that the new life into which he rose is possible in the realm of the Spirit. Michaels expresses this particularly clearly when he writes, "The meaning of the two datives is thus shaped by the respective participles they modify. If 'flesh' is the sphere of human limitations, of suffering, and of death (cf. 4:1), 'Spirit' is the sphere of power, vindication, and a new life … Both spheres affect Christ's (or anyone else's) whole person; one cannot be

---

[375] Elliott, *1 Peter*, 645.
[376] Wallace, *Greek Grammar beyond the Basics*, 343. Wallace argues that, because v. 18 may draw on hymn fragments, poetic license should be allowed to explain the difference in use between the two datives.
[377] Achtemeier, *1 Peter*, 250.
[378] Further discussions of the implications of this view can be found in the discussion of v. 19.
[379] Forbes, *1 Peter*, 123.
[380] Goppelt, *A Commentary on I Peter*, 253.

assigned to the body and the other to the soul."[381] Similarly, those who argue for the third view, a dative of respect, are pointing to the way in which the dative can serve to provide the frame in which what is presented is true.[382] This is captured well by Donelson who points readers towards the cosmic battle that may be signified by "flesh" and "spirit." Christ – living in the realm of the flesh, under the powers of the flesh, himself a proper member of the world of the flesh – was put to death; yet living in the world of spirit where God rules, Christ was made alive. The cosmic conflict between fleshly powers and spiritual ones would not be divided temporally (in terms of era) or spatially (as parts of the self or the world). Flesh and spirit work in the same place, at the same time. Christ, as subject to fleshly powers, is put to death. Christ, as cared for by God, is made alive."[383] While some have argued for an intermediate state in this passage between the death and resurrection of Christ, commentators from all three of the views above have affirmed that the totality of this phrase should be understood as referring to the death and resurrection of Christ. And while there are arguments in favor of all three views, the dative of sphere or the dative of respect seems most likely in this passage as these allow for parallel readings of the dative that remain within the broad contours of early Christian tradition with its emphasis on the physical death and bodily resurrection of Christ.

Verse 19 portrays Christ, after his resurrection, going and proclaiming a message to imprisoned spirits. This verse raises many questions, and each question has more than one possible answer.[384] The list of answers can be put together in ways that seem to generate an exponential amount of potential understandings of this verse. This has led more than one commentator to suggest that this verse is one of the most difficult interpretive conundrums in 1 Peter and maybe in the New Testament.[385] Some of the questions raised by this verse include: Where did Jesus go? Who are the

---

[381] Michaels, *1 Peter*, 204–5.

[382] Wallace, *Greek Grammar beyond the Basics*, 144.

[383] Donelson, *I & II Peter and Jude*, 111.

[384] Important academic studies of this verse include Dalton, *Christ's Proclamation to the Spirits*; Reicke, *The Disobedient Spirits and Christian Baptism*.

[385] Martin Luther himself describes the text as "strange" and "obscure" and says "I do not certainly know what St. Peter means" (*The Epistles of St. Peter and St. Jude Preached and Explained*, trans. E. H. Gillett (New York: Randolph, 1859). E-book: www.gutenberg.org/files/29678/29678-h/29678-h.htm, accessed September 2020).

imprisoned spirits to whom he spoke? What was the message that he brought? And, what is the background behind this verse? As with all letters, the author assumes that those who first heard this text would have had background knowledge that enabled them to make sense of this intriguing passage. Part of our work is to recover literary and historical backgrounds that are no longer as familiar to us as they were to the readers of the first century and then to suggest a plausible interpretation of this verse.

Here, we can be guided by a chart of the major options that have been proposed from the early days of the church until now. This chart is not comprehensive but should help readers see clearly the choices that have been made over the centuries. The three numbered segments present three major proposals, and the letters denote divisions within each of those proposals.

(1) *Christ's soul proclaims to the souls of Noah's contemporaries*
    (A). Christ's soul preached to the spirits to convert/save them
    (B) Christ's soul brought good tidings only to those converted prior to death
    (C) Christ's soul proclaimed condemnation to the souls of Noah's contemporaries
(2) *The preexistent Christ proclaimed through Noah to Noah's living contemporaries*
(3) *The spirits are fallen angels to whom Christ proclaimed his definitive victory*
    (A) Christ made this proclamation during his *descensus*
    (B) Christ made this proclamation at/during his ascension, and the prison is in the lower heavens or air[386]

Verse 19 begins with the words "in which" (ἐν ᾧ). These can either refer back to "the spirit" at the end of v. 18 (NRSV, ESV), or they can be used as a conjunction that joins the previous clause to the next with a translation such as "after" (NIV) or "so, thus" (NLT). Some English translations that choose "which" understand it as an instrumental dative and give the sense "by the Spirit he went" (CEB) meaning that the Holy Spirit enabled Jesus to

---

[386] This chart is drawn from information presented in Dalton, *Christ's Proclamation to the Spirits*, 15–41.

go and preach, either in the intermediate time and state between his death and resurrection or after his resurrection. Other English translations leave the meaning more ambiguous with "in which" most likely referencing the mode or sphere in which the preaching was accomplished. In this case it refers either to life enabled by the Spirit or the resurrected life in the Spirit. In the comments on v. 18 this commentary argued that Christ being put to death and made alive is a reference to his death and resurrection, and so this commentary argues that Christ went to the imprisoned spirits in his glorified state and not as a disembodied "soul" in the time between his death and resurrection. In light of that, this verse is a continuation of the movement that began in v. 18 with suffering, death, and resurrection, and which now begins to proceed towards the ascension of v. 22.

The language used in this text to describe Jesus' "going" is neither the explicit language of descent (to hell) nor of ascent (to heaven). Rather, it is the simple word for "went" (*poreuomai*). The language of "going" does not indicate either the direction Christ went or where the prison is located. However, this identical word is used again in this long sentence in v. 22 where it is part of the phrase "went into heaven." From this, we may assert that between the resurrection and the ascension to the right side of God, Christ's journey takes him to a prison where he proclaims a message to imprisoned spirits. This leads us to three questions: Who are these spirits, where are they imprisoned, and what message was proclaimed? The answers to these questions draw on the literary background of 1 Peter and the historical and literary contexts of the first century.

Who are the spirits? "Spirits" either refers to human beings or to fallen angels. Verse 20 provides a particular context by introducing Noah into the sentence. The identity of the spirits is further clarified in v. 20 with the phrase "who in former times did not obey, when God waited patiently in the days of Noah." The story of Noah is recounted in Genesis 6–8. But it was also a popular story that was retold in other Jewish literature.[387] The context provided by the Noah story could point to the first understanding of the spirits as referring to the souls of people who lived at the time of Noah. These people rejected God and are now imprisoned as spirits in hell

---

[387] Richard Bauckham, *Jude & 2 Peter*, Word Biblical Commentary: 50, David Allan Hubbard and Glenn W Barker (eds.), (Waco, TX: Word Books, 1983), 251–52.

because of their disobedience.[388] In this view, Christ is understood as descending to the prison where the spirits of Noah's contemporaries are held during the time between Christ's death and resurrection. Within this view there is debate over whether Christ proclaimed the gospel and thus offered to those who rejected God an opportunity of salvation; whether he proclaimed the gospel only to those who had repented prior to their death thus eliminating the possibility of conversion after death; or whether he preached a message of final victory and condemnation of their evil. Clement of Alexandria (d. 215 CE) was the first known proponent of the view that 1 Peter 3:19 refers to the *descensus*, and it came to be the general view of the early church prior to Augustine. Out of that perspective some came to understand that Christ preached not only to the spirits from the days of Noah but also to all who were in hell. Cyril of Alexandria (d. 444 CE) writes, "Going in his soul, he preached to those who were in hell, appearing to them as one soul to other souls."[389] The view that Christ preached to all who were imprisoned in hell has found acceptance among some modern scholars as well.[390] While this view is well supported among early church fathers, it misunderstands the contrast between "flesh" and "spirit" in v. 18 as referring to Christ's body and soul rather than understanding them as modes or spheres of activity as this commentary has already argued. Once it is clear that the larger phrase of which these are a part is a reference to the death and resurrection, this view is no longer sustainable. While there are a variety of positions within this view about the nature of the message that Jesus proclaimed, it is not necessarily the case that the preaching that Christ made was an offer of salvation. In addition, the word "spirits" does not normally refer to human beings in the New Testament. However, there are examples of the word referring to angelic or demonic beings.[391]

---

[388] Wayne A. Grudem, *1 Peter*, Tyndale New Testament Commentaries (Nottingham, England: IVP Academic, 2009), 204–5; Goppelt, *A Commentary on I Peter*, 258; Feldmeier, *The First Letter of Peter*, 203–6.

[389] Bray and Oden, *James, 1–2 Peter, 1–3 John, Jude*, 107.

[390] Charles Bigg, *A Critical and Exegetical Commentary on the Epistles of St. Peter and St. Jude* (New York: C. Scribner's Sons, 1901), 162–63.

[391] Note that Hebrews 12:23 does use *pneumata* with the qualifier "righteous" to refer to humans. Meanwhile, Hebrews 1:14 identifies angels as spirits as does Revelation 1:4; 3:4; 4:5; 5:6; elsewhere, *pneumata* is used of evil spirits (see Matt 8:16; Luke 10:20). *pneumata*

The second major view was introduced by Augustine and has a long history of acceptance by scholars following him. Augustine argued that the preexistent Christ preached to Noah's contemporaries while they were alive through the person of Noah. Augustine did not believe that conversion was possible after death. If one understood 1 Peter 3:19 as referring to Christ preaching salvation to imprisoned souls, then it seemed that there was an opportunity for salvation after death. Dalton shows that Augustine's solution to this problem can be supported from 1 Peter itself, which recognizes that "Christ was active in former ages."[392] In addition, 2 Peter 2:5 identifies Noah as a "herald of righteousness," but it is not clear that 1 Peter 3:19 is referencing this tradition.[393] This view extends from Augustine through Aquinas up until the Reformation. Today very few scholars put forward this view; although, Grudem is an exception.[394] Most scholars do not see the verb "going" as descriptive of Christ's activity in the Old Testament. Nor is it clear from this view how "spirits in prison" can be a reference to human beings alive in the time of Noah.

The third major view is that the spirits are fallen angels. The background for this view is drawn from the description in Genesis 6:1–4 of the sons of God who took earthly wives and whose offspring are described as giants. This story, which occurs immediately prior to the story of Noah at the opening of Genesis 6–8, precedes the description of wickedness that brought forth the flood. In light of that, the episode of the relations between the sons of God and the daughters of men came to be seen as part of the wickedness that caused the flood. The story hinted at in Genesis 6:1–4 was expanded in Jewish tradition and literature, especially in the book of *1 Enoch*.[395] Thus, in this view, Genesis 6–8 is only one part of the background to this text and a more expansive understanding of this story is to be found in literature that was well known by Jews during the first century. One question that can be raised about this view is why no one in the early church proposed such a view. This view of the background and meaning of "spirits" has been expounded in depth by Dalton who draws on

far more frequently refers to evil beings than to angels in the New Testament literature. Achtemeier, *1 Peter*, 255.

[392] Dalton, *Christ's Proclamation to the Spirits*, 14.

[393] Bauckham, *Jude & 2 Peter*, 251.

[394] Grudem, *1 Peter*, 205.

[395] Beare, *The First Epistle of Peter: The Greek Text with Introduction and Notes*, 146.

his own research alongside work by Spitta from the late 1800s and Reicke and Selwyn in the middle of the twentieth century. It seems that very early in the life of the church, many of the apocryphal books such as *1 Enoch* fell out of favor as the church grew. In fact, *1 Enoch* has only been preserved fully in an Ethiopian dialect, although fragments of it have been found in Latin and Greek, including fragments found among the Dead Sea Scrolls. As these books quickly became unknown and as the early church fathers relied on theological interpretation, it can be argued that the background of 1 Peter 3:19 became obscured. In the late nineteenth century in the middle of a hermeneutic time period that placed a high value on history and literary backgrounds and alongside the discovery of new materials (Enoch was first translated into English in 1821), a new understanding that "spirits" refers to fallen angels came to predominate, and this view is now the most widely held among modern commentators on 1 Peter.[396]

In the view that the "spirits in prison" refers to fallen angels the argument is that Christ proclaims a message of victory. This brings us to yet another question posed by this verse. We have seen that commentators have suggested a variety of messages that may have been proclaimed: a message of salvation (whether to the souls of Noah's contemporaries, those of Noah's contemporaries who may have repented before death, or all those imprisoned in hell) or a message of victory / condemnation in which the finality of Christ's triumph over evil is made known. The verb used here is *kērussō*, which is used to describe public announcements and proclamations and also means to "preach" or "proclaim." In other words, Christ is not described as preaching the good news (*euangelizō*) but as making a proclamation or announcement (*kērussō*). The verb *kērussō* does not in and of itself indicate the content of Christ's message. Some, particularly those who hold to the view of Christ's descent into hell, have argued that Christ's message was an invitation to hear the good news and repent. They point to the association of *kērussō* with the proclamation of the gospel elsewhere in the New Testament.[397] And, those who interpret 4:1–6 in a parallel fashion to 3:18–22 argue that the phrase "the gospel

---

[396] Achtemeier, *1 Peter*, 255; Elliott, *1 Peter*, 661; Peter H. Davids, *The First Epistle of Peter*, The New International Commentary on the New Testament (Grand Rapids, MI: Eerdmans, 1998), 140; Jobes, *1 Peter*, 245; Michaels, *1 Peter*, 208. Michaels argues that the spirits are the offspring of the fallen angels and not the fallen angels themselves.

[397] Goppelt, *A Commentary on I Peter*, 257.

was proclaimed to the dead" in 4:6 provides the background to understand 3:19 as also being a proclamation of salvation to dead humans.[398] Others have argued that Christ's message was a kingly message of triumph over the powers of evil, sin, and suffering and the announcement of his resurrection from the dead. This latter position is supported by the idea that the word used to describe Christ's message was "proclamation" and by the idea that those who hear the preaching are spirits (e.g., fallen angels) and thus beings to whom the biblical text does not offer the good news of salvation.[399] Selwyn writes: "Christ's work of redemption was achieved: it still needed to be proclaimed, even to the disobedient angels who could not, in the ordinary sense of the term, repent, but who could be brought into subjection (cf. verse 22)."[400] Further, the greater context of suffering argues for a message of triumph over enemies rather than evangelization of those who have failed to trust Christ in this life.

Finally, the last question to consider in relationship to 1 Peter 3:19 is the location of the prison. Those who understand this verse as describing the descent of Christ to preach to the dead understand the prison as either hell or Hades or "the place of the dead."[401] Those who ascribe to the position that this text is about imprisoned fallen angels also point to a tradition of imprisonment but indicate that the location of the prison is unspecified. The word "prison," which, as Dalton notes, refers to "being kept in custody, as prisoners awaiting trial" does not demand a particular location.[402] And the text itself does not directly indicate the location of the prison. Others have argued that the prison is "in the air" on the basis that Christ goes there during his ascent into heaven (v. 22).[403] Some who understand spirits as fallen angels see the prison as located in the lower reaches of heaven since heaven in the first century was understood as a

---

[398] Goppelt, *A Commentary on I Peter*, 259.

[399] Although Dalton notes that some liberal Protestants argue that the salvation proclaimed by Christ extends even to the fallen angels. Dalton, *Christ's Proclamation to the Spirits*, 37.

[400] Selwyn, *First Epistle of St. Peter*, 200.

[401] Dalton, *Christ's Proclamation to the Spirits*, 16–17.

[402] Dalton, *Christ's Proclamation to the Spirits*, 157–58. According to Dalton, prisons were a place to await judgement. "Modern prison sentences, where the chief punishment is the actual detention, were unknown" (158).

[403] Elliott, *1 Peter*, 655.

tiered space.[404] In this view, Christ proclaims his ultimate triumph over the fallen angels as part of his ascent into heaven (3:22). Finally, Michaels puts forth an unusual proposal. He understands the "spirits" to be the offspring of fallen angels (e.g., demons) and assumes that the audience of 1 Peter would associate the spirits with "the unclean spirits very much alive and at work in their world."[405] He then adds, "The point is simply that Christ went and announced his sovereignty to these spirits *wherever they might be*, in every place where they thought they were secure against their ancient divine Enemy."[406]

These spirits were kept in prison because they disobeyed (**v. 20**). This is the third time the verb "disobey" occurs in 1 Peter. In 2:8 those who do not believe stumble against the rock of offense because they disobey. Disobedience is directly connected to disbelief in or distrust of God and God's son Jesus Christ (2:6–7). In 3:1, the wives addressed are those who are married to husbands who disobey the word. The word is already associated with God, his enduring message, and the good news (1:23–25), so that disobedience in 2:8; 3:1; and 3:20 is a rejection of God's message and instruction and pursuit of one's own course over God's way. These spirits disobeyed in the time of Noah when God waited patiently. The story of Noah seems to have been fairly well known in Asia Minor by both Jews and Gentiles. Literary works like the *Sibylline Oracles* written in the first century include references to Noah.[407] And artifacts like coins from 193–253 CE portray Noah and his wife on one side and the ruling Roman emperor on the other, indicating a familiarity with the story of Noah.[408] With the short phrase "during the building of the ark" Peter alludes to the stretch of time between God's choosing of Noah and the flood. Many Jewish sources argued that this space of time may have been as long as 120 years and was a gift from God that was provided to give that generation time to repent.[409] First Peter then draws the audience's attention to the few who were saved, eight people (Noah and his wife, Noah's three sons and

---

[404] Elliott, *1 Peter*, 655.

[405] Michaels, *1 Peter*, 210.

[406] Michaels, *1 Peter*, 210.

[407] Jobes, *1 Peter*, 246.

[408] Jobes, *1 Peter*, 245; Paul R. Trebilco, *Jewish Communities in Asia Minor* (Cambridge: Cambridge University Press, 2006), 86–88.

[409] Katie Marcar, "In the days of Noah: Urzeit/Endzeit correspondence and the flood tradition in 1 Peter 3–4," *NTS* 63:4 (2017): 564.

their wives, Gen. 7:7) and indicates that they were saved by being able to pass through the waters of the flood. In the context of 1 Peter, this emphasis on the few who were saved may speak to the audience of exiles and aliens, those small groups scattered and dispersed across the communities of Asia Minor. The Old Testament story of Noah points to a man of integrity who lived rightly in relationship to God and others (Gen. 6:8–9). This may remind us of the righteousness of Christ already pointed out in 3:18.[410] God's seeing of the righteous is also reminiscent of Psalm 34/1 Peter 3:12 and the assertion that "the eyes of the Lord are on the righteous." Peter has focused on right behavior before God throughout his letter, and here he draws on the example of a man who heard the word of God, acted on it, and lived with integrity. In contrast, the great majority of people in the days of Noah were filling their world with evil and violence (Gen. 6:5–12), which may anticipate the sins of 1 Peter 4:3.[411] This man and his family experienced salvation from destruction by being carried on a boat through the flood. The verb "saved" is passive. It was not water that saved them; rather, they were saved by God's intervention. They passed through the water that had the potential to destroy them.[412] Noah and his deliverance from the flood is a message of encouragement to a group who also find themselves challenged to live rightly in a world that opposes and oppresses them.[413]

Peter now correlates this experience of being saved by passing through the waters of the flood to the Christian experience of baptism. These two events stand in a typological relationship to one another (NRSV: "prefigured"), so that the event in which God saves Noah from destruction

---

[410] Marcar, "In the days of Noah," 557.

[411] Marcar, "In the days of Noah," 559.

[412] There is debate about whether the water is the *instrument* of salvation, meaning the thing that carried them and brought about their salvation, or whether the water is the *location* of their salvation. Since Augustine, some have noted that the water of the flood was both the means of destruction for those who did not believe and the instrument of salvation for those in the ark (e.g., Jobes, *1 Peter*, 252.) While Jobes argues for the instrumental meaning "by water," the Greek preposition *dia* can have either meaning. In light of the ark and the passive verb, the locative meaning "through water" is more persuasive.

[413] The story of Noah immediately follows the story of the "sons of God" in Genesis 6. There is a long history of these two stories being treated together, and this may help to explain the interweaving of traditions preserved in *1 Enoch* and the story of Noah. Elliott, *1 Peter*, 697–705.

corresponds to the saving activity of God through baptism. The earlier activity of God is a symbol of the activity God is doing now, and is a similar type of deed. The use of an explicit analogy and the introduction of baptism "catches the readers' attention by including them in the analogy, and using it to exhort them and to encourage them."[414] The phrase "baptism . . . saves you" is unique in the New Testament. Many of the early church fathers saw the ark as a type for the church. In the same way that the ark was the place where Noah's salvation took place, so too, the church is the location in which saving baptism takes place.[415] Modern commentators have moved away from this typological understanding of the ark and the church and instead see the correspondence between vv. 20 and 21 in the saving activity of God. The means by which baptism saves is expressed at the end of the verse. It is "through the resurrection of Jesus Christ." We have already seen that the recipients of 1 Peter have entered into new birth "through the resurrection of Jesus Christ" (1:3). Baptism alone does not save but rather is joined with the power of God demonstrated in the raising of Christ from the dead. However, since baptism is a ritual of initiation into the household of God, the role of the church as the location in which baptism takes place can be assumed even though it is not explicitly stated.

In the middle of the verse is an aside that uses contrast to further define what baptism is: "not as a removal of dirt from the body, but as an appeal to God for a good conscience." Both pieces of this contrast present challenges to the interpreter. The first part of the contrast uses the words "flesh" (*sarx*, NRSV: "body"), "putting off" (*apotheosis*, NRSV: "removal"), and "dirt, filth" (*rhupos*, NRSV: "dirt"). Each of these words presents challenges to the interpreter. "Flesh" can simply refer to the physical body as in the NRSV but elsewhere in the New Testament can refer to humanity in its "weakness and misery."[416] The word *apotheosis* only occurs twice in the New Testament (here and 2 Pet. 1:14), but the cognate verb occurs about ten times including in 1 Peter 2:1: "rid yourselves of" a list of vices.

---

[414] Cynthia Long Westfall, "The relationship between the Resurrection, the proclamation to the spirits in prison and baptismal regeneration: 1 Peter 3:19–22," in Stanley E. Porter, Michael A. Hayes, and David Tombs (eds.), *Resurrection*, Journal for the Study of the New Testament Supplement Series: 186 (Sheffield: Sheffield Academic Press, 1999), 116.

[415] Jonathan P. Yates, "Salvation through water?: 1 Peter 3:20–21 in the ancient Latin tradition," *Worship* 92 (2018): 498.

[416] Dalton, *Christ's Proclamation to the Spirits*, 216.

Similarly, the word "dirt" (*rhupos*) occurs only here in the New Testament. It is used four times in the LXX and at least three of those passages refer to moral filth (Job 11:15; 14:4; Isa. 4:4). In light of this, some have suggested that the opening phrase of the contrast in 1 Peter refers to a moral cleansing so that "putting away/off the filth of the flesh" reflects putting aside the "'impulses' that governed the lives of his readers before they believed in Christ (cf. 1:14; 2:11 . . .). The 'removal of the filth of the flesh' is . . . a spiritual cleansing, and Peter's point is not that such cleansing is an unimportant or unnecessary thing, only that baptism is not it."[417] However, many commentators reject this view arguing that baptism does relate to purification and that the negation of "putting off the filth of the flesh" argues against this understanding of the phrase. Others have suggested that the phrase "not as a putting off of the filth of the flesh" could refer to the rite of circumcision. This interpretation relies on an understanding of Colossians 2:11 in which "putting off the body of the flesh" refers to circumcision.[418] However, both the broader context of Colossians and the vocabulary of that particular verse are different from the vocabulary in 1 Peter. If this referred to circumcision, Peter would be indicating that baptism is not merely an external rite associated with one's former life.[419] Many commentators and translations (NRSV, NIV, ESV, NASB, and CEB) understand the phrase in 1 Peter to refer to external purification of the body.[420] The contrast is between external cleaning and the internal conscience.[421]

The second part of the contrast is the Greek phrase *suneidēseōs agathēs eperōtēma eis theon* which can be translated in several different ways: either as "an appeal to God for a good conscience" (NRSV, NASB, ESV), or "the pledge of a clear conscience toward God" (NIV, NET), or "the pledge from a good conscience to God."[422] Like the first phrase in our

---

[417] Michaels, *1 Peter*, 216.

[418] Dalton, *Christ's Proclamation to the Spirits*, 217.

[419] Achtemeier, *1 Peter*, 269 but he indicates that such a meaning is far from certain. And Elliott rejects this meaning as too far of a stretch to be understood by the audience of 1 Peter; Elliott, *1 Peter*, 679.

[420] Goppelt, *A Commentary on I Peter*, 268.

[421] Elliott, *1 Peter*, 679.

[422] Davids, *The First Epistle of Peter*, 144–45. See also the marginal note in the NRSV which reads: "Or, 'a pledge to God from'" a good conscience. The differences in translation arise from questions about what type of genitive *suneidēseōs* ("conscience") is. "If objective, then it would refer to the pledge of a Christian to maintain a good conscience, but if subjective, it would be the good conscience from which a Christian

contrast, this phrase also contains a word that is used only here in the New Testament, *eperōtēma*, which has been translated in a wide variety of ways including: "appeal," "request," or "pledge." In the Greco-Roman literature, it can mean "inquiry," and some have extrapolated from this meaning to suggest the meaning "request."[423] The request that is being made is directed towards God and is a plea for a good conscience. While this is a possible meaning, it does not seem to make sense as a definition of baptism. Instead, the meaning of "pledge" is attested both in the interpretations of the early church and in contemporary commentaries.[424] This meaning is found both in contractual Greco-Roman literature and in the early church, where it is associated with confession.[425] Some have understood the content of the pledge as a commitment to maintain a good conscience.[426] But the most recent work shows that the early church understood the pledge as a commitment to the faith, a confession made from the good conscience of the one undertaking it.[427] Since this description of baptism takes place within a context containing creedal elements relating to the death, resurrection, and ascension of Christ, the content of the pledge may not need to be explicitly identified. This is especially true if some type of baptismal rite that included confession of one's relationship with God already existed in the earliest churches.

A Closer Look: Baptism in the New Testament

Baptism was known and practiced from the very beginning of the church.[428] The word "baptism" means a dipping or washing and is often connected to the

makes a commitment to God in baptism," according to Matthew R. Crawford in "'Confessing God from a good conscience': 1 Peter 3:21 and early Christian baptismal theology," *JTS* 67 (2016): 26. In addition, the word *eperōtēma* can mean either "pledge" or "appeal." Decisions about the meanings of these words are based on the context of 1 Peter and the use of these words and constructions elsewhere in the New Testament and broader Greco-Roman literature.

[423] Stephen Geiger, "A word about baptism: Ἐπερώτημα in 1 Peter 3:21," *Wisconsin Lutheran Quarterly* 113 (2016): 207.

[424] Crawford, "Confessing God," 35.

[425] Crawford, "Confessing God," 25.

[426] Achtemeier, *1 Peter*, 272; Dubis, *1 Peter*, 126.

[427] Crawford, "Confessing God," 35–37.

[428] George R. Beasley-Murray, "Baptism," in Gerald F. Hawthorne, Ralph P. Martin, and Daniel G. Reid *Dictionary of Paul and His Letters* (eds.) (Downers Grove, IL: IVP, 1993), 60.

ceremonial use of water to renew or begin a relationship with God.[429] John the Baptist practiced this type of baptism which is described in the opening chapters of the Gospels. Those who come to him for baptism confess their sins and engage in repentance (Matt 3:6, 11). Luke characterized this as "a baptism of repentance for the forgiveness of sins" (3:3). Those who came to John the Baptist were Jews seeking to renew their relationship with God. Jesus did not baptize with water.[430] Instead, his ministry was focused on inviting repentance and teaching about the kingdom of God. At the end of Matthew, after the resurrection, Jesus appears to the disciples and charges them to go "and make disciples of all nations, baptizing them in the name of the Father and of the Son and of the Holy Spirit, and teaching them to obey everything that I have commanded you" (28:19–20). This commission to make disciples is characterized by two things: baptism and teaching. Baptism into the threefold name or (in Acts) into the name of Jesus involves participation and solidarity with God and an act of cleansing.[431]

In the book of Acts, baptism continues to be a sign of repentance and entry into the Christian community. On Pentecost those who heard Peter's sermon and asked how to respond were told, "Repent, and be baptized every one of you in the name of Jesus Christ so that your sins may be forgiven; and you will receive the gift of the Holy Spirit" (Acts 2:38). Elsewhere in Acts, as significant barriers to the growth of the church were overcome, baptism was a mark of inclusion in the community. The Ethiopian eunuch (Acts 8:36–38) and Cornelius and his household (Acts 10:47–48) are notable examples of the inclusion within the new community of God's people of the formerly excluded. In the Pauline letters, baptism is assumed among those to whom Paul writes,[432] so he can remind them that they are children of God through faith, and that those who were baptized into Christ are clothed with Christ (Gal. 3:26–27). The practice of baptism is joined in Pauline thought with faith and participation in Christ who is the true Lord.

---

[429] BAGD

[430] John 3:22 is the only indication that Jesus baptized disciples. It says that "Jesus and his disciples went into the Judean countryside, and he spent some time there with them and baptized." However, in John 4:1–2, when the disciples of John the Baptist report that "Jesus is making and baptizing more disciples than John," the narrator quickly inserts an aside that states "although it was not Jesus himself but his disciples who baptized." There are no other reported instances of Jesus or his disciples baptizing people during Jesus' earthly ministry. Most scholars think that either Jesus did not engage in baptism or that if he did it was only briefly during the opening days of his ministry.

[431] John Nolland, *The Gospel of Matthew: A Commentary on the Greek Text*, Accordance electronic., New International Greek Testament Commentary (Grand Rapids, MI: Eerdmans, 2005), 1269.

[432] Lars Hartman, "Baptism," in Freedman (ed.), *Anchor Bible Dictionary*, 587.

First Peter's reference to baptism in a set of materials drawn from the traditions of the early church is not surprising since baptism was an integral part of the church from its inception. Baptism was an outward sign of repentance and faith in Jesus. Through immersion (the most well attested form of baptism in the New Testament) a person was cleansed and initiated into God's household. "Baptism was the public celebration of both a personal transformation and a social transition."[433]

The final verse (**v. 22**) in this long sentence announces Jesus' ascension into heaven and his position at the right hand of God where all angels, authorities, and powers are subject to him. The sentence that began with suffering for sin ends with Christ's triumphant reign alongside God. The very same participle (*poreutheis*) that was used to describe Christ's journey to the prison of the unbelieving spirits is here used to describe his journey into heaven. In both cases, the verb itself does not tell us about where he went or even how he went but rather our understanding of the direction of his journey is determined by the destination we are told about. Here, the destination is heaven, the place where God dwells and where the will of God is perfectly fulfilled. And Jesus is described as being on the right of God, a common description of a place of honor and power alongside the ruler. Jesus takes his place in the presence of God, reigning alongside God, and in that position there are three groups that explicitly submit to him. First Peter 2:13 began with the instruction to submit to every human authority and the household code continued with descriptions of what submission looks like for slaves and wives, but now our author makes clear that Christ reigns and that angels, authorities, and powers submit to him. Most commentators understand this triplet of beings as the enemies of God who seek to harm or destroy.[434] It is possible for "angels" to refer to either good or fallen angels and for that reason Michaels makes clear that all supernatural beings and powers are subject to Christ.[435] Peter's audience is assured that these powers are now subject to Christ even if that subjection is still hidden.[436] Christ's victory over enemies is assured.

---

[433] Elliott, *1 Peter*, 673.

[434] Achtemeier, *1 Peter*, 274; Davids, *The First Epistle of Peter*, 146; Elliott, *1 Peter*, 688–89; Keener, *1 Peter*, 289.

[435] Michaels, *1 Peter*, 220.

[436] Goppelt, *A Commentary on I Peter*, 272.

Verses 18–22 in the wider context of what has come before (3:13–17) are both an affirmation of the work accomplished by Jesus Christ in his death, resurrection, and ascension as well as a reminder that the Lord knows what it is to suffer (3:18). The audience to whom 1 Peter is addressed may experience suffering on account of their faith (3:13–17), but such suffering is not unfamiliar to the one they follow, Jesus Christ. However, Christ's suffering is of a different kind than theirs, for his suffering has the capacity to deal with sin. And while Christ died, he has also been raised from death, and in the resurrected body he proclaims a message of triumph over those spirits who disbelieved the message of God. Those who suffer are reminded of Noah, a man in right relationship with God who acted on the word of God to build an ark and was saved from the destroying flood. The audience is invited to understand that they too are saved through the resurrection of Jesus; their salvation is now marked by another watery reality – baptism. Those who suffer belong to one who has suffered and died, was buried, and rose again, and who has ascended into heaven where he reigns at the side of God. This is a message of solidarity and encouragement for a group that finds itself assailed by suffering on account of their relationship with God. This is also a message of suffering that addresses sin, of triumph over those who resist the true message of God, and of the reign of Christ now revealed. It is this message that the Christians offer with gentleness and courage to those who ask about the hope of those who suffer for their faith in this life (3:15).

Bridging the Horizons: Christians around the world continue to suffer for their faith. Some suffer imprisonment, physical abuse, and even death because of their allegiance to Jesus Christ and their alignment with the church. Others suffer by being excluded from social advancement and acceptance in societies that actively reject Christian faith and identity. For these Christians, 1 Peter is a word of encouragement that reminds them that they are not alone in their suffering and that the one to whom they have given their allegiance has also suffered. At the same time, they are reminded that Jesus' death has vindicated his position as the Son of God and enabled him to ascend to the realm of God where he now reigns. This is also an encouragement, as it has been for many communities over the centuries, that despite the suffering that is experienced now, God is ultimately in control.

At the same time, this message continues to offer a word of hope to those who have the ears to hear. The good news that sin has been addressed through Christ's suffering on the cross is announced. The triumphal reign of Christ over all the powers of this world and the supernatural world is proclaimed. Here we see both the triumph of God that is part of the apocalyptic worldview being proclaimed alongside the language of righteousness drawn from the domain of the law courts. We see that God's ability to make things right through Jesus Christ is connected both to the individual who participates in salvation through baptism and to the enemies of God who would reject and resist the work of God. Righteousness and rule work together to demonstrate the power of the suffering Christ to redeem the world.

Taking up the pledge made in baptism must come from a clear conscience before God. Throughout 1 Peter, salvation and ethics are intertwined. Those who have received the righteousness of Christ must seek to be people of righteousness with a clear conscience before God. They must be willing to suffer for the faith while also witnessing, when asked, to the God who has dealt with sin through the suffering and death of Jesus. Jesus has triumphed over the powers that would seek to usurp the place of God. And Jesus reigns with God. In light of this message, all Christians should seek to do what is right in the sight of God so that those around them may truly see God and give God glory when the fullness of his reign is revealed.

[1] Since therefore Christ suffered in the flesh, arm yourselves also with the same intention (for whoever has suffered in the flesh has finished with sin),

[2] so as to live for the rest of your earthly life no longer by human desires but by the will of God.

[3] You have already spent enough time in doing what the Gentiles like to do, living in licentiousness, passions, drunkenness, revels, carousing, and lawless idolatry.

[4] They are surprised that you no longer join them in the same excesses of dissipation, and so they blaspheme.

[5] But they will have to give an accounting to him who stands ready to judge the living and the dead.

[6] For this is the reason the gospel was proclaimed even to the dead, so that, though they had been judged in the flesh as everyone is judged, they might live in the spirit as God does.

After ending on a note of triumph, Peter returns in chapter 4 to the theme of suffering, picking up on the language of 3:18 – "Christ also suffered for sins." But now 1 Peter begins to draw out the implications for believers of taking on the same understanding of suffering that Christ had. Such a mindset only makes sense when believers are rightly oriented to time and understand that earthly time is short (4:3) and that God's judgment is a reality for all (4:5). Such an understanding of time allows believers to live faithfully in a hostile society.

Following the portrayal of Christ's reign in 3:22, our author returns to Christ's bodily suffering. Some of the ancient New Testament manuscripts add "for us" or "for you," which points back to the descriptions of Christ "bearing our sins" (2:24) and to Christ "suffering for sins" (3:18). These early additions in the manuscript tradition point to the scribal understanding that Christ's physical suffering was not simply a historical fact but was beneficial for believers.[437] Now, 1 Peter draws out a specific application of that suffering to the lives of those who have been brought into the presence of God through the suffering of Christ (3:18). Peter exhorts them to arm themselves with the same intention. Like some other metaphors in 1 Peter, the metaphor here draws from the military domain of preparing for war.[438] In 1:13, the audience was instructed to "gird up" their minds, using a deliberate metaphor associated with pulling up the tunic between one's legs in order to be free to move quickly and decisively. Now, they are encouraged to arm themselves. In 1 Peter, both metaphors are connected to the preparation of the mind for the challenge that lies ahead and indicate the need to be ready. They are to arm themselves with the same "intention." The word *ennoian* generally refers to "thought," "knowledge," or "insight"[439] and is used only here in the New Testament. It is found in multiple verses in Proverbs where it often refers to "discernment" (e.g., Prov. 1:4; 3:21). Following this trajectory some commentators point to "understanding" or "counsel" as the meaning here.[440] The content of the thought is acceptance of "the dying life."[441] Or, as Goppelt says, "What comes from Christ's whole path of blessing is the *understanding* that the flesh must be handed over to suffering unto death so that it may come to a life 'according to the Spirit' (3:18;4:6)."[442] But in the context of 1 Peter *ennoian* is probably best understood as a way of thinking, a disposition, or attitude (NRSV: "intention") that Christ had in the face of suffering,

---

[437] The reading "suffering" without the prepositional additions best explains how the other readings arose: Metzger, *Textual Commentary*, 624.

[438] BAGD

[439] BAGD

[440] Selwyn, *First Epistle of St. Peter*, 208; Goppelt, *A Commentary on I Peter*, 279.

[441] Selwyn, *First Epistle of St. Peter*, 208.

[442] Goppelt, *A Commentary on I Peter*, 279. Emphasis added.

similar to the kind of wise discernment we see in Proverbs.[443] In 2:22–23 we see this intention or disposition lived out. Christ did not sin nor resort to slander, deceit, or abuse when faced with suffering. In a similar way, Christians who suffer on account of their faith are to arm themselves with the same intent to live rightly in both speech and action even in the face of suffering.[444]

In the first part of v. 1, the author names Christ's suffering and encourages the audience to share Christ's purpose. But the next phrase presents a conundrum, which we can explore by comparing the NRSV, NASB, and NJB renderings of the Greek text.

NASB: "because he who has suffered in the flesh has ceased from sin"
NRSV: "for whoever has suffered in the flesh has finished with sin"
NJB: "that anyone who has undergone bodily suffering has broken with sin."

The first issue that presents itself is the translation of *hoti* as either a reason for what has come before (NASB, NRSV, "because," "for")[445] or as a clause expressing the content of the understanding or intention with which believers are to arm themselves (NJB, "that").[446] Both understandings are grammatically possible and difficult to choose between and ultimately the decision must be made based on the context. While *hoti* is used most frequently with the sense of "because" in 1 Peter there are at least two examples (1:12, 18) where it is used to express content (e.g., the content of the revelation in 1:12 and the content of what is known in 1:19). If *hoti* means "that," then it must refer to a thought that is shared between both Christ and believers. Many who reject the meaning "that" and lean towards "because" do so because they do not see the meaning of the phrase "he/whoever suffered in the flesh has finished with sin" as a thought shared by both Christ and believers. Instead, the argument from the context is that the *hoti* clause provides a further reason for believers to arm themselves.

Comparing the translations above shows that the next word is either "he" (NASB) or "whoever/anyone" (NRSV, NJB). The masculine singular

---

[443]   Davids, *The First Epistle of Peter*, 148.
[444]   Forbes, *1 Peter*, 136; Michaels, *1 Peter*, 225.
[445]   Goppelt, *A Commentary on I Peter*, 280; Michaels, *1 Peter*, 226.
[446]   Donald Senior and Daniel J. Harrington, *1 Peter, Jude and 2 Peter*, Sacra Pagina Series (Collegeville, MN: Liturgical Press, 2008), 113; Achtemeier, *1 Peter*, 278; Davids, *The First Epistle of Peter*, 148.

participle either refers to Christ ("he") or to an individual Christian ("whoever/anyone"). If it refers to the individual Christian, in what way might Christians be said to cease from (be finished with) sin because of their physical suffering? On the other hand, if it refers to Christ, in what way can we say that Christ ceased from sin if Christ is perfect? Either interpretation presents a puzzle.

One of the main objections to understanding the phrase "he who has suffered in the flesh has finished with sin" as referring to Christ derives from 1 Peter's repeated emphasis on Christ's sinless nature (1:19; 2:22). This makes it difficult to see Peter now suggesting that Christ has ceased from sin, implying that at one time he was sinning. However, there is certainly an echo from 2:21, 3:18, and the opening of 4:1 in the phrase "the one who suffered" that points directly to Christ as the subject of the clause. Michaels makes an extended argument for Christ as the subject by indicating that "in Greek usage the verb *pauesthai* could imply a contrast not only to one's own previous activity or behavior, but to a whole sphere of reality in which one had previously existed and by which one had been affected."[447] In other words, it was not that Christ was a sinner but that as a fully human person he lived in a sinful context and suffered from the sin around him both before he was crucified and on the cross. In that context, "ceasing from sin" would mean that his physical suffering due to sin had come to an end.[448]

However, many commentators understand this phrase as referring to the individual Christian.[449] The main verb in 4:1 is the imperative "arm yourselves." Since Peter has already begun an exhortation to his audience that will continue in 4:2, an argument from the context is that it is likely that this phrase describes Christians who have suffered rather than referring back to Christ.[450] Throughout 1 Peter Christians are invited to imitate Christ. In 2:4–5 Christ is the living stone and Christians are also living stones who are built into God's dwelling place. In 2:21 they are reminded that Christ sets an example for them of how to face suffering while living in the world. And now, in 4:1, Christians are invited to follow Christ's sinless

447   Michaels, *1 Peter*, 227, following A. Strobel, "Macht Leiden von Sünde frei? Zur Problematik von 1. Petr. 4,1f." *Theologische Zeitschrift* 19:6 (1963): 412–25.
448   Michaels, *1 Peter*, 227.
449   Elliott, *1 Peter*, 714; Feldmeier, *The First Letter of Peter*, 212.
450   Jobes, *1 Peter*, 263–64.

way of life in the midst of suffering. Since Christ suffered, and through his suffering and death Christ dealt with sin (3:18), Christians can also arm themselves with the same intention or resolve that Christ had to live without sin in the face of suffering. It is important to remember that Christ was fully human and faced the same temptations to sin that all humans face. Christ's sinlessness was not simply an aspect of his divine nature but was also an aspect of his righteous living as a human being in perfect relationship with the Father. Beare indicates that the Christian takes on "a mental concept of himself as 'crucified with Christ' – as having made an end, in imagination and thought, of the life of the flesh, and having begun to value the life of the spirit, the new life which is lived in and with Christ, as the only true life."[451]

But what does it mean that someone who has suffered in the flesh has ceased from sin? Achtemeier provides three possible understandings of this phrase: "(a) proverbial (Jewish) thought on the value of suffering, (b) a reflection of the Pauline idea of dying with Christ in baptism and thus dying to the power of sin,[452] or (c) a construct by which the author intended to link the Christian's suffering to that of Christ since both are in a way accomplishing God's will."[453] Achtemeier rightly shows that the proverbial context is limited to Jewish martyrdom and is most likely not applicable to this epistle and that "suffering" in 1 Peter is not the same as "dying" in Paul. However, 1 Peter does argue for imitation of Christ and the phrase is best understood in that way.[454] Davids more explicitly argues that "when a person suffers, he breaks the power of sin . . . over his life or atones for the sin in his life." This happens through Christ's suffering in which Christ shows that he is through with sin.[455] Here, sin, as elsewhere in 1 Peter refers to concrete actions or thoughts and not to sin as a power or force.[456] Those who have ceased from sin are those who pursue God's

---

[451] Beare, *The First Epistle of Peter: The Greek Text with Introduction and Notes*, 153.

[452] Also Feldmeier, *The First Letter of Peter*, 212.

[453] Achtemeier, *1 Peter*, 279.

[454] "[T]he point is analogous: Christ suffered due to sins even though the sins were not his own, while 'in the flesh' and in his resurrected state he no longer does. So Christians suffer now, but can do so in confidence that after their death they will no longer suffer due to sins, theirs, or anyone else's (e.g., their persecutors')," Davids, *The First Epistle of Peter*, 149.

[455] Davids, *The First Epistle of Peter*, 148–49.

[456] Contra Senior and Harrington, *1 Peter*, 114.

righteousness made available to them through the suffering of Christ (2:24). It is possible that the one who has suffered on account of faith in Jesus Christ and right behavior (good works) based on that faith is one who has turned aside from sins that would have led to evil behavior rather than good behavior. That person may have turned aside from inability to maintain allegiance to Christ in the face of social pressure and even abuse (see further on 4:3–4).[457] This is a practical demonstration of the holiness by which they have been identified earlier in the book (1:2) and of the holiness to which they have been called in response to the new birth they have received (1:15–16). Living out the holy lives that God calls them to may involve suffering and certainly does not promise wealth or status or any of the other means of security valued by those outside of Christ.

The purpose of arming oneself with the same intention as Christ is to live the rest of one's life guided by the will of God rather than by human desires (**v. 2**). The choice is between human desires that have already been described as springing from a former life in which they were ignorant of Jesus Christ and had not yet experienced new birth (1:14). These human desires wage war against Christians and seek to destroy them (2:12). Instead, people are to choose God's will. The will of God is first character-ized in 1 Peter as seeking to do good in the context of the wider society (2:15) because Christians know that they belong to God (2:16). This choice to do what is right and good might involve suffering (3:17), but that does not place the Christian outside the will of God. Everyone has one earthly life. The choice is between living that life seeking to satisfy human desires or seeking to live rightly in accordance with God's will.

The human desires of v. 2 are characterized more explicitly in **v. 3**. When Peter writes, "You have already spent enough time in doing what the Gentiles like to do," there is a certain irony in the word "enough." Any time spent in the activities that follow is too much time spent in that way.[458] The life of Christians is divided into three time periods: the past, before Christ; the present remaining time of the earthly life; and the last time, the time of final judgment (anticipated in 4:5, 7).[459] Christians' current experience of earthly life is characterized as exile (1:1; 2:11), as

---

[457] Donelson, *I & II Peter and Jude*, 119; Jobes, *1 Peter*, 265.
[458] Michaels, *1 Peter*, 230.
[459] Bechtler, *Following in His Steps*, 132.

temporary, and as such it should be lived in light of both their current experience of redemption and of their future hope of receiving the fullness of their inheritance as children of God.[460] The choices one makes about ways of living and the desires that drive these reflect the will to which one is submitted: the will (*thelēma*) of God (4:2) or the will/intention (*boulēma*, NRSV: "like") of the Gentiles (4:3). Those who joined in the will of the Gentiles in the past participated in the parties, drinking, and idolatry described in the second part of the verse. Such activities were often associated with civic festivals, and in a culture that knew no separation of church and state, such civic festivals were also religious in nature. "While practices that often accompanied those festivals bordered on the profligate, a normal part of the festival included fealty to the local gods and to the Roman emperor as the embodiment of the advantages conferred by Roman culture. Such activity could only appear as idolatry to the Christians, and as a result, they would not participate in many forms of these public festivities."[461]

Many commentators have argued that Jews are a distinctive people group who would not participate in idolatrous activities and that thus the audience of 1 Peter should be understood as mainly Gentiles. But Jeffers argued that "Jews in the cities adapted their lives to the larger Gentile society to greater or lesser degrees. Some gave up their religious beliefs and practices entirely. We have examples of people with Jewish names making dedications to pagan gods."[462] And indeed one of the significant accusations of the Old Testament prophets against the people of God was that they had turned from God and taken up idolatry (e.g., 2 Chron. 33:7; Isa. 10:11; Ezek. 23:29). So it is possible that Jewish members of Peter's audience were living in ways associated with the nations around them. However, more detailed work by Barclay on Jews throughout the diaspora has shown that "the Jews' abstention from . . . 'idolatry', and their limited participation in the main currents of civic life, were their fundamental crimes in the eyes of the Greeks."[463] In a culture in which religion and civic life were intimately intertwined, the Jews' refusal to worship at

---

[460] Bechtler characterizes this time as a liminal state in which they are betwixt and between two other states of being, Bechtler, *Following in His Steps*, 126–35.

[461] Paul J. Achtemeier, "1 Peter 4:1–8," *Interpretation* 65 (2011): 65.

[462] Jeffers, *The Greco-Roman World of the New Testament Era*, 216.

[463] Barclay, *Jews in the Mediterranean diaspora*, 274.

the local temple or participate in the local festivals was an affront to those around them. Such refusal undermined the attempt to restore political fortunes by means of civic pride, patronage, and benefaction.[464] For this reason, the vast majority of contemporary commentators have identified the audience of 1 Peter as mainly Gentiles. However, it is clear that both Jews and Gentiles could have formerly participated in the list of human sinful desires cataloged in 4:3, but this list would have been the normal experience of Gentiles prior to conversion while it would have been seen by many Jews as being sinful and contrary to the covenant relationship God had established with them. Finally, we can note that all those who have been brought into the community of God's people are now contrasted with "the Gentiles." First Peter has no indication of tension between Jew and Gentile but instead sets up a contrast between the church (now, God's people) and Gentiles, all those outside of God's household.

Verse 3 lists six sins that can be broken up into three groups. Group one is living in licentiousness and passions, or a lack of self-constraint. Instead of self-restraint, people seek to fulfill whatever desire they have. This is a notable contrast from the disciplined and sober-minded life Christians are called to (1:13; 4:7). Group two involves drunkenness, revels, and carousing. These three sins are all related to the excessive fulfillment of desires. Revels and carousing in the first century referred to excessive feasting and drinking parties. Some drinking parties were philosophical gatherings for discussion, but the activity described here is about too much wine and too much food. The final sin is in a group of its own: idolatry. The Greek *athemitos* describes practices that tradition saw as improper or unseemly. While most Gentiles would have been fully embedded in pagan worship including the use of idols, both Judaism and Christianity maintained strict prohibitions against idolatry and saw participation in the worship of other

---

[464] "For civic communities struggling to revive their political fortunes, the presence of burgeoning sub-communities less than fully committed to the social and cultural life of the city was an irritant. Like larger-scale nationalism, civic pride can respond violently to the influence of 'aliens', when society itself suffers deprivation or decline. In the case of Asian cities, the Jews, scattered as they were in different locations, in which different issues arose at various times, were spared any major or concerted onslaught. But they had to contend with repeated violations of their 'rights', as time and again their communal institutions were challenged and their religious customs ignored. To this extent they were victims of the social, economic, and political pressures bearing upon the Greek cities in these decades," in Barclay, *Jews in the Mediterranean diaspora*, 274.

gods as an affront to the true God. Thus, in the list of sins it is the only one listed with its own adjective; this draws out the deeply problematic nature of idol worship. Many of the activities described in this verse take place in the temple precincts or during the religious celebrations that marked cultural life in the cities of Asia Minor. Both Judaism and Early Christianity rejected the worship of other gods. This meant that Jews who came to understand Jesus as God's anointed king, the Messiah, continued to worship God alone but oriented their worship through their understanding of Jesus Christ and the Holy Spirit. However, for most Gentiles worship of God alone would be a dramatic shift from their former understanding in which the world was populated by gods and divine beings. Scattered across Asia Minor were famous temples to various gods in the Greek and Roman pantheon. And, as the first century progressed, more and more temples were built to honor the family of Caesar. These temples and shrines were the center of social and religious life but were idolatrous in the eyes of the church.

Indeed, Peter says in **4:4**, "They are surprised that you no longer join them in the same excesses of dissipation." When the Christians in Asia Minor became part of God's people, a household with different allegiances than those they knew in the past, they became strange to their former friends and neighbors. The Greek word *suntrechō* means to run together. Peter writes that the former friends and neighbors are surprised the Christians are no longer hurrying towards the activities they had formerly engaged in, activities Peter identifies as a "wide stream of excess" (BAGD)[465] Of course, in their former lives they would not have seen themselves as running towards immoral behavior but as simply participating in normal cultural activities. The language of sin, immorality, and eager participation are Peter's critical description of their previous life.[466] Their former friends and neighbors expressed surprise that they stopped participating in the social gatherings and rituals that contributed to the political and cultural cohesion of society. Such surprise could lead to the kind of abuse, slander, and suffering that we have seen throughout 1 Peter, because participation in what Christians understood as idolatry was a way of showing allegiance to both the city and the empire. Failure to participate

[465] BAGD
[466] Michaels, *1 Peter*, 233.

marked one at best as willfully shirking civic responsibility and at worst as subverting or undermining the authority and structures of civil society. If calamity struck the city or region, those who failed to participate in civic-religious activities could become scapegoats for their failure to properly please the gods. "And so they [those who are surprised] blaspheme." When the speech of those who are surprised is directed against God, it is blasphemy. If it is directed against people, it is abuse. The word *blasphēmountes* can be translated either way here, but since this word has not previously been associated with verbal abuse in 1 Peter it is probably best understood as blaspheming God.[467] Some commentators have suggested that perhaps Peter views abuse against God's people as blasphemy of God as well.[468] In any case, those who are surprised and who speak against God and his people will have to give an account (**v. 5**) to God, the true and final judge. The emphasis is on "the retribution which awaits the unbelieving and hostile pagans at the coming judgment."[469] The scene is that of the final courtroom in which those who were arrayed against God must account for their words and deeds. The text does not specify who the judge is before whom account is given. However, 1 Peter 1:17 attests to God the Father as judge and 2:23 portrays Christ entrusting himself to God, the one who judges justly. Although Christ is portrayed in other New Testament writings as the judge of the living and the dead (Acts 10:42), in 1 Peter he is portrayed as the suffering servant risen and glorified by God but not as judge. Thus, it is best to understand God as judge in this portion of 1 Peter as well. God's righteous judgment extends to all humanity and encompasses the living and the dead.

In **v. 6** we come to another challenging verse. As we will see, none of the solutions available for understanding this verse are completely satisfying. Verse 6 begins with the phrase "for this is the reason," which shows that this verse is linked both backwards to v. 5's declaration of the judgment of humanity and forward to the purpose statement (*hina*) that emphasizes living in the Spirit. The verse continues, "the gospel was proclaimed even to the dead." This immediately raises the question "who are the dead?" The

---

[467] Forbes, *1 Peter*, 140.
[468] Michaels, *1 Peter*, 234.
[469] Dalton, *Christ's Proclamation to the Spirits*, 266.

answer needs to correspond to our understanding of "the dead" from the immediately preceding phrase "the living and the dead" that concludes v. 5.

Over the centuries, there have been three main ways to understand to whom "the dead" in v. 6 refers. First, it may refer to those who are spiritually dead. In other words, the good news is proclaimed on earth to those who have not yet awakened to the message of Christ. This was the position of many in the early church who commented on this passage.[470] However, the dead in v. 5 clearly refers to people who have physically died, and 1 Peter does not elsewhere characterize people who have not yet come to faith as dead. Instead, they are characterized as disobedient or disbelieving (2:7, 8; 3:1) or rejecting (4:5). Since v. 6 is directly linked to v. 5, the meaning of "the dead" cannot change so drastically from physically to spiritually dead without some sort of signal.

Second, "the dead" may refer to those who have died either without hearing or without believing the good news. The idea then is that the good news was proclaimed to all the human dead in Hades.[471] This view is often held by those who understand 3:18–19 as describing Christ's descent into hell. In this view, those who are dead hear the gospel and have a chance to repent. The proclamation of Christ to the spirits is now extended to include a proclaiming of the gospel to all the dead. Horrell argues "If, then, the point of the verse is primarily to support the statement in v. 5 – that God stands ready to judge the living and the dead – then the immediate context could just as well lead us to see v. 6 as a statement about the universal announcement of the gospel as to see it as a promise of vindication for dead Christians: God can justly judge all people, both the living and the dead, since the gospel has been announced to all, to the dead as well as to the living."[472] Some might object that both 3:19 and 4:6 use aorist

---

[470] "This view was first proposed by Clement of Alexandria (*Adum.* 4:6 . . .). It was adopted also by Cyril of Alexandria (cited with approval by Theophylact (PG [*Patrologia Graeca*] 125.1237, 1240), Augustine (*Ep. Eud.* 164.21; PL [*Patrologia Latina*] 33, 717–18), Bede (PL [*Patrologia Latina*] 93.6A), Erasmus, Luther, and others and has been defended more recently by Gschwind ([*Die Niederfahrt Christi in die Unterwelt: Ein Beitrag zur Exegese des Neuen Testaments und zur Geschichte des Taufsymbols*, Münster: Aschendorff] 1911, 24–40)." Elliott, *1 Peter*, 733.

[471] Green, *1 Peter*, 127–28; Goppelt, *A Commentary on I Peter*, 289; Reicke, *The Disobedient Spirits and Christian Baptism*, 206.

[472] David G Horrell, "Who are 'the dead' and when was the Gospel preached to them? The interpretation of 1 Pet 4.6," *NTS* 49 (2003): 78.

verbs, indicating that the preaching is complete and that therefore this cannot be a universal event; however, Goppelt replies to that criticism with the indication that 1 Peter presents a view of the proclamation of Christ and not a view of the time or order in which it happens.[473] There are two main arguments against the view that 4:6 refers to Christ's descent to hell and the proclamation of the good news to the universal dead. First, the language of vv. 18–19 is significantly different from 4:6. In 3:18–19 the characters are "disobedient spirits" and what Christ does is to "proclaim" (*kerygma*), but here the language refers to dead people and they have heard the good news. In addition, Christ is obviously doing the proclaiming in 3:19, but there is no clear indication of who preaches in 4:6. So, those who hear are different ("spirits," 3:19; "the dead," 4:6), the message may be different as well ("proclamation" vs "gospel"), and the identity of the preacher is clear in one instance (3:19) and unnamed in the other (4:6). A second argument against this view comes from the wider canon, which does not present the idea that the dead receive a second chance after death.

The third, and currently most widely accepted, view of "the dead" is that it refers to believers who heard the gospel while they were alive, but who have since died.[474] Arguments for this view are derived from the immediate context, from the purpose of 1 Peter, and from consideration of the question of what happens to Christians after death which is familiar from the wider canon (1 Thessalonians in particular). In the immediate context the Christians are instructed to arm themselves with the same attitude that Christ had towards suffering and sin and are encouraged to live in accordance with the will of God (4:1–2). Then they are reminded that they have taken up a new life, a life of which their former neighbors disapprove (4:3–4). Indeed, their former associates abuse them and reject the good news, but will have to give an account to the true judge (4:5). "[T]he principle thought of 4:5" is the "condemnation of the unbeliever and . . . vindication of the faithful Christian."[475] Thus, in the immediate context, "the thought of the writer goes back to the *Christian* dead whose fate needs to be vindicated against anti-Christian taunts."[476] This interpretation of the

---

[473] Goppelt, *A Commentary on I Peter*, 289.
[474] Achtemeier, "1 Peter 4:1–8," 78; Forbes, *1 Peter*, 142; Jobes, *1 Peter*, 270–72; Michaels, *1 Peter*, 237; Selwyn, *First Epistle of St. Peter*, 214.
[475] Dalton, *Christ's Proclamation to the Spirits*, 266.
[476] Dalton, *Christ's Proclamation to the Spirits*, 271.

phrase also demonstrates the kind of pastoral care and encouragement for which 1 Peter is known (5:12). And, it fits with the broader canonical witness about Christians who have died. First Thessalonians 4:13–17 describes Christians who have died using both the language of "falling asleep" (1 Thess. 4:13–14) as well as the language of death: "the dead" (1 Thess. 4:16). Some who argue for a late dating of 1 Peter think that the issue of what happens to the Christian dead is no longer pressing in the later church. However, those facing suffering and persecution may well wonder whether their faithfulness is in vain and 4:5–6 points to God as the ultimate judge who vindicates. Those who object to this view do so on two main grounds. First, they argue that if "the dead" in v. 5 is to be understood broadly, then it should be understood broadly in v. 6 as well and not limited to Christians. Second, they argue that Christ preaches the good news; however, the more likely rendering of the verb is "the good news about Christ was proclaimed."[477] The text does not indicate who does the proclaiming.

For those Christians who heard the gospel and who have since died, the purpose is that "though they had been judged in the flesh as everyone is judged, they might live in the spirit as God does." This last phrase of v. 6 draws out a series of contrasts that is highlighted in the chart below drawn from the Greek text. Note that like 3:18, where the same structure is used, the emphasis falls on the second half of the comparison.

On the one hand/Although	On the other hand/Nevertheless[478]
Judged	Live
According to humans	According to God
In the flesh	In the spirit

The subject of the verbs "judged" and "live" are "the dead," and we have argued that this refers to those who heard and responded to the gospel in this life and then died. In what respect are such Christians judged? There are two possible ways to understand being judged in the flesh according to humans. First, it can be understood as referring to the common experience of death that is undergone by all humanity. Death is itself the consequence and result of sin and thus is the judgment that humanity experiences as a

---

[477]   Achtemeier, *1 Peter*, 287.
[478]   Achtemeier, *1 Peter*, 287.

result. This is the direction that the NRSV takes with the phrase "judged ... as everyone is judged." However, a closer look at the two spheres (flesh and spirit) in which judging and living take place indicates that "in the flesh" refers to embodied life in this world and that "in the spirit" refers to embodied life in the resurrection (cf. 3:18). If these are the spheres in which judging and living take place, then the second option is to understand the judgment that takes place as judgment according to human standards. As 4:4 states, the human reaction to followers of Jesus is first surprise and then blasphemy and abuse. This is the human judgment that they experienced from their neighbors prior to death. The contrast is with the resurrection life which they now live (present subjunctive). Although they experienced judgment from humans, the true life they now have "depends upon the new relationship to God which is established through the response of faith to the Gospel."[479] Just as Christ is made alive in the spiritual realm where God rules (3:18) so too Christians who have died, even those who have experienced the human judgment of their neighbors, live in the realm of the Spirit who gives life.

Before leaving 4:1–6, it is important to consider the relationship between 4:1–6 and 3:18–22, and this is best done by considering the flow of these two passages along with the broader context in which they are found. In 2:11–3:12, a household code instructed the people of God how to live when facing challenges from unbelievers (rulers, crooked masters, and disbelieving husbands). Then, in 3:13–17 Peter turned his attention to the possible experiences of suffering that were occurring among his audience. The passage 3:13–17 may be a direct response to those who indicate that doing good brings about suffering. This should not be a surprise to God's people. Our author then moves into 3:18–22, which serves as a reminder to the audience that Christ also suffered and that out of his suffering sin was addressed once for all time. Christ died and rose from the dead, and in his resurrected body he preached a message of triumph over his enemies and came to a place of authority over rulers and other authorities. When Christians join with the suffering, resurrected, triumphant Christ in baptism they experience salvation through his resurrection and pledge a life of purity. Once again, in 4:1–6, Peter reminds them that Christ suffered, but

---

[479] Beare, *The First Epistle of Peter: The Greek Text with Introduction and Notes*, 156.

now he turns to their experience of suffering, in particular, rejection by their friends and acquaintances when they refrain from engaging in the civic activities and celebrations that had previously been part of their life. Just as Christ preached a message of triumph over his enemies, so too those who continue to reject Christ and who blaspheme God and speak against God's followers will also experience judgment from God. Meanwhile, those who suffer on account of their faith (3:13–17) can be assured that the Spirit who raised Christ from death and the God who reigns in power also sees and knows their suffering. While they may be rejected by their family, friends, and neighbors, while they may lose positions of influence or experience abuse at the hands of other humans, they find acceptance in the eyes of God and true life in the realm of the Spirit. Together, these two passages (3:18–22 and 4:1–6) demonstrate that suffering on account of one's faith and familial identity as a child of God is not in vain, is not unseen by God, and that ultimately the Christian experiences the same resurrection life as Christ – life made available through the power of the Spirit.

Bridging the Horizons: The passage 4:1–6 begins with the instruction for Christians to imitate Christ by arming themselves with the same response to suffering that Christ had. This call to be like Christ in response to unjust suffering echoes the call to be holy as God is holy (1:15–16). In the early part of 1 Peter, God calls the Christian to holiness and then in 2:21–25 and 3:18–22, Christ, the one who did not sin, is described living out this holiness through non-retaliation and faithfulness to God in the face of suffering and death. Today's Christian, like Christ, may also suffer on account of faith. The temptation is to respond to persecution in kind: abuse for abuse, mockery for mockery. But 1 Peter uses military metaphors ("arm yourselves") to show that the power of the Christian lies not in violence but in the resolve to suffer as Christ suffered if called upon to do so. Fleming Rutledge reminds us that "the language of struggle and combat is not incompatible with a commitment to nonviolence … Military imagery like that in the Bible is used in nonviolent struggle to inspire, to encourage, and to interpret."[480] Rutledge goes on to recount the ways in which the civil rights movement in the United States (1953–1964) used the language of war for peaceful protest and resistance. She quotes journalist John Seigenthaler who says, "It was clear that there was a war on. We [journalists] could

---

[480] Fleming Rutledge, *The Crucifixion: Understanding the Death of Jesus Christ* (Grand Rapids, MI: Eerdmans, 2017), 384.

see that the weapons of non-violence were stronger than those of violence."[481] Christians have been born again into a new life characterized by holiness and love. Their capacity for nonviolent love and the resistance of evil through good works is derived from the new birth and the new identity they have as the people of God. Together, the church must determine what it looks like to do good and must be prepared to suffer as Christ did. During the civil rights movement, Martin Luther King Jr and other leaders called the church to peaceful resistance against evil and oppression and together as a group presented a vision of common humanity to a country beset by racism, prejudice, and segregation. In the twenty-first century, some members of the church in the West feel threatened by changes in the culture around them, a culture that is moving quickly towards a post-Christian era. In this context, the challenge will be to take up love, good works, and humility, all of which are characterized by non-retaliation and nonviolence. Perhaps, once again, journalists will see the church in action and know that the weapons of nonviolence are stronger. But this must be the work of the church together, for the imitation of Christ is an imitation taken up from within the community of God's people and not by individuals alone.

For the Christians addressed in 1 Peter, part of the suffering that they experienced was the scorn of their friends and neighbors as they withdrew from activities they had previously engaged in that were associated with the worship of other gods. This behavior is described in the text as excessive partying (drinking, feasting, and the like) and idolatry. In the first century this partying took place in the context of civic-religious worship (remember these are not separate at this time). This most likely included celebrations that were part of the imperial cult along with local celebrations dedicated to the gods and goddesses enshrined in particular cities. In other words, the idolatry that 1 Peter writes about is a social reality that governs the structures and norms of the society in which the Christians of the first century live. To reject such social norms was to stand apart from them and critique them. Earlier in 1 Peter, we see that Peter adopts the household code of the Roman Empire while also subverting it. He uses the code to draw out the capacity of slaves and women both to choose how they will respond to persecution and to serve as examples to the wider Christian community. When this approach to the culture is combined with 4:1–6, we see the necessity for a nuanced response to our social reality. On the one hand, certain forms and ways of living that come from the culture around may be adopted by Christians; however, such adoption must always be undertaken with care. For ultimately, the community of God's

---

[481]   Quote comes from the PBS series, *A Force More Powerful*, September 2000, quoted in Rutledge, *The Crucifixion*, 385.

people must be most fully shaped by the ethic of holiness, love, and good works laid out in 1 Peter rather than by the cultural customs of the day. Indeed, the practice of holy love and good works very well has the potential to subvert social structures that rely on the exercise of power for the purpose of social control. On the other hand, certain social and cultural norms must be rejected because they violate the ethic of love, holiness, and good works that should characterize Christians. Those who excuse themselves from participation in these rites and rituals will often find themselves at odds with their culture. Christians should not be surprised when this happens nor should they be surprised when they are the recipients of abuse on account of such choices. The challenge of this passage is not to respond to persecution with self-justification or a demand for certain civic or social "rights." Instead, Christians should be prepared to suffer as Christ did with faithfulness to God and nonviolence.

1 Peter 4:7–11: Life Together as the End Draws Near

[7] The end of all things is near; therefore be serious and discipline yourselves for the sake of your prayers.

[8] Above all, maintain constant love for one another, for love covers a multitude of sins.

[9] Be hospitable to one another without complaining.

[10] Like good stewards of the manifold grace of God, serve one another with whatever gift each of you has received.

[11] Whoever speaks must do so as one speaking the very words of God; whoever serves must do so with the strength that God supplies, so that God may be glorified in all things through Jesus Christ. To him belong the glory and the power forever and ever. Amen.

The major section that began at 2:11 draws to a close with this final paragraph. The author, having just finished with the judgment of the living and the dead (v.5), reminds the readers that the end is near (4:7a). Then, a set of ethical instructions are presented to guide the community in their life together (4:7b-11a). The section ends with a doxology (4:11b) that marks the closing of this major section.

Verse numbers were only added to the New Testament text in the 1500s, and it is interesting to note that some of the patristic commentators on **4:7a** actually placed the sentence "The end of all things is near" with v. 6 in their commentaries. By doing so they highlighted the connection between God's judgment and the last day.[482] In 1 Peter 2:12 we see that this major section began with a reference to the end – "in the day of visitation." Thus, the whole section with its household code, its delineation of suffering and response, its reminder of God's judgment, and its ethical instructions begins and ends with an eschatological framework. The audience hearing this letter is still living in the time of suffering. However, this time of suffering is a time of transition – a liminal period – between their former life prior to their new birth, and the fullness of the life to come when they receive the full hope of the resurrection. The last time is near, imminent, but not yet fully begun.[483] The death, resurrection, and ascension of Jesus Christ are the first event of the end, but the audience still awaits "the end of all things." They themselves participate in the new life made possible through this coming eschatological event while still awaiting the final judgment in which all things will be made right. The eschatological frame orients their life in this world. The same God who is ready to judge (4:5) is ready to reveal salvation (1:5). In light of this, they can live now as free people who belong to God (2:16), exercising their capacity to choose holiness, love, and good works. In other words, the eschatological frame is not a promise of future salvation so that they can ignore their very real suffering in this world. Instead, it is an awareness that the suffering they experience in this life on account of their faith is limited to this time of transition between their old life and the life to come when the end of all things fully arrives.

Since the audience knows that the end is near they are encouraged to be serious and self-disciplined. The word translated as "serious" in the NRSV, *sophronēsate*, refers to being in a sound state of mind or having a good, sensible approach to life. This is combined with the Greek word, *nēpsate*, which means "sober, free from drunkenness" in contexts outside the New Testament. But in the New Testament it is used metaphorically to mean "being free from every form of mental and spiritual drunkenness" and comes to have the sense of being well-balanced and self-controlled (BAGD). The same language of sobriety is used in 1:13 to describe the preparation for hope. Together, these words convey the call upon

---

[482] Dan Batovici, "Commenting on 1 Pt 4:7–11: A case study in patristic reception," *Annali Di Storia Dell'Esegesi* 36:1 (2019): 173.
[483] Bechtler, *Following in His Steps*, 130.

Christians to be composed and ready. This is the state that they are to have no matter how long they must wait until the fullness of the end arrives.[484] This clarity of mind is to be used for prayer. The word for prayer (*proseuchas*) used here appears frequently in the New Testament and refers to calling on God. Goppelt notes that "the commonly used plural brings to mind the plurality of acts of prayer. The life of the early Christian community was surrounded by appeal, intercession, thanksgiving, and adoration from both individuals and groups."[485] This is the second reference to prayer in 1 Peter. Previously, husbands were instructed to treat their wives well so that their prayers would not be hindered (3:7). Now, Christians are to be mentally alert. Both actions and attention can impact prayer.

The most important thing of all is to maintain love for one another in the family of God (**v. 8**). Elliott identifies love as "the emotional commitment and loyalty of believers to one another as . . . brothers and sisters of the household of God."[486] This has been an important theme in 1 Peter. In 1:22 they are to "love one another deeply from a pure heart," and in 2:17, alongside honoring the emperor and all people, they are to "love the family of believers." The household code ends with the reminder to have brotherly love for one another (3:8). This familial affection characterizes the life together of God's family. Such love is to be a constant marker of the church's community life together. Love for one another was a consistent identifying mark of the church across the New Testament (e.g., John 13:35; 1 Thess. 3:12). The second half of v. 8 provides the reason for maintaining love for one another: namely, "for love covers a multitude of sins." It is possible that Peter alludes to Proverbs 10:12 – "Hatred stirs up strife, but friendship covers all who are fond of strife" (NETS-LXX) – but there are significant differences between the text of 1 Peter and both the LXX or Hebrew text of Proverbs 10:12. If 1 Peter draws on this Old Testament text, it is only an allusion at best. The phrase "covers a multitude of sins" is close to James 5:20: "whoever brings back a sinner from wandering . . . will cover a multitude of sins." However, while the phrase "cover a multitude of sins" is shared between the two texts, the action which brings it about is different (love in 1 Peter, bringing back a wandering sinner in James). In light of this

---

[484]   Michaels, *1 Peter*, 245.
[485]   Goppelt, *A Commentary on I Peter*, 296.
[486]   Elliott, *1 Peter*, 750.

and the repeated instruction to the early church to love one another, it is possible that Peter draws on a maxim derived from the Old Testament but circulating freely in the early church.[487]

The application of this saying in the context of 1 Peter is open to a number of interpretations. In a recent article, David Downs lays out four main proposals about how love covers sins:

(1) God's love covers human sins;
(2) human love for others covers the sins (through forgiveness) of the objects of such love;
(3) human love for others suppresses sins in the sense that loving action prevents the occurrence of future transgressions among the people of God;
(4) human love for others atones for the sins of those who demonstrate such love, with the removal of sins coming either in the present or at the time of future, eschatological judgment.[488]

It is also possible for interpreters to hold more than one of these views at the same time. For example, those who understand that human love covers the sins of others may understand that love to be dependent on God's love.[489] Several things stand out. First, Schreiner points out that love is other-centered and for this reason rightly rejects love as the means of covering or atoning for one's own sins.[490] Second, the proverbial saying is embedded in a communal context. Michaels rightly points out that Western preoccupation with the individual has contributed to the debate over whose sins are forgiven, the one loving or the one having their sins covered. He sees this discussion as wrongheaded and, instead, argues that since sin is a social phenomenon, it is within the context of the Christian community that people experience forgiveness through loving and being loved.[491] Mutual love marks the whole community.[492] Such love characterizes the whole community so that all are honored (2:17) and so that the

---

[487] Elliott, *1 Peter*, 751.
[488] David J. Downs, "'Love covers a multitude of sins': Redemptive almsgiving in I Peter 4:8 and its early Christian reception," *JTS* 65 (2014): 490–91.
[489] Senior and Harrington, *1 Peter*, 120.
[490] Thomas R. Schreiner, *1, 2 Peter, Jude*, The New American Commentary: 37 (Nashville, TN: Broadman & Holman, 2003), 213.
[491] Michaels, *1 Peter*, 247.
[492] Achtemeier, *1 Peter*, 296.

group is marked by tenderness and humility towards one another. Third, 1 Peter does not specify any particular sins that are either covered or excluded from being covered. At the same time, it seems that covering in this context does not mean hiding sin under the rug or refusing to acknowledge wrongdoing, and it certainly cannot mean allowing sin in any form to continue. Rather, covering refers to "veiling or covering *before* God."[493] This concept is expressed using the same vocabulary in Psalm 32:1 (LXX: 33:1) in the words, "Happy are those whose transgression is forgiven, whose sin is covered." The covering over/forgiveness of sin ultimately derives from the love of God and is exercised in the community of the church for the sake of mutual love and encouragement. In considering what this might look like for the church, it is helpful to remember the social structure of the household code as "the institutional way of the world subverted to the Christian reality of love for one another and honor for one another. In this view, the slave and the women married to unbelievers become the examples of love and honor. They honor their masters and husbands and live towards them with goodness."[494] If this characterizes the life lived towards unbelievers, how much more the life of love lived towards believers? When we focus on the individual, the focus is consumed with whose sin is covered; when the focus is on the community, not as a hierarchy, but as a family and a body of priests, then we can see the communal expectation of love, honor, humility, and tenderness as unifying cultural expectations of the new community.

Verse 9 instructs the family of God to "be hospitable to one another without complaining." Hospitality was practiced by both Jews and Gentiles. In the Old Testament, there are many instances of hospitality. Two that stand out are the hospitality that is shown by Abraham to the three strangers who appear to him in Genesis 18. Abraham provides food and a place to rest in the heat of the day; they, in return, announce the fulfillment of God's promise of a son to Abraham and Sarah. Then, Abraham accompanies them on their way. Another example is Rahab's hospitality towards the spies who entered the city of Jericho (Josh. 2). They came to her house and she hid them when the king's men came looking for them. She declares awareness that God has given the land to Israel and asks

---

493 Selwyn, *First Epistle of St. Peter*, 217.
494 I am indebted to Dr Shively Smith for this insight in a private conversation in June 2020.

for her life. Once again, there is an exchange: "Our life for yours!" (Josh. 2:14). Both hosts and guests had obligations to one another and when hospitality was extended to strangers it brought about friendship. "Like love, hospitality forges social bonds. In fact it has been asserted that 'hospitality was the chief bond which brought the churches a sense of unity.'"[495] Selwyn echoes this sentiment and points out how early Christian hospitality was a household-to-household enterprise. In the early church hospitality towards other Christians might involve housing traveling ministers for a few days, but ministers were not to take advantage of such hospitality by overstaying their welcome. The Didache, written around the second century, advised, "Let every apostle who comes to you be welcomed as if he were the Lord. But he is not to stay for more than one day, unless there is need, in which case he may stay another. But if he stays three days, he is a false prophet" (Did. 11:4–5). The guest was not to take advantage of the host. On the other hand, those who offered hospitality were to do so with a willing spirit and not with reluctance or resentment expressed as grumbling or complaining. Some hospitality involved overnight guests, but believers also experienced hospitality when they worshiped in the homes of those who had space to accommodate a meeting and ate meals together, including celebration of the Lord's Supper (see 1 Cor. 11:17–34; Acts 2:46).

"Like good stewards" (**4:10**) introduces economic language that highlights the distribution and use of gifts within the family of God. The steward (*oikonomos*) was usually a slave who managed the master's household. Occasionally, the word might refer to a public treasurer. But here, where so much of the language of 1 Peter has drawn from the familial metaphor, it is best understood as a household steward. The family of God is reminded that they are not the owners or masters but rather the stewards who manage and care for that which they have received from their master. They are to be "good" stewards, faithful with whatever it is that they have received from God. In this case what has been received is the "manifold grace of God." The Greek word *charis*, grace, has three main meanings:

---

[495] Elliott, *1 Peter*, 752–53 quoting V. H. Kooy, "Hospitality," in George A. Buttrick (ed.), *The Interpreter's Dictionary of the Bible: An Illustrated Encyclopedia*, vol: 2 (New York: Abingdon, 1962), 654.

(1) outward grace or loveliness (not used much in the New Testament);[496] (2) a gift given or the attitude of benevolence from the gift giver; (3) gratitude or thanksgiving.[497] In 1 Peter, *charis* has already been used to describe the gift of salvation (1:10) and the response to it (2:19–20). Now, *charis* is described as a gift from God. This is not an inborn talent but rather a gift that God gives. God's gift is diverse (NRSV: manifold).[498] In 1 Corinthians, Paul describes the diversity of gifts this way: "Now there are varieties of gifts, but the same Spirit; and there are varieties of services, but the same Lord; and there are varieties of activities, but it is the same God who activates all of them in everyone" (1 Cor. 12:4–6). All the members of God's household are stewards of the diverse gift that comes from God. In the economy of God, each member of God's family receives a gift, but the purpose of that gift is to enable the community to serve one another. The word "serve" is particularly associated with "waiting on tables," "helping or offering assistance," and "being at the service of others."[499] As Christians steward what they have received and serve others with that gift, the family of God is strengthened and blessed. In God's economy all are clients (see, A Closer Look: Gifts and Patronage in the Greco-Roman World) who receive from their Father. And, in God's economy, all are patrons who steward what they receive from God for the sake of others and all are clients who receive from other members of the household of God. In such an economy, all receive and all give.

A Closer Look: Gifts and Patronage in the Greco-Roman World

Grace (*charis*) is a word that can have deeply nuanced meaning. John Barclay uses the anthropology of gifts and gift giving to help us understand grace as potentially referring to "the graciousness of the giver, the grace conveyed, and the gratitude returned."[500] Like the language of stewards, grace is also tied into economic language associated with gifts and gift giving in the first century. The Greco-Roman economic system was one of patronage and benefaction which relied heavily

---

[496] The LSJ has this as the first of three definitions. Barclay, *Paul and the Gift*, 576, who notes 1 Peter 2:19–20 as a possible use in this sense. Note that in 2:19–20, this commentary argues for the third meaning of *charis* in that context.

[497] Barclay, *Paul and the Gift*, 577.

[498] BAGD, "the grace of God, that manifests itself in various ways."

[499] BAGD

[500] Barclay, *Paul and the Gift*, 582.

upon relationships in order to keep the wheels of the economy turning. There were three different relational roles that made patronage work: patron, client, and broker. People could belong to all three groups. The patron is the person who gives a benefit or gift to another person. The client is the one who receives that gift or benefit. And the broker is a person who connects patrons and clients. We might illustrate this with a description. There is a wealthy man who lives in a city in Asia Minor. In the morning, his clients come to see him. To one he gives a few coins, to others he gives more. The clients enter to see him not in the order of their arrival but in the order of their status. Those of higher status enter first, while those of lower status must wait. When the wealthy man has seen all his clients, he goes out into the city to visit his own patron. He may receive a gift from his patron. Sometimes the clients will repay money that was loaned or will return the gift that they received in another form. It was always understood that gifts formed a relationship between two people with an obligation to respond to that gift. Such a gift might not be in kind. Rather, those of lower status might repay a portion of the gift by expressing gratitude for the giver and/or praising the giver in the marketplace. Such gratitude and praise raised the stature of the giver and was an important part of gaining honor in the cultural context. However the gift is returned, the patron and client have entered into a relationship of reciprocity. In our Western context, gifts are generally understood to be free and with no obligations attached. If there are obligations, it is often not thought of as a gift. However, this is not the understanding of gift in some contemporary non-Western cultures, and it does not appear to be the sense of gift in the first century. Not only do patrons give gifts to individual clients, they might also give such gifts (benefactions) to their local community. Examples of these types of benefactions include providing the funds to pay for a new building, a communal festival often associated with the temple of a local god or goddess, or the production of entertainment for the town such as a play or games. Patrons who made such benefactions to a city gained stature among their fellow citizens and were often honored with inscriptions to recognize the gift they had given.[501]

Verse **11** focuses on two forms of gifts believers receive from God: the gift of speech and the gift of service. Rather than spelling out a wide variety of the gifts that God gives to believers, as Paul does in his letters (e.g., 1 Cor. 12:7–10; Eph. 4:11–12), 1 Peter sums up all the gifts in these two categories. Speech has already been an important theme in the letter. First Peter 1:23

---

[501] deSilva, *Honor, Patronage, Kinship & Purity*, 95–156; Bruce W. Winter, *Seek the Welfare of the City: Christians as Benefactors and Citizens* (Grand Rapids, MI; Carlisle, Cumbria: Eerdmans; Paternoster Press, 1994), 21–41.

emphasizes the living *word* of God as the means of new life – a word about the Lord (1:25) that people can choose to either believe or to disobey or disbelieve (2:7–8; 3:1). And believers were to be able to share the hopeful message of the good news to anyone who asked (3:15). If believers experienced verbal abuse or evil speech, they were not to return such speech in kind (2:22–23) nor were they to speak deceitfully or slander others (2:1, 22). Now, in **4:11**, whoever speaks should speak as a person who has the opportunity to share the words of God. "Whoever speaks" does not designate a particular person such as a teacher, preacher, or prophet. Instead, when someone speaks, that person has the capacity to communicate divine words to the Christian body. Nor does the verse specify the context in which such speech may occur. It may be in the context of the Christian assembly but might also take place in other contexts. For example, 1 Peter has already indicated that Christians may be asked to give a defense for their hope. If this occurs, then the gift of speaking words from God extends beyond the Christian assembly itself. Peter has already shown that God's word is the living and enduring source of new birth (1:23) associated with the gospel (1:25). Now, Christians are invited to use the gift of speech to speak for God, whether in the context of worship or in the daily context of life faithful to the gospel.

In the ancient world, divine speech (*logia*) was often communicated through an oracle (as well as through prophets and priests), which can refer either to a person who delivered divine wisdom or to the words delivered by such a person.[502] Often those who participated in the religious systems of the ancient world and who sought to hear from the gods would seek out an oracle, a person known to have the ability to hear and communicate messages from the gods. A famous example of this is the oracle at Delphi in Greece. There was also an oracle of Apollo at Didyma on the western coast of Asia Minor. "Oracles were thought to provide supplicants with two types of information. Some prescribed tasks to be performed or instructions to be followed … The other function of oracles was to provide insight into future events."[503] While oracles are usually

---

[502] David E. Aune, "Religion, Greco Roman," in Craig A Evans and Stanley E. Porter (eds.), *Dictionary of New Testament Backgrounds* (Downers Grove, IL: IVP, 2000), 920.

[503] Travis B. Williams, "Delivering oracles from God: The nature of Christian communication in 1 Peter 4:11a," *HTR* 113:3 (2020): 237–38.

associated with speech, there are examples of oracles being written down in books, which were later consulted for guidance. However, even here it is not the book itself that is the oracle but rather the book is the receptacle for the oracle.[504] It is possible that the meaning of *logia* in 1 Peter is a reference to Scripture with the implication that those who speak are to allow Scripture to guide their speech.[505] However, the usual meaning of *logia* in the first century and its association with speaking in the first part of the verse, argues in favor of understanding *logia* "oracles" as divine speech.[506] Similarly, the parallel with the second portion of the verse also argues in favor of understanding this as "oracles from God." Just as strength to serve is supplied by God, so too words to be spoken come from God. In the Christian community, the oracles of God are particularly related to the gospel message about Jesus and its interpretation.

The second category of gifts that Peter discusses is service. "Whoever serves must do so with the strength that God supplies." Once again, Peter reminds the audience of God's economy. Everyone is invited to serve. Service would have been expected of the lowly and the slave, but in the Christian community all are invited to serve one another. They take on a shared posture of humble service in the context of the new household of God. The service that is given does not come from one's own resources but rather out of the strength that God supplies. God is the one who "defrays the expense" (BAGD) of the service that believers provide to one another. Thus, once again God is the patron who supplies what is needed to the clients (believers) in order that they may enter into relationships of service to one another, both giving and receiving in reciprocity with one another.

Our section ends in the same way that it began – with God receiving glory. In 2:12 God receives glory when outsiders see the good deeds of God's people and respond by giving glory to God. In 4:11, the result of speaking God's words and serving out of what God supplies is that God is glorified both within the community of God's people and implicitly in the surrounding community as well. God receives honor and praise as a result of the way that God's people speak and serve. Christians enter into relationship with God through the new birth that God brings about

---

504 Williams, "Delivering oracles from God," 341.
505 Achtemeier, *1 Peter*, 299.
506 Achtemeier, *1 Peter*, 299; Williams, "Delivering oracles from God," 342.

through Jesus Christ, and it is through this work of Jesus Christ that God receives glory. The divine words are tied to the message of the gospel that declares that God's anointed, Jesus Christ, has suffered and died to deal with sin and has risen and triumphed over his enemies and reigns with God over all the powers of this world. God is honored through Jesus Christ and all that he accomplished. It is not entirely clear whether the last phrase of 4:11 describes God or Jesus, but it is true of both – to him belong the glory and the power forever and ever. Amen. Since Jesus is the nearest referent, it is probably best ascribed to him. This mini doxology once again highlights the reign of Jesus Christ and draws this major section of the book (2:11–4:11) to a close.

Bridging the Horizons: The phrase "love covers a multitude of sins" can be disturbing in our contemporary contexts. There is a plethora of examples of churches that have "covered over" serious sins to the detriment of those who were sinned against and, ultimately, when such sin comes to light, to the detriment of the church and its leadership. Some of these cover-ups have been so large that when they became broadly known, they caused scandal not only in the church but in the wider world as well. Often such cover-ups have involved those least able to defend themselves from predatory behaviors. In addition, other types of systemic sins such as racism and abuse of power have been overlooked by churches with cultural majorities for decades and even centuries. "Love covers a multitude of sins" cannot and should not be used by the church to downplay, dismiss, excuse, or negate sin within a congregation, especially not sin committed by those with power. Instead, the church is invited to a mutual practice of love towards one another. What does such love look like practically in relationship to sin? First, it means caring deeply for one another. When Christians care deeply for one another they want to see each member of the congregation thrive. Such thriving must include the confession and forgiveness of sin. Hidden sin has the potential to destroy both the sinner and potentially the community. Dietrich Bonhoeffer in his book *Life Together* describes how sin loses all of its power when it is brought into the light and confessed in the presence of a loving brother or sister.[507] Love enables Christians to admit their own sin and not to be shocked at the sins of others. At the same time, Christians recognize that sin must be addressed through the healing sacrifice of Christ (1 Pet. 2:24; 3:18).

---

[507] Dietrich Bonhoeffer, *Life Together* (New York: Harper Collins, 1954), 112–13.

In God's economy all are stewards who receive from the Lord and all are enabled both to give and receive from others within the family of God. The reciprocity of God's economy invites several important responses from the church. First, there is the invitation to identify oneself as a steward rather than an owner. In North America, there is a tendency to focus on ownership and on what belongs to the individual. But being a steward means that a possession has been given to that person to care for and steward for the sake of God's community. The members of God's household are given many gifts, and it is important that we not limit what has been given to either material or spiritual things. Everything that a member of God's family has is a gift from God, including life itself (cf. 1 Peter 3:7, "coheirs of the gift of life"). Being able to identify as a steward rather than an owner can deepen a sense of responsibility for all that one has been given. Even those who "own" property of some type can understand both what they own as a gift and how they use it as stewardship. Such stewardship may require selling what one owns in order to serve others. Thinking that focuses on what is "mine" and that allows Christians to use their goods in any way they please because they "belong to me" no longer makes sense when one identifies as God's steward rather than as an owner. No longer do Christians need to have anxiety about securing their future because as stewards they remember that they belong to God (1 Pet. 2:16), that all they have received is gift, and that, like Christ, they can entrust themselves to God in all circumstances (1 Pet. 2:23).

Second, being a good steward can lessen unhelpful comparison between members of God's household. God gives to each member of the family a gift to steward. It is given as God pleases, and it is the responsibility of a good steward to manage it well for the sake of the wider Christian community. Jealousy or envy directed towards the gifts of others has no place in the Christian community. Instead, the church can affirm the shared stewardship of the whole by naming the ways in which diverse gifts are being stewarded by different people so that the larger Christian community can flourish. Recognition that everyone has a gift from the Lord opens up a capacity for generosity towards others with the gifts that one has. For example, those with homes engage in the practice of hospitality, whether in the form of meals or overnight stays, for the benefit of the wider church. One question that a Christian might ask (either privately or in the context of the community) is "what do I have in my hand?" or, in other words, "what has God given to me?" This demands a follow-up question: how will I steward what God has given? The life of a good steward is an invitation to be generous to others, especially to members of the household of God, because the grace-gifts of God are given in order to serve others. The challenge is to learn to use all the gifts that one has received – both material and spiritual – for the sake of others.

Finally, there is an invitation to receive what others give out of the treasure that God has bestowed on them. In some ways, this last invitation is the most challenging. For many, it is difficult to receive from others. One reason for this difficulty is that people who receive from others may feel indebted to the person from whom they received. This can begin a cycle in which someone is always keeping score to figure out how they can repay what has been given so they are no longer in debt. However, the vision of the church in 1 Peter is of a mutually loving community in which all are serving one another with the gifts they have been given. There is no idea of paying back what has been given. Instead, the whole community is filled with the gifts of God. A second reason that some people do not like to be on the receiving end of being served is that it requires a clear-eyed recognition that the individual is not self-sufficient (a highly prized Western value!). To be able to receive is to acknowledge that one needs the other members of the community in order to experience the various expressions of God's grace. When one is able to receive from other members of the community, the experience of grace is manifold. When one clings to what one has received and is unable to open the hands to receive from others, one's experience of God's gift becomes limited to the boundaries of the self. Receiving and giving are both needed. Similarly, the person who always has their hands out to receive but never gives is also truncated in their experience of the grace of God. God invites the family of God to a recognition of their identity as stewards, to openness to receive God's grace-gifts, and to a reciprocity of giving and receiving in their relationships with one another. Such an economy is an example to the world of the sincere love of Christians in action.

First Peter focuses on gifts of speech and service, and in our contemporary understanding these two gifts may be understood quite broadly as encompassing both the words and deeds of Christians. Loving service is demonstrated in a variety of ways, not least in the speech fellow Christians exhibit towards one another and in the service they provide to those within the Christian community. Speech and service, engaged in faithfully and with attention, have the potential to function as yeast both within God's community itself as well as within the larger society to which Christians belong. But these are the quiet ways of prayer, love, hospitality, and service. There is nothing flashy here, but there is a deep faithful response to the new life that God offers through new birth and a new family identity. Peter's repeated call for loving relationships within the household of God and good deeds oriented towards the community reminds us that godly speech seeks to build up the community while providing a gentle and reasonable defense of Christian faith to outsiders. In this way, the community is strengthened and the nature of God's love becomes evident, thus bringing honor and glory to God.

1 PETER 4:12–5:11: LIVING AS CHRISTIANS AMID SUFFERING

1 Peter 4:12–19: Suffering as Christians

[12] Beloved, do not be surprised at the fiery ordeal that is taking place among you to test you, as though something strange were happening to you.

[13] But rejoice insofar as you are sharing Christ's sufferings, so that you may also be glad and shout for joy when his glory is revealed.

[14] If you are reviled for the name of Christ, you are blessed, because the spirit of glory, which is the Spirit of God, is resting on you.

[15] But let none of you suffer as a murderer, a thief, a criminal, or even as a mischief maker.

[16] Yet if any of you suffers as a Christian, do not consider it a disgrace, but glorify God because you bear this name.

[17] For the time has come for judgment to begin with the household of God; if it begins with us, what will be the end for those who do not obey the gospel of God?

[18] And "If it is hard for the righteous to be saved, what will become of the ungodly and the sinners?"

[19] Therefore, let those suffering in accordance with God's will entrust themselves to a faithful Creator, while continuing to do good.

The third major section (4:12–5:11) of the letter begins here. It is marked by the direct address, "Beloved," last seen at the beginning of the second major section, 1 Peter 2:11–4:11. This section resumes the discussion of suffering, now, in an intensified form (4:12–19; 5:8–10). And, like the previous section, it ends with a brief doxology (4:11; 5:11). This major section is best broken up into three parts: (1) suffering as a Christian (4:12–19); (2) living and leading with humility (5:1–7); (3) resisting the devil (5:8–11).[508]

The theme of suffering begins in 1 Peter 1:6 and unfolds over the entire book before coming to a climax in 1 Peter 4:12–19. Peter has been preparing his audience for this message since the beginning of the book. From the start, Peter hints at the association between suffering and fire (1:7) while also unfolding a broader picture of suffering that includes a variety of trials (1:6). These trials include outsiders who speak evil about Christians because of their faith (2:12), masters who abuse their slaves for doing right

---

[508] Further comments on these divisions can be found at the beginning of each section.

(2:18–20), suffering by the household of God on account of right behavior (3:13–14), and suffering because the audience no longer participates in the civic-religious celebrations that mark the life of ordinary citizens (4:3–4). What might have been seen as a mild form of persecution in the earlier portions of 1 Peter is markedly more intense in this final extended passage on suffering.

The opening of this section begins with the direct address, "Beloved." This catches the readers' attention as they are reminded of their identity as those who are loved by God and cared for by the author of the epistle. This form of address was last seen at 2:11 where it also marked the beginning of a major section. This is the second time that the author uses the word "surprised." In 4:4, the former associates of the audience are surprised when those who are now part of God's household no longer join them in the orgies, drinking parties, and idolatry that were part of pagan life. Their former neighbors could not anticipate such a change in practice in the lives of Christians. Now, in **4:12**, Peter instructs his audience that in contrast to their pagan neighbors, they are not to be surprised when they encounter a "fiery ordeal." Those who encounter suffering on account of their faith are not to be startled by that encounter. Two suggestions have been made about why they should not be surprised. First, a period of suffering, trial, and tribulation was understood as coming before the final end and judgment of all humanity.[509] So, when Christians experience this type of suffering on account of their faith, they should not be surprised because this is a sign that they are living on the cusp of the final judgment. Second, in the broader philosophical tradition of the first century, there was an idea that people should prepare themselves for possible suffering by thinking about bad things that could happen to them. In this context, the phrase "nothing unexpected has happened" became a means of consoling those who encountered suffering by reminding them that they had anticipated it.[510] Thus, Greco-Roman, Jewish, and early Christian literature, for different reasons, anticipated suffering and felt that one should not be surprised

---

[509]   Dubis, *Messianic Woes in First Peter*, 5–35.
[510]   Paul A. Holloway, "Nihil inopinati accidisse – 'Nothing unexpected has happened': A Cyrenaic consolatory topos in 1 Pet 4.12ff," *NTS* 48 (2002): 436–37.

when it became reality. In the context of 1 Peter, the instruction not to be surprised is clearly set within an eschatological context. In 4:7, Peter has already reminded the audience that "the end of all things is near." Now, 4:12–19 begins with a fiery ordeal and ends with a depiction of God's judgment of both the righteous and sinners, further pointing to an eschatological framework. In light of both eschatology and an orientation to what may unfold in the future, Christians should not be surprised when they encounter persecution.

The word for fiery ordeal, *purōsis*, occurs here, twice in Revelation (Rev. 18:9, 18), and twice in the LXX (Prov. 27:21; Amos 4:9). Proverbs 27:21a, "Burning is a test for silver and gold" (NETS-LXX), provides one possible context for understanding the fiery ordeal. There, burning occurs in the context of testing metals (LXX: *dokimion*) for refining. The cognate verb "to burn" (*puroō*) occurs almost thirty times in the LXX and is often found in contexts that depict metal refining (e.g., LXX Ps. 11:7)[Eng. 12:6]; Jer. 9:7). Dubis argues that this context should apply to our understanding of the fiery ordeal. He writes, "[T]he persecutions that the readers are experiencing are the fires of God's furnace by which God tests the readers and their faith, authenticating the genuineness of their faith while also purging whatever dross may be present within them."[511] Such refinement and testing is often associated with the last times. Closer in time to 1 Peter, the *Didache* 16:5 also uses the concept of fiery ordeal in an eschatological sense: "Then human creation will come to the fire of testing [*tēn purōsin tēs dokimasias*], and many will fall away and perish, but those who endure in their faith will be saved by the curse itself."[512] This fiery imagery in 1 Peter evokes the eschatological frame since fire was often associated with God's judgment in Jewish and early Christian thought (e.g., Dan. 7:11; Zech. 13:9; Matt. 13:41–42; Rev. 20:9–10). Such fiery testing is meant to confirm Christian faith and life (cf. 1 Cor. 3:13–15).[513] Throughout the Old

---

[511] Dubis, *Messianic Woes in First Peter*, 78.

[512] Quoted in Michaels, *1 Peter*, 260.

[513] For more on the "testing of faith" see the commentary on 1:7. For more on persecution, see the Introduction to the commentary under "Situation."

Testament, testing was a common part of God's relationship with God's people and was used to determine if they would be faithfully obedient to the covenant relationship initiated by God.[514] For example, God tested Abraham (Gen. 22:1) by asking him to sacrifice the very son, Isaac, whom God had promised to him. Abraham's obedience was proof of his faith in God (Gen. 22:12). Similarly, God tested Israel as a nation. Moses says, "Remember the long way that the Lord your God has led you in these forty years in the wilderness, in order to humble you, *testing* [emphasis added] you to know what was in your heart, whether or not you would keep his commandments" (Deut. 8:2). The forty years of wandering are portrayed as a long test in which God seeks to know the heart of each person and their commitment to covenantal obedience. Dubis makes the following four points about the Jewish texts that reflect on God's testing:

(a) trials should not be interpreted as abandonment by God; (b) God sends trials upon his people in an attempt to ascertain their allegiance; (c) one's goal in testing should be to be 'approved' through faithful endurance and a humble acceptance of God's will; (d) the afflictions of God's people differ both in purpose and degree when compared to those of the wicked: God corrects his people as a father, while God condemningly punishes the wicked.[515]

In 1 Peter 1:6–7, testing is a significant part of the experience of suffering, and this is reiterated in 1 Peter 4:12. In chapter 1 that suffering is associated with "various trials," but in 4:12 that is replaced by a single fiery ordeal. Peter does not specify exactly what the ordeal is that Christians experience nor how long it will last, but it is associated with the tribulations and testing of the end times. And Peter has already indicated that the end times were inaugurated with the revelation of Christ to them (1:20). Christians should not be surprised when they encounter suffering because it is part of the unfolding of the final judgment, which they already know about and anticipate.

---

[514] Dubis, *Messianic Woes in First Peter*, 86.
[515] Dubis, *Messianic Woes in First Peter*, 89.

A Closer Look: Apocalyptic and Eschatology in 1 Peter

First Peter is written in the context of apocalyptic thinking. Apocalyptic is often associated with books like Revelation with its visions, heavenly messengers, and other worldly beings or with smaller portions of books like Matthew 24. But apocalyptic is not only a genre of literature but is also a worldview that was prominent, especially among Jews and Christians, in the first century. Apocalyptic asks the question "who is in control?" The answer to this comes from those who hold fast to faith despite facing persecution. In the twenty-first century, the word apocalypse is often associated with cataclysm. However, its original meaning is "unveiling," and apocalypticism as a worldview unveils the true power operative in this world. For, while it may seem that the governments of this world or forces beyond control are the reality in which humans live, apocalyptic thinking identifies God at work even if the ways in which God is at work are difficult to discern. Apocalyptic sees that, "The reign of God in this world is hidden and the struggle of God's elect must reckon with that fact ... The ambiguity of the mundane is clarified when put in relation to the events as seen from a heavenly advantage."[516] When examining books that do not belong to the apocalyptic genre, it is helpful to identify important aspects of apocalyptic that may show up in the worldview that is expressed in such writing. Robert Webb has identified a long list of apocalyptic and eschatological elements in 1 Peter.[517] Some of the most important elements he identifies include: first, references to primordial events (3:19–21); second, repeated evidence of persecution and suffering throughout the letter (1:6; 2:12; 3:17; 4:19; 5:10) since apocalyptic takes place in the context of social crisis; third, repeated references to judgment including both the church and all people (1:17; 2:12; 4:4–5; 4:17); fourth, identification of a great conflict between the devil who seeks to devour (5:8) and the God who strengthens and establishes God's people (5:10). Recognizing the apocalyptic worldview in 1 Peter allows the interpreter to see clearly the social crisis that Christians experience because of persecution and the way in which 1 Peter reminds readers that the ultimate battle is not against those who persecute them but against the devil. Indeed, they can be confident in their ongoing obedience to God because God is the one who controls history from the foundation of the world to the day when Christ is revealed. Those who are given apocalyptic insight are consoled with the understanding that the current suffering will only be for a little while (1:6–8; 5:10).[518]

---

[516] Gordon L. Isaac, "Eschatology vs. apocalyptic," *Liturgical Ministry* 19:1 (2010): 25.

[517] Robert L. Webb, "Intertexture and rhetorical strategy in First Peter's apocalyptic discourse: A study in sociorhetorical interpretation,"in Webb and Bauman-Martin (eds.) *Reading First Peter with New Eyes*, 80–83.

[518] Holloway, *Coping with Prejudice*, 150.

While apocalyptic as a worldview addresses the question of who is in control when God's people experience suffering, eschatology is closely related to time, especially the end time. In 1 Peter, the Christology of the text displays a significant connection to time. Christ was known before the foundation of the world and is now "revealed at the end of the ages" (1:20). This revelation of Christ took place through his death, resurrection, and ascension into heaven (3:18–22). And Christians anticipate a final day when Christ will return and they will experience the fullness of the salvation that is guarded in heaven for them (1:3–5). "As the opening of the letter-body in 1.13 makes clear, these anticipated events – the apocalypse of Christ and the final day of salvation – are effectively one and the same: the readers' hope is to be fixed on the [grace] that will be brought to them [in the revelation of Jesus Christ]."[519] Throughout 1 Peter that last time is referenced in a number of ways: "the last time" (1:5), "the revelation of Christ" (1:7, 13; 4:13), and "the day of visitation" (2:12). This final day is connected with the prominent eschatological theme of judgment in 1 Peter, which revolves around God as judge. God is identified as a judge who judges impartially (1:17) and justly (2:23). God judges the living and the dead (4:5) and will judge both the church and the ungodly (4:17–18). Like Christ, who entrusted himself to God who judges justly (2:23), so too Christians can entrust themselves to God, their Creator (4:19). There has been some debate among scholars over whether elements of judgment and visitation by God in 1 Peter should be understood as referring to the final eschatological judgment or to an opportunity when God visits nonbelievers to bring salvation, but "the author of 1 Peter holds these two concepts (the present and the future) in tension and … the two options are not mutually exclusive."[520] Understanding both apocalyptic and eschatology allows readers to see the ways in which God is in control despite any appearances to the contrary. It also reminds readers that history has an end in the great and final day of the Lord. And, in 1 Peter, such an understanding is always related to the ethics of the Christian church. Those who know that God is in control and that God is the just judge will live accordingly. On the one hand, they live in freedom as slaves of God alone (2:16) and, on the other, they practice the good behavior God calls out of them as a reverent response to the one they know as both Father and impartial judge (1:17).

Verse **13** begins with a strong contrasting "but" that highlights the difference between being surprised by the fiery ordeal of suffering and

---

[519]   David G. Horrell and Wei-Hsien Wan, "Christology, eschatology and the politics of time in 1 Peter," *JSNT* 38 (2016): 267.
[520]   Joseph, *A Narratological Reading of 1 Peter*, 110.

rejoicing to the extent that they share in the sufferings of the Christ. There are several ways that "sharing Christ's sufferings" can be understood. First, 1 Peter has already talked about imitating Christ and following in his footsteps when Christians experience unjust suffering.[521] When slaves experienced unjust suffering on account of their faith, they were reminded that Christ also suffered and that he suffered in an exemplary way (2:18–25). Similarly, in 4:1 Christians are to arm themselves with the same intention as Christ. In this view, the call to share in the sufferings of Christ is another call to imitate Christ's holy response to suffering.[522] Dubis objects by asserting that while imitation language is surely present in 1 Peter, "sharing" means more than just imitation.[523] The second view suggests sharing or "fellowship" (*koinōneō*) may refer to spiritual union with Christ and his sufferings. The idea here is one of mutual union. The church shares in Christ's suffering on the cross and Christ shares in the sufferings of his body, the church (cf. Acts 9:4–5). First Peter uses the phrase "in Christ" three times (3:16; 5:10, 14) with a likely meaning of union with Christ.[524] However, the theme of participation or union with Christ is not prominent in 1 Peter as it is in Paul, and while it may make sense of the idea of sharing, it does not fully explain "sharing in suffering." Dubis has proposed a third view that the Greek that is translated as "the sufferings of the Christ" should be understood as a reference to the messianic woes (a period of tribulation that inaugurates the end of the ages). Unusually, the phrase in 4:13 is the sufferings of "the Christ" (*tou Christou*), which is also repeated in 5:1. The unusual use of the article points either to an emphasis on the title of Messiah or to a particular aspect of messianic suffering anticipated in both Jewish and early Christian eschatology. Unlike Jewish eschatology, which anticipated such suffering during the advent of the Messiah, Dubis argues that these woes or tribulations are inaugurated in Christ's suffering on the cross.[525] Christians share in this suffering because they live in the eschatological end times. The eschatological focus of 4:12–19

---

[521] Michaels, *1 Peter*, 262.

[522] Selwyn, *First Epistle of St. Peter*, 221; Davids, *The First Epistle of Peter*, 166.

[523] Dubis, *Messianic Woes in First Peter*, 97.

[524] Elliott, *1 Peter*, 865.

[525] Dubis, *Messianic Woes in First Peter*, 99–102; Joseph agrees with the important caveat that suffering is not required in order to enter the Messianic age: Joseph, *A Narratological Reading of 1 Peter*, 115–16.

and the fiery trial of 4:12 both suggest this possible meaning. Finally, Hockey proposes that the term "sharing" refers to participation as solidarity.[526] By this she means that participation is about "to whom one belongs and to what truth and values one subscribes."[527] The social commitments that one makes as a Christian have the potential to cause suffering and the type of suffering Peter is talking about only comes about because one lives out the Christian commitment to doing good that is so evident throughout 1 Peter. These possible understandings of the phrase "sharing Christ's sufferings" are not mutually exclusive. First Peter has focused on the passion as a time of suffering for Christ, and the understanding that this is the inauguration of the end times is widely shared in the New Testament. First Peter also anticipates that Christians imitate Christ in his suffering and that the results of doing good may indeed be suffering through rejection by the society around. Perhaps the least satisfying proposal is "spiritual union," but even here the idea that Christians share in Christ's suffering and he in the sufferings of them is not unknown in the New Testament and may be alluded to, although briefly, in 1 Peter.

Christians are to rejoice insofar as they have the opportunity to participate in the sufferings of Christ. The recipients of 1 Peter were most likely already suffering on account of their faith. And they were experiencing surprise at the abuse and slander from their neighbors on account of their commitment to doing good and not participating in idolatrous civic practices. However, it is also clear that 1 Peter does not envision everyone necessarily suffering on account of their faith (cf. 3:13–14). In her work on emotions, Hockey argues that "joy is appropriate when something evaluated as good and beneficial is present."[528] She goes on to say that "by seeing suffering as the result of being united with Christ it means that suffering no longer needs to be evaluated negatively, because being united with Christ and God is good and secures the good."[529] It is good because it allows Christians to focus on how they are viewed by God rather than by society so that suffering for living well as a Christian is no longer a source of

---

[526] Hockey, *The Role of Emotion in 1 Peter*, 153.
[527] Hockey, *The Role of Emotion in 1 Peter*, 153.
[528] Hockey, *The Role of Emotion in 1 Peter*, 143.
[529] Hockey, *The Role of Emotion in 1 Peter*, 154.

shame for the believer. Indeed, it becomes possible to see such suffering as a reason for joy.

The sufferings of Christ are already referred to in 1 Peter 1:11 as something the prophets look ahead to; they look into Christ's sufferings and then into his subsequent glories. Similarly, in 4:13 the sufferings of the Christ are followed by the revelation of his glory. This pattern of suffering as a prelude to glory can also be seen in 1 Peter's unfolding narrative of Christ's suffering for sin (2:21–25) followed by his resurrection (3:18) and ascension (3:22). "Since Jesus' suffering was followed with his exaltation, it follows that participation in his suffering will lead to participation in his glory . . . The knowledge that one will be vindicated should affect how one interprets suffering."[530] In 4:13 Christians rejoice when they have the opportunity to share in Christ's sufferings *so that* they "may also be glad and shout for joy when his glory is revealed." The joy that they experience now in suffering with Christ is exponentially multiplied at the point when Christ's glory is fully revealed. The verb "rejoice" (*chaireō*) is repeated in both halves of the verse; in the second half, their rejoicing is intensified with the addition of the verb "to be exceedingly joyful" (also in 1:6, 8). A similar pattern of suffering, persecution, and rejoicing in the anticipated future is found in the words of Jesus in Matthew 5:11–12, and that may be reflected here in 1 Peter. Christians who share in the sufferings of Christ and who have already experienced the new life made possible through Christ's glorious resurrection anticipate the joy that will be theirs in the final revelation of Christ's saving power. Thus, the lives of faithful Christians are marked by joy both now and in the future. The Christian life is neither all suffering nor all triumph but rather a sharing in both the suffering and the glory of Jesus Christ. There is no hint of stoicism in the response to either suffering or glory; rather, participation in Christ's suffering and seeing the revelation of his glory are both causes for rejoicing, joy, and gladness.

Christians are not to be surprised by the fiery ordeal but are instead to rejoice when they have the opportunity to share in Christ's sufferings. **Verses 14–16** lay out the positive reason for suffering – namely, as a Christian (vv. 14, 16) – alongside negative reasons for suffering (v. 15).

---

[530]   Joseph, *A Narratological Reading of 1 Peter*, 106; also, Achtemeier, *1 Peter*, 307.

These reasons form a smaller unit within this paragraph with an A, B, C, A¹, B¹ structure.

A – If you are <u>reviled (suffer)</u> for the <u>name of Christ</u> you are blessed
    B – because the spirit of <u>glory</u>, which is the Spirit of God, is resting on you
        C – But let none of you <u>suffer</u> as a murderer, a thief, a criminal,
           or even as a mischief-maker.
A¹ – Yet if any of you <u>suffers</u> as a <u>Christian</u>, do not consider it a disgrace,
    B¹ – but <u>glorify</u> God because you bear this <u>name</u>.[531]

The parallelism is between suffering as a Christian (A, A¹) and the glory that comes out of such suffering (B, B¹). At the center is the clear instruction not to suffer for doing evil. Together, these verses reiterate the reason for suffering that has already been laid out in 1 Peter: good behavior and good works done as a result of faith in God and the experience of Christ's redemptive work (1:16, 17, 22; 2:12, 15; 3:13–14, 16). This is firmly reiterated in the midst of the more intense description of suffering in 4:12–19.

Using this structure, Peter reiterates a theme that has been prominent elsewhere in the epistle: Suffering is honorable when it comes about because of one's faith, Christian identity, and good works. But suffering on account of wrongdoing should not be a part of the Christian community. Verse 14 begins "If you are reviled for the name of Christ." "If" here introduces the real possibility that the audience is currently suffering.[532] Some commentators indicate that "if" (*ei*) presumes the reality of suffering and therefore translate the particle as "when."[533] However, as Michaels rightly notes, while the "if" in 4:14 presumes the reality of suffering for the audience, "Peter examines different possible cases or scenarios, some more remote and more drastic than others. Knowing that none of these will apply to all his readers and that some may not apply to any of them, he makes no attempt to distinguish levels of probability with the use of different types of conditional clauses."[534] Some in the audience may be experiencing suffering now on account of their faith while others may never experience such suffering. To be reviled is to be mocked or insulted

---

[531] Similarly, Elliott, *1 Peter*, 778.
[532] Dubis, *1 Peter*, 149.
[533] Achtemeier, *1 Peter*, 307; Elliott, *1 Peter*, 779.
[534] Michaels, *1 Peter*, 263.

and focuses on verbal abuse: "if you are reviled." Such speech is intended to shame the one who experiences it, to mark members of God's household as outsiders associated with the name of Christ. The abuse that they endure takes place "for the name of Christ." It is because they belong to Christ and have acted in allegiance to Christ that they experience the verbal abuse of their neighbors and former associates.[535] "Christ" is the title by which Jesus was identified as the true king of Israel and it is used of Jesus throughout 1 Peter. Those who associate with the name of Christ are those whose allegiance is first and foremost to the king whom God has raised up from death and made triumphant over the powers of this world. "If you are reviled for the name of Christ, you are blessed" is the second beatitude in 1 Peter and parallels 3:14, "if you do suffer for doing what is right, you are blessed." This second beatitude closely parallels Jesus' saying in Matt. 5:11, "Blessed are you when people revile you and persecute you and utter all kinds of evil against you falsely on my account" (parallel, Luke 6:22). For the household of God, blessing is associated with suffering on account of good works and righteousness and on account of identification with all that is represented by the name of Christ. In the context of the first century, the type of proverbial form that the blessing takes is a way of describing behavior that the larger community of Christians finds honorable.[536] Some have suggested translating the phrase as "how honored you are!"[537] And indeed, their association with Christ and with Christ's sufferings is honorable (note the instruction in 4:16 not to be ashamed).

The reason for and evidence of their honor is that "the spirit of glory, which is the Spirit of God, is resting on you." This phrase shares affinities with Isaiah 11:2, "And the spirit of God shall rest on him" (NETS-LXX). This is the only verse in the LXX where the vocabulary of "spirit," "God," and "resting" come together, so while the verse has been significantly altered in 1 Peter 4:14, it is reasonable to see an allusion to Isaiah 11:2. First, some of the significant differences between Isaiah and 1 Peter include

---

[535] The prepositional phrase "*en onomati*" can mean "because": Elliott, *1 Peter*, 779–80. It is often translated as "for" in English versions, but can also refer to a title or category (BAGD, Louw and Nida) and thus mean "in view of this" (Davids, *The First Epistle of Peter*, 323) or it can mean "in the name" (Michaels, *1 Peter*, 264), but note that the Greek article "the" is missing from the phrase.

[536] Kenneth C. Hanson, "How honorable! How shameful! A cultural analysis of Matthew's makarisms and reproaches," *Semeia* 68 (1994): 90.

[537] Elliott, *1 Peter*, 781.

the change from the spirit of God resting on one person, God's anointed Messiah, to the spirit of God resting on the whole community ("you" plural). Second, glory is not mentioned in the Isaiah text. Finally, the Spirit is something that is promised in the future "shall rest on him" whereas in 1 Peter the Spirit is presently resting on the community. In the eschatological context of 1 Peter 4:12–19, it is possible that these changes between the text of Isaiah 11:2 and I Peter 4:14b point to the fulfillment of this Isaianic promise in the community of the church. While the text of Isaiah points to the Spirit resting on the chosen king, other texts in Isaiah promise an outpouring of God's spirit on all Israelites when they have returned from exile (e.g., Isa. 59:21).[538] If this is the case then the spirit of God resting on the whole community of God's people in 1 Peter can be associated with their participation in the messianic community and their sharing in both Christ's suffering and glory. Their ongoing present experience of God's spirit resting upon them is a vindication of their choice to remain faithful to God despite suffering while continuing to practice good works.[539] As God's household, living on the cusp of the final judgment, their experience of suffering and glory echoes the experience of the one they follow, Jesus Christ, who suffered on their behalf and whom God vindicated by raising from the dead and who now receives glory forever (2:24; 3:18; 4:11). There is no indication that their experience of the spirit of God is only temporary or only occurs while they are suffering.[540] Thus, the beatitude of 4:14 is an encouragement to an audience experiencing both suffering and the glorious presence of the spirit of God at the same time.

Before we turn our attention to the next verse, we should pause for a moment over the phrase "the spirit of glory, which is the Spirit of God." If this phrase is translated word for word, it reads, "the of the glory and the of the God spirit." Several suggestions have been made about how to understand the awkward grammar of this phrase. Some, like the NRSV, take the second phrase "the spirit of God" as an explanation of the kind of glory that is resting on the congregation, namely that glory is the spirit of God. Dubis argues for this position based on similar explanatory constructions

---

[538] Dubis, *Messianic Woes in First Peter*, 122.
[539] Joseph, *A Narratological Reading of 1 Peter*, 166.
[540] Contra, Goppelt, *A Commentary on I Peter*, 324.

in Isaiah 11:2.[541] Others take the phrase as expressing a single idea along the lines of "the Spirit of the glorious God" (cf. NLT).[542] The repetition of "the" in the genitive case (the glory and God) lends itself to this interpretation; however the repetition of "the" (*to*) in the accusative case argues against it. There are too many uses of "the" in this Greek phrase! A third option is put forward by Selwyn who takes "the glory" as a substantive and suggests it refers to the Shekina glory of the Old Testament, the shining presence of God that filled God's temple. He argues that the link back to the glory revealed at the final judgment (4:13) appeals to this understanding of glory.[543] A more recent argument that "the spirit of glory" refers to the glory of God that rests on the temple has been linked to the description of God's people using the word *oikos* and other temple imagery in 2:5.[544] That temple (*oikos*) reference is repeated in 4:17. Some have objected that a reference to the spirit of glory that rested on the temple would need to be very clear from the context of 1 Peter, and it is not.[545] Yet, the repetition of the word "temple" (*oikos*) both earlier in the book and in the immediate context may encourage a reading in which the people of God, who are now the living temple of God, are filled by the spirit of God even in the midst of their suffering. Grammatically, this third option is the least likely, while both the first and second options are possible. However, it is probably best to see the second phrase as a further description of the glory that rests upon God's community, similarly to the NRSV translation.

As elsewhere in 1 Peter (2:20), Christians are not to suffer for doing wrong. Four types of wrongdoer are listed in **4:15**: murderer, thief, criminal, and mischief-maker. The first two are straightforward examples of wrong-doers that were agreed upon throughout the Greco-Roman world by both Jews and Gentiles alike.[546] The third, "criminal" is the translation of a broad category, "evildoer" (*kakopoios*), which can refer to any type of behavior society saw as evil, not just behavior that might be illegal according to the laws of the day. The fourth, "mischief maker," is the most

---

[541]   Dubis, *1 Peter*, 150. Forbes, *1 Peter*, 157 also recognizes this as one grammatical possibility.
[542]   Technically known as hendiadys, Elliott, *1 Peter*, 782.
[543]   Selwyn, *First Epistle of St. Peter*, 222.
[544]   Dennis E. Johnson, "Fire in God's house: Imagery from Malachi 3 in Peter's theology of suffering (1 Pet 4:12–19)," *JETS* 29 (1986): 290–91.
[545]   Goppelt, *A Commentary on I Peter*, 323.
[546]   Elliott, *1 Peter*, 783.

difficult. The Greek word *allotriepiskopos* is used, as far as we know, for the very first time in Greek literature here in 1 Peter and then is not used again until the fourth century.[547] This makes it difficult to determine the exact meaning of the word. This difficulty can be seen in the variety of English translations of the word: "mischief maker" (NRSV, RSV), "meddler" (ESV, NIV, and NASB), and "informer" (NJB). It is a compound word formed by adding the prefix *allotrios*, "belonging to another," to the word *episkopos*, "overseer." When Elliott compares similar constructions in which *allotrios* is added to a noun, he comes to the conclusion "that in such constructions *allotrios* always qualifies the activity *as involvement in something alien to the doer*, or engagement in matters not one's proper concern."[548] Thus, people who meddle are people who involve themselves in things that are not rightly theirs to oversee. In her study, Brown indicates that in the Greco-Roman world meddling was socially censored and frowned upon; it involved "attention to tasks outside of one's own designated sphere of activity."[549] Other scholars have suggested that meddling (or, in various other forms, mischief-maker or busybody) is too innocuous in relationship to the other items in the list and would not draw the rebuke that Peter makes here. However, Brown argues that while these English words are viewed as innocuous in our Western culture, meddling in Greco-Roman culture was a far more serious social offense. Those who have argued that the word demands a stronger connotation have put forward suggestions including "concealer of stolen goods," "spy," or "revolutionary."[550] Finally, Michaels rightly rejects the argument that the word refers to an impure bishop ("overseer") since the language of the list applies to the whole community and not only to leaders.[551] In any case, whether this particular form of wrongdoing is judged to be mild or severe, any suffering that Christians experience is not to be a result of rightful punishment for wrongdoing: such suffering would be shameful.

Instead, if they suffer, it should be on account of their Christian identity (**v. 16**). The name "Christian" is only used here and twice in Acts (11:26;

---

[547] Keener, *1 Peter*, 339.

[548] Elliott, *1 Peter*, 786.

[549] Jeannine K. Brown, "Just a busybody?: A look at the Greco-Roman topos of meddling for defining Ἀλλοτριεπίσκοπος in 1 Peter 4:15," *JBL* 125 (2006): 558.

[550] BAGD

[551] Michaels, *1 Peter*, 267.

26:28). Acts 11:26 indicates that "it was in Antioch that the disciples were first called 'Christians.'" Horrell makes the argument that since the Greek word "Christian" is, as scholars agree, derived from a Latin form, this may indicate that the label first came from encounters with Roman authorities.[552] As a label associated with criminals and mischief making, it was a label of shame applied by outsiders. In v. 15 a collection of dishonorable titles such as murderer, thief, criminal, and mischief-maker are laid out; these labels should never be true of the follower of Christ. At the same time, if members of God's household do come to the attention of outsiders, the name or label "Christian" should be a source of pride rather than shame. Scholars agree that the name began as a derogatory insult by outsiders.[553] But 1 Peter shows how that name has been turned from a shameful designation to a source of honor for those it describes. The epithet that was meant to stigmatize becomes a means of social cohesion within the group.[554] The suffering that Christians may be experiencing comes about in both a historical and an eschatological context. In the historical context, persecution is a reality. This persecution may extend from verbal slights and abuse all the way through execution.

Christians are experiencing hostility from the populace among whom they live, suffering verbal slander and accusation. This hostility can reach the level where it takes the form of legal accusations, which result in Christians being brought before the governor for trial. It is likely that the popular slander included some of the typical kinds of criminal accusation – that the Christians committed incest, were murderers, cannibals, and so on – and the accusations brought to the governor may also have included mention of such [crimes]. This again is confirmed in 1 Peter's account, where the likelihood of accusations of various kinds of evildoing is apparent (4.15) – and the author is concerned that no such accusations should stick. But the crucial accusation, in the end, would be that of being *Christianus*, the *nomen* [name] coined by Romans to designate such persons. This ... would most likely lead to suffering like Christ, suffering to death. And it is precisely such suffering that the author of 1 Peter insists is a noble experience which ... brings glory to God.[555]

[552]   David G. Horrell, "The label Χριστιανός: 1 Peter 4:16 and the formation of Christian identity," in Horrell, *Becoming Christian*, 168–69.
[553]   Achtemeier, *1 Peter*, 313.
[554]   Horrell, "Label," 198–202.
[555]   Horrell, "Label," 197.

If they suffer as Christians, a very real and present possibility, then they are not to be ashamed. Dubis remarks that vv. 15–16 happen in the middle of the most intensely eschatological passage in the whole of 1 Peter. In the eschatological context, where Christians live with an intense awareness that "the end of all things has drawn near" (author's translation) the instruction to not be ashamed ("do not consider it a disgrace") can be understood within the context of apostasy. In both Jewish and early Christian literature, the end times were associated with a rise in both lawlessness (4:15) and apostasy.[556] The temptation of those who experienced suffering on account of their faith would be to deny their association with Christ and to reject their Christian identity and association in order to avoid or reduce suffering.[557] It is the goal of name-calling to demean and belittle, but Christians have no need to be shamed by their identity as followers of Jesus. In place of shame, they are to glorify God because they bear this name, the name Christian.[558] This echoes the language of "bearing reproach for the name of Christ" (NRSV) in 4:14 or being "reviled" for it. Elliott notes that glorifying God in this name is the "fifth positive valuation of innocent suffering … Not only is suffering innocently a divine test of faith (v 12), a sign of solidarity with the suffering Christ (v 13a), a cause for

[556] Dubis, *Messianic Woes in First Peter*, 138–39.

[557] Indeed, such repudiation of the Christian faith was allowed in the Roman system as seen in the letters of Pliny. Although these letters are from the second century, it is possible that they represent earlier practice as well. Those who denied Christ, cursed the name of Christ, and made an offering to the Imperial cult were allowed to go free if being a Christian was their only "crime." If other crimes had been committed they would not have been allowed to go free. Horrell, "Label," 191–96.

[558] In the latest edition of the Greek New Testament (UBS5, NA[28]), the word "name" (*onomati*) has been replaced with "part/matter" (*merei*). The oldest manuscript (P[72]) and all the oldest and most significant codices (א, A, B, and a variety of minuscules) support the reading "name." The earliest manuscript evidence for the reading "matter" is from the eighth to ninth century and is found in a variety of minuscules as well as in the Majority text. However, the most recent Greek New Testament takes "in this matter" as the more difficult reading to be retained as original. Partly this is because it is hard to understand how "matter" arises from "name." One suggestion has been that "name" is used in an idiomatic manner to mean "for this reason," but this meaning is not well attested in the New Testament and the dominant sense "name" fits the context. A large quantity of witnesses support the reading "matter," and it is the more difficult reading. However, the reading "name" appears to be supported by an older and more diverse set of witnesses, and the reading "name" is suited to the context. "Matter/part" can be explained as a scribal gloss of an idiomatic understanding of "name." In light of this, "name" is to be preferred. For extended discussion see Horrell, "Label," 179–80.

rejoicing (v 13bc), and a mark of the Spirit's presence (v 14); it is also an opportunity for actively glorifying God."[559]

Verse 17 begins with "for" (*hoti*) and provides the cause or reason that God's people are experiencing suffering.[560] They are to recognize that their suffering is part of God's eschatological judgment. Peter states that such judgment begins with the household of God.[561] Jobes rightly points out that since they are suffering for being Christians and not, presumably, for evildoing, the judgment that is envisioned here must be associated with the final eschatological judgment rather than, for example, God's judgment for failure to live out covenant requirements or as punishment for sin.[562] Instead, Christians are to understand that the social hostility and suffering they experience is the beginning of God's judgment that unfolds at the end time. Jobes goes on to point out that "the likely sense of *to krima* [the judgment] in 1 Pet. 4:17a [is that] God will begin his process of judging humanity with his own people, to see which are truly Christ's."[563] Jobes points to Matthew 25:31–46 as an example of judging that begins with God's people (sheep) followed by those who do not belong to God (goats). Three points must be made here. First, the judgment of God's people serves to confirm and refine faith and thereby prepare those people for entrance to the kingdom of God,[564] which 1 Peter describes as receiving the outcome of faith, salvation (1:9). Those who persevere through suffering on account of their faith are fully vindicated at the second coming and experience the fullness of joy when Christ is finally revealed. Second, the association of judgment with "the time" places God's judgment in the

---

[559] Elliott, *1 Peter*, 797.

[560] "For" refers back to the theme of the whole paragraph, with Forbes, *1 Peter*, 160, and not just to the instruction to glorify God at the end of v. 16; contra Achtemeier, *1 Peter*, 315.

[561] The NRSV translates *oikos*, "house," as "household of God." John Elliott has long argued that the familial metaphor of house/household is the predominant metaphor for God's people in 1 Peter and that *oikos* does not refer to the temple (Elliott, *A Home for the Homeless*, 197–98). Many remain unconvinced by Elliott's argument and contend that "house of God" does describe the temple. For example, Dubis, *Messianic Woes in First Peter*, 152. In recent work, Mbuvi argues for a reference to the "temple-community" (Mbuvi, *Temple, Exile, and Identity in 1 Peter*, 119). That is the living community formed through the sprinkling of the blood of Jesus for the work of offering sacrifices and proclaiming God's wonderful deeds (2:4–10). In 1 Peter 4:17, God's judgment begins with God's own community.

[562] Jobes, *1 Peter*, 292; Bechtler, *Following in His Steps*, 155.

[563] Jobes, *1 Peter*, 293.

[564] Dubis, *Messianic Woes in First Peter*, 147.

eschatological frame that has already been so prominent in this portion of 1 Peter. Third, the connection of judgment to the eschatological framework also associates it with the time of tribulation or messianic woes that inaugurates the final judgment.[565] The audience of 1 Peter is not to be surprised when they suffer. Thus, the suffering that the church experiences at the hands of outsiders has the potential to refine faith. Such tribulations can be seen as a sign that the final judgment with its promise of vindication and revelation is approaching.

Several Old Testament texts have been suggested as potential background to the text of 1 Peter 4:17a: Jer. 25:15–29;[566] Ezekiel 9:6; Mal. 3:1–5; Zech. 13:9. The verbal parallels with any of these texts are minimal: Jeremiah 25 describes God's judgment beginning with God's people much as 1 Peter does. The Ezekiel passage also describes God's judgment beginning first in Jerusalem and indeed starting with the elders who are in the temple. Those who prefer Ezekiel 9:6 as a possible background text point to the shared vocabulary of "begin with" and "house" (*oikos*), with the latter being understood as a reference to the temple.[567] Those who argue against Ezekiel 9:6 point out that the context of Ezekiel 9:6 does not fit with the message of 1 Peter. Ezekiel 8–11 shows how the temple has been defiled and is in need of judgment, but in 1 Peter God's temple is formed from people who have been given new birth and made holy (1:1–3).[568] While Malachi does not share verbal references with 1 Peter, it too talks about God's judgment. The prophet Malachi has already been alluded to in 1:7 with its reference to refining fire. This refining starts with the "descendants of Levi" (Mal. 3:3), those who serve in the temple; they are purified so that they can present acceptable sacrifices in the temple (Mal. 3:4). Johnson argues that while 1 Peter shares verbal links with Ezekiel 9, Malachi provides the conceptual background for judgment that begins with God's temple (*oikos*) and expands to those who are not part of God's covenant.[569] Thus, the cleansing and refining of the temple and of those outside it is in view in both Malachi and 1 Peter. The problem with all of these texts, as Jobes

---

[565] Dubis, *Messianic Woes in First Peter*, 157.
[566] Jer. 25:15–29 = Jer. 32:15–29 LXX.
[567] Michaels, *1 Peter*, 271.
[568] With Elliott, *1 Peter*, 798–99; Liebengood, *The Eschatology of 1 Peter*, 147–48; Jobes, *1 Peter*, 292.
[569] Johnson, "Fire," 292.

points out, is that they generally present God's judgment of Israel as a judgment for sin.[570] But the judgment in 1 Peter is not a judgment of condemnation but rather an evaluating or discerning in regards to those being judged.[571] Zechariah 13:9 depicts a remnant who survive a time of tribulation. That remnant is refined and tested by fire, perhaps demonstrating an instance of suffering as a period of testing after the return of the shepherd. However, there are no verbal parallels between Zechariah and 1 Peter either. Overall, it is best to see the background for the idea of judgment beginning with the household of God as deriving from the generally well-known Old Testament idea that God is the judge of all the nations and that God's judgment begins with God's own people. This is demonstrated in multiple texts, including those above, but no single Old Testament text stands behind this portion of 4:17.

In the second half of v. 17, 1 Peter asks, "If it begins with us, what will be the end for those who do not obey the gospel of God?" The judgment that begins with God's people extends to all people. This is understood both from the Old Testament and from 1 Peter. As discussed in relationship to Malachi, above, but also seen in prophetic passages such as Amos 1:3–2:3 and Isaiah 13–19, God's judgment extends beyond Israel to the surrounding nations. And, in 1 Peter 4:5–6 God is seen as the judge of all humanity – both the living and dead, both the obedient and disobedient. Here, Peter asks the rhetorical question, if judgment begins with God's household what will the end or outcome be for those who do not believe? The word disbelieve/disobey (*apeithountōn*) has already occurred in 2:8 and 3:1 where it refers to those who reject Christ. In 4:17 this is further explained as those who disobey or reject the good news message that comes from God, the message about Christ as the suffering Messiah who has died for sins and been raised from death by God (2:22–25; 3:18–22). None escape God's judgment, but the contrast is between those who choose to trust and those who do not. If those who trust can expect God's judgment, how much more so those who do not believe? Since this is the case, and since the end is drawing near, and since God is the judge, what outcome can such a group expect? The rhetorical question implies that no good outcome can be expected for the nonbeliever. In the next verse (**v. 18**), Peter quotes

[570] Jobes, *1 Peter*, 292.
[571] Green, *1 Peter*, 155.

another rhetorical question from Proverbs 11:31 LXX to draw a parallel that extends the question posed in v. 17. "If it is hard for the righteous to be saved, what will become of the ungodly and the sinners?" In the context of 1 Peter, "the righteous" refers to the community of believers. The focus of the first half of the quotation is upon the salvation that the righteous experience. The adjective *molis* (NRSV: "hard") should be understood as describing a degree of difficulty indicating that salvation is not easy.[572] The Gospels point to God as the one who ultimately achieves salvation on behalf of believers. For example, when the disciples ask "who can be saved," Jesus replies, "For mortals it is impossible, but not for God; for God all things are possible" (Mark 10:26–27). The salvation offered to believers was achieved through the death of God's son Jesus Christ, surely a difficult way to bring about salvation. But if salvation for believers is difficult, "what will become of the ungodly and the sinners?" Again, the rhetorical question is unanswered but the implication is that their end will be destruction. The "ungodly" and "sinners" in this context refer to those who do not follow and trust Christ. In the context of the fiery ordeal (4:12) that the audience is experiencing, those who belong to God will be saved through the time of tribulation with difficulty. But the audience can rely upon the one who has promised to guard them for the purpose and outcome of salvation (1:5). Those who have chosen disbelief and disobedience will find that the tribulations that come before the eschatological end may bring about a different outcome than that promised to believers. While the NRSV asks "what will become of them?" A more literal rendering would be "where will the impious and sinner appear?" (RSV). Potentially, the answer is "nowhere."[573]

Peter sums up this paragraph, 4:12–19, on suffering with an entreaty that those who suffer according to God's will entrust themselves to their faithful Creator (**v. 19**). Those who suffer refers to believers who experience the type of suffering that has been described in this passage (e.g., the fiery ordeal, v.12; sharing in Christ's sufferings, v. 13; being reproached, v. 14; and suffering as a Christian, v. 16) and further back in 1 Peter where Christians suffer for doing good (3:14). Such suffering is within the will of God. This is

---

[572] BAGD; Joseph H. Thayer, *Greek – English Lexicon of the New Testament*, Accordance electronic (Altamonte Springs, FL: Oak Tree Software, 2004). Originally published in 1885.
[573] Dubis, *Messianic Woes in First Peter*, 167.

the fourth time the phrase "the will of God" has been used in 1 Peter. The phrase is repeatedly associated with doing good or living in a right manner (2:15; 3:17; 4:2). And in 3:17 it is particularly associated with suffering for doing good. Those who suffer because they have responded to God in faith and have chosen to live in obedience to God are within the will of God even if they suffer. Their unjust suffering is not a source of shame but rather a source of glory and honor. There are, of course, those who suffer rightly; in other words, they experience suffering because they have chosen to participate in doing wrong. This type of suffering will not bring honor in the eyes of God to the Christian who suffers. Those who suffer are to entrust themselves to the faithful Creator. This echoes the example of Jesus Christ in 2:23 who also suffered but did not respond to the suffering he experienced by causing others to suffer. Rather, he entrusted himself[574] to the one who judges rightly. These members of God's household can rely upon the faithfulness of their Creator even in the midst of suffering. The one who created them through new birth is faithful and reliable until the end. They can entrust their very selves to the one who has made the whole world and who remains always faithful to the covenant promise. Achtemeier notes, "While the noun 'creator' is used only here in the New Testament, the conviction that God is creator of all things pervades early Christian faith, and its use here suggests that ... the same power at work in the very creation of the universe is now at work for their salvation. That is why the readers can be encouraged to entrust their lives to the same God who brought them into existence."[575] The word "entrust" is a present imperative that defines their current way of life as a continuous response to the faithful Creator. The final phrase of this verse can be understood as either something they do while they are entrusting themselves; thus, the NRSV translates it as "while continuing to do good." Or, it can be understood as the means by which they entrust themselves; in the CEB this reads as "by doing what is right." The requirement that the household of God live rightly in relationship to God, to each other, and to the world around them extends through the whole of 1 Peter (2:15, 20; 3:6, 17). Suffering on account of one's faith is not a reason to abandon good works

---

574   The verb is different; *paradidōmi* in 2:23 and *paratithēmi* in 4:19.
575   Achtemeier, *1 Peter*, 318.

and right living. Indeed, elsewhere Peter made clear that good works performed in the midst of suffering bring glory to God (2:12).

Bridging the Horizons: Both Edwards and McKnight, writing in commentaries that have an explicit application section, "Contemporary Significance," note that the experience of suffering that was a reality in the lives of the early Christians is far removed from the experience of most Western Christians today.[576] While some, even within the Western context, may experience suffering on account of their faith, this has not been the norm. It is certainly true that some in the Western world do face suffering on account of decisions made out of a faithful response to God. For example, there are those who choose to live with integrity because of their faith in God and refuse to shade the truth for their employer, perhaps resulting in demotion or firing. There are some who have been mocked or insulted for their witness to Christ. But suffering on account of one's faith is not typical of the experience of most Christians in the Western world. It is also clear that as Western culture has moved from a majority Christian culture to a secular, humanist, and materialist culture, the values of society are changing. In the midst of this changing culture, Christians may become more susceptible to suffering for their faith. At the same time, it is important that Christians not consider every social or political decision of which they disapprove as a form of persecution. Those who live in a multicultural society will find themselves at odds with others, but not all opposition is persecution. Nor should Christians advocate for the persecution of other groups (secular or religious) with whom they disagree. Instead, whether or not Christians experience persecution, they will need to continue to make their witness known in broader society through their good works and their lives of holiness. This will take many forms. For example, there will be works of mercy that see Christians provide food, clothing, and shelter to those in need. There will be the good works that take place by developing relationships to provide counsel, comfort, and presence for those who are sick, imprisoned, or grieving. And, for those who are able, there is the good work of advocating for justice. In addition, Christians will need to be known for their integrity; their unwillingness to "spin" the truth; their rejection of lies and falsehoods and their advocacy for truth; their unwillingness to entertain slander or gossip or malicious speech about others. When Christians fail to live out the gospel with good works, they may unwittingly undermine the gospel itself and make the gospel "just words" rather than a new birth from God that transforms followers in such a way that holiness, love, and good works become their quintessential identity

---

[576] Edwards, *1 Peter*, 195; McKnight, *1 Peter*, 252–53.

markers. As Western society becomes more secular, Christians will be challenged to consistently demonstrate good works, and their commitment to good works may provide the opportunity to testify to God's good news in Jesus Christ. The temptation Christians living in the West face is the temptation to aggressively pursue a political solution to real or perceived persecution. Any political solutions should not come at the expense of others. And any political solutions must be accompanied by continued good works. Advocating for justice, feeding the hungry, and visiting those in need are the work of all Christians whether or not they experience persecution. Generally, Western Christians have not faced persecution on a similar scale with that experienced by the early Christians. In contrast, there are Christians around the world who do experience persecution on a regular basis. Such persecution may extend from such things as exclusion from the regular institutions of society, perhaps schools and government workplaces, to attacks, attacks on places of worship, to kidnapping and killing. Such stories make headlines even in secular newspapers in the Western world.[577] Other organizations are dedicated to highlighting the persecution faced by Christians around the world.[578] Contemporary Christians, like their first-century counterparts, should not be surprised when they encounter suffering that is a result of their faithful belief and practice as a Christian. At the same time, contemporary Christians should reject all forms of behavior that rightly bring about the judgment of society. But 1 Peter reminds Christians who suffer on account of their faith that sharing in the sufferings of Christ is an honor.

1 Peter 5:1–7: Leading and Living with Humility

[1] Now as an elder myself and a witness of the sufferings of Christ, as well as one who shares in the glory to be revealed, I exhort the elders among you

[2] to tend the flock of God that is in your charge, exercising the oversight, not under compulsion but willingly, as God would have you do it – not for sordid gain but eagerly.

[3] Do not lord it over those in your charge, but be examples to the flock.

[4] And when the chief shepherd appears, you will win the crown of glory that never fades away.

---

[577] Heba Farouk Mahfouz, "Coptic Christians describe bus attack in Egypt: 'Even the little children were targets,'" *Washington Post*, June 1, 2017. www.washingtonpost.com/news/worldviews/wp/2017/06/01/coptic-christians-describe-bus-attack-in-egypt-even-the-little-children-were-targets/

[578] Open Door USA, n.d., website, www.opendoorsusa.org/christian-persecution/world-watch-list/; www.persecution.com/about/

⁵ In the same way, you who are younger must accept the authority of the elders. And all of you must clothe yourselves with humility in your dealings with one another, for "God opposes the proud, but gives grace to the humble."

⁶ Humble yourselves therefore under the mighty hand of God, so that he may exalt you in due time.

⁷ Cast all your anxiety on him, because he cares for you.

First Peter 5:1–7 resumes the form and style of the household code (2:11–3:12) with instructions to "elders" and those who are "younger" and an emphasis on humility. The themes of holy life, mutual love, suffering, and dependence on God that were introduced in earlier parts of the letter continue in this section. Like the household code of 2:11–3:12, the instructions intended for the elders and the young people are given in a way that is instructive for all. A new section within the major unit (4:12–5:11) is signaled here by the use of "now" (*oun*), the change in form, and the introduction of two new groups, the elders and the younger ones. The unit ends with instruction to the whole group (5:5b) followed by a quotation from Scripture (5:5c). This follows the pattern of the previous household code, which also ended with an address to all (3:8) and a quotation from Scripture (3:10–12). Here, Peter follows his quotation from Proverbs with an application of that text to his audience (5:6–7).

First Peter **5:1** opens with a conjunction (NRSV: "now;" NASB: "therefore" [*oun*]) that invites consideration of the relationship between what preceded in 4:12–19 and what comes now in chapter 5. The introduction of elders, who are mentioned here for the first time, seems like an abrupt shift from the topic of suffering under a fiery ordeal (4:12) and the judgment that begins with God's own house (4:17). However, the introduction of the elders at this point may reflect the prior topic of judgment that begins with God's house.[579] Often, God's judgment begins not with Israel as a whole but with the leaders of Israel. In Ezekiel 9:6, which some scholars have seen as the background for 4:17, the elders are listed first among those who are judged followed by "young men" (*neaniskon*), a term similar to "younger" ones (*neōteroi*) in 5:5. The move from judgment of the house of God to elders may be a reminder that those who have responsibility over God's people are also subject to God's judgment. However, this

---

[579] Schutter, *Hermeneutic*, 79. Also, Campbell, *Honor, Shame, and the Rhetoric of 1 Peter*, 216.

commentary has already noted that Ezekiel 9:6 may not be the best background for 4:17 and a similar assertion can be made here. In Ezekiel, the elders are judged for their sinful ways, but there is no hint of such judgment in 1 Peter 5:1–4. Others have suggested that the description of the severe trials that the congregation faces necessarily turns the apostle's attention to the leadership needed when God's people face suffering.[580] In any case, this section addressed to elders shares similarities with the larger themes that have come before. Peter identifies himself as one who has witnessed the sufferings of Christ (cf. 4:13) and leaders are instructed to act in ways that reflect the holiness, love, and humility that is to characterize all Christians. The text surrounding the opening of chapter 5 makes it clear that these church leaders take on their task in an environment where persecution from society is present (4:12) and where resistance against evil is necessary (5:8–9). And, just as the slaves and wives served as examples to the whole community of how to live in the midst of unjust suffering, so too the elders are explicitly urged to serve as examples to the community.

For the second time Peter exhorts (cf. 2:11) his audience, but this time his exhortation is specifically directed to the elders among them. Peter, who opened his letter by identifying himself as an apostle of Jesus Christ (1:1), now identifies himself more fully with three descriptors: first, as a fellow elder; second, as an eyewitness of the sufferings of Christ; and, third, as one who will partake in the glory that will be revealed. The word for "fellow elder," *sumpresbuteros*, is found only here in the biblical text and is not found in other Greek literature until much later.[581] Peter puts himself on the same level and in the same position with those he addresses. "In this respect, there is no implication here that Peter is the *only* proper shepherd; nor is there any hint of a succession of Petrine ministry so defined."[582] Peter identifies himself as a fellow elder alongside the elders of the churches in Asia Minor. Jobes notes that "Peter personally understands their responsibilities, their fears, and the pressures that assail them because he also bears the responsibilities of an elder. The apostle embraces his calling as a leader in the church, a calling that will lead to his martyrdom in

---

580 Forbes, *1 Peter*, 166.

581 Elliott, *1 Peter*, 816.

582 While Bockmuehl is speaking directly about John 21, his observation applies to 1 Peter as well. Markus N. A. Bockmuehl, *Simon Peter in Scripture and Memory: The New Testament Apostle in the Early Church* (Grand Rapids, MI: Baker Academic, 2012), 65.

Rome."[583] As a fellow leader, he provides an example for the elders he addresses on how to lead – not by commanding but by urging; not by demanding but with collegiality; not by holding up glory but rather by testifying to Christ's suffering. It is his witness of Christ's sufferings that he holds up next. A witness is one who sees and testifies to the truth, whether in a court setting or as a divine messenger.[584] Peter, as demonstrated in Acts, was the first apostle after Pentecost to witness to the death and resurrection of Jesus (Acts 2:14–40) and he continued to be a witness to the sufferings of Christ.[585] In the ancient world, it was expected that such testimony from a reliable witness was faithful and true, but it was also recognized that testimony had to be evaluated.[586] Testimony always involves both the experience of the one who testifies and the interpretation of that experience by the one who testifies. Even if the testimony involves quotation, it still involves selection, which is interpretive. Over the last several hundred years there has been a long focus on objective history, but recent scholarly work has focused attention on the reality that much of what we know about the world we learn on the basis of the testimony of others.[587] So too, Peter now testifies about the sufferings of Jesus Christ. In 1 Peter, the focus has been on the suffering that Christ experienced through verbal abuse and crucifixion. While Peter was not present at the crucifixion, he was certainly able to testify to its reality and to the sufferings of Christ before and during that event. Finally, Peter identifies himself as one who "shares in the glory to be revealed." Just as the introduction to 1 Peter refers to "the sufferings destined for Christ and the subsequent glory" (1:11), so too Peter sees himself as participating in both Christ's sufferings and in the glory that follows, even as other Christians share in both Christ's sufferings and glory (4:13).[588] The eschatological horizon extends from the suffering of Christ's death to the revelation of God's glory, and Peter

---

[583] Jobes, *1 Peter*, 300.
[584] BAGD
[585] Note that this phrase, "the sufferings of Christ," is identical to the phrase in 4:13, although there the emphasis is on sharing in Christ's sufferings. See the commentary at 4:13 for further comment on "the sufferings of Christ."
[586] Gene L. Green, *Vox Petri: A Theology of Peter* (Eugene, OR: Cascade Books, 2019), 29–30.
[587] For more on eyewitnesses see, Richard Bauckham, *Jesus and the Eyewitnesses: The Gospels as Eyewitness Testimony*, second edition (Grand Rapids, MI: Eerdmans, 2017).
[588] Schutter, *Hermeneutic*, 108.

locates himself solidly within that horizon. Christ's suffering and his vindication when his glory is revealed is a pattern for Peter's life and for the lives of all believers who live in the time inaugurated at the cross and vindicated at the last day.[589]

Peter addresses himself to the "elders among you." The use of the phrase "among you" is seldom commented on by scholars, but it should be noted that it immediately frames the role of the elders in relationship to the community. And, it is a reminder that the elders who are addressed are spoken to in the context of a community that is listening in. This is not private communication to a special group of leaders but rather an appeal to which the larger community are witness. The word "elder" can refer either to a leadership role[590] within the church or to a person who is older.[591] "Elders" was a term used to designate leaders in the Jewish synagogue as well as in the early Christian communities.[592] The same term was also used in both the Greco-Roman and Jewish culture to refer to older men who were the heads of their households, men of honor and status within society.[593] Both its use in the synagogue as well as its broader social use may have influenced its adoption among the early house churches. While the term was well known in the first century, Elliott argues that it is only with Ignatius of Antioch around 106 CE that we have a fully formalized threefold organizational structure (bishop, elders, and deacons) for the church.[594] While the Pastorals may come close to this structure, the leadership that we see in 1 Peter is less formalized. Indeed, it is focused on the character and motivation of those who lead rather than on a list of qualifications. Throughout the New Testament, elders generally appear as a group who seem to work together, and the elders in 1 Peter are addressed as a group. "The elders met as a group with the apostles to consider the

---

[589]   Elliott, *1 Peter*, 821.

[590]   John Hall Elliott, "Elders as leaders in 1 Peter and the early church," *Hervormde Teologiese Studies* 64:2 (2008): 555; Achtemeier, *1 Peter*, 323; Beare, *The First Epistle of Peter: The Greek Text with Introduction and Notes*, 171; Green, *1 Peter*, 164–65.

[591]   Against the majority, Donelson argues that at best 1 Peter refers to a "loose organizational structure," and that "the call to shepherd the flock suggests the ancient Mediterranean pattern of giving honor and responsibility to the elderly in the community." Donelson, *I & II Peter and Jude*, 143.

[592]   Achtemeier, *1 Peter*, 322; Michaels, *1 Peter*, 279.

[593]   Elliott, *1 Peter*, 814.

[594]   Elliott, "Elders as leaders in 1 Peter and the early church," 554.

question of circumcision (Acts 15); all the Jerusalem elders met with Paul and discussed the crisis at hand (Acts 21:17–26); a council of elders laid hands on Timothy (1 Tim. 4:14); and a group of elders prayed over a sick believer (James 5:14) … it appears that local church elders … functioned as a group of equals."[595] Since 1 Peter 5:2–3 gives specific instructions on the manner in which God's flock should be tended, it is best to understand the elders referred to here are leaders within the Christian community.

The imperative given to elders in **5:2** is to tend God's flock. Most likely, the epistle would have originally been read out in house churches where everyone – elders and younger people, slaves and wives of unbelievers, and the rest of the church – would have heard it together. Instructions directed to particular groups of people were heard by all. In one sense, this makes the elders who are instructed by Peter accountable to the congregations who also hear this instruction. The congregation and its leaders have a mutually interdependent relationship.[596] First Peter makes use of the familiar Old Testament metaphor of shepherd and flock. "In Jewish and OT texts, the theme of God as shepherd delegating authority to human religious or political 'shepherds' is a commonplace (see, e.g., Jer. 23:1–5; Ezek. 34:2–24; Zech. 11:3–17) … The New Testament likewise affirms this derivative role for Christian leaders as shepherds more generally, including in 1 Peter."[597] The Old Testament also repeatedly describes the people of Israel as God's flock and Old Testament leaders who fail to adequately care for God's flock are punished or destroyed (Ezek. 34:10–12; Jer. 13:17; Isa. 40:11; Zech. 10:3). The elders are reminded that the people they care for do not belong to them but rather to God. Peter, who has identified himself as a fellow elder, was instructed by Jesus to shepherd the flock (John 21:15–17). The instruction to shepherd the flock is now passed on to the elders of the churches in Asia Minor. They shepherd by exercising oversight (*episkopountes*).[598] Louw and Nida note that "in translating

---

[595] Matthew D. McDill, "The authority of church elders in the New Testament" (PhD dissertation, Southeastern Baptist Theological Seminary, 2009), 181.

[596] Gert Breed, "The diakonia of the elder according to 1 Peter," *In Die Skriflig* 50:3 (2016): 2.

[597] Bockmuehl, *Simon Peter in Scripture and Memory*, 65.

[598] The NRSV rightly notes that some early manuscripts lack the word for "exercising oversight," but the committee retains it in the most recent revision of NA28. The participle can be read as either attendant circumstance ("while exercising oversight") or as means ("by exercising oversight"). The verb does not, in our context, refer to bishops as it does in later early Christian texts.

episkopē (53.69), *episkopeo* (53.70), or *episkopos*, it is important to try to combine the concepts of both service and leadership, in other words, the responsibility of caring for the needs of a congregation as well as directing the activities of the membership. In some translations an equivalent may be 'helper and leader.'"[599] In the context of 1 Peter, God's people are living in a volatile situation and part of the work of shepherding involves caring for the vulnerable, being on the alert for danger to the flock.

The kind of oversight the elders are to exercise is further qualified using three contrasting pairs. For each negative description of a leader, a positive description is also provided:

not under compulsion but willingly;
not for sordid gain but eagerly; and
not lording it over but being examples.

Those who shepherd God's flock are not to do so because they have been forced or compelled into such a position. Instead, the image of willingly volunteering to serve underlies the description here (BAGD). The position of elder carried with it responsibility for the care of others and might be a position that some wished to avoid. In the context of suffering, saying "yes" to the position of elder might open one up to greater potential risk for difficulties as the leader of a group despised and rejected by wider society. It is possible that the position of elder was an appointed or elected position and that Peter is encouraging those appointed to take up their position willingly.[600] Second, elders are not to take up positions of leadership in the church in order to gain financially through dishonesty or greed. The word for "sordid gain" (*aischrokerdos*) is only used here in the Bible. When paired with the word "eagerly," it becomes clear that the motivation of the elders is in focus. Elders are not to seek a position of oversight among God's people for the purpose of making money. Elliott rightly notes that elders may receive a wide variety of benefits on account of their work. This might include money, food, clothes, or even honor.[601] None of this is problematic unless elders find that they desire not service to God and

---

[599] Louw and Nida, 53.71.
[600] Goppelt, *A Commentary on I Peter*, 345; although, note that others express uncertainty about whether elders were elected; Achtemeier, *1 Peter*, 326.
[601] Elliott, *1 Peter*, 829.

God's flock but rather the acquisition of benefits for themselves. Elsewhere, the New Testament makes clear that "a laborer is worthy of his wages" (1 Tim. 5:18), but it also warns against "the love of money" (1 Tim. 6:10). In contrast to being motivated by sordid gain, the elders are to shepherd the flock "eagerly." The attitude should be one of being eager to be of service and to meet the needs of others, doing so freely and willingly.[602] Both Christians and the broader Greco-Roman society saw "leadership undertaken for ulterior motives [as] dangerous and immoral."[603] Finally (**v. 3**), elders are not to "lord it over" the flock. The word translated as "lord it over" (*katakurieuontes*) means to rule in a domineering fashion. The elders are to shepherd the flock not by domineering over them. First Peter 5:3 may contain an allusion to the saying of Jesus in Mark 10:45 where Jesus also makes use of the same word for "lord it over." There, Jesus indicates that the rulers of this world lord it over those under their control, but his disciples are to be servants. Likewise, in 1 Peter 5:3, the leaders of the church are not to lord it over those in their charge (*kleros*, "lot, portion"), the group that has been apportioned to each elder. Both the saying in Mark and the instruction in 1 Peter point to an emphasis on humility among Jesus' disciples. This focus on humility will be made explicit in 5:5–6. The elders are to be an example to the flock, echoing the posture of a servant from Mark's gospel.[604] In 2:21, Christ himself left an example for the whole church of how to live while suffering. His example is one of non-retaliation in the face of abuse, of holiness of life in the face of evil, and of purity of speech when confronted with threats. Ultimately, Christ entrusts himself to God, who judges justly. In the same way, the whole congregation has been instructed to entrust themselves to their faithful Creator (4:19). Now, the elders are called to live their lives as examples to all people of God on how to live faithfully while practicing holiness, love, and good works in the midst of suffering. The elders are to be the example to those in their charge of right living in light of the new birth. The three antitheses with their negative and positive motivations for leadership describe shameful ways of leading to be avoided and honorable ways to lead in the service of God.[605]

---

[602] BAGD
[603] Donelson, *I & II Peter and Jude*, 145.
[604] Elliott, "Elders as leaders in 1 Peter and the early church," 556.
[605] Green, *1 Peter*, 163.

The author repeatedly emphasizes an attitude of willingness alongside the humility of setting an example rather than making demands.

"When the chief shepherd appears" (**v. 4**):[606] Once again, the eschatological horizon of the epistle is drawn into the present activity of the congregation. The service of the elders is undertaken in anticipation of the day of Christ's return, a day already described as a day when praise and glory will accrue to Jesus Christ (1:7), a day when the full gift of Jesus Christ will be made known (1:13), a day of visitation (2:12), and a day of rejoicing for those who see the glory of Christ (4:13). The congregations anticipate the day this full revelation of Christ will take place and understand that the time for such a revelation is near at hand (4:7). Christ is now identified as the chief shepherd. And, with this, 1 Peter continues the metaphor of shepherding God's flock while making it clear that Jesus Christ is the true and great shepherd. While the title "chief shepherd" is only used here in the Bible, the identification of Christ as a shepherd is known in other New Testament texts. Jesus identifies himself as the good shepherd who lays down his life for the sheep (John 10:11). And when Jesus sees the people without a shepherd, he feels compassion (Matt. 9:6; Mark 6:34).

Those who have served faithfully and well can anticipate receiving "the crown of glory that never fades away" when Christ returns. In the Greco-Roman world the crown was widely recognized as a reward given to those who completed public service with distinction.[607] In addition, crowns were given to those who achieved victory in racing and other games; although such crowns were often garlands made from plant leaves and were thus not "unfading."[608] These crowns were designed to raise the honor and status of the recipient and were a way of acknowledging the contribution that had been made. Perhaps the greatest source of honor is not the crown but the recognition that comes with it. In this case, the elders are recognized and rewarded by the chief shepherd for the service they have rendered – a service based in their exemplary life of humility on behalf of God's flock.

---

[606] The participle *phanerōthentos* is part of a genitive absolute construction and can be taken as either middle ("when the chief shepherd appears," NRSV) or passive ("is revealed"). If passive, God would be the implied revealer. Cf. the use of the identical verb in 1:20 with the passive sense "He ... was revealed at the end of the ages ..." (NRSV). See also, Dubis, *1 Peter*, 162.

[607] Achtemeier, *1 Peter*, 329.

[608] Elliott, *1 Peter*, 831.

Here, those who serve the church are acknowledged by their chief shepherd as worthy of recognition and honor for the work that they have done. In addition, the crown given by the chief shepherd is imperishable and reminds the audience of the imperishable inheritance received by those birthed into God's family (1:3–4). And, unlike crowns made of plants or even of precious metals, this is a crown made of glory (another word within the honor domain). Once again, those who do good, in this case by living with humility as leaders of the flock, are vindicated with an opportunity to share in the glory that most rightfully belongs to Christ, the chief shepherd. The elders were important members of the community but they faced suffering on account of their faith just like the rest of the congregation. While wider society outside the church mocks and abuses them, rather than crowning them, they receive true honor in recognition by the chief shepherd himself.[609]

"In the same way" introduces a second group of people, the "younger" ones. The wives in 3:1 and husbands in 3:7 were introduced as groups using the same Greek word. A similar usage to introduce a new group with new instructions can be seen here. Achtemeier also notes that in 3:1–7 there is a long section devoted to the wives of unbelieving husbands (3:1–6), followed by a short instruction to husbands (3:7). Similarly, here we also have a longer instruction to elders (5:1–4), followed by a short instruction to the younger ones (5:5a).[610] Using the same form that was used in 2:13 and echoed in the participles of 2:18 and 3:1, the younger are told simply to submit themselves to the elders. There is some debate over the meaning of the word "elders" in the instruction "you who are younger must accept the authority of the elders." It could mean that those who are younger must accept the authority of the leaders, which is how "elders" was used in 5:4, or it could mean that the younger ones must submit to the older ones in the congregation. As many have noted, it seems implausible to argue for a shift from "leader" to "older person" without a specific indication of that shift in

---

[609] My thinking on the crowns as a source of honor for a group who were of lower status in the eyes of broader society has been influenced by the unpublished work of John R. Wright, "'The unfading crown of glory' as conceptual key: Mimicry and symbolic inversion of honorifics in 1 Peter," May 2020, General Epistles, NT921, Asbury Theological Seminary.

[610] Achtemeier, *1 Peter*, 331.

the text;[611] since it is clear that "elders" refers to leaders in 5:1–4, it is best to retain that meaning in 5:5. It is not entirely clear who constitutes the group of younger people (*neōteroi*). Several possibilities have been suggested: (1) those younger in the faith (recent converts); (2) the remainder of the congregation apart from elders; (3) younger men who had some particular role in the church; and (4) younger members of the congregation.[612] Many English translations favor the fourth option (NRSV, "you who are younger"), focusing on the age of the younger ones. Davids argues that this group refers to younger people in the congregation who may have thought they were ready for leadership. He suggests that such younger people may have been impatient with their elders and might not always have thought through the ramifications of their actions, thus potentially endangering the church.[613]

Other scholars have argued that the younger ones are not a specific group in the congregation but rather all those who are not elders.[614] Jobes writes:

The contrast is … between those who have the seniority and the commensurate standing that qualifies them to be *presbyteroi* in contrast to those who, for whatever reason, do not. Official elders of the church were naturally chosen from those who held seniority in the faith, which most often also corresponded to physical age. Those not (yet) qualified to be elders were "younger" in standing in the church. The term … therefore refers 'to those who were not elders, that is to say all other church members.'[615]

However, in the previous household code segment, groups were addressed separately, while the whole congregation was addressed at both the beginning and the end. Similarly, it seems that we have an address to two groups (elders and younger ones) and an address to everyone (5:5b).

---

[611] Feldmeier, *The First Letter of Peter*, 237.

[612] Forbes, *1 Peter*, 170.

[613] Davids, *The First Epistle of Peter*, 182; Other commentators who argue for an age-related meaning include Beare, *The First Epistle of Peter: The Greek Text with Introduction and Notes*, 175; Green, *1 Peter*, 169; Grudem, *1 Peter*, 192–93.

[614] Feldmeier, the rest of Christians (by analogy), in Feldmeier, *The First Letter of Peter*, 238; Goppelt, *A Commentary on I Peter*, 351; Michaels, *1 Peter*, 289; Senior and Harrington, *1 Peter*, 141.

[615] Jobes, *1 Peter*, 307, following R. A. Campbell, *The Elders: Seniority within Earliest Christianity* (Edinburgh: T&T Clark, 1994).

So, rather than drawing a strict line between age, office, and rank in the early church, it is probably best to see these identity markers as intertwined. Donelson notes:

Early Christian notions of equality before God did not, for the most part, undo social hierarchies. However, it is not clear in this verse who is being asked to submit to whom and what the character of that submission might be. The most likely explanation is that "elders" and "young people" refer loosely to both age and status in the community. The admonition to elders not to rule in a domineering way does not permit the young people to ignore their authority … Elders should rule, but they should do so in a gentle way. Young people should, in turn, submit to this noncoercive authority.[616]

This is the first time in 1 Peter that submission takes place between Christians. In the earlier instructions, submission was to outsiders (rulers, masters whether good or bad, and unbelieving husbands). Here, those who are younger are instructed to submit to those who have responsibility for the care of the flock. There is reciprocity in these instructions. While the younger ones are to submit to the elders, the elders are to act in ways that demonstrate their worthiness to lead. This reciprocity is enhanced by the instruction that follows in the next clause: all the members of the church are to clothe themselves with humility. This echoes the structure of 2:11–3:12 where, after addressing slaves, wives of unbelievers, and believing husbands, Peter addresses the whole community and instructs them to practice unity, love, and humility (3:8). In 5:5, all are to clothe themselves with humility. The idea of putting on moral virtue or taking off vice is well known in the New Testament even though the exact word for "clothe yourselves" (*enkombōsasthe*) occurs only here in the Bible (cf. Col. 3:12). First Peter 2:1 instructs believers to put off such things as evil, malice, and envy. And, other clothing metaphors are found in 1 Peter 1:13 ("girding up") and 4:1 ("arming yourselves") but none of the military nuances are found in the instruction to clothe themselves in 5:5. Indeed, Elliott suggests that the etymology of the Greek word may relate to the action of tying a serving cloth around one's waist.[617] Humility has already been listed as a characteristic of the Christian community in 3:8, but now it is found as the

---

[616] Donelson, *I & II Peter and Jude*, 146; similarly, Achtemeier, *1 Peter*, 332.
[617] Elliott, *1 Peter*, 846. An argument for the definition of a word based on the meaning of each component of that word must always, however, be held loosely.

singular focus of 5:5. The attitude of humility went against Greco-Roman ideals, especially when such humility included association with the poor and the despised. It was one thing to be merciful and even gentle. Such qualities could even be seen as noble in a leader as long as such a person did not debase himself.[618] But generally, humility was seen as an attitude worthy of slaves.[619] First Peter has already identified those who hear this letter as God's slaves (2:16) and so it is perhaps not surprising that the whole congregation is instructed to take up a quality deemed by the larger society as one suited for slaves. It is this way of being that they are instructed to exhibit with one another. And, it is the very quality that Christ himself exhibited when he humbled himself by suffering on the cross and entrusting his life to the one who judges justly. This demonstration of humility on the part of Jesus is evident both in 1 Peter and in other parts of the New Testament. For example, in Philippians 2:8 Christ humbled himself to the point of death on a cross. Peter supports this instruction that the church practice humility with a quotation from Proverbs 3:34 LXX. The subject of the Proverb is God. God opposes (*antitassetai*) those who are arrogant. The verb can be used generally to mean opposing but can also be used in specific contexts to refer to waging battle against someone.[620] God stands in opposition to those who are arrogant or haughty. Goppelt notes that "'Pride' shows itself in disobedience against the gospel and passes away with acceptance of it."[621] Those who reject the chosen stone in 2:7 and who disobey the gospel (4:17) show themselves to be people who have set themselves up as knowing more than or being greater than God, thus proud or arrogant. In the New Testament, arrogance is either contrasted negatively with humility (e.g., Luke 1:51–52) or found in vice lists (e.g., Rom. 1:30). In contrast to the arrogant, who God opposes, God shows favor ("grace") to those who are humble. God's grace has been a repeated theme in 1 Peter with such grace linked to God's salvation, whether in the present or at the moment of Christ's revelation (1:10, 13), and to the breadth of God's gifts to the church (4:10). The gracious gifts of salvation and empowerment for ministry are given to

---

[618] Keener, *1 Peter*, 376.

[619] Goppelt, *A Commentary on I Peter*, 353.

[620] LSJ and Thayer both give military connotations to the word and refer to its use to describe opposing in battle; for "oppose," see BAGD.

[621] Goppelt, *A Commentary on I Peter*, 354.

the humble and are available to the whole church, leaders and other members alike. Throughout this Proverb, God is the actor, and it is God's activity towards the arrogant or the humble that is described.

The quotation from Proverbs 3:34 stands between the exhortation to the community to clothe itself with humility and the instruction to be humble under the hand of God (**5:6**).[622] In this way, the quotation from the Old Testament Scriptures is a means of instructing the whole community while also providing the transition between the leadership instructions and the general teaching directed to the whole congregation.[623] What follows in vv. 6–7 unpacks the meaning of the proverbial saying for the church in Asia Minor.

In 5:6–7 Peter continues with the theme of humility in relationship to God and provides an interpretive comment on the text of the Proverb from 1 Peter 5:5. The verb in 5:6 can be either a middle voice meaning "humble yourselves" or a passive voice, "be humbled."[624] In either case, the humility that characterizes God's household is humility in relationship to God. In other words, even if the humble position that they experience comes from the world through suffering on account of their faith,[625] such a humble position is in God's will (3:17; 4:19) and is under the control of the mighty hand of God. The mighty hand of God is referred to throughout the Old Testament where it can indicate both God's powerful judgment and discipline (e.g., Job 30:21) or God's power to deliver. The phrase is used repeatedly to refer to God's power to rescue Israel from the Egyptian empire. Moses speaks to the Israelites and asks them, "[H]as any god ever attempted to go

---

[622] Many commentaries have a break between 1 Peter 5:5 and 1 Peter 5:6. Reasons for the introduction of a break ranges from the use of "therefore" to mark a new section, the list of three imperatival instructions beginning at v. 6, or a shift in focus from the internal community to the external society. Elliott, in an unusual move, creates a break between 5:5a and a unit that runs from 5:5b–11 while noting that this is a minor break: Elliott, *1 Peter*, 845. It seems to me that there is a movement from instructing leaders (5:1–4) to the broader community, and even to the threats that the community faces from external sources. But the flow of these transitions is so tightly woven that a break at this point seems unnatural. Thus, this commentary presents a longer section (5:1–7) at this point.

[623] Sargent, *Written to Serve*, 98.

[624] In form, the verb is an aorist passive imperative. Some recent scholars have argued that during the koine period the passive endings came to represent both the middle and passive forms of the verb. See Chrys C. Caragounis, *The Development of Greek and the New Testament: Morphology, Syntax, Phonology, and Textual Transmission* (Grand Rapids, MI: Baker Academic, 2006), 153; Dubis, *1 Peter*, 166. Others continue to argue for a true passive sense of the verb; Forbes, *1 Peter*, 175; Elliott, *1 Peter*, 850.

[625] Achtemeier, *1 Peter*, 338.

and take a nation for himself from the midst of another nation, by trials, by signs and wonders, by war, by a *mighty hand* [emphasis added] and an outstretched arm, and by terrifying displays of power, as the LORD your God did for you in Egypt before your very eyes?" (Deut. 4:34; other examples include Exod. 3:19; 6:1; 13:9; Deut. 9:26; Dan. 9:15). In the eyes of the Egyptians, the Israelites were a despised group of slaves, but under the mighty hand of God, they were delivered from oppression in order to become God's people. God has the power to deliver God's people from Egypt, and God has the power to watch over and care for God's flock who find themselves living in a hostile social setting. Those who follow Christ and Christ's example of humility in the midst of a society that mocks and abuses them will experience being humbled under God's mighty hand. This is part of the acknowledgment of God's power and sovereignty. It is God who humbles, and it is God who raises up. Any position that the church obtains or any honor or glory that it receives is given by God. In many ways this group of Christians – scattered and exiled – is already humble, far from the places of power and on the margins of society. Yet, they are not instructed to raise themselves up or to make their own way to places of power, rather they are to exist in humility in relationship to God and to one another. And then, the Lord will exalt them. Again, it is the activity and action of God that raises up. "God 'exalts' by granting a share in the glory that Christ received by his exaltation (1:11; 3:22), a share in a life free of evil and pain" in the last day.[626] This exaltation happens in due time – at the time of God's choosing. Elsewhere in 1 Peter, "time" (*kairos*) refers either to the last time (1:5; 4:17) or to the time of Christ's suffering and subsequent glory (1:11). It should be understood in a similar fashion here, as it continues the theme that God will vindicate God's people. "[I]n 1 Peter, God is arbiter of honour and shame (2.6–7, 13, 19–20; 3.12; 5.5–6). He is the one whose approval the believers live for and seek."[627] Whether humbled in relationship to God or raised up in the last day, believers are honored by God's activity on their behalf.

"Cast all your anxiety on him" (5:7). As elsewhere in 1 Peter, the participle has been translated in the NRSV as an imperative, and it does rightly derive imperatival force from the imperative in 5:6.[628] Other English

---

[626] Goppelt, *A Commentary on I Peter*, 357.
[627] Joseph, *A Narratological Reading of 1 Peter*, 168.
[628] Forbes, *1 Peter*, 175.

translations treat it as a participle of attendant circumstance (e.g., ESV, KJV, "casting"). But it is also possible to understand this participle as describing the means by which God's people accept their humble circumstances.[629] In the midst of their humble circumstances, they show their reliance upon God by casting every care, worry, or anxiety on God. The wording of this saying echoes the saying of Jesus: "Therefore I tell you, do not worry about your life, what you will eat or what you will drink, or about your body, what you will wear" (Matt. 6:25). The teaching of Jesus goes on to enumerate God's care for the needs of the disciples (Matt. 6:25–34). First Peter sums it up as "because he cares for you." Believers do not rely on themselves to address their concerns but instead turn to God. As a group on the margins of the Greco-Roman society and with fears and worries about their very survival as a group, they can be assured that even in the depths of their suffering God cares for them. "They may … hand over to God the fear for their existence … that presses in on them with society's discrimination."[630] They follow the example of Christ who entrusted himself to God (2:21–25) and live out the instruction to entrust themselves to the faithful Creator (4:19).

Bridging the Horizons: One way to think about humility is to consider it within the context of power. Humility is associated with lowness, being small, and even being weak. The majority of those who first heard Peter's epistle were not the powerful of their society but rather the humble – slaves, wives of unbelievers, those under the governance of the empire. But their humble position in society is not explicitly pointed out by 1 Peter, rather, it is assumed, and it is helpful for twenty-first century readers to acknowledge it. These people living on the margins of society are not instructed to become powerful or to straighten their backs or to lift their heads. Rather, they are invited to acknowledge their humble status before God, the Almighty. Their status in life is not connected to their status in society but rather to their status before God. Their status is located in the favor that God shows them as they continue in right behavior flowing from their faith. They are the people who recognize God's wonderful ways and deeds and acknowledge their humble status before God. This is what it means to clothe oneself with humility. These are the

---

[629] Achtemeier, *1 Peter*, 339; Forbes, *1 Peter*, 175–76.
[630] Goppelt, *A Commentary on I Peter*, 358.

people whom God will lift up when God sees fit. Here, in the phrase "lifting up," we might hear an echo of the crucifixion and glorification of Christ. John's gospel speaks of the Son of Man being lifted up (John 8:28), and of the hour of Christ's suffering as being the hour of Christ's glory (John 12:27–32). It is at the point when Christ is lifted up on the cross that he is enthroned as king. What was meant for his humiliation became the means of his glorification and of his ability to offer eternal life to all. For these Christians who suffer degrading insults and humiliating persecution, this is a reminder that God's exaltation of them happens in God's time, and even the suffering and humiliation can become an avenue to God's exaltation in God's time. The instruction on humility reminds Christians that their position is always in relationship not to the society that surrounds them but to the Almighty God who stoops down to death on a cross, who proclaims good news to all, and who triumphs over sin and death. In humility Christians recognize that God works through the small, the weak, the meek, the grieving, and that God is at work through the suffering they endure and the opposition they face.

Being lifted up does not involve the absence of humility. The Christian will always be humble in relationship to Almighty God. Even if God chooses to raise up Christians in this life to places of power in this world, such places are small – places of humility – compared to God and God's power. Whether God chooses to raise up the Christian who experiences humiliation, this is done in God's time. Still, Christians will come to share in the glory of Christ at the resurrection, the final echo of the idea of being lifted up. God may choose to raise up Christians into God's presence, and there they will find that they have been exalted while remaining humble. The Christian is enabled to live in the presence of the Holy God without being destroyed. Humility is not just something to be taken on for a period of time in order to attain power or position (e.g., being exalted or lifted up). That will always be a temptation for humanity – to use humility as a way to power. Those who heard 1 Peter were humble because of their exilic relationship to society and the persecution they faced. In the midst of suffering – whether suffering of an individual or of the community – the humble know who they are in the presence of God: they are the children of God, invited into a glorious inheritance made possible through the resurrection. And they anticipate continuing in humble relationship with their Father and Creator both now and when they are raised up for all eternity. For the promise given is not the promise of power but rather the promise of eternal relationship with the God who restores humanity and creation so that they live together in humility with one another and with God, sharing in Christ's glory. Humility is not to be forced on others, nor are Christians to humiliate others. Instead, Christians proclaim the wonderful deeds of God and invite others into relationship with God where they too accept the posture of humility.

1 Peter 5:8–11: Resisting the Devil

[8] Discipline yourselves, keep alert. Like a roaring lion your adversary the devil prowls around, looking for someone to devour.

[9] Resist him, steadfast in your faith, for you know that your brothers and sisters in all the world are undergoing the same kinds of suffering.

[10] And after you have suffered for a little while, the God of all grace, who has called you to his eternal glory in Christ, will himself restore, support, strengthen, and establish you.

[11] To him be the power forever and ever. Amen.

First Peter 5:8–11 continues, like 5:1–7, to use the imperative in these final instructions addressed to the whole church. However, it begins with a double imperative that signals heightened attention to the eschatological context. And, it introduces a new character, the devil (5:8), who has not been encountered before while returning to the explicit theme of suffering (5:9). It ends with a contrast between the devil who devours and the God who strengthens and establishes (5:10–11).

For the fourth time in 1 Peter, the church is instructed to be sober (NRSV, "discipline yourselves,"1:13; 4:7; 5:8), and this time they are also instructed to keep watch (**5:8**). These two imperatives occur with no conjunction joining them together. Placed next to each other, they emphasize the vigilance that should characterize the church. These verbs are also used in other eschatological texts that encourage believers to be ready for the day of the Lord (e.g., Matt. 24:42; 25:13; 1 Thess. 5:6).[631] It becomes immediately apparent why the church must be attentive: "Like a roaring lion your adversary the devil prowls around." The noun "adversary" occurs here and in the Gospels (Matt. 5:25; Luke 12:58; 18:3) where it refers to the "accuser," the private individual who brings charges in court against another. In the LXX it can refer both to an adversary in court (Prov. 18:17; Jer. 27:34; 28:36) as well as to adversaries more generally (1 Sam 2:10; Hosea 5:11). In the Roman court system the accuser pressed charges against the defendant. Here, the devil is portrayed as that accuser waiting to bring charges against Christians, perhaps the charge of apostasy or disobedience.[632] The church experiences

---

[631] Christopher Byrley, "Persecution and the 'adversary' of 1 Peter 5:8," *The Southern Baptist Journal of Theology* 21:3 (2017): 91.

[632] Dominique Charles, "'Votre Adversaire Le Diable Rôde Comme Un Lion Rugissant' (1 P 5,8)," *RB* 120:3 (2013): 421.

social hostility coming from those around who see them as subversive and rebellious. In these circumstances, the danger the church faces is that of becoming complacent or reticent in the face of social pressure that may extend to persecution. The danger they face comes from the devil. This is the title used to refer to the primary transcendent evil being and is also used by the LXX to translate the Hebrew *satan*, which means "accuser."[633] Revelation 12:9 brings together many of these descriptions of the evil being opposed to God: "The great dragon was thrown down, that ancient serpent, who is called the Devil and Satan, the deceiver of the whole world." The association of the devil with slanderous accusation is noteworthy in light of the abuse and slander that Christians in Asia Minor face from their neighbors. The devil is both the accuser and the opponent of Christians. This is the one who "seeks to hinder the eschatological event of salvation and to wrest believers from the life with God through bodily harm and, above all, through temptation."[634] The identity of the devil as a transcendent being in opposition to God shows that the fight that Christians are engaged in is not simply against the hostile rejection of their neighbors. Elliott has argued that "1 Peter ... expresses no anxiety over or hatred for the power of Rome."[635] But this does not fully take into account the source of the conflict between Christians and wider society. Williams argues:

Evidence from the letter suggests that the author blames the imperial system for the readers' troubles just as much as he does the general populace. First, the subtle resistance to the dominant Empire evidenced throughout the epistle ... suggests that Rome is a major problem. Second, the threat to which the author refers in 1 Peter 5.9 (*viz.*, being devoured by the "roaring lion") seems to have involved both imperial agents and private citizens. At issue is the turning aside from the Christian faith amidst pressure to conform to the expectations of Greco-Roman society. But it is not just friends and neighbors that would be pressuring the readers to apostatize. On a larger level, the Empire is also responsible, since it facilitated many of the institutions that were causing the social conflict (e.g., emperor worship, Roman court system, entertainment, etc.). Thus, it is doubtful that the author would have differentiated between the people in general and the Empire more specifically.[636]

---

[633] BAGD

[634] Goppelt, *A Commentary on I Peter*, 361.

[635] Elliott, *1 Peter*, 858.

[636] Williams, *Good Works in 1 Peter*, 239.

Behind the hostile actions of their neighbors lie the systemic forces of the Roman Empire. And behind those forces lies a greater force that is intent on devouring them.

In order to draw the audience into his final argument, 1 Peter makes use of a vivid metaphor that contains sound ("roaring"), movement ("prowls"), and destruction ("devour"). In verse 8, the devil is portrayed as a roaring lion that prowls around seeking someone to devour. This vivid metaphor placed at the end of Peter's letter brings an image to the mind of the audience that helps focus their attention on the main message to "stand firm in the faith."[637] Nowhere else in the Bible is the devil compared with a lion. This has led scholars to debate the background for this metaphor. Most propose a background drawn from the Old Testament[638] while a few argue for a reference to the material culture of the first century.[639] The lion was used to depict the enemies of Israel in the Old Testament. For example, in Jeremiah 50:17, appears the phrase "Israel is a hunted sheep driven away by lions," and in Psalm 22:21, a Psalm used to depict Jesus' passion, the Psalmist pleads, "Save me from the mouth of the lion!" The lion could be depicted as the enemy of the faithful people of God, and God was the means of deliverance from such a fearsome enemy. Jobes notes that "Fierce animal imagery is also used in Daniel and Revelation to symbolize world systems deformed by the powers of darkness and sin."[640] She goes on to say, "Peter may be implying with the lion imagery that satanic powers are at work in the sociopolitical system of the Roman Empire, under which his readers are suffering."[641] However, the Old Testament was not the only source for lion imagery in the first century. Lion imagery was ubiquitous in Asia Minor and is found in statuary, coins, and even in some mosaics in wealthy homes, where a lion is depicted battling other lions or a human hunter.[642] But the most common place to see lions was at one of the most popular forms of entertainment in the

---

[637] David G. Horrell, Bradley Arnold, and Travis B. Williams, "Visuality, vivid description, and the message of 1 Peter: The significance of the roaring lion (1 Peter 5:8)," *JBL* 132 (2013): 715–16.

[638] Elliott, *1 Peter*, 856–57; Achtemeier, *1 Peter*, 341.

[639] Boris A. Paschke, "The Roman *ad bestias* execution as a possible historical background for 1 Peter 5.8," *JSNT* 28 (2006): 489–500.

[640] Jobes, *1 Peter*, 314.

[641] Jobes, *1 Peter*, 314.

[642] Horrell, Arnold, and Williams, "Visuality," 706–7.

Roman world: the theatrical spectacle of the games. These involved animal hunts or fights in the morning, execution of criminals around noon, and gladiator contests in the afternoon.[643] Executions by beast (*ad bestias*) were one of the highly anticipated features of these events, and executions by lion were the most highly anticipated of all.[644] Paschke has shown that Christians were executed by being thrown to the beasts as early as Nero.[645] And Horrell's research has shown that the same kind of executions were practiced throughout Asia Minor during the time period in which 1 Peter was most likely written.[646] Such executions would have ended with the lion devouring its prey. In other words, the vivid metaphor of the devil as the roaring lion seeking to devour its pray may draw on the cultural reality of the first century as well as the Old Testament depiction of the lion as the enemy of the righteous.[647] The imagery of the lion atop its prey consuming the prey it has stalked, attacked, and killed strikes the audience as a terrifying danger signal in the face of potential complacency. "The devil is not physically persecuting the believers himself; instead, most understand this verse as a reference to the devil's influence and empowerment of intermediate agents who perform the acts of persecution against Christians."[648] Such agents may be hostile neighbors or perhaps this is a reference to the various rulers of the Roman Empire. By portraying the true adversary of Christians in this vivid manner, 1 Peter catches the attention of the audience and prepares them for the imperative that follows.

The people of God are to resist (**5:9**) their opponent, the devil. It is not enough to be alert and watchful, there must also be active resistance in the face of evil. Both Ephesians 6:13 and James 4:7 use the same word, *anthistēmi*, to speak of resisting the cosmic forces of evil and the devil. First Peter 5:9 shares the same idea that Christians are involved in a battle against spiritual forces.[649] Asumang has shown that the New Testament

---

[643] Horrell, Arnold, and Williams, "Visuality," 708.

[644] Horrell, Arnold, and Williams, "Visuality," 708–9.

[645] Paschke, "Roman *ad bestias* execution," 496.

[646] Horrell, Arnold, and Williams, "Visuality," 712.

[647] I am indebted to Tyler Hallstrom for his work on the metaphor of the roaring lion in 1 Peter 5:8 presented as an unpublished paper, "'Like a lion': Assessing the source domain of the leonine metaphor in 1 Peter 5:8," May 7, 2020, NT941, Asbury Theological Seminary.

[648] Williams, *Good Works in 1 Peter*, 238.

[649] Achtemeier, *1 Peter*, 342.

takes up ideas of a cosmic spiritual war from the Old Testament and embeds them in the apocalyptic narrative of a battle between God and the forces of evil, a battle that culminates in the eschatological day of judgment when God's people will experience salvation and vindication.[650] The idea that the Christians of Asia Minor are involved in a spiritual war has already been hinted at by the use of such military metaphors as "arm yourselves" (4:1) and the instruction to "gird up the loins of your mind."[651] In addition, the reference to the devil points to a spiritual and cosmic conflict rather than a solely local and material conflict. Finally, the Christians have been instructed to be "sober" (*nēpsate*, NRSV, "discipline yourselves"), a word used in other New Testament contexts related to being alert on the last day (e.g., 1 Thess. 5:6–8; Rom. 13:11–14). All of this points to resistance as part of the cosmic battle against the devil and the forces of evil. What is the manner by which such resistance takes place? That resistance is based on the firm, solid nature of faith. From the moment of new birth, faith was an essential part of salvation (1:5); faith has been tested by suffering (1:7) on the way to the final salvation anticipated at Christ's return (1:9). This faith is rooted in the death and resurrection of Jesus and directed towards God (1:20–21). Now, at the end of the epistle, Peter reminds those hearing his words to be firm in faith. In this strength, they resist the predatory enemy that seeks to destroy them, and they remain ready for the fullness of salvation. The Christians of Asia Minor are engaged in a spiritual battle, and the weapon for that battle is the very trust they have in God as the just judge and faithful Creator (2:25; 4:19). And while the devil may lie behind the attacks they face from society, there is no hint of retaliation in their resistance, for the epistle has made quite clear that resistance to abuse is characterized by non-retaliation (but not necessarily acquiescence).[652] Finally, Peter reminds them that they are not alone in suffering on account of their identity as Christians (4:16).[653] The verb "being accomplished" (*epiteleisthai*, NRSV: "undergoing") in the

---

[650] Annang Asumang, "'Resist him' (1 Pet 5:9): Holiness and non-retaliatory responses to unjust suffering as 'holy war' in 1 Peter," *Conspectus* 11 (2011): 21.

[651] Asumang, "'Resist him,'" 31–32, 36. Asumang notes that "girding up the loins" can be used in both general and military contexts.

[652] Asumang, "'Resist him,'" 37.

[653] The grammar of the phrase "the same kinds of sufferings" (*ta auta tōn pathēmatōn*) is awkward, but the sense of either "the same sufferings" or "the same sort of sufferings" is clear enough. Elliott, *1 Peter*, 861.

passive has the sense of something being brought to an end or goal or being completed, but in this context most English versions translate it with a sense of "undergoing" or "happening." However, the passive form and the goal-oriented direction of the verb remind the readers that "the sufferings of Christian believers are not a matter of chance but a necessary part of God's purpose."[654] Even though their suffering originates with the devil, it is part of God's will because "that suffering means the Christians remain faithful to their trust in God. In the choice between suffering and apostasy, it is God's will that Christians [reject] apostasy even when that means inevitably that suffering will be inflicted upon them."[655] This suffering on account of their faithfulness to God is not unique to the church in Asia Minor. Throughout the world, other members of the household of God are experiencing the same kind of suffering that the churches in Asia Minor are experiencing. The book of Acts shows a variety of different types of suffering and persecution experienced by the early church including trials (Acts 20:19), imprisonment (Acts 4:3; 16:23; 21:33), and martyrdom (Acts 7). This portrait of the early church makes it clear that suffering and persecution were part of the church's experience from the beginning. Persecution took place in Jerusalem as well as in the other provinces the apostles visited. When Peter addresses those in Asia Minor, he reminds them that they are not alone in their experience of suffering on account of their faith. Indeed, those who followed the crucified and suffering Christ should not be surprised when they too encounter suffering on account of their identity.

Peter finishes the main body of the letter with a doxology (**5:10–11**) that reminds the audience of the character and calling of God. In Greek, the verse in fact begins with a contrast: "but" marks the divergence between the prowling devil looking for prey and God who is identified as "the God of all grace." While enduring suffering and facing their opponent they are reminded that God's "divine beneficence has been lavishly bestowed on the people of God" (1:10; 4:10; 5:5).[656] All grace in its many variations (4:10) flows from God and is a gift to those who suffer on account of their faithfulness to the God who has called them: "the God of all grace, who has called you." It is God's character to summon or invite and in 1 Peter

---

[654] Michaels, *1 Peter*, 302.
[655] Achtemeier, *1 Peter*, 344.
[656] Williams, "Reciprocity and suffering in 1 Peter 2,19–20," 432.

God calls those who have received new life into a new identity. In 1:15 the God who calls invites them to resemble God through holiness that resembles God's own. And in 2:9 the God who calls moves them from darkness into God's own light. The church is called to imitation of God (2:21; 3:9), but such imitation is only made possible by God's own gift of new birth, new identity, and new way of living in holiness and love. Members of the church are called by God into "his eternal glory in Christ." The calling has already happened, and the eternal future is secured; the glory of God is secured for them by their participation in Christ.[657] God's glory has been shared with God's son Jesus Christ through the resurrection, ascension, and rule of Christ (1:11; 3:21–22). Now, God's people anticipate their entrance into the fullness of God's glory, for they as people who are in Christ share in the glory that the Trinity has secured on their behalf. The God who calls makes their new birth possible through the resurrection of the Son in the sphere of the Spirit. God's people anticipate the final day when they will live in glory with the Father and the Son. Right now, God's people live in between the past calling of God and the future participation in eternal glory, yet they live already as participants in Christ. And, in the in-between space the challenge is to live as members of God's people: loving one another, living in holiness, and doing good. That in-between time may very well be one of suffering, but such suffering is "for a little while." The beginning of 1 Peter pointed to a time of grief and trials that was also characterized as being short (1:6), and, as the letter draws to a close, the same encouragement is offered in 5:10. This may be a time of suffering, but it will not go on forever. And, the church can expect that God will "restore, support, strengthen, and establish" them. Together, these four verbs all point to the activity of God to secure God's people. Here, we see that God will restore them, mending what has been broken by their suffering and making them whole.[658] God will support them. The verb used here (*stērizō*) has the meaning of strengthen or establish.[659] In eschatological contexts such as we see in 1 Peter it most often means "strengthen,"[660] and can have the nuance of reinforcing someone who is

---

[657]   Elliott, *1 Peter*, 865.
[658]   Achtemeier, *1 Peter*, 346.
[659]   BAGD
[660]   Achtemeier, *1 Peter*, 346.

suffering.[661] The third verb, strengthen (*sthenoō*), occurs only here in Greek literature and has the meaning of making strong.[662] It is a synonym of the previous verb and Michaels suggests that the multiplication of synonyms related to strength may reinforce the important phrase "steadfast in your faith" from 5:9.[663] The final verb in the series is "establish". This relates to the work of laying a foundation and metaphorically it refers to providing a secure basis for the life of faith. "God will give the Christians an unshakable grounding by including them in his eschatological glory. The fact that the verbs are also what is needed during the suffering, that is, strong and unshakable confidence in God, is not accidental. Christians are already to show the kind of reality that will be theirs at the time of the eschatological fulfillment."[664] In the eyes of the world this little community that is experiencing suffering might be seen as a disgrace, but they are the recipients of many gifts from God. They are God's people welcomed into his glorious presence and honored by the sure foundation and strength that God provides. The one who establishes them is the one to whom power belongs forever (**5:11**). This final verse of the section is a very short doxology, which is very similar to but shorter than the one in 4:11. The emphasis is on the power of God and serves to confirm the capacity of God to fulfill the promises that have been made to a people in adversity. Most major commentators agree that the verb supplied is the present indicative and that the translation should draw out the fact that power or dominion belongs to God.[665] This is not a wish for God to have power but a statement that emphasizes the power that God already has and uses.

Bridging the Horizons: The main instructions of this passage are to be alert and watchful (5:8) and to resist the devil (5:9). In our churches, there are often two extremes: (1) churches that never talk about the devil or Satan; and (2) churches that blame every small thing that goes wrong in a person's life on the devil. In 1 Peter, the

[661] Elliott, *1 Peter*, 866.
[662] Achtemeier, *1 Peter*, 346.
[663] Michaels, *1 Peter*, 303.
[664] Achtemeier, *1 Peter*, 346.
[665] Achtemeier, *1 Peter*, 346; Elliott, *1 Peter*, 867; Goppelt, *A Commentary on I Peter*, 366; Michaels, *1 Peter*, 304.

devil is the force behind the persecution that Christians experience, and the devil is to be resisted by continuing in faithfulness to God and the pursuit of love, holiness, and good deeds. But Peter does not place the devil behind every adverse circumstance that Christians face. Fleming Rutledge gives three pieces of advice about Christians and the devil: (1) do not use the devil to shift blame away from oneself (e.g., "the devil made me do it"); (2) avoid using the devil as a way of projecting evil onto other groups of people; and (3) recognize both that Satan is God's enemy and that Satan cannot exist apart from God (he "has no independent ontological status of his own").[666] In the context of 1 Peter, we are reminded that sin is driven by human desires and choices (4:2). There is no hint that those who are outsiders to the Christian group are despised or hated or blamed or treated as evil by Christians (e.g., there is no projection of devilish intent upon those persecuting Christians, even if the devil is behind that persecution). Instead, Christians are repeatedly instructed to live in ways that are good in the eyes of God with the awareness that living in that way will finally reveal God's truth to those who oppose them (whether through conversion or on the final day when Christ is revealed). At the same time, Christians should be fully aware that there is an enemy of God in this world. In a world that is inclined to dismiss belief in the devil or Satan, Christians are able to remind the world that there is indeed an enemy power that seeks to destroy and to devour all that is good, all that comes from God. While 1 Peter focuses on the suffering that comes about because of persecution and the roving lion that seeks to destroy, contemporary Christians are aware that the power of evil shows up not only in direct persecution, but in such malignant ways that they "require us to speak of a power far more monstrous than the mere sum of individual transgressions."[667] Here, for a start, we might think of the various genocides that have marked the last 100 years in places such as Russia, the Third Reich, Armenia, and Rwanda. Christians must not forget that there is an Enemy of God in this world. At the same time, Christians must be fully aware that their power to resist the devil happens in two ways. First, God is the one who enables Christian resistance to the power of evil. It is God who strengthens, who establishes, and who empowers. Second, resisting the devil is done together in community. The command, like all the instructions in 1 Peter, is in the plural. The church together is to resist the devil. Such resistance takes place through the community work of loving one another, living holy lives with one another, and pursuing good works and good behavior as a community with all those with whom the church has relationship. It is together in mutual relationship with God and with one another that the church that God has established finds the power to stand against the Enemy.

[666] Rutledge, *The Crucifixion*, 438.
[667] Rutledge, *The Crucifixion*, 438.

1 PETER 5:12–14: LETTER CLOSING

[12] Through Silvanus, whom I consider a faithful brother, I have written this short letter to encourage you and to testify that this is the true grace of God. Stand fast in it.

[13] Your sister church in Babylon, chosen together with you, sends you greetings; and so does my son Mark.

[14] Greet one another with a kiss of love. Peace to all of you who are in Christ.

The last three verses of the epistle follow the format of many New Testament letters. Important persons are identified, greetings are sent, and a final closing instruction and benediction are given.

The closing section of the epistle starts with the introduction of Silvanus **(5:12)**. The name Silvanus was common in Greco-Roman culture and perhaps this Silvanus is someone who is otherwise unknown to us today.[668] However, it is likely that the same Silvanus who is identified as Paul's companion in 2 Corinthians 1:19 and as the coauthor of 1–2 Thessalonians is also meant here. Further, it is likely that Silas, known to us from Acts (esp. Acts 15:22–41), and Silvanus are the same person. "Silas and Silvanus are probably the Greek and Latin forms of the same Jewish name."[669] Peter indicates that he wrote "through Silvanus." There are two possible ways to understand this. Silvanus may be either the carrier of the letter who delivered it to the churches in Asia Minor or he may be the scribe who helped Peter compose it. It is, of course, conceivable that Silvanus both delivered the letter and had some role in its composition.

Many recent scholars have argued that Silvanus is the carrier of the letter. Evidence in support of this position includes: (1) the use of the formula elsewhere in the New Testament. Acts 15:22–23 describes the selection of Silas as one of the men who would deliver a letter from the apostles to the church in Antioch. The letter was "written through their hands" (Acts 15:23). The letter is clearly from the apostles and the elders and the phrase refers to their work as the bearers of the letter;[670] (2) The same formula "through a particular person or group" is used in

---

[668] Achtemeier, *1 Peter*, 351.

[669] Ernest Best, *1 Peter*, New Century Bible Commentary (Grand Rapids, MI: Eerdmans, 1982), 55; Selwyn, *First Epistle of St. Peter*, 241.

[670] Elliott, *1 Peter*, 873.

extrabiblical literature to refer to the letter carrier;[671] (3) The commendation of letter carriers was common since the letter carrier was the personal link between the author and the audience. Silvanus' commendation as a "faithful brother" is further evidence that he was the letter carrier;[672] (4) If the Silvanus of 1 Peter is the Silvanus/Silas who traveled with Paul, he already has experience as a letter carrier. Arguments that Silvanus would be too prominent to be merely the delivery person underestimate the importance of the letter carrier. The letter bearer was not merely a mail delivery person, he or she was also often the reader and interpreter of the letter, a person able to communicate the thought and intention of the author.

Those who argue that Silvanus was the scribe who helped compose the letter argue for this position on the following evidence: (1) Many scholars assume that Peter would not have been able to write the kind of sophisticated level of Greek contained in 1 Peter. Selwyn writes, "We may be confident that [Silvanus] would have had his own contribution to make to the substance no less than to the language of the letter, or in other words, that he drafted, or helped to draft, it; and the receptive mind of the Apostle would have welcomed his help;"[673] (2) Davids argues that writing "briefly" makes the idea that Silvanus is the letter carrier less likely;[674] (3) Some have argued that the journey would have been too great for a single letter carrier;[675] (4) Those who date the letter late think that Silvanus would have been too old to make such a journey and that it is therefore more likely that he is the scribe.[676] In other words, most of the assertions about Silvanus as the letter's scribe have been based on assumptions about Peter's linguistic capability or the capacity of Silvanus to make the journey; and (5) However, more recently Craig Keener has provided extensive research that shows that the formula "through a person's name" can refer to scribes as well as letter carriers.[677]

---

671 Elliott, *1 Peter*, 872.
672 E. Randolph Richards, "Silvanus was not Peter's secretary: Theological bias in interpreting διὰ Σιλουανψου … εγραψα in 1 Peter 5:12," *JETS* 43:3 (2000): 417–32, 420.
673 Selwyn, *First Epistle of St. Peter*, 11; also Davids, *The First Epistle of Peter*, 6.
674 Davids, *The First Epistle of Peter*, 198.
675 Goppelt, *A Commentary on I Peter*, 369.
676 Achtemeier, *1 Peter*, 351.
677 Keener, *1 Peter*, 393–402.

In evaluating the evidence for both positions, a few comments can be made. First, if Peter was the author of 1 Peter as the epistle itself claims and as the church endorsed for hundreds of years, he may very well have used a scribe to help physically write the letter. This would have been a common practice. However, to suggest that Peter was unable to orally compose a letter of 1 Peter's quality is to deny the oral and rhetorical skills for which he was known. Peter was the first preacher of the apostles (Acts 2) and as such may well have had rhetorically persuasive speech that evidenced the kind of oral qualities that we see in the Greek of 1 Peter (e.g., attention to alliteration, colorful turns of phrase, vivid imagery, and the invention of new words). Furthermore, Karen Jobes has shown in her work that the Greek of 1 Peter shows Semitic influence and was most likely composed by someone whose native language was not Greek.[678] It does show some finesse in its style but is not on the same level as the Greek of Josephus, another non-native who wrote in Greek. It is quite possible that Peter's oral capacity to communicate in Greek was honed in his ministry after Pentecost and that while the letter itself may have been written with the help of a scribe it reflects the message and thought of Peter. It is possible that this scribe may have been Silvanus, but that is not completely clear from the language used in 1 Peter. It is noteworthy that Silvanus is not cited at the beginning of the letter as a coauthor as he was in 1–2 Thessalonians. In light of this, it is better to retain our understanding of Peter as the author and Silvanus as a helper (whether as a scribe, a letter carrier, or both).[679] At the same time, some scholars have argued that the language "through Silvanus" could *only* point to Silvanus as the letter carrier and not as a scribe.[680] However, Keener's more recent work cited above shows that the evidence is not as decisive as some thought. It is possible, perhaps likely, that Silvanus is the letter carrier, but that is not the only way to understand the language of the text. As the letter carrier, Silvanus would have read and interpreted the letter for the congregations in Asia Minor.

---

[678]   Jobes, *1 Peter*, 331–38.

[679]   These comments, of course, are based on the idea that Peter is the author of 1 Peter and that the letter is not pseudonymous. See the section on authorship in the introduction for further discussion. Those who affirm pseudonymous authorship struggle to explain the reference to Silvanus. Schreiner, *1, 2 Peter, Jude*, 247.

[680]   Elliott, *1 Peter*, 874; Richards, "Silvanus," 418.

Peter gives Silvanus his own endorsement, referring to him as a "faithful brother." This commendation serves to identify Silvanus as a fellow member of the Christian community. Although this is the only time the word "brother" is used in 1 Peter, such kinship language was regularly used to identify members of the church (e.g., 1 Cor. 1:1; 1 Thess. 1:4; 2 Thess. 1:3; Philem. 1:1, etc.). He is faithful, and so can be relied upon as a loyal and trustworthy person. Such a commendation may further point to the possibility that Silvanus is the letter carrier as his affirmation by Peter serves to secure his role as the reader/interpreter of the letter.[681]

A Closer Look: Writing and Sending Letters in the Ancient World

Writing and sending letters in the ancient world involved varying degrees of literacy, a broad category. It can be as basic as having the ability to sign one's name. A higher degree of literacy would include the ability to read and decipher simple messages. And, at the highest level, literacy would involve the ability to compose and read a complex argument or narrative. It is hard to know exactly what percentage of the population in the ancient Roman Empire was able to read and write the kind of complex composition found in 1 Peter, but most estimates range between 10–30 percent. There was no system of free public elementary education throughout the Roman Empire that taught basic reading and writing skills. Those who learned to read either received local private education in groups or were taught by a private tutor. Writing skills were sometimes taught separately, which meant that some might learn how to read without learning how to write.[682] On the other hand, the Jewish people valued being able to read Scripture and did educate their male children in reading so that they could read the Hebrew Scriptures. Thus, Jews most likely had a higher level of literacy than the general populace of the Roman Empire. There is, however, less likelihood that Jews living in Israel had the same level of literacy in Greek, which would have been a second language.

The ability to write was valued. Writing was a more difficult undertaking in the ancient world than it is today. The tools for writing involved rough paper made from the papyrus plant and a reed pen dipped in ink. Those with the means could purchase parchment, called vellum, made from stretched and treated goat or calf skin.[683] Writing

---

[681]   Keener notes, however, that commendations can be given to those who perform a variety of functions and are not reserved solely for letter carriers. Keener, *1 Peter*, 395.

[682]   Harry Y. Gamble, *Books and Readers in the Early Church: A History of Early Christian Texts* (New Haven: Yale University Press, 1995), 2–10.

[683]   Andre LeMaire, "Writing and writing materials," in Freedman (ed.), *Anchor Bible Dictionary*, 1004.

with these materials required patience and care. In light of this, many people made use of scribes to communicate in writing. Those who were wealthy might own a slave who functioned as a secretary; others could hire a scribe to write on their behalf. Scribes might write many different types of documents from letters of various lengths to legal documents such as wills or marriage certificates. Almost all of our New Testament letters were written by scribes. In Romans, the scribe identifies himself as "Tertius, the writer of this letter" (Rom. 16:22). And in Philemon, Paul indicates that he wrote that short letter himself (Phil. 19, 21). Scribes could either have taken dictation using shorthand on wax tablets and then prepared the letter for the sender or they may have been given greater freedom to construct the letter's message. In any case, the writing would have been read back and approved by the author.[684]

Once a letter was prepared, it needed to be sent to its destination. The delivery of mail, especially to destinations over a great distance, was slow. The average walking pace is three to four miles per hour on a good road, and a person walking most of the day might average around twenty miles per day. The average speed by horse was about fifty miles per day on good Roman roads and slower when traveling over paths that were less well maintained. Just the journey from Rome to the northern part of Asia Minor would have been at least 1,600 miles by land or over 1,300 miles combining land and sea travel. Just getting the letter from Rome to Asia Minor would have taken many weeks. Further travels of many weeks would have been needed to deliver the letter to the five provinces named in 1 Peter. This is why some scholars suggest that the letter carrier brought the letter to Asia Minor where it was copied and distributed by several different couriers to the churches.[685] This is, of course, speculative but not impossible. Travel was also expensive with the need for food, lodging, and other necessities along the way. While there was a state-run postal system, it was reserved for administrative use by the government of the Roman Empire. Anyone wishing to send a private letter had to find someone to carry it to its destination. For example, one letter writer noted, "I have already written to you through your camel driver."[686] Often people sent letters with those they knew who were already traveling to the destination the letter needed to go. Those with the means could, of course, send a slave or hire a courier. It does seem that when a letter carrier is named in the letter, that carrier often had "an important role in the communication process."[687] A study of Josephus shows that even in

---

[684] Torrey Seland, *Strangers in the Light: Philonic Perspectives on Christian Identity in 1 Peter*, Biblical Interpretation Series: 76 (Leiden; Boston: Brill, 2005), 12.

[685] Seland, *Strangers in the Light*, 36.

[686] Keener, *1 Peter*, 394.

[687] Peter M. Head, "Letter carriers in the ancient Jewish epistolary material," in *Jewish and Christian Scripture as Artifact and Canon*, ed. Craig A. Evans and H. Daniel Zacharias,

informal correspondence "letter carriers can reinforce the message of the letter in person, or carry conversation further, or bring news back of how the letter was received."[688] Letters were a significant means of communication in the ancient world and both scribes and letter carriers played an important part in their creation and distribution.

Following the introduction of Silvanus, Peter lays out the purpose of this short letter. It was convention to refer to a letter as short even when, as with 1 Peter, it was fairly long in comparison to most. It may also be a way to indicate that more could be said on the subject than has been written in the letter.[689] The letter has a dual purpose. First, it is meant to be an encouragement to the churches. The Greek word for the verb "to encourage," *parakaleo*, has already been used in 2:11 and 5:1 as Peter urges his readers to continue to live faithfully in light of their new identity as God's family. Now, he indicates that his whole letter has been meant as a means of such encouragement. Second, the letter serves as a witness. Peter has already identified himself as a witness of the sufferings of Christ (5:1) and now indicates that he fully bears witness (*epimartureō*). The word is used only here in the New Testament but carries the meaning of affirming that something is true.[690] The object of the testimony is "this is the true grace of God." The word "this" may refer to the letter itself and therefore to the message or content of the letter; the word "epistle" would be implied.[691] Or, it could refer to the antecedent "grace" (5:10) with which it agrees,[692] though Michaels notes that this creates a repetitive statement along the lines of "the grace God holds in store for us is true grace from God."[693] In a recent article, Williams has argued that "the most likely referent . . . is the suffering experienced by the Anatolian Christians."[694] He goes on to say

Studies in Scripture in Early Judaism and Christianity: 13 (London: T&T Clark, 2009), 219.

[688] Head, "Letter carriers in the ancient Jewish epistolary material," 218.

[689] Forbes, *1 Peter*, 184.

[690] BAGD

[691] Achtemeier, *1 Peter*, 352; Forbes, *1 Peter*, 182; Jobes, *1 Peter*, 324.

[692] Elliott, *1 Peter*, 878; Elliot quotes Brox who understands grace as being "able to hope under the present precarious conditions;" see also Feldmeier, *The First Letter of Peter*, 254.

[693] Michaels, *1 Peter*, 309.

[694] Williams, "Reciprocity and suffering in 1 Peter 2,19–20," 435.

that grace is redefined for this audience so that it is no longer about receiving pleasurable benefits but rather it is about understanding that "the conflict which they were experiencing was actually part of God's bestowal of lavish munificence."[695] While Williams makes a good point about God's grace, the same argument can be made from the message and context of the epistle. In other words, it does not rest on understanding "this" as referring to suffering. It is better to understand "this" as referring to the letter and its message.

In this epistle, Peter has encouraged them with a reminder of their identity as the new family of God, exhorting them to live holy, loving lives characterized by good conduct in the midst of suffering. And Peter has repeatedly shown that God's grace is present even in suffering. This grace includes the blessings of salvation and hope located in the resurrection of Christ as well as the knowledge that the suffering experienced on account of faith is within the will of God. They are to stand firm in this grace. The command to stand firm is reminiscent of other instructions in this epistle such as being prepared by girding themselves (1:13) or arming themselves (4:1). It also echoes the recent instruction to resist the devil by being firm in faith (5:9). At the same time, it is clear that God is the one with the power to strengthen and establish them (5:10) and that what they experience is a gift from God, whether salvation, favor, or being in the center of God's will.

The beginning and the ending of the letter reflect similar ideas. The letter opens by addressing the "elect" (1:1) and now the "co-elect" (5:13) send their greetings. This parallelism is reinforced by the description of the audience as "exiles of the Dispersion" and the community from which the letter originates as those located "in Babylon." Neither the sender nor the recipients are at home. And the letter ends, as it began, with a wish for the community to experience peace (1:2; 5:14).[696] The letter, like many of Paul's letters (Rom. 16:21; 1 Cor. 16:19; Phil. 4:21–22), draws to a close with final greetings. The first greeting comes from, literally, "the co-elect." The NRSV translates this as "your sister church." The word co-elect (*suneklektē*), which is not used elsewhere in the New Testament, is a feminine singular adjective functioning as a substantive. There are two main proposals about its meaning. First, it is possible that it refers to a

---

[695] Williams, "Reciprocity and suffering in 1 Peter 2,19–20," 435.
[696] Schutter, *Hermeneutic*, 28; Michaels, *1 Peter*, 311.

specific woman, perhaps Peter's wife, who sends her greetings. However, the identity of any particular woman would have to be surmised from the known relationships of Peter (Mark 1:30; 1 Cor. 9:5), the sender of the letter. Second, it is more likely that it refers to the church in Rome. Other New Testament passages refer to the church as the elect sister (2 John 13) and the singular can function as a collective noun (e.g., "the church"), and that is its likely referent here.

The church that sends its greetings is identified as being "in Babylon," most likely a symbolic reference to Rome. In the Old Testament, Babylon was the capital of the Babylonian Empire and became the enemy of Jerusalem and God's people (2 Kings 24:10; Jer. 20:4). At the time that the New Testament was written, the actual city of Babylon had been abandoned and was mainly ruins.[697] Thus, when 1 Peter refers to the greetings as coming from the co-elect in Babylon, this is a symbolic reference to Rome, the capital city of the current empire. While 1 Peter recognizes the power and authority of the Roman Empire (2:13–14), it also subtly subverts that power with awareness of God and the assertion that all people are God's creation and that all people are to be equally honored. By referring to the church as being "in Babylon," the author makes use of a symbol for a city that is set against God and God's people, a place where they dwell as foreigners, people of the diaspora (1:1). In Rome they live a life in which they are both embedded in the social structures of a place that is not their home while at the same time being keenly aware of their identity as exiles, like the original exiles from Jerusalem who had to make a home in Babylon. The identification of Rome with Babylon became prominent among Jewish and Christian authors after 70 CE when Jerusalem and the temple were destroyed. Both of these empires were known as having governments that had destroyed God's dwelling place and scattered and killed God's people. Many scholars have argued that, among other reasons, 1 Peter's reference to Rome as Babylon suggests the book was most likely written after 70 CE and is thus pseudonymous.[698] However, the book of Daniel and the understanding of the Four Kingdoms points to Rome as the successor of Babylon even prior to 70 CE.[699] New Testament books that are

---

[697] Achtemeier, *1 Peter*, 353.
[698] For just one example, Elliott, *1 Peter*, 887.
[699] Achtemeier, *1 Peter*, 47–48; Keener, *1 Peter*, 405.

likely to have been written after 70 CE do use the name Babylon to refer to Rome (e.g., Rev. 14:8; 18:2) showing that this association between Rome and Babylon became solidified after the destruction of Jerusalem. Tradition and the testimony of the church as early as the second century has long placed Peter in Rome for his final ministry and his martyrdom.[700] Thus, when Peter indicates that the co-elect in Babylon send greetings, it is best to understand this as a reference to the church in Rome. Peter also identifies Mark as his son who sends greetings. There is a long historical association between Peter and John Mark. When Peter is released from prison, he went to the home of John Mark's mother (Acts 12:12), and John Mark became one of the original traveling companions of Paul (Acts 12:25). Mark is understood as the author of the gospel of Mark, and it reflects Peter's eyewitness accounts of the life, death, and resurrection of Jesus.[701] Mark is most likely a spiritual son or protégé of Peter.

Peter instructs the family of God to "greet one another with a kiss of love" (5:14), which is a final mark of the familial relationship between the members of the community. Throughout 1 Peter members of the church have been instructed to practice love towards one another (1:22; 2:17; 3:8; 4:8). Now, that love is demonstrated with a kiss. This is the affectionate practice of family and disregards the social hierarchy so prized in the world at that time. The kiss becomes an embodiment of the church's theology of love.[702] The book then closes with a wish that all those who are in Christ experience God's peace. "In Christ" is another way of expressing their new birth and their participation in the new family of God. Peace is a state of being that comes not from a lack of suffering or an absence of emotion – both are prominent throughout 1 Peter – but from right relationship with God and with the members of God's household, and, to the best of the churches' ability, with the culture surrounding it. The letter begins and ends with both grace and peace (1:2; 5:12, 14), and echoes the Proverb quoted in 3:11: "seek peace and pursue it." It is a fitting end to a book exploring the identity of God's people, and their way of life in a world opposed to their faith in God.

[700] Larry R. Helyer, *The Life and Witness of Peter* (Downers Grove, IL: IVP Academic, 2012), 273–77.
[701] Green, *Vox Petri*, 43.
[702] Joel B. Green, "Embodying the Gospel: Two exemplary practices," *Journal of Spiritual Formation & Soul Care* 7:1 (2014): 21.

Bridging the Horizons: One of the defining cultural values in North America is individualism: a focus on being independent and self-reliant. Yet, at the end of 1 Peter it becomes clear that Peter did not do his work alone. He had associates who were part of the work of ministry: Silvanus, the church in Rome, and Mark. Dennis Edwards notes at the end of his commentary the need that church leaders have to be in partnership with others in the work of ministry.[703] This applies to the rest of the church just as much as to leaders. In 1 Peter the whole church is called to lives of holiness, love, and good works. The church is repeatedly addressed using the plural "you," making it clear that the whole community is called to this life together. It is not the work solely of the leaders but of the whole church. But it is not easy to live lives of holiness, love, and good works, especially not in the context of a society that rejects such a way of living. It is much easier to live in this way when Christians participate in groups that encourage examining oneself for sin, attention to holiness, reflection on the concrete practice of love, and joint participation in good works. In recent years, there has been a revival of small Wesleyan groups that seek to reflect together on Scripture, spiritual disciplines, and mission while seeking together to see God at work in their daily lives. At their best, these groups are an encouragement to pursue deeper relationship with God and with God's people for the sake of reaching out to others as God gives the opportunity. Legalistic participation in such groups generally does not promote the kind of longing for God (2:3) that makes holiness a gift rather than a burden. Instead, these groups function best when together people seek to grow into the life God has promised. In a beautiful reflection of the new family that God is forming the church itself finds that hierarchies and social barriers are broken down and a new family is formed based on the new birth that God has given (1:3). The members of the contemporary church may not greet each other with a kiss, but it is important that we do symbolize that familial relationship with an embodied greeting that signifies the peace that should be inherent to the family of God.

---

[703]   Edwards, *1 Peter*, 216–19.

General Index

Achtemeier, P. J., 67, 72, 78, 85, 106, 112–13, 117,
125, 132, 143, 145, 154, 156, 162, 165, 169, 176,
183–84, 197–98, 203, 211, 216–17, 222–23,
225, 229, 231, 233, 238–39, 246, 252, 264–65,
270, 272, 276, 282, 284, 286–87, 289, 291,
293, 297–98, 300–2, 304–5, 309, 311
Adeyemo, T., 35
Arnold, B., 297
Aronson, E., 111
Asumang, A., 298–99
Aune, D. E., 251

Bain, K., 175
Balch, D. L., 131, 142
Barclay, J. M. G., 22, 57, 155, 233–34, 249
Barton, S. C., 3
Bates, M. W., 53
Batovici, D., 244
Batten, A. J., 170, 174
Bauckham, R., 114, 189, 214, 216, 281
Beach, L., 54
Beale, G. K., 31
Beare, F. W., 34, 78, 113, 216, 231, 240, 282, 288
Beasley-Murray, G. R., 223
Bechtler, S. R., 118, 142–43, 233, 244, 272
Beetham, C. A., 166
Best, E., 304
Bigg, C., 34, 215
Bird, J. G., 131
Bockmuehl, M., 280, 283
Bond, H. K., 16
Bonhoeffer, D., 253
Borgman, P., 178

Boring, M. E., 29
Brandt, C., 109
Bray, G. L., 21, 215
Breed, G., 283
Brewer, D. I., 173
Brooke, G. J., 114
Brown, J. K., 269
Byrley, C., 295

Callan, T., 104
Campbell, B. L., 27–28, 63, 90, 93, 115, 154, 195,
279, 288
Caragounis, C. C., 291
Carson, D. A., 31
Carter, W., 146–47, 191
Chamy, F. A., 53, 67
Charles, D., 295
Chester, A., 157
Christensen, S. M., 189–90
Crawford, M. R., 223
Cullmann, O., 16

Dalton, W. J., 208, 212–13, 216, 218, 221–22, 236,
238
Davids, P. H., 37, 170, 174, 217, 222, 225, 229, 231,
262, 266, 288, 305
DeSilva, D. A., 64, 67, 91, 202
Dimant, D., 115
Dinkler, M. B., 183
Donelson, L. R., 97, 210, 212, 232, 282, 285, 289
Downs, D. J., 246
Drury, K. W., 108
Dryden, J. de W., 26, 29

Scripture Index

Genesis

1, 99
2:7, 77
6, 220
6:1–4, 216
6:5–12, 220
6:8–9, 220
6–8, 210, 216
7:7, 220
11:29–30, 177
12:3, 188
12:11–12, 178
16:2, 112
18, 247
18:12, 177
20:11, 178
20:12, 177
20:13, 178
22:1, 259
22:12, 259
23:4, 188
30:3, 112

Exodus

3:19, 292
6:1, 292
6:6, 91
12:5, 93
12:37–38, 128
12:38, 128
13:9, 292
13:32, 67
15:13, 91
19, 53, 123, 125
19:2, 53

19:5–6, 123
19:6, 42, 113, 123
19:10, 96
19–24, 88
24:2–8, 58
24:16, 79, 96
25–40, 88
32, 23
40:34, 96

Leviticus

1:3, 93
1–17, 88
3:1, 93
3:7, 209
3:12, 209
4:3, 209
4:14, 209
4:23, 93
5:15, 93
9:23, 96
11, 88
11:44, 88
17–18, 102
18–27, 88
19, 88
19:2, 88
19:3, 88
19:36, 88
19–20, 88
20, 88
20:7, 88
26, 88
28, 93
45, 88

CPSIA information can be obtained
at www.ICGtesting.com
Printed in the USA
BVHW050756250522
637954BV00009B/21